PORTAGE PATHWAYS

Loris C. Troyer

# PORTAGE PATHWAYS

*Loris C. Troyer*

THE KENT STATE UNIVERSITY PRESS
Kent, Ohio, and London, England

© 1998 by The Kent State University Press, Kent, Ohio 44242
All rights reserved
Library of Congress Catalog Card Number 97-38126
ISBN 0-87338-600-0
Manufactured in the United States of America

LIBRARY OF CONGRESS CATALOGING-IN-PUBLICATION DATA

Troyer, Loris C., 1914–
    Portage pathways / Loris C. Troyer.
        p.      cm.
    A collection of columns originally published in the Ravenna-Kent
    (Ohio) Record-Courier.
    Includes index.
    ISBN 0-87338-600-0 (cloth : alk. paper) ∞
    1. Portage County (Ohio)—Civilization.      I. Title.
F497.P8T76  1998                                                    97-38126
977.1'37—dc21                                                       CIP

British Library Cataloging-in-Publication data are available.

# CONTENTS

# FOREWORD

Loris C. Troyer, editor emeritus, has been such a pivotal figure for so long at the *Record-Courier* and in the Portage County community that it would be difficult to consider the twentieth-century history of either without his name coming quickly to mind.

My family, the Dix family, entered the newspaper business in this county in 1926, 71 years ago, and for more than 60 of those years Loris has been associated with the newspaper, the majority of that time serving as editor and then executive editor.

As such, he has played a major role chronicling some of our community's most dramatic events. Loris was the reporter who broke the news in 1940 that the federal government, apparently in anticipation of the coming world war, was secretly acquiring land to build a large arsenal east of Ravenna, our county seat. This 22,000-acre complex became a major provider of ammunition for our nation's defenses during World War II and, later, during the Korean War and the war in Vietnam. At its highest periods of activity, it has by far been Portage County's biggest employer.

Himself one of Kent State University's illustrious graduates, Loris has reported on the exciting developments at his alma mater for more than 60 years. His years of reportage began in 1936, when the University's enrollment numbered in the hundreds, and continues right up to the present day, when Kent State's multicampus complex provides education for an enrollment of more than 25,000 students and offers many cultural, educational, and entertainment opportunities that greatly enrich our community. During his watch as editor, he witnessed what was probably the University's saddest moment, the slaying of four students during a civil disobedience action on the Kent Campus on May 4, 1970.

Loris spent thousands of hours during those days providing the *Record-Courier* with editorial leadership as it attempted to explain this bewildering tragedy and its aftermath to the people of Portage County.

What a wonderful guide to our community he has been and continues to be. Readers of "Portage Pathways," the weekly historical column he has written since retiring from full-time duties, are treated to an anecdotal history of our community, as told by a person of steadied perspective, one not easily ruffled by life's ups and downs. They also read community history authored by a writer with a healthy sense of humor who genuinely likes people and finds their everyday lives of engagement and challenge interesting—the substance, in fact, that makes up the history of our community.

Those qualities have made Loris a special person, one who often ends up playing an important role in many of our community's most successful civic undertakings. On a lighter side, they have made Loris a most sought-after speaker at many a get-together, where his ability to tell a story enlivens such occasions. Those same qualities have also enhanced the appeal of the *Record-Courier*, helping it fulfill its role as the newspaper of record for Portage County and giving the *R-C* a special flavor it might not otherwise have.

Over the many years they worked together, my father, the late Robert C. Dix, as publisher of the newspaper, found Loris invaluable. Invariably, the two of them began their workdays together over early-morning coffee discussing the community and the newspaper's mission. Those discussions helped mold the personality of the *Record-Courier* and helped set its editorial direction.

Growing up in that newspaper environment, even as a youngster I sensed the great esteem in which Loris was held. By the time I entered adulthood, and eventually employment at the *Record-Courier*, Loris had become for me one of two or three figures whose guidance was the equivalent of 24-carat gold.

One day, in 1982, some years after I had succeeded my father as publisher, Loris walked into my office and informed me that, at age 68, he wanted to retire from the day-to-day pressures of deadlines. I took a deep breath as panic set in. "You'll get along," he assured me, and then he presented me with a "retirement" proposition. He said he would contribute a weekly column to the *Record-Courier* about the history of Portage County. "I've been thinking it over for some time," he said, "and it's something I'd like to do."

Not knowing as much as I should about Portage County, I mentally calculated that the column would run dry in about a year or two but consented to give it a try. How wrong that computation proved to be! After 15 years and more than 700 weekly columns, Loris continues to mine the history of our community, each week finding historical "discoveries" and then polishing them into the gems his columns have become, making "Portage Pathways" easily one of the best-read features of the newspaper.

If you are not familiar with "Portage Pathways" but want to know more about our county and its history, you are in for a treat when you delve into this volume. And if you are already a regular reader of "Portage Pathways" in the *Record-Courier,* I think you will join me in feeling grateful to Loris for what has become a major contribution to the compilation of Portage County history. I know you will join me in extending thanks to the excellent efforts of the Kent Historical Society, The Kent State University Press, John T. Hubbell, and Sandra Halem, who with this book have helped preserve these wonderful, informative, and entertaining columns for posterity.

DAVID E. DIX, PUBLISHER
*Record-Courier*

## A NEWSMAN RECALLS HIS SIX DECADES
## WITH THE *RECORD-COURIER*

*August 18, 1996*

I was working in Massillon the summer of 1936. It was beastly hot, with temperatures about 95 degrees day after day. Despite the heat, Paul Brown and his Massillon Tigers, not baseball, were the major topic of conversation. On many evenings, Brown held court in a downtown cigar store as he regaled his listeners with his prospect for the upcoming football season.

What was I doing in Massillon in 1936? Well, summer jobs for college students were hard to come by in those Depression years. For want of a better one, I was selling Singer sewing machines and vacuum cleaners. To better acquaint me with sales procedures, I was required to learn how to use all those fancy sewing gadgets—hemstitchers, buttonholers, and basters. My means of transportation was a 1930 Model-A Ford coupe. Its leaky radiator, which required filling a couple of times each day, was my main concern as I made my sales rounds. I really wasn't "into" selling sewing machines; in fact, to me it was pure drudgery. All I made was the equivalent of bare meal money.

In that state of mind, I certainly welcomed a call from Bob Dix, a gentleman I hardly knew. Upon the recommendation of a friend, George Urban, he offered me a part-time job at the *Kent Courier-Tribune*, at the magnificent sum of $10 per week. He said my main responsibility would be covering Kent State University news, but I soon discovered that was hardly the extent of my duties, nor were the hours part-time. On August 19, 1936 (60 years ago Monday), I started my newspaper career, all of it with the same company. And, after six decades, I'm miraculously still here.

In 1936 the *Kent Courier* was housed in a small wooden building at 138 East Main Street Actually, the *Courier* was two papers, the *Daily*

*Courier-Tribune*, published in association with Ravenna's *Evening Record*. The page 1 masthead was interchanged and some stories on page 1 were made over to accommodate each community. Also, there was the semi-weekly *Courier*, published on Tuesday and Friday with only local news. That news was usually warmed-over stuff saved from the previous days.

The production department in the Ravenna plant included a bank of clunky linotype machines that set stories and ad type on single-line metal, which was placed in page-size chases. Then we graduated to teletype machines. Operators set stories into reams of paper tape with perforated symbols that was fed into automatic linotype machines that set the metal type. Later, after the presses were converted to offset machinery, we advanced to scanners that scanned a page of news copy and reproduced it into column-wide paper type.

After several other technological advances, today the *Record-Courier* is completely computerized. Stories are written on terminals—not typewriters—and through fascinating production facilities are converted to column-sized paper columns. Even more sophisticated technological production advances are in the offing for the *Record-Courier*.

I often wonder how editors such as E. Y. Lacey, a minister-lawyer turned editor, or Johnny Paxton or N. J. A. Minnich would marvel at such production developments. In their day, type was handset one letter at a time.

Those are the production advances I have witnessed. The people side of journalism is far more interesting, as it well should be. Imagine the passing parade of people in 60 years—hundreds upon hundreds of public servants, business people, teachers, lawyers, farmers, social workers, professors, college presidents, athletes, civic leaders, ministers, and *Record-Courier* employees. The list goes on and on. Many of them are now long gone.

In 1939, I moved to the Ravenna office, where I covered the courthouse, city hall, schools, and scads of organizations in every Portage County community, reporting with writing and camera. There I was associated with Angelo Sicuro, one of the most dedicated, versatile, and accomplished editors I ever have known. Besides, he was (and is) a most painstaking and knowledgeable grammarian.

In 1948, I returned to Kent as the Kent editor, and in 1963 I became executive editor. As editors, Ange and I retired on the same date, October 1, 1982, with a combined total of 99 years of service to the *Record-Courier* and the Dix family.

People accustomed to the movie version of journalism view our work as one filled with glamour. Young people entering the profession soon learn otherwise. It's hard work with long hours and is always under the discerning scrutiny of the public. But, at the same time, it has many rewards. There are opportunities to meet famous people. My travels have taken me into the presence of seven American presidents, a passing glance at two others, lunch with Ronald Reagan in the White House, and elbow-rubbings with dozens of movie and TV stars, big-time athletes, and internationally known scholars. I have been to Europe a couple of times and have visited enough castles and cathedrals to last me the rest of my life. Not that such adventures aren't broadening.

One of the real perks of newspapering with the *Record-Courier* has been the opportunity to participate in civic and community life. Bob Dix, my boss and mentor for so many years, believed intensely in that premise, and he allowed time for his people to take part in community matters. In fact, he almost insisted upon it for his editors.

In my mind, the real heroes are on the homefront . . . good, law-abiding, hard-working people. They take care of their families, see to their children's good behavior and education, support and participate in their churches and their schools, keep abreast of the doings of their government (national, state, or local), help build their communities, and serve their neighbors in times of distress or need. Portage County is generously populated by people like this. Those are what present politicians describe as family values. They make them appear to be a recent invention when, in fact, true Americans have been following those practices ever since our country was born.

After my retirement in 1982, I began writing "Portage Pathways" each week, based upon the knowledge and interest I accumulated from many years of chronicling the news of local communities.

No, despite this 60th anniversary, this is not my swan song. God willing, and with continuing health, mental capacity, and the blessing of readers, I shall continue. Certainly, it is an understatement to say that the past six decades have constituted a merry ride. They really have.

PART ONE

# PORTAGE COUNTY HISTORY
# AND HISTORIANS

# IT'S QUIZ TIME!

## Test Your Knowledge of Portage

*September 5, 1993*

This is a different type of column. Some might say it's the type of column one writes when there exists a shortage of material. And there's an element of truth in that conclusion. But there's never a shortage of historical stuff. It's a never-ending saga. This week's column arrives in the form of a historical quiz including 10 questions and, of course, 10 answers.

If you come up with seven correct answers consider yourself quite historically smart. That's the first prize, your contentment in the knowledge that you're quite above average. Five out of the 10 isn't all that bad. Your prize has been mislaid and you had better start boning up by getting ahold of some of Portage County's volumes of recorded history. If you wind up with fewer than five correct answers, assess yourself as one who is historically disinterested. You, too, can recover by reading a bit more local history.

So, here goes the test:

1. What was the original name of Freedom Township?
2. What was the maiden name of President James A. Garfield's wife?
3. What serious fire in Kent resulted in the organization of the Chamber of Commerce and, indirectly, in the location of the Kent Normal School (today's Kent State University) in Kent?
4. For whom was the Hubbard squash named?
5. Who wrote *Recollections of an Old Settler?*
6. What was the length of Capt. Samuel Brady's leap across the Cuyahoga River in Kent?
7. Who was the judge in the first session of the Portage County Common Pleas Court in 1808?
8. What was the original name of what today is the city of Kent?
9. What was the original name of the present Hiram College?
10. What was the source of the name for the city of Ravenna?

And the answers are:

1. Freedom Township was settled in 1818 by Mr. and Mrs. Charles Paine. The family originally was from Painesville, and that city was named for his father. Because she was the first female in the township, Mrs. Paine was given the privilege of naming the township. Being a highly patriotic individual, she chose the name "Liberty." Then it was determined that there was another township by that name in Ohio, so she turned to the name "Freedom" as a substitute.

2. Lucretia Rudolph, daughter of a farm couple, Mr. and Mrs. Zeb Rudolph of Hiram, became President Garfield's bride in 1858. Garfield, born in Orange in Cuyahoga County in 1831, started school at the new Western Reserve Eclectic Institute in Hiram after it opened in 1850. He later taught there and served as principal of the school from 1857 to 1861. He was a trustee of the institution when he was assassinated in 1881.

3. On December 10, 1909, the Seneca Chain Company plant on West Main Street in Kent was struck by a serious fire. Because the plant was one of the town's principal employers, people acted quickly in hopes of restoring the concern. In February 1910 a group of Kent civic leaders met to organize the Kent Board of Trade (ancestor of the Kent Area Chamber of Commerce) to promote rebuilding of the plant. As a result, a public stock sale was instituted, the plant was rebuilt, and operations were resumed. Seneca Chain was located in the complex later housing the Twin Coach Company. Almost simultaneously, the Ohio General Assembly approved legislation to create two normal schools in northeast and northwest Ohio. John Paxton, editor of the *Kent Courier*, challenged the new Board of Trade when he wrote: "If we want that normal school, let's go after it." A committee was organized by the board. A plan was developed and presented to the Ohio site selection commission in July 1910. Later that year, the town was jubilant when Governor Harmon announced that the normal school would be located in Kent. Incidentally, KSU is named for William S. Kent, donor of the original land, and not for the community of Kent.

4. Story has it that the Hubbard squash was named for Bela Hubbard, first settler of Randolph Township in 1802. He obtained the seeds from southern Ohio, planted them on his farm in Randolph, and was so pleased with the result that the squash from that time on has borne his name.

5. Christian Cackler Jr. wrote *Recollections of an Old Settler* in 1870. The book, reprinted many times, is the best source of early history in Portage County, particularly Franklin Township. Cackler came to Hudson (then part of Portage County) in 1804. He later moved to Franklin Township. His marriage in 1814 to Theresa Nighman was the first in Franklin. The old Cackler homestead still stands on Cackler Road. Cackler was with Commodore Perry in the Battle of Lake Erie in the War of 1812.

6. The best source for the length of Brady's Leap across the Cuyahoga (at a spot off Gougler Avenue) again was Christian Cackler. He said it was 21 feet, based upon a measurement made some years later. When the canal was built, rock on the river's east side was removed and the gorge widened.

7. Calvin Pease was Portage County's first common pleas judge. He was appointed by the Ohio General Assembly to serve the new county of Portage which was organized in 1807. The first court session was held at the Robert Eaton home at Campbellsport on August 23, 1808. The first case involved defendant William Simcock of Franklin Township, who was accused of breaking the quiet of the Sabbath "by sporting and hunting game with guns and hounds." He was found guilty and fined $1.50.

8. The original name for the City of Kent was Franklin Mills. The name was changed to Kent in 1867 in honor of Marvin Kent in appreciation for his bringing the Atlantic and Great Western Railroad into the village, a move which resulted in considerable prosperity. The name "Franklin" honors Franklin Olmstead, son of Aaron Olmstead, original owner of Franklin Township.

9. The original name of Hiram College was the Western Reserve Eclectic Institute. The school was established by the Disciples of Ohio in 1850. It was chartered in March of that year and went into operation the following November. In 1867, the institution became a full-fledged college and the name changed to Hiram College. Today, Hiram is one of the premier liberal arts colleges in the nation.

10. Ravenna received its name even before any settlers arrived in the township. Benjamin Tappan Sr. purchased two-thirds of the township and then sent his son, Benjamin Jr., to settle the land and serve as his

agent. Benjamin Jr. later wrote that other owners of township parcels wanted to give the settlement the name "Tappan." "I could not agree to their proposition and I proposed the name of 'Ravenna.'" That meeting took place back in Massachusetts. Tappan never had been to Ravenna, Italy, the source of the name. It is believed that his fiancée, Nancy Wright, liked the name and influenced him. Tappan arrived in Ravenna in 1799. He wrote that due to a surveyor's error, the Tappan family really believed they had purchased land that today is in Randolph Township.

## PORTAGE COUNTY RICH IN PREHISTORIC ARTIFACTS

*n.d.*

The ancient peoples and the levels of their cultures, located in prehistoric times in Portage County and other areas of Ohio, always have provided fascination for historians and archaeologists.

While Portage County is not as noted as the mound area near Chillicothe for prehistoric civilizations, there is bountiful evidence of their presence here. Two such mounds were excavated many years ago near Brady Lake, and at least 18 other mounds have been located in widely scattered areas of the county.

Dr. Phillip R. Shriver, writing in *Portage Heritage*, a history published by the Portage County Historical Society in 1957, related that a highly advanced group of ancient people, the Adena, were here in Ohio between approximately 800 B.C. and A.D. 700. The Adena were expertly artistic in carving bone and stone and shaping copper and mica into ornaments. They were the first of the so-called moundbuilders.

Dr. Shriver, one of Ohio's most knowledgeable historians, led the excavation of an Adena mound on the south shore of Lake Rockwell in 1955. Adena knives were among artifacts unearthed. Dr. Shriver, then a professor and later a dean at Kent State University, became president of Miami University, a position from which he now has retired.

In his historical treatise, Dr. Shriver revealed that the most advanced of prehistoric peoples in this area were the Hopewell, who inhabited

Ohio from A.D. 300 to 1200. The Hopewells were noted for their geometric earthworks, examples of which can be found near Newark, Ohio, and a group of mounds at Mound City near Chillicothe. They were excellent craftsmen and were skilled in making pottery.

Most noteworthy evidence of the Hopewell presence in Portage County is the Indian mound located in Towner's Woods Park near Brady Lake. The mound, situated atop a lofty point overlooking Lake Pippin, was excavated during the summer of 1932 on property then owned by the late George B. Towner. Eleven prehistoric burials were unearthed in that excavation, revealing a large quantity of copper beads, slate ornaments, large sheets of worked mica, and flake knives, all of which testify to the extensive trade relations of this primitive people in Portage County. Some of the artifacts unearthed in that excavation, as well as others found in the Berlin Reservoir area, were turned over to the Portage County Historical Society's museum in Ravenna.

The Towner's Woods Indian mound is marked by a large stone carved with notations of the Hopewell presence that, with the 11 burials and unique artifacts, contributed to a better understanding of the ancient peoples of northern Ohio. The park, owned by Portage County, with its wooded trails, picnic shelters, and sylvan setting on the shore of beautiful Lake Pippin, is an excellent public asset as well as a fitting memorial to a fine, public-spirited gentleman, the late George B. Towner Sr.

Prehistoric earthworks, more than 30 of them, have been located within Portage County borders. Eighteen mounds are known to exist in Mantua, Nelson, Hiram, Streetsboro, Franklin, Charlestown, Edinburg, and Palmyra. In addition, Shriver wrote 30 years ago that village sites have been discovered in Nelson, Streetsboro, Franklin, and Palmyra, and burials and cemeteries have been located in Hiram, Nelson, Streetsboro, Shalersville, Windham, Paris, Palmyra, and Edinburg.

All of these sites are reminders of prehistoric civilizations that existed in this area many centuries before the Indian tribes who greeted our first Western Reserve settlers in the late 1700s and early 1800s.

————

# PORTAGE COUNTY RICH IN NATIVE
# AMERICAN HISTORY

*March 2, 1985*

Two hundred years ago, no one ventured into what is now Portage County without consent of the Indians. The Indians were protective of their lands, a wilderness that sustained their abodes and their hunting grounds.

Although southern Ohio, particularly the area surrounding Chillicothe, is much more famous for its early moundbuilders, there is evidence that prehistoric earthworks existed in Portage. At least 18 mounds have been located in Mantua, Hiram, Nelson, Streetsboro, Franklin Township, and Palmyra.

One such mound was unearthed in 1932 on the George Towner property on the south shore of Pippin Lake, today part of Towner's Woods park. There, 11 burials were uncovered on the summit of a lofty hill overlooking the lake. According to Dr. Phillip R. Shriver, onetime Ohio history professor at Kent State University and later president of Miami University, copper beads, slate ornaments, projectile points, and many flake knives were unearthed, testifying to the existence of these primitive peoples in our county.

Later, this area was populated by the Senecas, who had their headquarters near the Cuyahoga River in Streetsboro Township. The Senecas were led by Chief Bigson, a powerful man who was known for his upright dealings with the white settlers. When the first settlers arrived in Windham, a few decaying wigwams still existed a short distance northwest of today's village. The Cayugas frequently made camp in Hiram and at Nelson Ledges.

In Palmyra, a number of Indian families belonging to the Onondagas and Oneida tribes still existed when the first settlers arrived. The same tribes had a village at Aurora. The Palmyra settlement was on the "Great Trail" that extended from Fort McIntosh, where Beaver, Pennsylvania, is now located, to Sandusky. The Big Beaver Trail passed up the left branch of the Mahoning River into Trumbull County, through Milton and into the upper portion of Palmyra, then through Edinburg into Ravenna and Franklin Townships, crossing the Cuyahoga at Standing

Rock, which stands in the river at the rear of today's Standing Rock Cemetery, and thence northwesterly to Sandusky. Even after the first settlers had taken possession of Portage County lands beginning in 1798, parties of Indians frequently passed over that trail.

Portage County received its name from the old Indian Portage Path between the Cuyahoga and Tuscarawas Rivers, which at one time was within the limits of the county to which it gave its name. Since 1840, when Summit County was created, Portage Path has been located in Summit County, ten townships having been removed from Portage to create the new Summit County.

Actually, Portage County's first settlers apparently lived on fairly good terms with the Indians. Christian Cackler Jr., who came to Hudson with his father in 1804 and later settled in Franklin Township, relates in his *Recollections of an Old Settler* an eyewitness account of his relationship with Chief Bigson, whom he knew well. He tells about the big wigwam where the tribe gathered for the winter in Streetsboro and then dispersed for the warm months to their individual family hunting grounds. Cackler described the Portage County Indian as "the happiest man in the world," adding that Indians "got drunk often."

Four significant incidents in early Portage County history relate to dealings with the Indians. The first of these, Capt. Samuel Brady's famous leap across the Cuyahoga in Kent in 1780 while being pursued by Indians, has been related may times. The three others are lesser known.

The first of these events took place in 1803. Capt. Delaun Mills of Nelson, known as the "Daniel Boone of Portage," was hunting when the track of an Indian following him put him on his guard. Mills, one of Nelson's founders, put his hat on his gun and stuck it out so the Indian could see it. Sure enough, the Indian shot a hole through the hat. The Indian, tomahawk in hand, ran forward. Mills stepped out from his hiding place, killed the Indian, and buried him. Mills also is said to have killed Chief Big Cayuga and Snip Nose Cayuga.

The shooting of Daniel Diver of Deerfield in 1806 is one of Portage County's most famous Indian stories. John Diver traded a horse with Nickshaw, an old Indian, for an Indian pony. Nickshaw claimed he was cheated and sent another Indian, John Mohawk, to kill Diver. Mohawk made a slight mistake—he shot Dan Diver, John's brother, in the head, severing his optic nerve and blinding him for life. A group of settlers mistakenly went after Nickshaw. Heman Oviatt, David Hudson, and Owen Brown (John Brown's father) supposedly found the Indian dead. Two men were charged with murder but were acquitted in a Warren court. This was a case of mistaken identity on both sides.

Another bit of Indian lore concerns the Haymaker family, first settlers of Franklin. John, his wife, Sally, and their three children stayed the winter of 1805–1806 in a former surveyor's hut at what today is the west end of the Crain Avenue bridge in Kent. That fall, an Indian woman bearing a baby came to visit. She stood the baby on its board outside the hut. A wild hog grasped the baby and ran off with the squaw in pursuit. She clubbed the hog and retrieved her baby.

Cackler said he first saw Standing Rock in the fall of 1804. At that time, there were two trees on top. Whenever an Indian passed by, he fastened a piece of bark to one of the trees, pointing the direction he had gone. "There were many pieces of bark still clinging to the tree when I first saw it," Cackler said. Standing Rock still today is one of Kent's most historic landmarks.

———

## HUNTS HELPED TAME THE WILDERNESS
## IN PORTAGE COUNTY
### May 4, 1985

Portage County during its early days was teeming with wildlife. Wild animals roamed the forests at will, presenting many dangers to our first settlers and to their domestic animals. There are many stories of near escapes from enraged bears, wolves, and wildcats, which at one time were more plentiful in the county than cattle, sheep, and hogs.

To combat the danger from marauding wild animals, pioneers in nearly every township staged huge game hunts that resulted in wholesale slaughter of animals by the hundreds. The 1885 *History of Portage County*, which was reprinted by the Portage County Historical Society several years ago, provides a vivid account of these hunts.

Here's how these hunts were conducted. An entire township would be surrounded by hundreds of men and boys, and at a prearranged signal hunters would begin marching toward the township's center. As the circle contracted, animals were driven into an ever-shrinking area. Those that tried to escape through the line of hunters were gunned down. At the ring's center, all the animals and fowl were slaughtered.

The first of these hunts was held in Freedom Township in December 1818, accounting for 23 bears, 36 deer, 7 wolves, plus scores of wild turkeys and smaller game animals. A few days later, on Christmas Day, another hunt took place in Windham Township when 21 bears, 68 deer, a wolf, a wildcat, and an uncounted number of fowl and smaller animals were slaughtered.

The story was much the same in other townships. An 1818 hunt in Edinburg netted 7 bears, 5 wolves, 100 deer, and 400 turkeys; and the next year a hunt in Atwater and part of Edinburg Township felled 21 bears, 18 wolves, 103 deer, and 300 turkeys. That same year, 5 bears, 4 wolves, 60 deer, and considerable numbers of smaller animals and fowl were killed in a Streetsboro hunt. These hunts were sometimes referred to as "ring" or "army" hunts.

Why were our forefathers so ruthless in the slaughter of wild animals? Apparently there were several reasons. They killed animals, especially the larger ones, to protect themselves and their livestock. Also, there was a financial consideration. Bounties were paid for the scalps of the more dangerous animals. And certainly the hunts also put meat on the table.

Desecration of vast numbers of the animal kingdom appears to have been a way of life among our settlers. The most graphic example of these practices was the ruthless slaughter of our vast buffalo herds as settlers moved west to homestead new areas in the later years of the nineteenth century. Many "professional" buffalo hunters killed the animals to reap profits from their hides. Had we not put buffalo on the protected list, they would be extinct today.

The valleys of the Mahoning and Cuyahoga Rivers at one time were teeming with wildlife. In the swamps of Brimfield, bears were so numerous that the township once was known as "Bear Town."

The organized hunts had a telling effect in lessening wild game population and by the late 1830s had become increasingly unpopular. So
much opposition on the part of a certain class of citizens developed that
organized hunts finally were abandoned. Records indicate that the last
wolf in Streetsboro Township was shot by Merril Stanton on March 6,
1838. By that time, the large, more troublesome animals had pretty much
disappeared from the county.

Rattlesnakes were another problem for our early settlers, particularly
in the ledges area of northern Portage County. Regular hunting parties
were organized in the springtime to invade their dens to do away with
them. Settlers called them "yellow-skins." The first death in Portage
County was attributed to a rattlesnake bite. A boy named Bixby was
bitten by a rattler and died in 1799. His coffin was a log, split in half and
hollowed out to contain his body. Today, the sighting of a rattlesnake
would be big news.

Contrast the game hunts of olden times with the efforts government
organizations and wildlife groups expend today to retain and to propagate our supply of game. For example, an article in this month's *Kiwanis
Magazine* describes in detail the cooperative efforts of the United States
and Canadian governments to rebuild a plentiful supply of game in
both countries. Tranquilized moose are airlifted by helicopter from
Algonquin Provincial Park in Canada to a base camp where they begin
a long truck ride to the Upper Peninsula of Michigan, where moose
were once plentiful but disappeared following a turn-of-the-century
cutting of their habitat. On the Peninsula the transplanted moose form
a new herd. In exchange, wild turkeys captured in the United States are
making new homes in southwest Ontario, where they had become nonexistent. The same cooperative plan is resulting in forming new colonies of caribou, whooping cranes, grizzly bear, and other forms of wildlife in the United States.

All of this happens because of effective management by both countries and the perception of what the quality of life should be. Man has
the nasty habit of learning too late the importance of preserving nature's
balance. Perhaps had we not wantonly slaughtered many of our animals
as long ago as 165 years, we would not now have to be engaged in costly
programs to preserve and replenish our near-extinct colonies of some

species. Instead, we failed to learn from our predecessors, the Indians, who killed only enough to supply their food, clothing, and shelter needs.

———

## ANY WAY YOU LOOK AT IT, DEATH HASN'T CHANGED

*July 19, 1987*

Life was fragile on the Portage frontier. Death was a frequent and morbid caller. The raw civilization in the early 1800s, as our first settlers carved new homes from the Western Reserve wilderness, spawned hardships, disease, and a high death rate. Lack of sanitation, poor food preparation, a most humble level of medical technology, and natural hazards all contributed to the poor life expectancy.

Gravestones in our oldest county cemeteries bear silent witness to the prevalence of early death, as do genealogies of our earliest families. Cemeteries contain hundreds of graves of children under three years of age. Listings of children in family records all too frequently include the notation "died in infancy." Families who raised six to eight children fully expected to lose two or three others. An early Mantua writer observed that of 67 deaths in that community during a 25-year period, 45 were children under the age of three.

In those spartan days a male could expect to achieve age 40, if he was lucky. Even as recently as 1900, a baby born that year had a life expectancy of only 47.3 years compared with today's 73.8. In 1915, 999 of 100,000 babies died before they reached one year of age.

One of the first deaths in what now is Portage County (with the exception of Indians) was that of Hugh Blair, a rider with a pack train of horses which transported goods from Pittsburgh to the mouth of the Cuyahoga on Lake Erie. In 1800 his horse stumbled and threw him off in the vicinity of Breakneck Creek. He died of a broken neck. Supposedly, that's how the stream achieved its name.

Another of the county's earliest deaths was that of an Indian boy in Deerfield in 1809. Compassionate settlers buried his remains east of the center in a handmade coffin stained by the juice of a maple tree. And in

Rootstown, Harvey Davenport, a young man who came to Rootstown with the community's namesake, Ephriam Root, in 1800, died soon thereafter, becoming the first deceased in that community.

Of course, there were exceptions. All of the early deaths were not those of young people. George Austin of Rootstown lived to the ripe age of 106. Old history books are filled with drawings of early residents who appear ancient. Perhaps they only looked old, considering their beard embellishments.

Early burials in Portage County were made on the deceased's own premises in family cemeteries. For the lack of suitable coffins, hollowed-out logs customarily were substituted. The lack of roads sometimes posed a troublesome problem, even in death. Again in Rootstown, in 1809 the body of Nathan Chapman Sr., one of the town's earliest settlers, was carried on a bier for more than a mile to his grave in what is known as the Old Cemetery.

Malaria, or ague, was one of the common ailments of that day, claiming many victims. No doubt the prevalence of stagnant water had much to do with the onset of the disease. Quinine was accepted as the common antimalaria medicine. Homemade nostrums, some of them descending from the Indians, were common. Their ingredients were scrounged from the forests.

Naturally, some hucksters were brazen in the promotion of their cures. For example, in 1835 an advertisement in the *Western Courier*, published in Ravenna, extolled the curing properties of "Napoleon's Fomentation," claiming that it was a sure cure for hydrophobia, cancers, piles, and snake bites, among others in a long list of ailments. Our early doctors rode horseback to see their patients. Their out-of-town calls were priced at 25 cents. Hospitals were nonexistent.

Accidents, too, took their toll. Life was rugged and equipment was crude at best. One such accident claimed the life of William Price of Kent, who went to Lisbon to haul a new grinding stone back to his mill in the Stow Street area in 1831. On the return trip, the wagon upset and Price was crushed to death under the weight of the huge millstone.

Mortuary science was unknown in that day, as were commercial coffins. Bodies were preserved in ice until funeral services. Embalming was not then required by law. Coffins were handmade, most often by the

The Riddle Coach and Hearse Company of Ravenna made carriages and horse-drawn hearses.

community cabinetmaker. Arvillus Larkcom of Freedom must have spent most of his lifetime making coffins. When he died in 1883, it was estimated that his hands had fashioned three thousand of them.

In earlier days funeral services were held at the home or at the church, many times in both places. Early funeral directors provided chairs to accommodate mourners in homes. Church bells were tolled in mourning for one hour prior to the time of service. An artificial wreath, provided by the funeral director, was placed at the entrance of the deceased's home to let the public know that a death had occurred.

Earlier funeral costs were modest. Charles Dudley of Freedom in 1878 recorded them as follows: casket, $30; hearse, $3; grave digging, $4; sermon, $5; doctor's last bill, $10.50; and monument, $132.50. The S. C. Bissler and Sons Funeral Home in Kent has record books of the firm's predecessor, the Ira L. Herriff Funeral Home. Costs ranged from $39 to $101 in the 1880s.

Death was responsible for one of Ravenna's most prosperous industries for many years. Henry W. Riddle, a woodworker, arrived in Ravenna in 1860 and then took over the old N. D. Clark and Company carriage works, founded in 1832, to form Merts and Riddle for the manufacture of horse-drawn hearses. In 1890, this became the Riddle Coach and Hearse Company, whose intricately carved hearses were much in demand. Four presidents were carried to their graves in Riddle hearses.

During our long history, death has not changed. Only its frequency and the progressing customs we employ to accommodate it.

-------

## 1810 STOW STREET CEMETERY HOLDS
## HISTORY SECRETS
*May 26, 1991*

Each day thousands of motorists drive by one of Portage County's oldest landmarks. They pay little attention and hardly give this pioneer shrine a passing glance. Indeed, it's a safe guess that many of them don't recognize its existence. We're referring to the Stow Street Cemetery in Kent, located a long stone's throw from the city's downtown along the banks of the Cuyahoga River and adjacent to Fred Fuller Park.

Those who travel Stow Street probably are aware of its presence, but motorists who use Haymaker Parkway would be less conscious of this hallowed burial ground, at 181 years one of the most ancient in Portage County. It is appropriate that Haymaker Parkway, dating back only to 1975, should be located in such close proximity to the cemetery. The cemetery was created by Kent's founding Haymaker family and the first burial—that of Eve Haymaker—was made there in the fall of 1810. It is appropriate, too, that this cemetery's history be recounted this Memorial Day weekend as the nation pays tribute to its dead of all wars and as Americans decorate the resting places of their loved ones.

Stow Street Cemetery has not been in general use for more than 130 years, but it remains a public cemetery under the jurisdiction of the community's Cemetery Board of Trustees, a body that includes a city councilman, a Franklin Township trustee, and one member appointed from the community-at-large. That board is responsible for maintenance of the Stow Street Cemetery as it is for the upkeep of Standing Rock Cemetery and Green Cemetery on Hudson Road.

Stow Street Cemetery is tied as closely to the history of Kent as the Haymaker family itself. Jacob Haymaker purchased land in today's Franklin Township and sent his son, John, wife Sally, and their three children to settle the land in the fall of 1805. Jacob and his wife, Eve, arrived the next spring, as did another son, George, and the settlement began in earnest. The Haymakers built a cabin in the Stow Street area, planted crops, and built the community's first mill, albeit a crude one.

When Eve Haymaker died on October 11, 1810, the Haymaker family set out a two-acre plot along the banks of the Cuyahoga for use as a family burial ground. A year later, the family deeded the property to the Franklin Township trustees to serve as a community cemetery. For 48 years, the cemetery was the community's only burial ground, serving until Standing Rock Cemetery was opened along North Mantua Street in 1859.

Names on the tombstones in the Stow Street Cemetery provide a slice of Kent's earliest history. It is there that many of the community's pioneers are buried, some of them in graves whose markings are all but obscured by time. Other markers have been broken, propped up in a sad and awkward fashion against markers still upright.

Besides the several members of the Haymaker family, pioneers in their final resting places at the Stow Street Cemetery include such familiar family names as Woodard, Kelso, Burt, Parmelee, Russell, Root, Clapp, Rockwell, DePeyster, Wolcott, and Earl, among many others. The last burial in the cemetery was that of William A. DePeyster in 1914. He joined ten other members of the DePeyster family, one of whom was George B., who was commissioned the community's first postmaster in 1820.

The oldest burial visible on a headstone was that of James Oviatt, a young man of 19 years in 1818. That doesn't jibe, timewise, with the burial of Eve Haymaker there in 1810, a disparity that requires explanation. During the years that followed the opening of Standing Rock Cemetery, graves of many of the early settlers were moved from Stow Street to the new cemetery in the 1860s. Headstones also were moved. Although five Haymaker burials still are listed for the Stow Street Cemetery, graves of Jacob and Eve are not among them. Presumably, their graves were moved to Standing Rock.

The Stow Street Cemetery is a quiet, pastoral scene. There are large trees, considerable unused, open space, and the songs of birds chiming in with the rushing waters of the Cuyahoga. But all is not well with the cemetery. Like a stepchild, the cemetery appears to come out second best to the larger, more prominent Standing Rock. Crews mow the grass, but little else is done to keep the cemetery shipshape. This is not intended as a criticism of the Cemetery Board of Trustees. It's a simple case of the currently used cemetery getting most of the attention.

Surrounded by a chainlink fence, the two-acre plot is a gorgeous spot. But overgrown trees send their boughs over the fence, some of them almost submerging nearby graves. An attractive wrought-iron gateway is desperately in need of a new coat of paint. Tree trimming and painting would do much to bring the cemetery up to a condition befitting its role as the final resting place of our earliest settlers. And the cemetery would benefit from more frequent mowing and trimming.

The Kent Historical Society would like to see the Stow Street Cemetery restored to a more prominent place in Kent's history. What form the project will take still is an open matter. Perhaps the Society will organize a general clean-up and renovation of the ancient burial ground, in which case other community organizations most likely would become involved. Tours of the cemetery and its more than 200 graves are a possibility. Likely, a plaque will memorialize these pioneers.

In any event, stay tuned. Stow Street Cemetery most likely will play a more prominent, and more deserved, role in the community's current history.

***

## PORTAGE VOLUNTEERS PLAYED PROUD ROLE IN WAR OF 1812

*November 8, 1986*

Several of Portage County's townships had not yet been settled when General Meigs issued a call to county volunteers to defend the frontier in May 1812. Portage County, as a result of legislation passed in 1803–1804 by the Ohio General Assembly only months after Ohio became a state, already had its First Brigade of the Ohio Militia for home defense. The brigade was composed of all male inhabitants of military age in Trumbull County, of which Portage then was still a part.

Capt. John Campbell, founder of Charlestown who resided at Campbellsport, organized a company of rifleman on May 23, 1812, and war was declared against the British on June 18. Soon after the declaration of war, Campbell's company received orders to meet at Campbell's house, and on July 1 the citizen-soldiers pitched their tents, made of homespun linen sheets, along the banks of Barrel Run near Campbell's home. The militiamen had no uniforms, but each man was armed with rifle, tomahawk, and a large knife that were furnished by the public.

To John Harmon of Ravenna, a member of that 1812 militia, historians are indebted for a firsthand description of Portage County's role in the War of 1812. He wrote his report 57 years following the end of the war and had only a written roster of the regiment's personnel. The remainder of the report was based upon his recollections.

On May 23, when the prospective volunteers gathered in Ravenna, musicians—a drum and fife—went to the front of the crowd and men were told to step out and follow the music if they wanted to volunteer. When the music stopped, 51 citizens had volunteered to join up. It should be remembered that in 1812 Portage had a population of only 3,000, and 51 probably was considered a goodly number of volunteers for this "Second War of Independence."

The group was marched to the south side of the courthouse where their names were duly recorded. That night, a company of officers was elected at the home of William Tappan, which stood a short distance northeast of Courthouse Square. Campbell was elected the regiment's colonel.

On that roll of volunteers are many Portage County names familiar to succeeding generations of Portage Countians. Besides Campbell, Alva Day, John Caris, Lewis Ely Jr., Joshua Woodard, and Delaun Mills were among the officers. The corps of officers represented Deerfield, Rootstown, Ravenna, Atwater, Mantua, Randolph, and Palmyra, and the regiment's privates represented an even broader area of the county.

On July 4 the men were treated to an Independence Day dinner, and on July 6 their long, tedious, dangerous march began. They camped in

Hudson, Cleveland, and Sandusky bound for Detroit, where they were to help defend, with the aid of the main army, the fort against the British. They sailed on Lake Erie, finally arriving in Michigan. Many of the men were ill, presumably from eating spoiled beef furnished by an Indian whom they considered friendly.

Then, on August 17, a British officer arrived to demand the garrison's surrender, bringing with him articles of capitulation from General Hull's army. Indeed, General Hull had surrendered, a move that was considered near-treason by other American military authorities. The last word the Portage soldiers had heard of Hull was that he had successfully invaded Canada.

By that time, the Portage County company had been reduced to 21 by death and transfers. All were imprisoned by the British but were permitted, as parolees, to return home. They sailed for Cleveland, landing there on August 31.

Harmon later wrote of the Portage County contingent's exploits: "Although we were so unfortunate as to contract sickness and did little toward the defense of the frontier, it was because we had no opportunity, having been captured before we saw the enemy. We at least showed a willingness to do our duty in defense of our homes."

Meanwhile, during the brief war, all was not quiet on the home front in Portage County. When the Portage citizen soldiers left to defend the frontier, they left only Erastus Carter, who had a lame arm, to defend the women and children of Ravenna. Preliminary arrangements had been made that, should the fortunes of the war worsen, women and children should flee to Pittsburgh to escape a British and Indian invasion.

There was considerable anxiety when Hull surrendered his American forces and preparations for flight began in earnest. The cannonading between Comm. Oliver Hazard Perry and British vessels on Lake Erie was heard in northern Ohio, and soon a night messenger came riding through Portage to warn people to flee for their lives. The messenger said Indians were about to swoop down on settlers.

As flight preparations went forward, another messenger arrived. A horn was heard in the direction of Shalersville and a horseman came dashing along the road shouting, "Hurrah, hurrah, Perry is victorious." Dread of the moment turned to joy as settlers received the glad tidings.

The British had been defeated, and they could return to the tasks of carving an existence from the Western Reserve wilderness.

———

## UNDERGROUND RAILROAD DID
## ITS SHARE IN PORTAGE

*March 13, 1988*

The Portage area has had many railroads during its long history. Its most unusual one had no rails, ran no trains, carried no freight or paying passengers, and was not intended for profit. This railroad had no station buildings or station agents. However, it did have unofficial stations and agents who worked without pay and at considerable personal risk. What's more, its operations never were advertised, and no inducements were held out for public acceptance. This was the Underground Railroad, which was neither underground nor really a railroad.

The Underground Railroad was a highly complex, yet not a formally organized, system for helping southern slaves escape to the northern states and into Canada prior to the onset of the Civil War. It took its name from the secret, swift way in which slaves were transported to freedom. Free Negroes in both the North and the South as well as devout white abolitionists in the North assisted the slaves in their flight to freedom.

Ohio and Pennsylvania were important branches in this maze of clandestine operations, and Portage County was by no means an exception. In this area, scattered operations of the Underground Railroad are historically preserved largely through hearsay, a natural result of the railroad's secret nature. But there are documented incidents in the railroad's success, and to this day some residents of historical bent will point out sites that were customary stops and hiding places for the fleeing slaves. Some of those are a matter of historical record; others are mere conjecture.

Portage County was no stranger to slavery; in fact, several easterners brought slaves with them when they settled in Portage in the early 1800s, despite a provision in the Northwest Ordinance of 1787 that strictly forbade slavery in the Northwest Territory. When John Garrett came from Delaware to Nelson Township in 1804, he brought with him two Negro girls. He did so with a notarized writ which pledged they would be set free at the age of 18. In Palmyra, Noah Smith was prosecuted for holding a girl in bondage. A fine was imposed against him, but before punishment could be meted out, a higher court set aside the judgment against him.

Pre–Civil War years were emotionally charged over the slavery issue in Portage County. Differing views were so intense that even family relationships sometimes were strained. Schisms extended even to membership of churches. As early as 1834 a riot is said to have occurred in Aurora as a result of the slavery issue. Generally, Portage Countians were violently opposed to slavery, as evidenced by an antislavery rally in Ravenna on July 4, 1855, which drew a crowd estimated at 15,000.

The issue also involved partisan politics, and the label of "slavery party" was tagged on the Democrats. Published election results actually identified some candidates as "slave Democrats." Perhaps some of the antislavery sentiment stemmed from the most famous abolitionist, John Brown, a Kent resident in the mid-1830s. In any event, bells tolled in sympathy and protest when Brown was hanged in 1859 for his Harpers Ferry raid.

Another outcropping of the antislavery movement was an 1848 petition from Randolph residents to the Ohio General Assembly for the state to secede from the Union. The unsuccessful action was based upon the premise that Ohio's remaining in the Union placed the state on the side of southern slave states. With such an outpouring of antislavery sentiment, it was natural that Portage should be a prominent hub on the Underground Railroad. Although the railroad system was a loosely organized one, it is known that Kent had a bona fide committee charged with the duty of assisting escaped slaves.

The first instance of the railroad's existence here was in 1825 when two Negro men, three women, and a baby—all weary and half-starved—stopped at Woodard's Tavern located at the corner of North Mantua Street and Fairchild Avenue. Joshua Woodard fed and befriended them, and in the dark of night they were secreted in a wagon covered with hay, bound for Cleveland and a hoped-for trip across the lake into Canada. Young James Woodard, then only 15 years old, was assigned as the driver. North of town, the wagon was halted by two men whom

Woodard rightly guessed were seeking slave runaways. They asked what he had in the wagon, and he said produce for the Cleveland market. He went on his way, whistling a merry tune.

Young Woodard had declined to take the baby with him on grounds that he would cry out and reveal the slaves' presence. He remained behind with the Woodards, with the mother promising to return and reclaim him someday. She did, but the boy didn't recognize her. He remained with the Woodards and was raised into manhood by them.

Charlotte Weaver, grandmother of the late Dudley Weaver, prominent Portage County historian, told another interesting story involving the Underground Railroad. Her uncle and aunt ran the Cuyahoga House at the corner of North Mantua and Cuyahoga Streets in Kent. She watched as her aunt, Eliza, packed a basket with food which she said was for some hungry people. That day, two men arrived at the inn seeking runaway slaves. They searched every inch of the house and the barn, sticking pitchforks into the haymows, but failed to find the slaves who were secreted in a hollowed-out barn wall. "That night a wagonload of grain left the premises," Charlotte Weaver wrote. "Slaves—I never knew how many—were hidden among the sacks."

These are only two examples of encounters runaway slaves had with slave-seekers from the South. No doubt there are many more reposing within the dim pages of history or among handed-down recollections.

It is estimated that 75,000 escaped slaves gained their freedom via the Underground Railroad. The total is only a smidgen of the four million slaves in the southern states at the outbreak of the Civil War. They would be freed only after four years of the bloodiest war in American history.

———

## EX-SLAVES CHERISHED FREEDOM HERE

*May 14, 1989*

During the years of their youth, Henry and Rebecca Brantley held out only dim hopes of ultimately enjoying the blessings of freedom and peace. They were slaves who were sold on the auction block, destined to lives of toil in the fields of the Deep South and to endure the cruelties and indignities commonly directed toward Negroes during the pre–Civil War days. They were chattel, accustomed only to years of back-breaking labor and eventual death on the southern plantation.

But Henry and Rebecca at long last found freedom and peace, not in the South but in Ravenna, Ohio, where they spent the remainder of their lives in contentment, earned respect, and solid citizenship. Their lives were not unlike those of thousands of other former slaves who won their freedom by the blood spilled on Civil War battlefields.

A towering monument over their graves in Maple Grove Cemetery in Ravenna bears witness to the lives of travail led by Henry and Rebecca. The monument bears the word "Emancipation" with shackles falling from two carved hands. An inscription tells pertinent facts of their lives: "Henry Brantley born 1825, died April 15, 1888. Rebecca Brantley, born August 1833, died Oct. 26, 1880. Born slaves near Clarkesville, Montgomery County, Tennessee. Married 1852, Springhill, Mo. Fugitives from bondage, they came to Ravenna Aug. 28, 1862, where they lived honest and industrious lives."

Those brief words cannot adequately describe the lives of Henry and Rebecca. As with other slaves, they took their surname from their first owner, Abraham Brantley. At his death, Henry became the property of a son, Everett Brantley, and Rebecca was inherited by Everett's brother, Joel. The brothers subsequently moved from Tennessee to Springhill, Missouri. Henry and Rebecca were married there prior to the death of Joel Brantley. Rebecca then was sold to Washington Sides at public auction for $830. A drunken, cruel master, Sides forced her to pull a plow and do other field chores besides serving as housemaid. When the Civil War broke out, Sides took Rebecca and his other slaves to Arkansas to prevent them from escaping to the North.

Meanwhile, Everett Brantley, Henry's master, died and Henry became the property of the estate. While being transported to Arkansas, Henry escaped and made his way to the Union lines. By a stroke of good fortune, he became employed by Captain Seaton of Ravenna. In June 1862, Henry succeeded in locating Rebecca and took her to the Union army where she was given employment.

In August 1862, Captain Seaton was wounded and given a furlough to his home in Ravenna. He brought Henry with him. Rebecca followed in November. Although the war was far from over, Henry and Rebecca were free at last. And thus began useful lives for the former slave couple.

Henry became a plasterer and also worked as a handyman and care-taker for Judge C. A. Reed, for whom Reed Memorial Library is named. Rebecca worked in the judge's home. Rebecca was active in the Dis-ciples Church and earned a reputation as a skilled cook, being much in demand at parties and social gatherings. She learned to read after she was 30 years of age.

There exist two versions concerning the tall, striking monument that marks their graves. One version holds that Henry erected the monu-ment in memory of his wife. The other version contends that following Henry's death in 1888, Judge Reed ruled that the couple's savings be used to erect the impressive marker.

More than forty years ago, I took a photo of two Civil War veterans, John Grate, then 102, of Atwater, and Alvin Smith, 104, of Akron, and Ravenna historian John Lowrie posing with the Brantley monu-ment. Mr. Grate and Mr. Smith, a former slave, knew all about slavery. They fought four long years to eliminate this scourge from America's system . . . forever!

---

## SLAVERY PROTEST FUELED SECESSION
## BID IN RANDOLPH

*October 26, 1985*

During the pre–Civil War years, slavery feelings were emotionally charged in Portage County. So intense were differing views on the sla-very question that friendships were severed, family relationships were strained, and even schisms developed between church members. As early as 1834, a riot is said to have occurred in Aurora over the slavery issue. Generally, Portage Countians, harking back to their New England heri-tage, were opposed to slavery, and they backed their views with refer-ence to the Constitution's guarantee that all Americans are created free and equal.

These high emotions prompted mammoth antislavery rallies in the
1850s. One such was held in Ravenna on July 4, 1855, when 15,000
Portage Countians massed to hear spellbinding antislavery speeches.
One of the speakers was Ben Wade, who later became president of the
Senate and missed becoming president of the United States by one vote
when Andrew Johnson was impeached. James A. Garfield of Hiram was
a frequent speaker at such rallies. Only a few years later he would become a major general in the Union forces.

The slavery issue permeated Portage County politics during the pre–
Civil War years, Republicans charging that the Democrats were the
"slavery party." Published election reports actually identified some
Democratic candidates as "slave Democrats."

Stories of blacks fleeing to the North via the devious Underground
Railroad were common in local newspapers of that day. One escape incident concerned the family of Joshua Woodard, prominent Kent businessman who operated Woodard's Tavern at the corner of Fairchild Avenue and North Mantua Street. As the story goes, a slave couple and
their baby arrived at the tavern one night and were protected by the
Woodards. They were secreted in the Woodard home, located on the
western hilltop of Fairchild Avenue. Joshua's son, James, the next day
hid the couple in a load of produce and started for Cleveland from whence
they could flee to Canada. James declined to take the baby, fearing he
would cry out and divulge the slaves' hiding place. North of town, a
band of slave searchers stopped the wagon and probed the load with
pitchforks. Not finding the slaves, they permitted the wagon to proceed
to Cleveland where the couple went on to freedom. The slave couple had
agreed to return for their young son after antislavery sentiment died down.
When they did so several years later, the child did not recognize them,
and he was left in the Woodards' care to be raised to young manhood.

The community of Randolph was the hottest of antislavery hotbeds
in the days that preceded the Civil War. And thereupon hangs one of
the strangest tales during the pre–Civil War days when antislavery feelings were most intense. In the fall of 1818, residents of Randolph, many
of the community's most prominent men among them, petitioned the
Ohio General Assembly to take the necessary steps for the state of Ohio
to secede from the Union. Their reasons were directly opposed to those

of pro-slavery southern states who some years later seceded en masse. The Randolph secessionists, bitterly opposed to slavery, based their movement upon constitutional guarantees and also contended that by remaining in the Union Ohio actually supported the South's favor of slavery.

A petition signed by 80 residents of southern Portage County earnestly beseeched the Ohio General Assembly to call a convention of the people of Ohio "to concert measures for effecting a speedy and peaceable secession of this state from the Union for some or all of the following reasons." The 12 reasons, enumerating in detail many opinions of Randolph residents, were based upon the premise that, by remaining in the Union, Ohio actually condoned the views of slave states. To be specific, the petition said: "Because the state of Ohio with the Union is voluntary and a free state cannot be voluntarily associated in political relations with slave states without giving the countenance and sanction of that voluntary association to slavery of these slave states, on the principle that a state, as well as a man, is known by the company he keeps and, therefore, Ohio keeping company with the southern states, is responsible for their slavery and is by means of that connection, actually one of the slave states."

The petition went on to say that by remaining in the Union, Ohio, with its two million people, was in fact "throwing a shield of respectability over 300,000 slave-holders as a screen from the rebukes due to their horrible crimes, on the principle that respectability goes with numbers." The petition described slavery as the "scum of crimes" and stated that Ohio, by remaining in the Union, was "protecting the most heinous system of wickedness that ever existed."

The petition also alleged that Ohio, knowing of slave states in the Union, had no right to join the Union in 1803 and that Ohio representatives and senators could not take their seats in Congress alongside slave holders from the South "without recognizing those tyrants."

Some of the Randolph petition signers' names are recognizable today—137 years after signing the document. For example, William Stedman later served during the Civil War and emerged a general. Following the war, he served as consul at Santiago, Cuba, and died there of yellow fever in 1869. Dr. Joseph Price, a Randolph physician, was the father of Dr. E. W. Price of Kent who, in turn, was the father of Lucien Price, a gifted writer who achieved national prominence. Perhaps some of the signers have descendants in Randolph to this day—Case, Ensign, Churchill, Anderson, Merriman, Kendrick, Spees, and Smally, among others.

To Walter J. Dickerson we owe the preservation of this significant piece of Randolph history. Most of his writings concerning early days in Randolph up to 1880 were in the form of letters to newspapers. In 1953, Mr. and Mrs. W. H. Widener collected Dickerson's writings and published them in book form.

What was the outcome of Randolph's petition for Ohio to secede? The petition was presented to the Ohio General Assembly during the 1848–1849 session. Although considerable support was evident, no action was taken. And, thus, when southern states seceded 12 years later, Ohio was spared the odium that most certainly would have followed.

––––––

## GENERAL HAZEN'S REPLY DIDN'T AMUSE
## GENERAL SHERIDAN

*January 10, 1988*

Maj. Gen. William B. Hazen, one of six Portage County generals during the Civil War, apparently had a sense of humor. And it got him into big trouble with his military boss. *Portage Heritage*, the 1957 history of our county, tells an interesting story concerning this top military figure in the War Between the States.

During the Missionary Ridge campaign, Gen. Philip Sheridan asked him for a written report on a certain aspect of the battle. Hazen thought everyone, including General Sheridan, knew about that phase of the campaign, so, apparently with tongue in cheek, he filed a rather flippant report with Sheridan. His boss in the Union forces didn't deem his reply amusing, nor did he appreciate his flippancy. He ordered him arrested as a matter of army discipline.

The incident did not appear to have a detrimental bearing on his later military career. He became a brigade commander in the Army of

West Virginia and fought at Corinth, Pittsburgh Landing, and Murfreesboro. Following the Chickamauga campaign, he was promoted to major general. Major General Hazen was Portage County's only West Pointer to serve during the Civil War. Most of the county's other Civil War commissioned officers came from the Ohio Militia, were granted commissions, or were promoted from the ranks.

Born in Vermont in 1830, Hazen came to Nelson Township with his parents as a young boy. It was during his student days at the Western Reserve Eclectic Institute (now Hiram College) that he became a friend of James A. Garfield, then Hiram's president. While still a student he received an appointment to West Point, where he graduated from in 1855.

He took part in Indian wars on the Pacific coast and then went to Texas and New Mexico, serving several years in frontier wars while a lieutenant. He was wounded by an Indian arrow and was unable to rejoin the army when the Civil War broke out. He became a colonel in the 41st Ohio Volunteer Infantry in August 1861 and was promoted to brigadier general late in 1862.

General Hazen remained in the regular army following the war until his retirement. He spent his retirement years in eastern Hiram Township, where his home grounds reflected his love of military life. He modeled the grounds after a military camp, with trees standing as sentries around his property and other trees representing the camp headquarters, guards, and other camp points. Following the general's death, his widow married Adm. George Dewey, hero of Manila Bay known for his famous wartime order, "You may fire when you are ready, Gridley."

Garfield, of course, became the best known of the five other Portage generals during the Civil War. He was president of Hiram College and a state senator when the war broke out, and he received a colonel's commission. Following the West Virginia campaign and Battle of Shiloh, he became a member of General Rosencrans's staff at Chickamauga, where Rosencrans praised him for gallantry and good judgment.

Garfield resigned his major general's commission in 1863 following his election to Congress and had not yet been seated following his election as U.S. senator when he was nominated for president in 1880. He was shot in July 1881 and died the following September.

Perhaps Gen. Erastus B. Tyler, a Ravenna hatmaker who had his shop on Cedar Street, was one of Portage's most active and best-known generals. Prior to the Civil War, he had been an Ohio militia general and he entered the war as a colonel in command of the 7th Ohio Volunteer Infantry. He achieved the rank of brigadier general in 1862.

Tyler led forces at Antietam, Chancellorsville, and Fredericksburg, but it was during the Confederate siege of Washington that he won his glory. His force held back the southern troops at Monocacy near the capital, a victory that won for him praise from President Lincoln, who said, "The country is more indebted to General Tyler than any other man for the salvation of Washington."

Gen. William Stedman of Randolph, who was a state representative when the war broke out, commanded the 6th Ohio Cavalry and was mustered out in 1864. He was breveted a brigadier general in 1865 shortly before the war's end. Orlando Risdon served the 53rd U.S. Colored Infantry as a first lieutenant and in 1863 became a colonel in the 53rd, serving until 1864 when he resigned. He was breveted a brigadier general in 1865. Gen. Edwin B. Atwood, a native of Garrettsville, served during the Civil War and emerged a major. During action in the Philippines he was named a brigadier general. The general later commanded the Chicago military district. He is buried in Arlington National Cemetery.

Portage had two other generals, both of the Ohio militia, who were active during the Civil War with the home guard, organized to oppose possible raiding forces. John B. King of Ravenna commanded the unit known as "Squirrel Hunters." David McIntosh, the Shalersville patriot who later bequeathed a still-existing flag fund to Portage County, helped to recruit army volunteers and worked with the home guard.

Correctly, the Civil War many times has been described as our country's bloodiest. Of the 2,070 Portage Countians who served, 312 died, an appalling 15 percent fatality rate. Contrast that toll with 57 of 2,400 in World War I and 137 of 5,565 in World War II.

———

## MASON ACTIVITY DATES TO PIONEER
## DAYS OF PORTAGE AREA

*April 7, 1984*

Back in 1793 President George Washington officiated at the cornerstone-laying ceremony for the U.S. Capitol in Washington, D.C. Wearing his Masonic apron, he troweled the mortar to set the stone for perhaps America's most revered government office. The fact that he wore his Masonic apron was not unusual inasmuch as the Grand Lodge of Maryland sponsored the cornerstone ceremony. His symbolism also bespoke his strong affection for the Masonic Lodge, which had its American beginning in 1717 when four colonial lodges united under the banner of the Grand Lodge of England.

The ideals and rituals of the Masonic Order stem from the centuries of cathedral building in Europe from 900 to the 1600s. European stone masons organized guilds. Freemasons transferred from town to town wherever work took them. With the decline of cathedral building in the late 1600s, those guilds or lodges began accepting members who never had been stone masons. Thus, the largest fraternal organization in the world was born.

As a natural consequence, many of the early colonists had been Masons in Europe who transferred interests in their order to America during the colonial settlement period. During the early days of American Freemasonry, the order engaged in numerous political activities, and some historians are of the opinion that Masons spearheaded the 1773 Boston Tea Party. By 1832, Masons (nationally, but not locally) had abandoned involvement in political matters, and the order became fraternal and social in character. A strong belief in God as the "great architect of the universe" is the basic tenet of the Masonic creed.

During its early days in Portage County, the Masonic Order was not without its problems. Ravenna was said to be the Ohio headquarters for an anti-Masonic party that spawned sweeping political and social implications.

Unity Lodge No. 12, F. & A.M. in Ravenna, organized in 1810 and the oldest lodge in our county, was forced to "go underground" during the anti-Masonic movement. The *Ohio Star*, a Ravenna newspaper that began publication in 1830, was recognized as both anti-Masonic and anti-Catholic. The *Star* was the pioneer paper in the publishing evolution which is represented by today's *Record-Courier*. The anti-Masonic movement in the 1830s and early 1840s was a powerful political force. Darius Lyman, a Ravenna lawyer, ran for governor of Ohio in 1832 as a Whig party candidate with a strong anti-Masonic backing. He carried Portage County and narrowly missed being elected governor.

During that period of anti-Masonic sentiment, the Ravenna lodge suspended operations. Gen. Lucius Bierce took charge of the lodge charter and property until the lodge resumed open activity in 1852. In Portage County communities, men who were nonmembers of the Masonic Order were dubbed "Jack Masons."

Today, Portage County has six Masonic Lodges. Two of them—Palmyra and Mantua—celebrated centennials in 1983, and the Garrettsville Lodge is 130 years old this year. Rockton Lodge No. 316 in Kent celebrates its 125th anniversary this year. The Aurora lodge was organized in 1910. The Ravenna lodge is 174 years old. The Mantua lodge actually was organized in 1818, but, for unknown reasons, it went into a period of inactivity, causing a 65-year lapse. Its charter was called and the lodge was not rechartered until 1883.

The old Marvin S. Kent home on West Main Street, owned since 1923 by Rockton Lodge, is one of Kent's most historic buildings. Following the cornerstone laying on June 7, 1880, Marvin S. Kent searched far and wide for the choicest woods, which were rendered by expert carvers into the elegant woodwork which remains today.

Kent was one of the first four men to petition for membership into the lodge following its chartering in 1859; hence, purchase of the Kent home for a Masonic Temple had deep meaning for the lodge.

Four presidents—Benjamin Harrison, William McKinley, William Howard Taft, and Warren G. Harding—visited the Kent home, and the guest room where they slept remains intact to this day.

Organizers of Rockton Lodge had intended to name it Kent Lodge to honor the Kent family. About that time, there was growing sentiment to change the name of Franklin Mills to Kent. Marvin Kent actually favored Rockton as the town's new name, but village officials and residents prevailed on the Kent issue. When the lodge noted the strong sentiment for Kent as the town's name, it turned to Rockton, which recognizes Standing Rock, another of Kent's historic landmarks.

———

## RANDOLPH FAIR IS A THRIVING REMINDER
## OF A BYGONE ERA
### July 27, 1985

For 160 years, the invitation "Come to the fair" has not been an idle one in Portage County. Proud of their agricultural heritage, Portage Countians have staged fairs almost continuously since 1825 in various locations and under numerous sponsorships. Beginning during the county's early settlement days, fairs have been held in at least eight Portage County communities.

Today, only one fair survives, the Portage County Randolph Fair, which will celebrate its 127th year when it opens Tuesday, August 20, for a six-day run. The well-managed Randolph Fair, which since 1973 has enjoyed state-granted county status, has succeeded when others have failed. Although the fair has changed with the times, it has retained its basic agricultural flavor. There is truth to the statement that the Randolph fair's best advertisement is the fair itself.

The demise of other community fairs, particularly the long-running Portage County fair in Ravenna, bespeaks the rocky road those fairs traveled the past 160 years. Only 27 years following the county's first settlement, a Portage County Agricultural Society was organized at a courthouse meeting on May 9, 1825. The cadre of first officers included prominent names in county history: Joshua Woodard of Franklin Township, president; Elias Harmon of Mantua, first vice president; Owen Brown of Deerfield and Hudson (John Brown's father), second vice president; Frederick Wadsworth of Edinburg, corresponding secretary; Samuel D. Harris of Ravenna, recording secretary; William Coolman Jr. of Ravenna, treasurer; and Jonathon Sloane of Ravenna, auditor.

The first fair and cattle show was held on October 18, 1825, on Sloane's 15-acre lot on East Main Street in Ravenna. The highlight of the exhibition was the awarding of a $3 prize to Seth Harmon of Mantua for the best corn crop of the season—a hundred bushels and one peck on one acre of ground.

That fair prevailed until 1830. In 1839, the Ohio General Assembly approved its first act to encourage agricultural societies, and another society in Portage County was organized on June 20 of that year with William Wetmore as president.

That society sponsored a fair on October 20 and 21 of 1841, and then a severe farm drout eliminated fairs in 1845. A year later a new agricultural society sponsored a fair in Ravenna. David McIntosh of Shalersville then was in the House of Representatives and Wetmore was a member of the Ohio Senate. McIntosh later became president of the society. The society rented land in the east end of Ravenna for a fair site, and fairs operated there until 1879.

Meanwhile, Garrettsville organized the Highland Agricultural Association with the expectation of taking over county fairs from the distressed county organization. Garrettsville operated fairs until 1890. The 1885 *History of Portage County* was plain spoken in defaming the independent fair organizations around the county, pointing out that "these societies detract from the interest and usefulness of the county organization and had better be abolished." As it turned out, the independent organizations, notably that in Randolph, were more successful than the county group. The most distinctive feature of the Garrettsville fair was an appearance there by Horace Greeley when he was a candidate for president against Ulysses S. Grant in 1872. He delivered a campaign speech at the fair. He was swamped by Grant in the election and died less than a month later.

Other communities which sponsored fairs at various times included Deerfield, which organized in 1858 and sponsored a fair until 1890 on grounds just west of the Center; Edinburg, which held a fair as early as 1861; Mantua, where a fair operated in the 1890s; Rootstown in the early 1870s; Palmyra, which ran a farm fair in the 1880s, plus its Welsh horse fair which began in 1830; and Ravenna, where the fair ran into financial difficulties during the Civil War years. At that time, Horace Y. Beebe led a campaign to raise funds to bail out the fair. Following that period, fairs were held regularly for 50 years in Ravenna on grounds off

North Freedom Street. New buildings were added, and horse-racing meets were held at other times. In 1890, 20,000 attended the Portage County fair in Ravenna.

At the turn of the century, special attractions were added to the Ravenna fair program, including balloon ascensions and parachute jumps. But in 1909 many of the buildings were destroyed by fire. Among secretaries of the county fair in those days were Lafayette Smith, H. W. Campbell, Charlie Sharp, and Fred Knapp.

Then, the fair again ran into trouble, and for a number of years no fairs were held. Enter Dan Hanna, owner of Cottage Hill Farms east of Ravenna. He contributed money and naturally became the fair board president. He initiated a bond sale, put in $10,000 of his personal funds and guaranteed bank credit to get the fair going again. Later, he foreclosed on the fairgrounds to redeem his bonds, another group bid for the fair property, and the fair resumed. Voters in 1916 defeated a $20,000 bond issue to finance the fair. Portage County fairs with harness races and other attractions continued without interruption until 1925 when public interest waned. H. Warner Riddle was president of the fair board when the last county fair was held in 1929.

A disastrous fire on August 2, 1932, swept the fairgrounds, destroying the North Freedom Street buildings. The fire doomed any hope of resuming the fairs, although Ravennan Merle Patch, with the aid of Ravenna Jaycees, revived the fair with the use of tents in 1946 and 1947. Then the grounds were sold, and that area today is the site of the Fairlawn housing allotment.

While other fairs were passing out of existence or undergoing severe financial stress, the Randolph Fair, founded in 1858 with Bela Hubbard, the community's first settler in 1802, as president, continued to grow. The fair was staged on several temporary locations prior to its 1875 move to its present site on Fairgrounds Road. Today, the fair organization owns 86 acres and 43 buildings for display of farm products and animals, plus a grandstand for special events such as tractor pulls.

When you attend the Randolph Fair next month, pause for a moment to appreciate the excellent job the fair board has done for 127 years and to reflect upon the less-than-illustrious history of numerous other Portage County fairs.

## PALMYRA MAYFAIR IS GONE, BUT THE
## MEMORIES LINGER

*April 30, 1983*

It has been said that anytime two Welshmen get together, they form a chorus—so fond of singing are the descendants of Wales! This coming Monday would have been a big day in Palmyra, an eastern Portage County community known for its heavy concentration of people of Welsh descent. For nearly 150 years the ordinary pursuits of life came to a halt in Palmyra on the first Monday in May to celebrate a gathering of the clan with food-laden tables, singing and speeches in the native Welsh tongue, and reminiscing.

In the early days, dating back to 1830, this community event was known as the Welsh Horse Fair, a time when proud owners brought their prize horses to the square of town for exhibition. The automobile age doomed the horse fair, but not the enthusiasm of Palmyra's Welsh population to continue the event. For many years, the festivities were known as the Mayfair or, simply, the fair.

Like too many events that once served to preserve the American heritage, the Mayfair now has passed out of existence. The last Palmyra fair was held about 10 years ago, and the event was abandoned because so many of the "old-timers" had died and enthusiasm among their descendants to continue the event had waned.

Too bad! In my early reporting days the Palmyra Mayfair was a standard event on my annual calendar. It couldn't be excelled for old-fashioned congeniality. Native Palmyrans returned each year to their home community to join with former residents in paying tribute to their Welsh ancestors. Old-timers took advantage of this one opportunity each year to sing the old Welsh tunes in what they referred to as a "gymanfa ganu." In non-Welsh terms, that's a songfest. Someone with more than ordinary articulation in the Welsh language would deliver an oration or sermon in the native tongue.

There was plenty of talk of the olden days and then everyone would await a repetition of the program a year later. Always on hand for these affairs was one of Palmyra's most prominent Welsh sons, Dr. Howard W.

Jones, president of Youngstown State University. Dr. Jones, born in Palmyra in 1895, died about a year ago.

Naturally, all of the Welsh family names—Jones, Lewis, Griffith, Davis, Johns, Williams, Evans, or Reese—were particularly evident at fair time. Palmyra's historical writings reveal that there once were 19 Jones families on the same mail route, a revelation that breeds sympathy for the mailman.

The Welsh phenomenon in Palmyra is of historic interest. The community was settled in 1799 not by the Welsh but by people from Connecticut. The first settlers were David Daniels and his family from Grattan, Connecticut. The Welsh came later—about 1830—to work Palmyra's coal mines. They learned that trade in their native Wales, which is known for its rich veins of coal and other minerals. Those hardy souls, plus people such as David Enoch Jones who came directly from Wales in 1859, brought with them a cultural slice of their native land.

Singing and other arts—poetry, painting, sculpture—are much a part of the Welsh life-style even today. Each year in August, the National Eisteddfad is held in Wales, bringing together Welsh artisans from throughout the world. It is a time to honor people of the arts in a massive competition. Wales is a country of tradition, despite the country's union with England, which took place in 1536. It is said that one of three Welshmen speak both English and their native tongue. On St. David's Day, March 1, many Wales residents wear leeks (similar to an onion) in their hats to honor the country's patron saint.

The Welsh people take pride in their kindliness and warm hospitality. And more than 65 years later, they'll let you know that David Lloyd George, World War I prime minister of Great Britain, was born in Wales. That fierce pride is one of the traditions and personal attributes Welsh families brought with them to Palmyra, a name not of Welsh origin but a city in Syria.

There are hundreds of descendants of those early Welsh families in Portage County. But, for them, there will be no Palmyra Mayfair this coming Monday. Only memories of fairs that were!

————

## ACTIVE PIONEER GROUP MET WITH
## A MYSTERIOUS END

*February 16, 1985*

Can you imagine a crowd ranging from 3,000 to 6,000 attending an annual meeting of any organization in Portage County? A crowd of that number cannot be comprehended in today's circles, but one of such proportions was commonplace more than a hundred years ago for the annual meetings of the Pioneer Association of Portage and Summit Counties. The story of the Pioneer Association is one of the most fascinating in local annals . . . a story gleaned from a handsome, bound volume of the association's secretary minutes from 1874 to 1913. In itself, the volume constitutes a lesson in local history.

In recent weeks, two bound volumes of the Pioneer Association have come to me by a circuitous route. A Kent woman intensely interested in local history acquired the volumes—the handwritten secretary's minutes and the treasurer's reports—from an Akron bookstore. How the volumes managed to find their way into the bookseller's hands is anyone's guess. The two volumes are obvious treasurers in the storehouse of county records—moving, descriptive reports of an organization that at one time held a position of prominence. Names of influential people—pioneers and descendants of local pioneers—comprise a who's who of Portage-Summit residents of that day.

The cover of one volume says the association was organized in 1873, at which time the 1874 meeting was scheduled. The secretary's first entry describes the first meeting of the association, held at the home of Mr. and Mrs. Samuel Olin in Streetsboro on February 19, 1874. Seventy-nine were present, most of them upon the invitation of Mrs. J. B. Stratton, Mr. Olin's sister. A peculiar twist of the secretary's report of the first meeting is the listing of the total weight—11,973 pounds—of those who attended. Christian Cackler won honors as the heaviest individual, at 212 pounds.

That same year, on October 30, the second meeting was held at the Cackler home on today's Cackler Road with the Reverend Andrew Willson, prominent Christian Church minister of Kent and Ravenna, in charge. At that meeting a constitution was adopted, Cackler was elected president and Dr. A. M. Sherman of Kent as secretary with Luther Parmelee as his assistant.

The organization had a simple goal: "to cultivate social relations and to perpetuate the memories of the early settlers of this section of the country." At the outset, the geographic area encompassed by the association included Franklin, Streetsboro, and Ravenna in Portage County and abutting townships Hudson, Stow, and Tallmadge in Summit County. Later, that area was expanded to include all of Portage and Summit Counties.

Beginning in 1875 and extending until 1887, the annual meetings were held in Kent's Grove, an area owned by Marvin S. Kent, which was located between Pioneer and Park Avenues between North Mantua and North Prospect Streets in Kent. It was from that association that Pioneer Avenue derived its name.

Marvin Kent was elected president at the first session held in his grove. So crushing were the crowds that multiple sittings were required for the big dinner. Minutes of the 1880 meeting relate that four dinner sittings were required to accommodate the picnic crowd of 3,000.

Programs at the annual meetings included election of a board of trustees and officers, music by the pioneer band, and usually a speech by one designated by the association as "orator," plus a lot of handshaking and exchanging of greetings. At each annual meeting the secretary presented a "mortuary report," a listing of members who had passed on during the previous year. Astonishingly, many of the listings included residents who had lived into their high nineties. Priscilla Spooner lived to be 103. It was not uncommon for the ages of the deceased members to average in the high seventies and into the eighties in an era when the mortality rate was quite high.

After leaving the Kent grove, the Pioneer Association had several annual meetings at Randolph Park at Silver Lake. Then, on September 6, 1888, the association came of age—it dedicated its own grounds in Franklin Township between East Main Street and Crain Avenue. The eight acres abutted the east village limits of Kent which then extended to what today is the University Drive area. Enos Brainerd, Ravenna merchant, was association president, presiding over ceremonies attended by 4,000. For the dedication ceremonies, the village of Kent put on its finest holiday attire to greet the visiting Pioneers. Schools were dismissed and factories closed for the day.

The site was purchased by the association from the heirs of George Kent for $1,600. A well was drilled, the area was fenced, and a building for storage of the association's tables and a platform was erected. After eight years, the association encountered financial troubles and was forced to turn over the grounds to a trustee. The group was unable to pay lease fees and in 1896 was forced to forsake all rights to the grounds. The association then moved to Silver Lake for its meetings and in 1903 began meeting at the Brady Lake resort. A park handbill at the time when D. A. Hartman of Ravenna was park manager details the Brady Lake Park arrangement with the association.

The association's volume terminates with the 1913 minutes of the 39th annual meeting on August 7. No mention is made in the minutes of disbanding the association, and several hundred blank pages remain in the secretary and treasurer's volumes. The last treasurer's entry shows a balance of $76.14.

More than a thousand attended the 1913 meeting, a crowd that would indicate the association still was a vibrant group. The association's unexplained demise raises many questions that remain unanswered in the research of local history records—What happened to the association's effects, including many photographs of pioneers? Who was responsible for the termination of a 40-year-old organization? And how did the association's records wind up in an Akron bookstore? We will probably never know.

———

## GRISMER'S *HISTORY OF KENT* IS A VALUABLE TOOL

*June 17, 1990*

Books are abiding friends of mankind. Some entertain. Others amuse, inform, chronicle the major events of time, or quench man's thirst for knowledge. Books are timeless; once written they assume their role in the realm of literature (good or bad) and are forever part of the grist of human existence. Their permanence is what makes them unique, particularly in this hurry-up world in which we live.

Books that treat historical matters and recall for ages to come man's quest for progress are special, not only for the information they provide for future historians, but also simply because they enlighten those who wish to know more about their town, state, nation, or the world.

Portage County has several such historical volumes—an 1874 atlas, a rather voluminous 1875 history of the county, the Christian Cackler Jr. 1870 *Recollections of an Old Settler*, the 1957 *Portage Heritage*, several histories of communities, and Karl H. Grismer's 1932 *History of Kent*.

It is the last in this list that currently draws our attention. Grismer's *History of Kent*, 304 pages that trace the history of Franklin Township and Kent from the days of the Indians until the dark days of the Depression, is a marvelous book. Written in vivid, interesting style, the book not only is entertaining reading but also a valuable tool for use by historians.

Grismer's book is not novelistic; it is more encyclopedic in the information it offers. If you want to know who served in World War I, his rank and outfit, and where he served, you will find the information there. Likewise, if you want to know when the present stone-arch bridge was built, who built it, and what it cost, you'll find that, too. There is hardly any limit to the historical information the volume provides.

There are 11 general chapters ranging from the days before Franklin Mills (Kent) was settled until the early 1930s, written in specific periods of time. Twenty-one specialized chapters follow on such topics as industry, clubs, churches, newspapers, Kent State University, public officials, sports, prohibition, and the like.

The book concludes with 75 biographies of residents and leaders, beginning with Zenas Kent, who helped to build the community. The biographies were included at a fee; that's how the volume was financed.

Grismer was a onetime employee of the Davey Tree Expert Company, and later he was on the staff of the *Beacon Journal*. He spent seven months interviewing old-timers and poring over the files of the *Kent Courier*, the *Kent Tribune*, and the *Kent Bulletin*. He visited libraries and the Western Reserve Historical Society to seek information and to confirm his research.

Publication of the history was announced in the August 9, 1932, issue of the *Courier-Tribune* as a "treasured possession forever by any family." The *Courier* published ads for several weeks to announce the book's availability at the amazing, low price of $3.50 for an attractive, hard-bound copy. If you wanted one sent by mail, you needed to add 25 cents for wrapping and postage. That's quite a contrast with today's prices. Only on occasion does a copy of the book surface, most times rescued from the remote reaches of an attic or a dusty shelf in a collection-type bookstore. In the last sale of the book coming to my attention, the original volume went for $150. That price tells us that copies of Grismer's history are scarce. Libraries have the book, but they are not loaned out; they must be read on site. My own volume is under lock and key.

The rarity of the *History of Kent* copies prompts the mission of this column. The board of trustees of the Kent Historical Society is planning to reprint and update the present volume by adding happenings and other material since 1932. One problem—a most important one— an author is needed. The author will need to do all of the research by scanning newspaper files of the past 58 years and collecting factual material from public records and other sources. And, of course, some interviewing of older residents may be involved.

When Grismer's *History of Kent* was published in 1932, it was the first in Franklin Township since Christian Cackler's *Recollections of an Old Settler* in 1870. That was a time span of 62 years.

Now 58 more years have elapsed. It's time for publication of another history.

———

## JOHN LOWRIE

### A Vast Cornucopia of History

*April 10, 1988*

Several times during many years of our association, John Lowrie told me that he had never known a day without a headache. What an affliction, I thought at the time, not to live a day without pain. There were those who expressed little surprise at John Lowrie's headache sufferings, considering that his head was crammed with thousands of historical items whose emergence he seemed able to command at the slightest provocation. He had an insatiable hunger for all matters of history and an extraordinary memory to recall with astounding accuracy events, dates, names, places, and people over years and decades of Portage County history.

John Lowrie was never happier than when he was sharing some of his historical knowledge, and I was flattered that he should want to share with me some of the choice tidbits from his vast storehouse.

It was he who pointed out a spot along Barrel Run at Campbellsport where Ohio militia general Joshua Woodard trained volunteer riflemen to defend the frontier during the War of 1812. And it was John, too, who spent a sunny afternoon with me at the old Robert Eaton home along S. R. 14 near Campbellsport, where the first session of the Portage County Common Pleas Court was held on August 23, 1808. He delighted in retelling how Judge Calvin Pease had fined William Simcock $1.50 for "sporting with guns and hounds" on the Sabbath in the county's first criminal docket case.

In southwest Kent, we spent a delightful afternoon as he explained the intricate engineering involved at the P. & O. Canal's crossover with Plum Creek. John had a particular attachment to the canal; his father, George, a shepherd boy in his native Scotland, had helped to build the canal in the late 1830s shortly after he came to America. Also, John was a carpenter and a building mover, and all matters of construction held a strong fascination for him.

And we spent many an afternoon in his Ravenna home, which was packed with historic relics, artifacts, and scores of newspaper clipping scrapbooks . . . a veritable storehouse of items relating to earlier Portage County days. Luckily, his wife, Alta, shared his interest in local history.

John Lowrie was not a patient man. He always seemed to be in a hurry in his quest for historic knowledge, and he became weary of those not inclined to proceed at his pace to accomplish community goals, particularly the establishment of a county museum.

Although his formal education was somewhat abbreviated, he made up for such shortfall by becoming a voracious reader. He wanted to know as much as possible about the world around him; thus, in 1932–1933 he and Alta took a round-the-world trip. One can well imagine how they must have marveled when they visited the ancient Pyramids and King Tut's tomb. That trip became part of a vast accumulation of treasured memories.

Probably more than that of any other Portage Countian, John Lowrie's focused attention upon the county's past inspired an interest that eventually led to the organization of the Portage County Historical Society in 1951. Even then he was impatient with the establishment of a museum, and he gave some of the couple's collection to the Summit County Historical Society. It was the Lowries' gift of one of their homes at the corner of East Main and Clinton Streets that made a museum a reality. One of the conditions for the property's transfer required that the society achieve a membership of 600. That figure was oversubscribed by 200.

That building later was sold and razed, and the society purchased the Charlotte Strickland home on North Chestnut Street, which was used as a museum until the new Lowrie-Beatty Museum building was opened in 1968. Today's society complex includes several historic buildings and is graced by the clock tower, which displays the 1882 clock salvaged from the old county courthouse. The tower was dedicated in 1973.

Except for his world trip, John Lowrie never strayed far from Ravenna. He was born in 1866 on North Freedom Street across from the old Portage County Fairgrounds.

He was physically, as well as mentally, tough. In September 1958 he was struck by a car while crossing the East Main–Clinton Street intersection. Three days later he was the honored guest as relatives and friends helped him celebrate his 92nd birthday. The following October 7, while he and a friend were visiting in Edinburg, he suffered a fatal stroke.

With him died a vast store of Portage County's history. But he left a more lasting legacy—an appreciation of the historical strands that wove a revered piece of fabric.

# DEDICATED DUDLEY WEAVER,
# A HISTORIAN'S HISTORIAN

*April 27, 1985*

Dudley S. Weaver completed many personal missions during his interesting and contributing lifetime. Dudley was a historian, in my mind one of the most skilled Portage County has ever known. But, as with all historians, his work was not finished when he died on August 16, 1984.

An admirer and student of President Abraham Lincoln, right up until his death Dudley had worked toward the dedication of the spot in Ravenna where Lincoln's train halted for a few precious moments on February 15, 1861, en route to his inaugural in Washington. His longtime dream was fulfilled last Saturday when the Portage County Historical Society, in cooperation with Wendy's Restaurant, dedicated the site in an impressive ceremony. Fittingly, the site was dedicated in Dudley's memory.

I have many fond memories of my friend and fellow historian. A painstaking and exacting researcher, Dudley probably researched and recorded more local history happenings than any other Portage Countian. He was an accommodating source-person who always could be counted on to provide historical notes to those less skilled in such matters. There was a time during his long employment at AMETEK-Lamb Electric in Kent that he arose regularly four hours early to research and write Portage history before reporting for work. Such dedication to a cause is rare.

For 20 years he spent his vacations tracing the battlefield footsteps of his grandfather, Adam Weaver, a boy soldier with the Union army. In 1965 during the Civil War centennial, he waded into a swamp near old Fort Anderson, North Carolina, the spot where his grandfather was shot and severely wounded. In reverence to his grandfather's memory, he stood there quietly. Then he took a flask of water and poured it over the spot where his grandfather had fallen. This was his personal act of consecration. He had taken the water from a well on his grandparents' farm, which was located on Morris Road in Kent.

Dudley's interest in local history was spawned at the knee of his grand-mother, Charlotte. He was fascinated by her recollections of local happenings . . . stories of Indians, the Civil War, the trials of early settlers as they eked a bare existence from the lands of Portage County. Dudley developed an abiding respect for our forebears, an interest that inspired so many people and organizations including the Portage County Historical Society, which he helped to establish and which he served as trustee, researcher, historian, and editor of its newsletter for 20 years.

Railroading and streetcars also were among Dudley's hobbies, an interest that probably dated back to his grade school days in Kent when he worked early in the morning as a car checker before leaving for school. For many years he edited a newsletter that circulated among interurban car hobbyists and he built more than 400 model trains and streetcars.

Dudley's collection of historical memorabilia, much of it now in the Portage County Historical Society's archives, was immense. Throughout his lifetime he collected old-time photographs. Those he borrowed he copied on a view camera, in itself a collector's item.

In the mid 1950s, when Franklin Township and Kent were celebrating their sesquicentennials, the *Record-Courier* published a commemorative edition. Dudley was our main source of historical materials. I recall visiting his Brady Lake home and selecting from hundreds upon hundreds of photos, prime items for publication in the edition. He always was willing to help in such efforts.

Every local historian can count other history buffs among his mentors. For Dudley, the fabled John Lowrie, in addition to his grandmother, was his mentor. John was a storehouse of historical information, but he carried much of it in his head without troubling to record it. Dudley extracted much of John's material and developed records that will serve Portage County's future generations.

Dudley was my friend and the best of my mentors.

———

# KENT HISTORY BUFFS OWE DEBT TO ART TRORY
## Early Scenes Captured on Film by "Modern Mathew Brady"
### *December 1, 1994*

How quickly we forget!

The other day someone asked me, "Who was Art Trory?" His question was prompted by an announcement by the Kent Historical Society that the organization was selling, among other historical items, the Art Trory book.

Art Trory did not write books. The book in question was published by Kent State University when Art's vast collection of photos and negatives was put on display in the KSU Archives at the University Library. The book is organized by topic and includes some reproductions of photos he took in Kent and other sections of Portage County during 78 years as an amateur photographer.

I like to remember Art Trory as a more modern Mathew Brady (who was considered the father of news photography and who became distinguished for his battle photos during the Civil War). Mathew Brady died in 1896. Seven years prior to Brady's death, Arthur James Trory received a simple box camera as a birthday present. That modest gift began for him a lifelong affection for photography. And that affection gave to this area a fine collection of photographs that captures our historical progress, encapsulates the pleasant happenings of his lifetime, and bespeaks the warmth and zest for living that he displayed.

I knew Art Trory during his advanced years. He was genuine. He was a beautiful human being. He was forever enraptured with all of the newness around him. With rather crude photographic equipment he did an excellent job of preserving on film the scenes, the happy as well as the tragic events, and the people of his time.

Art Trory's daughter, Betty McCormick, perhaps described best the character of her father. In the preface of the book which introduced his copious photo collection, she wrote: "He was a man of unlimited enthusiasms and had an insatiable interest in people, nature and life in general. In his 88 years he had acquired and enjoyed a multitude of friendships of fellowmen from all walks of life. He expressed surprise that the Good Lord should have allowed him to live so many good years and enjoy every minute of the journey. A few minutes before his death [in 1967] he looked out the window at early morning sunshine and said, 'Isn't it a beautiful morning? It's going to be my kind of day.'"

Art Trory was not a photographer by profession. But his photos have found their way into many collections of historic artifacts. If he ever made any money from his photography hobby, no one knows about it. At the same time, he was certainly one of Ohio's most prolific and most accomplished amateur photographers.

A native of Lyons, Ohio, in Fulton County, he came to Kent after completing high school. He attended Ohio Northern University and graduated in 1899 with a degree in pharmacy. He was a druggist, but his life touched many other fields besides photography.

After working with his brother, Fred, in a Kent drugstore, he opened a bakery, which he sold in 1902. Then he opened a bookstore on North Water Street in Kent, after which he became a purchasing agent for the Mason Tire and Rubber Company on Lake Street. In partnership with Oliver Young, later Kent's water superintendent, he went into the grocery business on North Mantua Street. He was manager of the Kent Automobile Club and secretary and president of the Kent Chamber of Commerce. He operated drugstores in Hudson, Massillon, and Ellet before returning in 1949 to Kent, where a half-century before he had photographed most of the important happenings in town.

When Art Trory died, his daughter contributed his extensive photo collection to Kent State University. In 1976, as part of the Bicentennial celebration, the Arthur J. Trory Photographic Collection was opened to public viewing in the Student Center Gallery. That showing followed a massive undertaking of printing, cataloging, titling, and identifying his remarkable photographs. The scope of the collection really is immense.

There are family pictures, turn-of-the-century scenes, gatherings of the Riverside Cycle Club, civic events, train accidents, ravages of the 1913 flood, the 1901 snowstorm, the fire that destroyed the ice house at Brady Lake, life at Ohio Northern during his student days, his family life, cityscapes that reflect the changing life of his hometown. The list goes on and on. Many historic postcards depicting local scenes were made from Trory photos. How fortunate it is that his valuable photo-graphs have been preserved for future generations to see and to appreci-ate and for historians to evaluate.

Art Trory considered himself blessed by many good fortunes, most important among them his 62-year marriage with the former Mabel Loretta Kelso.

On Thanksgiving Day in 1967 Art Trory took pictures at a family gathering. Two days later he died, bringing to a close 88 years of zestful, productive living and a 78-year love affair with amateur photography that began with a simple box camera.

———

PART TWO

# MEN AND WOMEN OF
# PORTAGE COUNTY

# NO SHORTAGE OF NOMINEES FOR
# PORTAGE HALL OF FAME

*November 22, 1986*

On November 27, 1961, an article in the *Record-Courier* under the by-line of J. B. Holm, Portage County historian and onetime newspaper editor, detailed plans for a Portage County Hall of Fame, a project envisioned by the Portage County Historical Society. The article reported that the society's trustees had authorized the project and that nominations of famous Portage Countians were being sought for inclusion in the hall. Twenty-five years have elapsed, and the Hall of Fame has not materialized. Many nominations were received at the time, and the society's trustees selected 10 famous men and women for the first phase of the Hall of Fame.

The late Dudley Weaver, society archivist, undertook the project. He attempted to accumulate photographs of the 10, some of them without success. With his death, the project was relegated to the "back burner" but, according to the society's Jerry and Marie Osborne, has not been forgotten. With many other matters requiring the society's attention, the Hall of Fame has not been one with prime priority, valid as its purpose may be.

Portage has had many outstanding men and women in many fields—the military, the judiciary, public life, music, letters, industry, theater, education, athletics, science, art, religion, entertainment, agriculture. To honor them in a Hall of Fame appears the least we could do to preserve their distinguished accomplishments for future generations.

Consider the following prominent men and women for a Portage County Hall of Fame:

MILITARY—Gens. W. B. Hazen of Nelson, E. B. Tyler of Ravenna, William Stedman of Randolph, all in the Civil War; Col. Bill Bower of Ravenna, one of Gen. Jimmy Doolittle's Tokyo raiders, and Col. Frank Goettge of Kent during World War II; Lucius Bierce of Ravenna, leader of the "Army of Canadian Liberation"; Adm. Calvin Bolster of Ravenna.

JUDICIARY—William R. Day of Ravenna, justice of the U.S. Supreme Court and secretary of state; Luther Day of Ravenna, justice of the Ohio Supreme Court; Perry Stevens of Ravenna, an appellate judge.

PUBLIC LIFE—James A. Garfield of Hiram, U.S. president, assassinated in 1881, a congressman and Civil War general; Benjamin Tappan of Ravenna, U.S. senator and federal judge; Congressmen Daniel Tilden of Hiram, Ezra B. Taylor and Jonathon Sloane of Ravenna, Robert Cook of Kent and Ravenna (also an appellate judge); Martin L. Davey of Kent, two-time governor of Ohio; Isaac Swift of Ravenna, noted physician; Clarence Patterson of Kent, governor of Oregon; Samuel Huntington of Aurora, third governor of Pennsylvania; A. L. Humphrey of Randolph, governor of Kansas; Warren Forward of Aurora, secretary of Treasury under President Tyler and minister to Denmark; Royal Taylor of Aurora, first U.S. pension agent; James R. Garfield of Hiram, the president's son, secretary of the Interior; Chancey Black of Hiram, governor of Pennsylvania; Lucius Fairchild of Kent, governor of Wisconsin; Henry Swift of Ravenna, governor of Minnesota; Samuel Huntington of Aurora, governor of Ohio.

MUSIC—Jessie Brown Pounds of Hiram, writer of many hymns, including "Beautiful Isle of Somewhere"; Frederick Loudin, Charlestown native and onetime Ravenna resident who directed the Loudin Jubilee Singers, who became internationally known; Francesco DeLeone, Ravenna pianist and composer.

LETTERS—John S. Kenyon of Hiram, internationally recognized expert on English-language pronunciation; A. G. Riddle of Mantua, author of *The Portrait*; writers Lucien Price and Jim Tully of Kent; Halsey and Harlan Hall of Ravenna, who became famous publishers of Minneapolis and St. Paul newspapers; Martin Williams of Palmyra, editor of the *Minneapolis Tribune*; Luther McGahan of Ravenna, who founded an early daily newspaper in Los Angeles; Albert Dix I of Atwater and Palmyra, founder of the Dix Communications network; Emily Doty McBride and Ella Eckert of Ravenna, both of whom became well-known writers; poet Hart Crane of Garrettsville; Maxwell Riddle of Ravenna, internationally known writer about dogs and judges; Harriet Upton Taylor of Ravenna and Nelson, writer and historian; Fannie Ward of Ravenna, syndicated writer.

INDUSTRY—Robert Cross of Ravenna, founder of Lockheed Aircraft; John Davey of Kent, father of tree surgery science and founder of Davey Tree Expert Company; Cyrus Prentiss of Ravenna, promoter and president of the

C. & P. Railroad; Marvin S. Kent of Kent, promoter and first president of the Atlantic and Great Western Railroad; F. R. and W. B. Fageol of Kent, bus developers and founders of the Twin Coach Company.

ENTERTAINMENT—Etta Reed Payton of Ravenna, star of the Broadway stage; Vaughn Monroe, onetime Kent schoolboy and a radio and television star; Clark Gable, who lived at one time in Edinburg and who became famous as a movie star; Albert Hodge and Peggy King of Ravenna, television stars; Emma Vaders of Ravenna, a stage star.

RELIGION—Joseph Smith, onetime Hiram resident, founder of the Mormon Church; Lorenzo Snow of Mantua, president of the Mormons.

AGRICULTURE—F. A. Derthick of Mantua, Ohio dairy and food commissioner and head of the Ohio Grange; Perry Green of Hiram, state director of agriculture, Ohio Farm Bureau head, and state representative.

———

## CAPT. SAMUEL BRADY

### In Short, a Fascinating Man

*September 27, 1987*

For many years, historians have labored under the delusion that Capt. Samuel Brady merely was a whale of a broadjumper and Indian fighter. He was both of those, as we know from historical accounts of his hefty leap across the Cuyahoga River in Kent and his prowess in eluding pursuing Indians. While we have come to know him in history as a jumper who could have challenged present-day Olympians, there appears to have been more to Captain Brady than his famous leap. Much more!

For starters, he was a Revolutionary War hero who distinguished himself, along with his father and brother, in several Battles. Enlisting as a private at 19, Brady participated in Battles around Boston and Long Island in 1778, where he demonstrated his bravery and was promoted to a lieutenant's rank. He was in the Battles of Trenton and Princeton, and for gallant service in the Battle of Brandywine and Germantown he won a captain's rank at only 21 years of age. He was dispatched into the Ohio country by George Washington to quell Indian uprisings and as chief of the Rangers won acclaim as the "Daniel Boone of Ohio."

Capt. Samuel Brady, an Indian scout and Revolutionary War army officer, leaped over the Cuyahoga River in Kent in 1780 to escape pursuing Indians.

All of the above have been learned from the most complete biography of Captain Brady to come into Portage County, where he won
legendary fame for his leap across the Cuyahoga River in 1780. The
biography arrives here by a circuitous and unknown trail. The account,
the most complete I have ever come across in my historical meanderings,
was written by Rev. Ralph Emmett Fall and was published in *West Virginia
History*, a quarterly magazine, in April 1968. West Virginia lays claim to
Brady by virtue of his burial in West Liberty in that state. The treatise
came my way by way of Bonnie Hilliard, a *Record-Courier* reporter, who
obtained it from her father.

The Brady roots are traced to Ireland where one of his ancestors,
Hugh Brady, was the first Protestant bishop of Meath. Actually, the biography notes, the Brady pedigree traces back to Milesius of Spain, who
conquered Ireland prior to the Christian era.

The Brady presence in the United States goes back to Hugh Brady,
great-great-grandson of the original Hugh, who migrated to Delaware
and later to Shippensburg, Pennsylvania. First of the Bradys to the New
World, he was the grandfather of our subject, Samuel Brady, who was
the oldest of 13 children, born to John and Mary Quigley Brady in
1756.

Captain Brady won his spurs as a fighter at the hands of his father, a
captain in the Revolution. Father John Brady fought the Indians in the
Ohio country in the 1760s, and he fought alongside his sons, Sam and
John, then only 15, at Brandywine. Another son, James, was killed by
Indians in 1778. The father lost his life in a battle with Indians in 1779
in Pennsylvania.

When Capt. John Brady returned from earlier wars to his home in
Shippensburg, Pennsylvania, in 1756, he found that his wife had given
birth to their firstborn. The mother already had named him Samuel for
his uncle, another Revolutionary War soldier. Indians in three states
would learn to respect the capabilities of that youngster who was destined to become chief of the Rangers.

There was plentiful cause for Sam Brady to align himself against the
Indians. They had killed his father and a brother and he had seen them
cart off and scalp women and children. Even so, his descendants related
that he was a Christian man and a devout Presbyterian who could recite

Bible verses without reference to the Book. To family and friends, he was considered kind and generous. To Indians, he was a killer. To families on the frontier, he was considered a savior.

The story of the Indians' pursuit of Brady and his leap across the Cuyahoga has been told and retold thousands of times. The version told by Reverend Fall was obtained from a Brady descendant who said it had been passed down through the family. Captain Brady led a party of Rangers into Portage County in pursuit of Sandusky Indians. The Rangers ambushed them at a small lake (today's Brady Lake). Most of the Indians had been killed when a second and larger party of Indians arrived on the scene. Brady was captured. Most of his men were killed and scalped, but the Indians deferred torturing and killing Brady until they could take him to their Sandusky headquarters.

He was stripped of his clothing and bound to a stake. Fires were set. When the Indians' watch relaxed, Brady, a tall, muscular man, broke his bounds. One account says the heat of the fire loosened his bounds. Brady is said to have seized an Indian, a woman or a baby, and flung the person into the fire and escaped during the confusion. He dashed through the woods without clothing, food, or weapons. The chase must have lasted several days.

Arriving in what today is Kent, he intended to cross at Standing Rock, located on the Indian trail. But Indians intercepted him there. Instead, he came downstream to a spot along today's Gougler Avenue and in a gigantic leap crossed the river. Historians have placed the length of the leap anywhere between 21 and 30 feet. Christian Cackler, in his writings of 1870, placed the distance at 21 feet. He had talked to Ravenna and Hudson builders of a bridge at that spot in 1803 and they were friends of Brady. At any rate, the width of the river was smaller then; the gorge was later widened to accommodate the canal and, later, the railroad. The rest of the story is well known. Brady, shot in the thigh, made his way to the lake that bears his name, submerged, and breathed through a reed. The Indians gave him up for dead.

Captain Brady, who had escaped death at the hands of Indians on dozens of occasions and during the Revolution, ultimately died a natural death. His tombstone in West Liberty, West Virginia, says he died January 1, 1796, at 37. That doesn't add up with his birth year of 1756.

There is more to the Brady story . . . much more. This biography will be placed in the Kent Free Library for all to read. Meanwhile, the Kent Area Chamber of Commerce is honoring Brady through the sale of his portrait, originally a cigar box label, matted and framed for $12.50. That's the portrait accompanying this column.

––––––

## AMZI ATWATER WAS A PORTAGE COUNTY "LEGEND"

*March 15, 1992*

Amzi is not exactly a household given name. But it was that of a man named Atwater who was a legendary Portage County pioneer.

Amzi Atwater's connection with Portage County precedes the arrival of our original settlers. He was a leader of a surveying party that laid out this county and other areas of the Western Reserve into a conclave of townships that beckoned courageous people, most of them from Connecticut and Massachusetts, to the western frontier.

Contrary to what you may believe, Amzi Atwater had no relationship with the infant community of Atwater Township except that he was called upon to survey that land as well as other wilderness areas of the Western Reserve. Atwater Township was named for Caleb Atwater, one of six residents of Wallingford, Connecticut, who migrated here in 1799. Amzi Atwater and his family came from Hamden, Connecticut. Modern maps indicate that Hamden is located a short distance north of Hartford. The town of Wallingford doesn't even appear on modern maps. So it's really unknown whether or not Amzi and Caleb were related or if they knew each other in their native state. What is known is that Amzi really made a name for himself as a Mantua resident and as a popular and contributing person on the Portage County scene.

Historians know that Moses Cleaveland (with an extra *a*) led the original surveying party into the Western Reserve to lay out townships and ranges for the Connecticut Land Company in 1795. Cleveland was named for him, but I really never have seen a plausible reason why the first *a* in his name was dropped when it came to naming the new city for him.

Amzi Atwater came into this area in 1796 as the leader of the Reserve's second surveying party. The hardships he and his men experienced are almost beyond belief. While surveying in northern Palmyra Township in 1797, Miner Bickwell, one of the party, became violently ill with a fever. Atwater took two poles and fashioned a bed between two horses to make him as comfortable as possible. Bickwell was carried that way for five days. Finally, when they reached what is now Independence in Cuyahoga County, Bickwell died. His was the second death in the Western Reserve; the first was a member of the surveying party who drowned in the Grand River. Others in the surveying party later were fatally stricken, and when the party boarded boats to return home, almost all of them were ill or exhausted.

Amzi Atwater settled in Mantua in 1800 to begin a long career of public service in Portage County. Here's what the 1885 *History of Portage County* had to say about Atwater: "Being of hardy constitution and determined will, combined with a buoyancy of disposition, he was especially adapted to the life of a pioneer and a surveyor. He was possessed of a great versatility of talent, vigor and intelligence. He was courageous rather than daring, persevering, resolute and of sound judgment." Atwater was to prove throughout his lifetime the truth of that appraisal.

He was married in 1801 in Aurora to Huldah Sheldon, daughter of Ebenezer Sheldon, Aurora's first settler in 1799. That ceremony must have been a real privilege for Sheldon, then a justice of the peace. He performed the ceremony that joined his daughter and Atwater. What must have made the ceremony unique and pleasurable for him was the fact that the ceremony was Sheldon's only official act during a three-year term as justice of the peace.

Atwater was one of the 88 voters to cast ballots in Portage County's very first election, held June 8, 1808, at Benjamin Tappan's home in Ravenna Township. The Ohio General Assembly appointed him one of the county's first common pleas judges, a position he held with distinction for many years. He was one of three judges who presided during the county's second Common Pleas Court session in December of 1808. In 1813, in another case when he served as a judge, a jury acquitted John McManus of Ravenna Township of murdering his wife.

Amzi Atwater's life was not without its humorous aspects. Once, Asa Keyes, the county's first prosecutor, borrowed a horse from him to go to Warren. Upon his return he told the judge that he had changed the horse's bridle, causing Atwater to respond, "Yes, and the horse, too." It seems that Keyes and another lawyer had imbibed rather freely throughout the day. When they departed Warren each got on the wrong horse and rode away, unmindful that they had the wrong horses until they reached home.

Apparently drinking was rather common during courtroom proceedings in that day. On another occasion during a hearing in which Atwater was involved, the bottle apparently was passed about rather freely. Participants and members of the audience became boisterous to the point that one man was found in contempt and fined five dollars.

Many firsts were attached to Atwater's name: his home in Mantua was the site of that community's first school in 1807. He established the first hotel in Mantua. He was a member of the commission that was charged with overseeing construction of the Pennsylvania and Ohio Canal through Portage County. He surveyed the first road between Ravenna and Parkman by way of Mantua and also a road that coursed from Mantua over Hiram's south line and on into Garrettsville. The ultimate target of that road was Garrett's Mill.

Add to the foregoing attributes of Atwater his prominence as a poet and his service as a county commissioner, as an occasional preacher, and as the county's first surveyor (now county engineer). Besides all of those firsts, as a justice of the peace he performed Mantua's first marriage ceremony in 1803.

---

## MOSES JABE GILBERT, LEGENDARY COUNTY PIONEER

*October 9, 1994*

In today's world we may be inclined to believe that there exists a more than usual number of "characters." A close look at local history tells us that throughout the course of goings-on in these parts such characters have existed in every era. For example, consider the Portage County wag during the pioneer days who said, "Corn is our main crop. There's no market for corn so we make it into whiskey so we drink it."

That might have been good comedy, but it was not quite accurate. There was a market for whiskey. History tells us that some storekeepers kept a barrel of the stuff in a handy spot to treat customers. A dipper was on hand near the barrel for the steady customers to quench their thirst. Whiskey was a rather common medium of exchange. It was used to buy vittles. Teachers and even preachers were said to have accepted their salaries in whiskey rather than scarce currency.

A reference to characters brings us to Jabez Gilbert. He was a hard-working guy who came to Palmyra from Connecticut in 1811. No one knew him by his given name. He punctuated almost every vow to accomplish a job with "By Moses, I'll do it." As a result he was commonly known as Moses Jabe Gilbert. My first acquaintance with the legendary Moses Jabe Gilbert dates back to the late 1930s and early 1940s. At that time I had a landlord named Gilbert who made the claim that he was a descendant of Moses Jabe. There certainly wasn't any dishonor attached to such ancestry because Moses Jabe was a man of determination and iron will. When he had a job to do, he did it, sometimes under almost impossible circumstances.

Gilbert ran a tavern in Palmyra, among his many other job descriptions. For many years he contracted to haul the mail from Pittsburgh to Cleveland over roads that were hardly more than Indian trails. He started that assignment with a two-horse coach, delivering the mail once each week. He "graduated" to a four-horse hitch and increased his trips to twice weekly. Eventually he increased that pace to three times weekly. Considering the conditions of roads in those days, that was quite a feat. When roads became impassable during the winter snows and spring thaws and he found the conditions unbearable for his teams, he placed the mail in a bag on his back and walked the distance. Moses Jabe also contracted to haul steam boilers from Pittsburgh to Cleveland to power steamboats on the Great Lakes. He chose sturdy oxen for that pulling job.

He also was a stagecoach driver during the pre-canal days, when that form of passenger transportation was considered a big step forward from horseback travel. By 1823, stagecoaches were running in all directions from Gilbert's home community of Palmyra. One came from Warren, traveling in a westward direction through Ravenna and into Franklin Mills (now Kent) and on into Cleveland. The Wellsville-Cleveland stage came through Deerfield and on to Ravenna. Another traveled through Nelson, Garrettsville, and Hiram; there was another which went from east to west through Atwater; and still others ran north and south from Ravenna. A history of Suffield tells us that in 1829 Moses Jabe pulled into that community in a shiny, new stagecoach drawn by four horses. In 1826 he started a new stage route from Beaver, Pennsylvania, to Cleveland via Ravenna.

One wonders how Moses Jabe found time for all his pursuits. Besides his tavern and his contract hauling, he also operated an ashery in Palmyra. And during the War of 1812 he served in the First Company, Second Battalion of the local militia. His outfit received orders to prepare to march, but the war ended before the order was enforced.

His tavern in Palmyra figured indirectly in the first murder in Ravenna Township. On August 20, 1814, Epaphras Matthews, a peddler, was killed for his money at Cotton Corners east of Ravenna. Matthews and a man named Henry Aunghst had been traveling together and had been at Gilbert's Palmyra tavern the night before the killing. Aunghst was tracked down and convicted. He was hanged in 1816 from gallows that were erected on South Sycamore Street in Ravenna. His body was buried at the foot of the scaffold.

Moses Jabe Gilbert appears to have been a man one would want to know. He was a busy, hard-working character whose determination and iron will helped to build our county during its infancy.

---

## "FOUR-TOWNSHIP HOUSE"
## RICH IN PORTAGE HISTORY

*June 13, 1987*

John C. Campbell had a dilemma—one of his own making. During the first decade of the 1800s he built a house at Campbellsport, his namesake center, on the corners of four townships. At Campbellsport, located along S.R. 14 southeast of Ravenna, the townships of Ravenna,

Charlestown, Rootstown, and Edinburg converge. He selected that point and located his house so that it stood partly on all four townships.

One cannot help but wonder how John Campbell's residency was calculated for purposes of voting, paying of taxes, and receiving township services. Did the specific location of his living room determine his official residence for such purposes? Or, in those pioneer days did people pay little mind to such specifics?

At any rate, John Campbell was quite an active citizen, and historical writings credit him and his wife, Sarah, as being the first settlers of Charlestown Township in 1805, although they were not the first to occupy the land in that area. He held the progressive ranks of captain, colonel, and general in the Ohio militia. He and Gen. Joshua Woodard trained men for service in the War of 1812 on a field near Barrel Run in Campbellsport, adjacent to Campbell's residence. He was sheriff of Portage County in 1811, and he served a term in the Ohio Senate. About 1812 he erected a pretentious frame building on West Main Street in Ravenna where the renovated Etna Hotel now stands. He had intended to operate a hotel in the building but changed his mind and rented it to a Pennsylvanian for a store.

John Campbell came into Portage County in 1800, settling in Deerfield. In the spring of that year he married Sarah Ely, daughter of Lewis Ely, Deerfield's first settler, in 1799. Theirs was the first marriage in Deerfield Township. In 1805 the Campbells moved to Charlestown.

In 1809 Campbell was appointed land agent for Samuel Hinckley of Northampton, Massachusetts, who had come into possession of Charlestown Township lands from the Connecticut Land Company. He went to Granville and Blandford, Massachusetts, to organize a company of residents from that area for settlement of Hinckley's lands. The following year, he built a brick land office in Charlestown, more specifically at Campbellsport, approximately at the spot where S.R. 14 today passes through the once thriving center. That land office where sales of land were made to the incoming settlers is believed to be the oldest land office in the Western Reserve.

The land office remains today, although moved from that spot. In 1964, the Portage County Historical Society acquired the small building and moved it to the society's grounds on North Chestnut Street in

Ravenna. Its restoration was completed in 1978, and it occupies a place of honor among the buildings in the society's complex. In addition to serving as a land office, the building also is said to have been a headquarters for the mustering of volunteers in the War of 1812 and a hospital.

Incidentally, Charlestown from the time of its settlement until 1814, when the township was organized officially, was known as Hinckley, named for the original land owner. A creek in the township still goes by that name. The Charlestown designation evolved from a strange set of circumstances. When settlers were accepting donations to build a town hall, Charles Curtiss offered a barrel of whiskey to the project on condition the township be named for him. Such an offer was not to be declined.

John Campbell's house was the nucleus of the once bustling center which bears his name. Once it was known as Campbell's Port, an important shipping point on the Pennsylvania and Ohio Canal. At one time the center was also known as Breadport, so called because farmers brought their wheat there for shipment. Its glory days ceased with the passing of the canal.

John Campbell died in 1827. Tragedy stalked members of his family in strange coincidences. Two of his sons and a grandson died in separate steamer accidents on the Mississippi River and another son shot himself while working on the Mississippi.

---

## BENJAMIN TAPPAN WAS A BRILLIANT BUT UNPOPULAR PIONEER

*April 9, 1983*

Benjamin Tappan Jr. was a brilliant lawyer, linguist, and scholar, a leader with profound influence. Yet, the settler of Ravenna Township in 1799 was not a popular figure among his pioneering peers.

Perhaps his standing in the infant community explains why the first court session in the county on August 23, 1808, was not held at Tappan's home, as had been dictated by the Ohio General Assembly. A. B. Griffin, historian and onetime Ravenna mayor, had this to say about Tappan in 1869: "Mr. Tappan, at that time, was for some reason held in bad repute by some of his neighbors; so much so that his life was in constant jeopardy. Indeed, he was obliged to devise means to protect himself from bullets which made their way into his house at nightfall." He went on to say that the first court session was held outdoors on a plot of ground located on the road to Campbell's Corners (now Campbellsport). The court met in the morning and adjourned that afternoon to the Robert Eaton home, located alongside what is now S.R. 14 at Campbellsport. That home served as the court scene until a frame courthouse and a log jail were completed in Ravenna in 1810. Another unsubstantiated bit of history holds that Tappan's house burned down the previous night.

Additional credence that Tappan was not popular in his home county came in 1826, 17 years after he had departed from Ravenna. In that year he ran for governor of Ohio, receiving only seven votes in Portage County, which he had helped to organize. It should be remembered that Portage County in those days included its present confines plus 10 townships in the present Summit County, including what is now the city of Akron.

Tappan was Portage County's first lawyer and its third prosecuting attorney, a public office that launched a career that eventually led to the U.S. Senate. The Ravenna founder, the son of a Massachusetts minister, was a Yale graduate and was admitted to the bar in that state in 1799, the same year he made his perilous journey to inspect his father's newly purchased holdings in the Western Reserve. That journey is in itself an epic in the settlement of this Western Reserve area and is a clear indication that, despite any other failings, he was not short on courage.

As far as is known, Tappan is the only one among Portage County's early settlers who came "by sea" rather than overland. In April 1799 he set out from his father's home in Northampton, Massachusetts, to occupy his father's lands and to serve as sales manager in disposing of the holdings to settlers.

He started the long trip on horseback, taking with him a yoke of oxen, a cow, and tools. On the trip was his uncle, Benjamin Holmes, who in New York state was sent overland with animals and tools. Tappan

came by way of Lakes Ontario and Erie. On the trip, he met up with
David Hudson, who was on his way to settle what is now Hudson, and
overtook Elias Harmon and his wife who were bound for Mantua.

At Niagara, they found the river filled with ice and were forced to
portage their boats around and above the falls. Floating ice impeded
their progress. The lake trip was a perilous one. Near what is now
Ashtabula, one of the boats was dashed to pieces in the storm. Tappan
and his companions traveled along the shore until they reached Cleveland and then they entered the Cuyahoga River. They landed at a point
that now is Boston Township in Summit County, left their goods under
a tent, and began cutting a road through the wilderness to Ravenna.

The pioneering party reached what is now Ravenna on June 5, 1799,
only to find that uncle Benjamin Holmes, who had made the trip by
land, already had arrived. So Holmes, rather than Tappan, was the first
to glimpse Ravenna soil. The settlers finished a log cabin in 1800, then
Tappan returned east to get married and returned with his bride to the
wilderness. Later, Tappan built a house about a mile east of present-day
Ravenna at Campbellsport.

An interesting historical sidelight—the name "Ravenna" was selected
as a name for the settlement back in Massachusetts before the area was
settled. The name "Tappan" was proposed, but Tappan disdained. It is
said that he proposed the Ravenna name because he and his bride liked
the ring of the word, although neither had ever been to Ravenna, Italy.
Ravenna means "roots and flowers."

Tappan only lived here 10 years, leaving in 1809 for Steubenville,
where he became prominent in the bar, a U.S. judge and U.S. senator.
In legal history, "Tappan's Reports" are well known. He died in 1857
at 84.

Today, a Ravenna elementary school and a street named for him are
the only historic reminders of the man whose courageous journey led to
the community's founding.

———

## SAD SAGA OF NATHAN MUZZY LEFT AREA
## A LASTING LEGACY

*December 7, 1986*

Love, it has been said, conquers all! Not always so, at least not in the case of Nathan Muzzy, one of the most tragic figures in early Portage County history.

Had it not been for love, and his rejection by Emma Hale, the girl of his dreams, Nathan Muzzy probably would not have left his native Massachusetts to seek a better life in the Portage County wilderness. His disappointment in love as a young man ruled Nathan Muzzy's entire life . . . a life that accrued few successes and many failures. Had it not been for his deep disappointment, a body of water in Rootstown Township today would bear another name, as would a street, also in Rootstown.

A native of Worcester, Massachusetts, Nathan Muzzy was a soldier in the Revolutionary War. An intelligent young man, he graduated from Yale or Dartmouth, depending upon which version one accepts from the writings of county historians. E. Y. Lacey, fabled Ravenna newspaperman whose accuracy on historical matters was seldom questioned, labeled him a Yale graduate in writings more than 50 years ago. The 1957 county history, *Portage Heritage*, has him a Dartmouth graduate.

Whichever, at this late date, is not important. He had trained in college to be a Congregational minister and received his license. Then the blow fell . . . Emma Hale turned away his amorous pursuits, and Nathan, in his grief, left his native state for the Ohio frontier early in the nineteenth century.

Muzzy left the ministry and opted for the carpentry trade, seeking his fortune in the new Ohio country. He first came to Marietta, the first settlement in Ohio, and not long thereafter moved to Deerfield. With that Portage County community as his base, Muzzy worked in Rootstown, Randolph, Shalersville, and Palmyra. In the spring of 1801, Ephraim Root and his brother, David, teamed with carpenter Muzzy to erect a log house in the new settlement of Rootstown.

In Randolph, Muzzy erected a log house for himself, and shortly thereafter he built the first clapboard house in the township. In a display of his eccentricity, which apparently stemmed from his lost love, Muzzy burned down his first cabin and used the remaining framework for his new structure.

In front of the house, he erected a large gate with high posts and an overhead archway. On the arch he carved the name "Emma Hale," for the girl who had rejected him back in Massachusetts. Although the gateway was not connected to any fences, Muzzy always passed through the archway when he left or entered the house. Throughout his property he carved "Emma Hale" on the outbuildings and on trees, a visible indication that, despite his transfer from the East, he had not forgotten his onetime love.

Shalersville is one of the Portage County communities that gave shelter and work opportunities to Muzzy. In a drawing held by the Connecticut Land Company in 1795, the township known as Town 4, Range 8 in the Western Reserve fell by lot to Gen. Nathaniel Shaler, a resident of Middletown, Connecticut. Shaler never settled in Shalersville, yet the community took its name from its first owner. Joel Baker, his wife, and child settled the land in 1806, only a year before Portage County was separated from Trumbull County and organized as a county of its own.

Muzzy went into Shalersville in 1812 to locate a site for a sawmill, which he erected for Stephen Mason, who that same year was elected sheriff of Portage County. He selected a spot along the Cuyahoga River in the western section of the township for the new business venture, which later was expanded by Mason with the addition of a grist mill.

Many years ago, the lake in Rootstown Township south of Sandy Lake Road and west of today's S.R. 44 was given the name Muzzy Lake. The lake has played a prominent role in local history. In 1885, Ravenna voters approved a $75,000 bond issue to build a waterworks at Mother Ward's Pond (now Crystal Lake). Some years later, the pumping station at Crystal Lake was connected by pipeline to Muzzy Lake to augment the city's water resources.

Back in the 1940s when Rootstown, primarily through the efforts of attorney Ward Davis, still a Rootstown resident, made a pitch for Ravenna water, the fact that Crystal and Muzzy Lakes were located in Rootstown Township was offered as an inducement to achieve the Rootstown system. Ravenna City Council accepted the plan, and through the years the water service served to gird the community's residential and industrial development.

Nathan Muzzy died a pauper . . . a broken man. In his aged years he was taken in by Palmyra residents who cared for him until his death. He was buried in Palmyra.

Nathan Muzzy . . . a man who never forgot his lost love!

---

## FIRST SETTLER IN NELSON FAMED AS
## AN INDIAN FIGHTER

*September 13, 1986*

In most historical writings, Capt. Samuel Brady gets most of the public notice as a famous Indian fighter. Yet Portage County had an early settler whose adventurous exploits and notoriety as an Indian fighter led to his being dubbed a "Daniel Boone."

Capt. Delaun Mills, the first settler of Nelson Township, was a large, muscular man whose strength, cunning nature, and faultless aim with a rifle won him a wide reputation, not only as a foe of Indians but as a military leader. Early historical writings describe him as fearless and "brave to excess." Captain Mills probably never killed as many Indians as claimed by handed-down stories concerning this earliest of Nelson residents, but he had plenty of brushes with the tribes which once occupied Portage County lands.

Mills was born in Massachusetts in 1776 and came from Becket in that state to Nelson in 1800 to occupy lands that had been purchased from the Connecticut Land Company by Urial Holmes, Ephraim Root, Timothy Burr, and Appolos Hitchcock. He and his two brothers, Asahel and Isaac, set out for the Western Reserve in the spring of 1800 when Delaun was 24. He had married at 16. In the settling party were two wives and four children.

When the brothers reached Youngstown they had only 25 cents among them, a condition that required them to seek employment. They signed on as axemen to help clear the wilderness for the surveying party led by Amzi Atwater, who later would become a revered Portage County citizen. Isaac returned to the East, and Asahel delayed his coming to Nelson until the spring of 1801. Delaun in 1800 moved onto Holmes's land and erected a cabin for him and his family. He planted wheat, harvesting 43 bushels from three pecks of seed.

The many stories that circulated about Captain Mills would presume that he spent most of his time hunting down the many Indians that populated the county at that time. Not so. He operated a tavern in Nelson on the strategic route from Youngstown to Cleveland, and, as with all taverns of that day, he always kept a plentiful store of whiskey. It is said that the availability of whiskey added to his problems with Indians.

No doubt the stories about Mills's prowess as an Indian fighter were expanded with each telling. According to some historians, Mills would shoot a couple of Indians and throw their bodies onto a burning log pile; or kill an Indian, put his body under an uprooted tree, and then cut off the top branches to allow the stump to snap back and bury the body. There seems little doubt that he possessed an abiding dislike for Indians, a departure from most early settlers' treatment of the Indians, with whom they got along reasonably well.

The only authentic account of his exploits came from his son, Urial (probably named for Urial Holmes), who wrote from his home in Illinois an account in 1879 of Delaun's Indian warfare as handed down to him by his mother. Said Urial:

About 1803 an Indian got mad at my father and said he would kill him. Father was in the habit of hunting through the fall. One day in crossing the trail in the snow, he found the track of an Indian following him. This put him on his guard. He soon saw the Indian. They both sheltered themselves behind trees. Father put his hat on his gun stock and stuck it out so that the Indian could see it. The Indian shot a hole through the hat and when it fell he ran toward father with his tomahawk in his hand. Father stepped out from behind the tree, shot him and buried him.

Another time, we saw ten Indians, painted for war, coming. They came into our house, shook hands with my father but the last, who uttered an oath and seized him by the throat. Father caught him by the shoulders, jerked him off the floor and swung him around. The calves of his leg hit the sharp leg of a table. Father dragged him outdoors, took him by the

hair, pounded his head upon a rock and left him. The Indians put a pole
through a blanket and carried him off to camp. They said if he died they
would kill father. While he was confined they shot Diver of Deerfield.
This created quite a bit of excitement and the Indians all left for Sandusky,
leaving the crippled one in camp. Sometime later, when father was away,
he came to our house in the evening and asked if he could stay. Mother
told him he could. She did not sleep any that night, believing that he had
come to kill us. In the morning, he got up and cooked his breakfast of
bear's meat. Then he went out and returned with the hind quarters of a
bear which he gave to my mother, then bid her goodbye and left. She was
as glad to see him go as any visitor she had ever had.

This was quite a gesture of friendship from one who earlier had sought
to kill Mills. Mills is said to have killed both Big Cayuga when the chief
drew a knife on him and also the chief's nephew, Snip-Nose Cayuga.
Mills got his captain's title from his leadership in the Ohio militia. During the War of 1812 he served with distinction as a company commander
in the Battle of Mackinaw.

Captain Mills's life was spared in many confrontations with Indians
but he met his death in a less glorious way. He was bitten by a rattlesnake, one of the many that once infested the Nelson Ledges area in
great numbers. He was desperately ill, blood flowing from his eyes and
nose, and he was partially paralyzed. The usual remedy in those days
was to fill the patient with whiskey. Apparently that saved Mills from
the rattlesnake bite, but he never fully recovered from its effects. He
died on April 20, 1824, at 48, an untimely end to one of the more colorful characters on Portage County's Western Reserve frontier.

---

## BENEFITS ENDURE FROM PATRIOTISM
## OF PORTAGE GENERAL

*April 16, 1983*

Bequests sometimes are forgotten with the passing of time. Certainly,
this has not been the case with a bequest from Shalersville's Gen. David
McIntosh a century ago. A supreme patriot, General McIntosh died

100 years ago this month, leaving a $1,000 bequest to Portage County to buy flags for Portage County's townships. His wish has been meticulously carried out for the past century. Throughout the years, the Portage County auditor and the county commissioners have been guardians of the general's "flag fund."

Portage County Auditor Victor Biasella reports $274.74 in the McIntosh flag fund as of this moment, adding that the fund earns interest of approximately $32.50 per year. Ever since the general backed up his patriotism with a money bequest, county records have retained these funds in a separate account for the sole purpose of buying flags for the townships. Biasella says township halls throughout the county display flags that were purchased from the McIntosh fund. In recent years, the county has standardized the quality and size of flags at two-by-four feet. The auditor orders four flags at a time to assure that flags will be on hand when townships file requests.

His generous gesture a century ago tells a lot about General McIntosh and his patriotic fervor. But, really, who was General McIntosh? No doubt, in his era he was one of Shalersville's most prominent men. He was born in 1794 in New Hampshire and migrated to Ohio when still a child, settling in Shalersville Township.

Young David obtained work with Judge Amzi Atwater, who took a keen interest in the lad and sent him to school. In 1817 he cut through the center road from Shalersville into Freedom. As a young man, he joined the Twentieth Division of the Ohio militia and rose to the rank of major general. In 1844–1845 he represented Portage County in the Ohio General Assembly.

It was only natural that his patriotism would cause him to be an ardent supporter of the Union forces during the Civil War. Hence, Ravenna's Post 327 of the Grand Army of the Republic, an organization for Union veterans, would be named the David McIntosh Post in his honor.

General McIntosh had another important association with county government. As early as 1833, Portage County had made attempts to establish a "poor house." But, it wasn't until 1839 that the county purchased a 100 acres of land, buildings, stock, and farming implements from General McIntosh.

That center, located along what is now Infirmary Road, became Portage County's first poor house or infirmary. General McIntosh was its first director. The infirmary was operated by a board of directors until 1913, when it became the operating responsibility of the county commissioners. The "poor house" label was dropped in 1925 and the establishment then became known as the "County Home." Today we know it as the Portage County Nursing Home.

In the early days, persons afflicted with mental illness were housed at the county home along with those who had no place else to go for food, shelter, and care. In 1858 a brick building was erected on the Infirmary Road site, and in 1882 a wing was added. Then, in 1952 the present new home was erected.

General McIntosh built a square-topped house east of Shalersville center on the south side of what today is S.R. 303. It was there that he died 100 years ago this month at age 89.

For many years, a large photograph of the general hung in the treasurer's office of the old Portage County Courthouse. Somehow, such a display is the least Portage Countians could do for a patriot whose passion for "Old Glory" was so intense that he provided a fund to guarantee a perpetual supply of American flags to our townships. A century later, he is remembered!

----

## JOHN BROWN

### You Loved Him or You Hated Him

*October 4, 1987*

John Brown. An eccentric ne'er-do-well businessman, a zealot, a Bible-reading fanatic, a murderer. One of his biographers describes him as a man who "has been and perhaps always will be the subject of controversy." To others he was a martyr, a saint, and a hero for his attempts to obliterate slavery. Still others considered him a treasonous American whose view that force was a proper means to accomplish his purpose could not be justified.

Reverence or disdain for John Brown depends upon your point of view. At any rate, 128 years following his execution, few would argue against his antislavery motives, only against his hell-bent course of violence to bring about change, a premise prevalent in more recent years concerning other public issues.

John Brown had deep roots in Portage County. His father, Owen, came from Connecticut to Hudson, then in Portage County, in the early 1800s. Owen, who also later resided in Deerfield, served as a Portage County commissioner from 1813 to 1819. Owen's second wife (not John's mother) was the former Sallie Root of Aurora. A street in Hudson to this day bears the name of Owen Brown. John was born in Torrington, Connecticut, in 1800 and was only five when the family came to Hudson. In Deerfield, he was associated with the Grant family, ancestors of Ulysses S. Grant.

Brown's life from his boyhood days in Portage until his return some years later apparently was spent, for the most part, in Pennsylvania. In 1835 he was postmaster in Randolph, Pennsylvania, his location when he and Zenas Kent negotiated for Brown to erect a tannery in Franklin Mills (now Kent). Work on the tannery just west of the Stow Street bridge began in that year and was completed in 1836. Brown, for a brief period, managed the tannery for Kent. Then he bought a farm along Mogadore Road and he and a man named Thompson laid out the area into a subdivision. Even today, on tax maps the area is known as the Brown-Thompson Addition.

Brown resided on Mogadore Road. He erected a building at the corner of West Summit and Franklin Avenue for a hotel but, like Brown's other ventures, it didn't pan out. The building was moved by Marvin Kent to North Water Street in 1882. The old tannery building was razed several years ago, and that area, thanks to the Kent Environmental Council, now is John Brown Tannery Park.

Brown attended the Kent Congregational Church during the mid-1830s and caused a tiff among church members when he objected to blacks being relegated to rear pews for services. He left Kent soon thereafter and went to work for Simon Perkins in Akron. His principal duty was managing Perkins's sheep herd. His house at the corner of Copley and Diagonal Roads, across from Perkins's house, today is owned by the Summit County Historical Society.

As early as 1834 Brown planned a school for Negroes, and in 1839 he and members of his family took an oath to help in the abolition of slavery. In 1849, he settled on a farm in North Elba, New York, where a Negro colony had been established. His prominence as a national figure by that time was developing. In 1855, Brown and five of his sons went to Kansas, where passage of the Kansas-Nebraska Bill had raised the slavery issue into an intense rivalry between the Free State party and the pro-slavery advocates, a situation that erupted into violence at the famed Pottawatomie Massacre on May 25, 1856. Although Brown did not actually participate, several of his sons did, and five pro-slavery advocates were murdered. John Brown said the killings were "decreed by God."

About that time he hatched the Virginia scheme, a plan to seize the federal arsenal at Harpers Ferry and, with an armed force, make slave-liberating forays into the South. With 19 men, on October 16, 1859, he surprised and captured the arsenal. Two of his sons, Watson and Oliver, were killed in the raid. Another son, Fred, had died in the Kansas warfare. Two days following the raid, the wounded John Brown was taken prisoner by U.S. troops led by Robert E. Lee, then a colonel. He was convicted for treason and murder.

On December 2, when Brown was hanged, bells throughout Portage County tolled in mourning for their onetime fellow citizen. Indignant mass meetings were held in both Kent and Ravenna. Brown's attack heightened the bitterness between the North and South and probably hastened the Civil War.

What happens to families of people such as John Brown? This much we know, Brown sired 20 children, seven by his first wife and 13 by his second wife. There must be countless Brown descendants in the country. In 1864, his second wife, three daughters, and a son, Salmon, headed west in three wagons. They escaped an attack by Sioux Indians in Nebraska and finally settled in Red Bluff, California. This information is contained in a 1975 article in *True West* magazine kindly mailed to me by Pearl Collage of Atwater. The family received a good reception, and members of the community contributed funds for them to buy a house.

This euphoria waned as a result of differences of opinion people held for the causes of the North and South. Six years later, Mary sold the house and moved to a ranch bought by son Salmon in another California county. She died in 1884.

The article also includes a 1906 interview with Salmon, then an aged and crippled man, who described his father's Bible sessions with his large family. "He was a kind and loving father," Salmon said as he recounted the family's notification of John Brown's execution. The body was returned by special guard to New York, where it was interred near the old farmhouse. A huge rock marks his grave.

During the Civil War, Union troops sang a popular war song, which had for its refrain: "John Brown's body lies a mouldering in the grave, but his soul goes marching on."

————

## A. M. SHERMAN
### An Unusual Man . . . and a Gifted One
*September 11, 1988*

Dr. Aaron Morgan Sherman never strayed very far from his beloved Brimfield, Ohio, nor from his ancestral roots in Brimfield, Massachusetts. And during his long lifetime, he had few peers in guarding zealously the memories of our settlers whose pioneering spirit, hard work, and determination brought forth new homes, farms, and crude but prospering industries onto the Western Reserve scene.

Dr. Sherman—known always by his initials, A.M., instead of his given name—was an unusual man . . . and a gifted one. He combined his multiple talents and interests in helping to build the communities of Brimfield and Kent and, for a brief period, Garrettsville. Revered as a physician during a long practice, Dr. Sherman also was, at various times, a druggist, teacher-educator, historian, soldier, musician. Few industrial community enterprises passed him by or were not touched by his able hand.

Born in 1826 in Brimfield, Hampden County, Massachusetts, Dr. Sherman traced his ancestry to a young man who emigrated from England to

Massachusetts. It was a natural turn of events, considering the family's hometown of Brimfield, Massachusetts, that Captain Harris and Sally Sherman would migrate from New England to Brimfield in Portage County in 1831, only 15 years following the community's settlement, when the future doctor was only five years of age. Sherman spent his early years on his parents' Brimfield farm, attending school in the winter months and then a select school for a brief period. The latter apparently prepared him to teach for four years in daytime schools and singing classes in an evening school.

Higher aspirations called him to "study" medicine under Dr. John Knowlton in Garrettsville, beginning when he was 21. He also studied medicine at Western Reserve College in Cleveland, graduating in 1851. He launched his practice in Garrettsville, then moved to Kent, where he temporarily strayed from medicine for a brief venture into the drug business. Medicine, fortunately, called him back. Throughout his remaining years (he lived into his nineties), he attended to the ills of his friends and neighbors. But there were many diversions from his practice, one of them his service as assistant surgeon in a Washington hospital during the Civil War.

Another was his election as state representative from Portage County in 1883. The doctor was an energetic promoter of enterprise. He was particularly active in helping establish industries in Kent during the 1880s. He served on a community committee to attract the Connotton Valley Railroad, as well as the Turner Brothers' alpaca mill to the giant industrial building that still stands on the west shore of the Cuyahoga in Kent. When C. A. and Scott Williams established the Peerless Roller Mills, forerunner of the Williams Brothers Mill, Dr. Sherman helped to raise public subscriptions during a community support campaign.

While a resident of Garrettsville, Dr. Sherman became a member of the Masonic Lodge. His move to Franklin Township in 1857 prompted him to lead the organization of Kent's Rockton Masonic Lodge, chartered in 1859, in which the doctor served as master for ten years.

He was a charter member of the Portage County Medical Society in 1866 and also of the Portage-Summit Pioneer Association, organized in 1874. He served the latter as secretary-treasurer for many years. And he was a firm believer in educating young people, hence his membership on the Kent school board for many years.

Perhaps Dr. Sherman's crowning legacy was his authorship of a history of Brimfield Township in 1881. His history, dating back to the community's settlement in 1816, was the township's first. On July 4 of that same year, during Brimfield's 65th anniversary celebration, he based his address upon his written words.

In 1916, when he was 90, Dr. Sherman attended Brimfield's centennial celebration. At that time, he expressed fear that the early settlers would be forgotten. Through the writings of Dr. Edgar McCormick, the Brimfield Memorial House Association, and the efforts of others, their light still shines.

———

## BRAINERD

### A Citizen's Success over Adversity

*October 18, 1987*

Chronicles of Western Reserve history are profuse with examples of people with humble—even sparse—beginnings who ultimately became prominent in a variety of businesses, professions, or civic life.

With hardly more than a common school education, they rose above limitations imposed by their earlier lives, assumed leadership roles, and wielded high influence in the upward struggle to build new communities. Their accomplishments were forged from a regimen whose principal ingredient was unstinting effort coupled with basic wisdom.

Such a man was Enos P. Brainerd, whose entrepreneurship on the Portage County scene in the 1800s can be held out as a striking example of citizen success over early adversity. Today only historians or descendants would recognize the Enos Brainerd name. Yet, in his era few of his Portage County contemporaries would not have known him or would not have been familiar with his many associations and accomplishments.

Enos Brainerd was born in 1814 in Lewis County, New York, of English stock that dated back to settlement in Connecticut in the late

1600s. His education was obtained in common schools, with a brief period in an academy. At 16, he was the oldest of four sons when his father died. Despite his mother's wish that he be educated to pursue a profession, he opted to take up the harness-making and carriage-trimming trade, a reasonable one considering the use of horses and carriages.

He was only 20 years old when he came to Ohio and settled in Cuyahoga Falls, then located in Portage County. He married a Ravenna woman two years later, and then in 1839 moved to Randolph, where he pursued his trade and where he really was launched into a life of public service. He was elected Randolph justice of the peace in 1843 and two years later was successful in his bid for county treasurer. He served one term, moved to the county seat, and thereafter was a Ravenna resident.

Following his brief fling with public office, Brainerd turned to business enterprises, the eventual hallmark of his local fame. Upon leaving the treasurer's office in 1848, he entered into partnership with his brother-in-law, Samuel Mason, to conduct a hardware store and tinning business in Ravenna. Only four years later, his business life took another turn when he became cashier of the Franklin Bank of Portage County, which had been established by Zenas Kent in Franklin Mills (Kent) in 1849.

His association with Mr. Kent led to higher business prominence when in 1855 he was elected treasurer of the Atlantic and Great Western Railroad Company. The railroad, then chartered but not yet built, did not become a reality until 1863, when its first trains came into Portage County from the east. His railroad interests, which spanned 14 years, included the office of secretary and member of the board of directors. Simultaneously he was a director, treasurer, and financial officer of the Silver Creek Mining Company in Wayne and Medina counties.

During his railroad years, he held a directorship in the Portage County branch of the State Bank of Ohio in Ravenna and in 1863 became the bank's president. His last bank association was that of a director of the newly organized First National Bank of Ravenna. He served, too, as treasurer of the Farmers Insurance Company of Portage County, an association that likely inspired his service as treasurer and president of the Portage County Agricultural Society.

Brainerd, who descended from Revolutionary War stock, was a patriot who believed in involvement with governmental and political affairs. Originally, he was a Whig. He voted the Free Soil ticket, and when the Republican party was organized he served for many years as chairman of the county's central committee. One of his main interests in the later 1880s was the Portage-Summit Pioneer Association, which he served as a director and historian.

But his business career was not yet finished. In 1870 he entered into partnership with his son, Charles W., to conduct a Ravenna drug business, a venture which extended to 1882, when his son transferred to a Mantua drugstore.

Despite his own limited education, Brainerd was a warm friend of education. Prior to the union school system, he was director of common schools and for several years was president of the Ravenna Board of Education.

The Brainerd house still stands at 533 East Main St. in Ravenna. Built about 1855 by Charles Lawrence, for whom Lawrence Street is named, the home was purchased by Common Pleas Judge A. S. Cole in 1914 and now is the insurance business headquarters and home of Larry McCardel.

The house is included in East Main Historic District, which has gained admission to the National Register of Historic Places through efforts of the Ravenna Heritage Association. Enos P. Brainerd would be pleased with that honor.

———

## RIDDLE'S NOVEL RESEMBLES HIS MANTUA
## FRONTIER LIFE

*December 20, 1986*

*The Portrait,* an 1874 novel, was written by Albert Gallatin Riddle. Was it really an almost tearful, moving recollection of his own early life as a bright and sometimes misunderstood and tormented youth on the Mantua frontier? The slices of life as lived by the book's hero, Fred Warden, who grew into manhood as a brilliant lawyer and political orator, closely parallel Riddle's own career.

A. G. Riddle is no stranger to Portage County historians. Born in Monson, Massachusetts, in 1816, he came to the Western Reserve with

his family when only a year old. Biographers say the family settled in
Geauga County, yet it is known that Riddle spent time in Mantua, and
it is that community which serves as the setting for *The Portrait*.

Names and places in the novel are those we know today—the
Cuyahoga River, Mantua Center, Mantua Corners, and many families
whose names are familiar to area residents, including Skinner, Atwater,
Chapman, Snow, Johnson, Carmen, as well as the story of Joseph Smith
and Sidney Rigdon and the Mormons and the old tavern on the "state
road."

Although I had known of Riddle as a man of letters and Mantua's
claim upon him, only in recent days did I read *The Portrait*, one of at
least 15 novels Riddle wrote after tiring of his law practice and his service as an Ohio representative and as a U.S. congressman. The book
was reprinted by the Mantua Historical Society ten years ago as a tribute to the Bicentennial celebration.

Now, back to Fred Warden. Fred was bound out to a farmer as a young
boy, following the death of the woman he believed to be his mother.
But on her deathbed, she told him otherwise, a revelation that was to
confound him until he was 29 years old, when he learned the real truth.
The farmer to whom Warden was bound was William Skinner, a prominent farmer who in the early 1800s lived just east of S.R. 44.

There were parallels between Warden and author Riddle. Early on,
Fred showed signs unlike those of his youthful colleagues. He was
thoughtful, intelligent, hard working, and he displayed deeper and more
profound motivations than most of his peers. As he grew older, he showed
exceptional talents as a public speaker. Riddle was an accomplished orator
who loaned his talents to the William Henry Harrison presidential campaign of 1840. The book's hero, Warden, studied under a lawyer in
Massillon; Riddle read law under Seabury Ford in Geauga County. That
Seabury Ford, last Whig governor of Ohio, was the great-grandfather of
Portage County's present Seabury Ford, Aurora and Ravenna attorney.

The second time young Fred Warden was "bound out," it was to the
owner of the tavern, where he worked around the barroom, cut wood,
and did other chores contrived by his not-too-upstanding master. Riddle,
after serving his time on the Mantua farm, joined his two older brothers
in doing carpentry work. Money left over from sustaining himself went

for the purchase of books. In 1835 he went to Western Reserve College in Hudson and then to a Painesville academy, all the while dreaming of the day when he could use his speaking talent to further his career.

He was admitted to the bar in 1840, and three weeks thereafter was nominated for prosecuting attorney in Geauga County. He called the meeting in Chardon that resulted in the formation of the Free Soil party in Ohio, and he ultimately became one of the organizers of the emergent Republican party. Following six years as prosecutor, he was elected to the Ohio House and immediately became one of its recognized leaders. A Whig and bitterly opposed to slavery, he served in Congress from 1861 to 1863. The most famous law case in which he was involved was as a government prosecutor in the trial of John Surratt for the murder of Abraham Lincoln.

His public service was not at an end following his years in Congress. He settled into a law practice in Washington, D.C., became law officer for the District of Columbia, headed the law department at Howard University, and served as a consul in Cuba. During the Civil War years he claimed women had the right to vote on the basis of the Fourteenth and Fifteenth Amendments.

But writing was his first love and he shed his government career and his law practice to devote all of his time to its pursuit. *Bart Ridgeley: A Story of Northern Ohio* was his first book, published in 1873. His prolific pen turned out book after book, stories for periodicals and newspapers, and legal treatises. Included in his writings was a book on another Portage Countian, James A. Garfield.

In 1845, Fred, the hero of *The Portrait*, married the beautiful Belle. That's the same year Riddle married Caroline Avery, the daughter of a Geauga judge. Ultimately the central figure in Riddle's book learned his true heritage and he met his real mother, a South Carolinian. There the parallels between Fred and Riddle separated; Riddle knew his heritage. His grandfather had come from Ireland and his parents from Massachusetts.

A. G. Riddle died in 1902 and was buried in Rock Creek Cemetery in Washington, D.C. His books are his legacy.

———

# FREDERICK LOUDIN'S SONG
## A Triumph over Racism
*March 22, 1986*

Three decades before the Civil War, life was not easy for black people in a white man's world. In New England, about 1830, whites burned down a school and jailed the teacher for admitting black students. Permission to build a college was denied when it was learned that Negro boys would be admitted.

Faced with such conditions, a young black couple in Vermont decided to seek a better life in the Western Reserve wilderness. Jeremiah and Sybil Loudin loaded all of their possessions into a wagon drawn by a team of oxen and headed westward. They arrived in Portage County's Charlestown Township following a grueling, three-month trip. There they would prosper on a farm. From those humble and troubled beginnings emerged Frederick J. Loudin, born in Charlestown in 1836, who became Portage County's most illustrious, internationally known black man.

The Loudin children attended school in Charlestown, but later Mrs. Loudin moved her children to Ravenna to take advantage of a better system of education. Frederick was a diligent and intelligent boy. Yet he was not to escape deliberate instances of discrimination against his race. Seats in the Ravenna schools were at that time assigned in accordance with scholarship. Although he stood at the top of his class, the scholarship standard did not apply to him.

Frederick became a printer's apprentice in Ravenna, earning $45 per year, $5 of which he contributed to the church he attended. He possessed a fine bass voice and made application to join the church choir. He was denied because of his color, and it is said that he never troubled the church with his presence thereafter.

Young Frederick went to Pennsylvania, where he married Harriet Johnson in 1872. Meanwhile, in Nashville, Tennessee, first steps were taken to establish a Negro university. It opened in 1866 with a thousand students of all ages, some of whom could not even read and write.

To raise funds for the infant school, which was to become Fisk University, 11 young black singers were assembled to make appearances, the meager funds they earned to be contributed to Fisk. It is believed that young Frederick attended one of their concerts in Cleveland. Whatever, three years later he was a member of the Fisk Jubilee Singers. And five or six years after that, when that singing group disbanded, the small group of musicians was performing throughout the United States and Europe under the name of the Loudin Jubilee Singers, with Frederick Loudin as the leader.

Frederick kept a diary during his years of travel as leader of the famed singers. He wrote of his days in Germany during a concert tour of that country's principal cities. In 1884, his niece, Leota Henson, who had attended Ravenna schools, left with her Aunt Harriet for Germany to study piano. Two years later, her Uncle Frederick, due to arrive in London for concerts, sent for Leota to serve as the group's accompanist.

The group toured England, Scotland, Ireland, and Wales, and its members visited many historical places, such as Westminster Abbey, the Tower of London, Windsor Castle, and Shakespeare's home at Stratford-upon-Avon. Leota's diary included autographs of Queen Victoria, King Edward VII, Kaiser Wilhelm, Ralph Waldo Emerson, Theodore Roosevelt, and James A. Garfield, among others. The crowned heads of Europe and other prominent people of that era were treated to the Loudin Singers' music and Frederick's classic rendition of "Rocked in the Cradle of the Deep" in his booming bass voice. Everywhere they went, the singers were encored and wildly acclaimed.

Following two years in Great Britain, the Loudin Singers set out for Australia, their six-week trip by boat including stops in Naples, Pompeii, Cairo, Port Said. They saw the Pyramids, the Sahara Desert, the Arabian bazaars, plus many other international attractions, before they arrived in Melbourne. Their concerts took them to every principal town in Australia, New Zealand, and Tasmania. After three and a half years there, they returned by way of India, China, and Japan. They visited the Taj Mahal, and alongside its tombs they sang "Steal Away to Jesus"— a Christian song, in a temple of another faith.

Home at last, the Loudin Jubilee Singers presented a concert in Kent on September 29, 1891. Their advance billing said they had just returned from a six-year, around-the-world tour and had appeared in 17 countries and before six crowned heads of Europe, four U.S. presidents, two governors general of Canada, six governors of Australian colonies, the viceroy of India, and the governor of Bombay.

Maturity and success had healed the hurts and disappointments of Frederick Loudin's early life. He had achieved fame and now was acclaimed as a hero in his hometown of Ravenna.

At one time, Loudin operated a shoe factory in Ravenna, first on South Chestnut Street and then at the corner of North Chestnut Street and Central Avenue. The South Chestnut factory, which employed both blacks and whites, was located in an old building which later became part of the Redfern Mills, a building that now houses some of the Oak Rubber Company's manufacturing facilities. Loudin also was an inventor. He held patents for a fastener to meet rails on window sashes and for a key fastener.

Throughout their many travels, Mr. and Mrs. Loudin purchased logs and many objets d'art and shipped them home. The logs, representing many types of wood, were cut into lumber and used to build their home at 401 South Walnut Street, at the corner of Walnut and East Riddle Avenue in Ravenna. That home, which stands today, the Loudins named "Otira."

The singers made more tours of Europe, and it was in 1902 in Scotland that Loudin suffered a nervous collapse. He returned in 1903 to Otira, where he died on November 3, 1904. Frederick and Harriet Loudin are buried in Maple Grove Cemetery. Their grave is marked by a fine, granite tombstone that he selected several years prior to his death.

Frederick Loudin dared to dream in an era when black people had no cause to dream. He fulfilled that dream through God-given musical talent, a talent that won him acclaim throughout the world.

———

## GOLD WAS A POWERFUL LURE FOR
## TIMOTHY PARSONS
*n.d.*

Ever since several thousand years B.C., gold has been a powerful lure. No one knows for certain when gold was discovered, but golden artifacts date back to at least 3500 B.C. If gold were used in manufacture that early, its discovery certainly occurred prior to that time. During the ensuing centuries men have sought it with a passion. They have dug for it, panned for it, and even killed for this precious metal. And thereby hands a tale of one of Portage County's most prominent men who, like many other young men of his generation, could not resist the spirit of adventure generated by the discovery of gold in the West.

It was on January 28, 1848, that James Wilson Marshall discovered gold at Sutter's Mill in California, setting off the gold rush during that year and 1849. On horseback, by boat, and on foot folk went to seek quick riches in the gold fields of California. Most of them were disappointed. After years of backbreaking work, few realized their dream. Timothy Graves Parsons was one of those who sought adventure and elusive wealth in the California goldfields. Much to the dismay and anxiety of his parents—Edward and Clementia Parsons, a Massachusetts-born farm couple who settled in Brimfield in 1831—Timothy, at age 21, set out by boat for California in 1853.

Timothy was born in Brimfield in 1832, and no doubt his parents envisioned for him a career as a farmer, businessman, or teacher. But the spirit of adventure and the lure of California gold were powerful inducements to this young Brimfield man.

For seven long years he labored in the new American state. He spent two years in Alameda County and then spent five years seeking his fortune in Toulumne County. All the while, his anxious parents and his brothers and sisters wrote him faithfully, and his mother, with concerned anxiety, reminded him repeatedly that he had planned to remain for two years to seek his fortune.

That collection of 42 letters from home and Tim's responses is a historical treasure trove, excerpted in Edgar McCormick's *Brimfield and Its People.* Significant sections of those letters bear repeating.

From his mother in 1854: "A young man from Brecksville returned last week from Cal. via the overland route and was smart and healthy. He journeyed all the way in his mining costume with his long hair and beard. We would not care how long the beard or the hair could we but see you. Your father is almost worn out with waiting upon cattle." 1855: "There is no want of business here. It may not yield as much gold but I think it would be better in the end. Think of your board bill, my son.

Mother will board you much cheaper and if you are sick it shall not cost you anything but the comfort of home."

Tim was kept up on news from home—family matters, community happenings, marriages, deaths, life on the farm. He saved all the letters, and his messages to his family and friends also were preserved. Tim finally did come home in November of 1859. He did not strike it rich.

He farmed for a spell, and then in 1861 enlisted in the 42nd Regiment of the Ohio Volunteers. Meanwhile, his brother, Edward A. Parsons, had started a planing mill and lumber business in 1863. That was the beginning of the Parsons Lumber Company, a highly successful business which would prevail in Kent for 109 years.

Brother Edward for a brief period had a partner, Porter B. Hall, great-grandfather of the present Porter B. Hall of Twin Lakes. Following the end of the Civil War, Timothy Parsons joined his brother as a partner and in 1869 bought out his brother. From that day on, the company went under the name of the T. G. Parsons Lumber Company.

Timothy Parsons died in 1923 at 91. The business passed to a second generation, his sons, Edward, Dwight, and John, all of whom had been active in the firm with their father. Dwight's son, Charles A., now a Florida resident, was manager of the business when it ceased operations in 1972. The Parsons buildings on Franklin Avenue in Kent were razed in the mid-1980s for the site to become the new location of the Kent Post Office.

Timothy Parsons's quest for elusive gold was not completely fruitless. In 1866, when he married Eleanor Maria Sawyer, his gifts to her were a wedding ring made from gold he had mined with his own hands and a bar pin with gold dust in its center ornament. No doubt, those treasured mementos were the capstones of his California adventure.

———

## PHINEAS TOMSON, A REVERED AND
## INFLUENTIAL TEACHER

*September 1, 1984*

Some described him as unusual. Others as colorful. Whatever the description, during his era he was a teacher revered by all except the most critical and loved by generations of students. Phineas Butler Tomson was Portage County's best-known teacher during the late 1800s and early 1900s. Born in Shalersville Township in 1848, he taught for more than 50 years in nine Portage County rural school districts as well as others in Mahoning and Stark counties and in Michigan.

So influential was Mr. Tomson that for years following his retirement, Tomson school reunions attracted hundreds of his former pupils. The last of those reunions was held in 1928 in the Freedom Congregational Church, when Common Pleas Judge C. B. Newton, the main speaker, paid glowing tribute to Tomson.

Perhaps one of the most immeasurable of qualities is the lasting influence teachers have upon the future careers of their charges. Almost everyone can recall a teacher who had a profound influence upon him during his school years. Successful men and women often speak of special teachers who helped to shape their lives. No doubt, older residents of Portage County who had Tomson as a teacher would confirm the influence he had upon them. His was a remarkable career. He may not have considered it so, because he often remarked that he wanted nothing more than to be a good rural schoolteacher. The esteem with which he was held leaves little doubt he achieved that mission.

Tomson worked on a Shalersville farm during his boyhood. He attended school in a one-room district building with homemade seats, benches, and blackboards. A box stove located in the middle of the room provided heat. From that school he went on to the Shalersville Academy, located at the center of the township, and then to Mount Union College.

He began his teaching career at 18 in the Pinney district of Paris Township. Tomson moved frequently. He taught in Franklin, Ravenna, Brady Lake, Shalersville, Freedom, Hiram, Randolph, Rootstown,

Atwater, Charlestown, and Newton Falls, plus stints in Mahoning and Stark counties and a brief period in Michigan.

He only made one venture into city school administration. That was in 1889 and 1890 when he served as principal of DePeyster School in Kent. Despite good service testimonials, he moved on, stating he preferred rural teaching and supervision and he could do the most good in that sphere of education.

Today's students would have a little difficulty visualizing the schools in Tomson's day. So would the teachers. It is said that when he entered a new district he arrived several days early to tidy up the building and school grounds. He wallpapered, did carpentry work, and performed other tasks not commonly included in a teacher's portfolio. Also, he visited parents of pupils who would be attending his classes.

Students soon discovered they were there to learn. He had few rules, but he meant them to be abided. Most of his rules of conduct were dictated by his powerful personality.

Tomson valued his students, and he followed their later progress. He meticulously recorded the names of more than 1,300. Those names he included in his book, *Fifty Years in the School Room*, which he wrote following his retirement.

Throughout his teaching years, Tomson always used the fabled "McGuffey Readers," which he cherished not only as a teaching aid but also for the series's moral persuasions. It was only natural that he should found the Portage County McGuffey Association in 1929. He was the association's first president, an office he held until his death.

Auto magnate Henry Ford wrote him, expressing his interest in McGuffey and in keeping alive the memory of the "little red schoolhouse." Ford had read *Fifty Years in the Schoolroom* and invited Tomson to visit the Ford collection of Americana in Dearborn, Michigan. That association culminated in Ford's presenting him with a complete set of the 1857 edition of McGuffey Readers.

When Tomson died in 1933, E. Y. Lacey, whom I remember as a fine historical writer for the *Ravenna Republican*, wrote: "Teacher Tomson chose to be a common pedagogue because he felt that he could do the most good in that sphere of his profession. What he has accomplished is written high on the memorial shaft."

Twenty years before he died, Tomson directed a marker be placed upon his future grave in beautiful Hillside Cemetery in Shalersville Township within sight of a school where he once taught. He wrote his own epitaph: "School is out. Teacher has gone home."

----

## FREEDOM MAN RAILROADING'S INVENTIVE GENIUS

*April 19, 1992*

Portage County has produced many men and women who have won national and international pursuits. Certainly among them must be considered a Freedom Township native with the unlikely given name of Plimmon. Plimmon H. Dudley was his complete handle. This unusual name didn't deter him from achieving a worldwide reputation as an inventor and one of railroading's best-known figures during the era when trains were "king of the road."

Plimmon Dudley was born in Freedom in 1843. His father and mother were pioneers of that township. His father's name was Charles, hence his unusual given name appears a bit of a mystery. After spending his youth on a Limeridge Road farm, he entered Hiram College. There began a relationship that endured for many years and signaled a most unusual married life. At Hiram he met Lucy Bronson, a fellow student, from Peninsula, and they were married in 1871.

Plimmon Dudley was an engineer, obviously a brilliant one, considering that his work in railroading took him throughout the world and brought him fame as an inventor of railroad testing equipment. But back to his married life. He and his wife resided for 40 years in a railroad car, a rolling home and office on wheels. This was no ordinary railroad car, although it appeared so on the exterior. The interior was a different story.

The car contained Dudley's private office and invention workroom, with a variety of complicated instruments, as well as a generous library filled with scientific volumes. The other end of the railroad car included the couple's parlor, dining room, kitchen, and bedroom. Mrs. Dudley's grand piano had a place of honor, as did her sewing machine, plus a generous supply of kitchen utensils.

That railroad car traveled from Maine to California and even into Mexico. From the car—and from Dudley's brilliant mind—came some of the most radical improvements made in railroad history. There he developed the *Empire State Express*, which was capable of speeds up to 70 mph. He was a consulting engineer for the New York Central Railway, and it is said that he had a special talent for solving the knottiest of railroad problems.

He invented the Dynagraph, a machine capable of detecting irregularities in tracks and low joints. His device recorded that information by use of pens which wrote as the railroad car moved. At the end of a run, Dudley simply handed a roll of paper which provided an exact record to the railroad's general manager so that crews could make proper corrections to the trackage. He also invented the Strematograph, a vest-pocket instrument which measured the stress of rails under a passing train. He believed implicitly in hard nails, thus his nickname of "Hard Dudley" among railroaders.

Dudley's reputation took him and his wife throughout Europe and Asia. Both were multilingual, so they never had any difficulty among people of other countries. The Dudleys were entertained many times by the crowned heads of Europe.

Dudley was not a pretentious man. One time when he and his three brothers returned to the family homestead in Freedom, they were comparing suits. One of them, a judge, said his cost $80, a large sum in those days. Plimmon, probably the wealthiest among them, said he bought his for $16.50 at Montgomery Ward's in New York City.

Dudley had two other claims to fame. He was a boyhood friend of James A. Garfield, a relationship which continued until the president's assassination. And when he was civil engineer, he placed the Meridian monument and Meridian stone on the Portage County Courthouse grounds. Wonder if they're still there.

His fame in railroading is everlasting. His interesting railroad car, his inventions, and his manuscripts are housed in the Smithsonian Institution in Washington, D.C.

# FRED FULLER LIVES ON IN BEAUTIFUL KENT PARK

*February 16, 1992*

Thousands of people each year enjoy the facilities and appreciate the pristine beauty of Fred Fuller Park along the Cuyahoga River in west Kent. Only older park patrons probably would have the faintest notion who Fred Fuller was and why the park was named for him. Also, they might wonder why the bridge which provides access to the "island's" baseball field was named in honor of Harvey Redmond. Or why the park's shelter-house honors Roy H. Smith.

For the record, the beautifully treed park was named for Fred Fuller to recognize his long, unstinting, and ultimately successful effort to achieve a park for his home community. As for the bridge, it was named for Harvey Redmond, a World War I veteran, who in 1940 led a Kent American Legion fund campaign for a city park. Roy Smith, onetime mayor of Kent and president and chairman of the Lamson and Sessions Company, was recognized for his personal contributions and those of his company toward the park development

The passing of time tends to obscure the accomplishments of people and their unselfish civic contributions. Remembrances of them diminish with each successive generation. That is why it is deemed important to take notice of their accomplishments and to make certain they receive their rightful place in local history.

When he retired in 1937, following a long and successful career in the steel business, Fred Fuller could have retired to a life of ease. He chose a different course. That he should return to his native Franklin Township was a natural turn of events. He had deep roots here.

Fuller was born in 1872 at Cackler's Corners in northwestern Franklin Township. He was proud of his heritage, particularly that he was a great-great-grandson of Christian Cackler Jr., who settled here in 1804. It was Cackler who, in his 1870 *Recollections of an Old Settler*, chronicled the early history of Franklin Township and Portage County that was the first, and remains the best, eyewitness history of this area.

During his boyhood years, Fuller delivered newspapers in Kent and then became a printer's devil at the old *Kent Bulletin*. For four years he served as assistant Kent postmaster. Interspersed during those years was a stint at Western Reserve Academy in Hudson.

In 1894 he joined the Falcon Iron and Nail Company in Niles, launching a career of 43 years in the steel business. That firm merged with the American Tin Plate Company, taking Fuller to Chicago and giving him a promotion to chief clerk. Then he was transferred to New York City, and then to Pittsburgh following the merger of the American Tin Plate Company with the American Sheet Steel Company. When that firm merged with the Carnegie Illinois Steel Company. Fuller became general sales manager with offices in Pittsburgh.

While still in Pittsburgh, he acquired the old Pioneer grounds on Linden Road in Kent and allotted the area for development. When he returned to Kent in 1938, Linden Road became his address.

In retirement, Fuller immersed himself in civic betterment projects. He became president of the Kent Rotary Club, served as a vestryman of Christ Church Episcopal and a member of the Kent Free Library Board, as a member of the city planning commission, and eventually he became a member and longtime chairman of the Kent City Park Board. The latter service was the capstone of his civic career.

He prodded, cajoled, pleaded with city officials, industry, clubs, and fellow citizens in his campaign to achieve a city park for Kent. Lamson and Sessions gave some of the land, organizations raised funds to build shelters and other facilities, Harvey Redmond raised funds to help, and Roy Smith used his influence and provided funds to gain eventual success for the park project.

In January of 1946 Fred Fuller was recognized by a grateful community for his efforts. That month the Kent Area Chamber of Commerce awarded him its first Kent Medal for Public Service. And the following December he was accorded his highest honor when Kent City Council approved legislation to name the park for him.

Fred Fuller died in 1955. But his name and the community's gratitude to him live on in beautiful Fred Fuller Park.

# MONDAY IS THE HUNDREDTH ANNIVERSARY
# OF CARIS'S BIRTH

*February 11, 1990*

He was born in Ravenna on February 12, Abraham Lincoln's birthday. Appropriately, he was given Lincoln as his middle name. Tomorrow is the hundredth anniversary of Albert Lincoln Caris's birthdate.

Albert Lincoln Caris has been described by friends and fellow barristers in many ways: one possessed of the sharpest of legal minds, the most accomplished trial lawyer of his era, a fair, honest judge who believed deeply in the law and impartial justice for all, a legend in his own time, certainly one of Portage County's all-time outstanding citizens. He was all of those.

I have many fond recollections of this man whom I considered a good and loyal friend. As a young reporter I covered many trials during which he was the defense attorney. Never have I witnessed a better one. His quick, sharp knowledge of the law, his gift for oratory, and his knowledge of the Bible, the classics, or Shakespeare, which he demonstrated profusely, constituted a legal drama that will not soon be matched. And they won for him most of his court trials.

Big-city lawyers who may have anticipated a country bumpkin most times were left mumbling to themselves when he finished with them. On one occasion, I actually witnessed a physical encounter between him and a Cleveland attorney when, during a trial recess, the big-city legal beagle made a remark which clearly questioned Caris's honesty. He would have none of that. His honesty and integrity were not to be disparaged.

It always has been my view that Albert Caris could have achieved anything he desired in the way of public office. He was the most accomplished, eloquent public speaker I ever encountered. His charm, brilliance, simplicity of delivery, and logic would have won him a majority of voters. Who would not have voted for him for congressman, U.S. senator, governor, or justice of the Ohio Supreme Court after hearing him speak? And he had the learning, wisdom, and ability to get things done to back up his oratorical gift. He disdained that type of public life.

He never forsook his Portage County roots, although he won acclaim as one of Ohio's most sagacious and accomplished trial lawyers and distinguished jurists.

Amazingly, Albert Caris never had the advantage of a law education. He studied law under Attorney H. R. Loomis for three years, then took the Ohio bar examination. He humbly noted that he placed second in the examination, his only superior being a Harvard Law School graduate.

Despite his success and lofty respect as a judge, he was as much at home with those of lesser stature as he was with the high and mighty. He counted among his close friends people in all walks of life. He did not forget their accomplishments nor their times of despair. Over the years, my mail brought many laudatory messages from him when he deemed I had done something worthwhile. Who would not cherish memories of such a man?

Unlike his middle namesake, our first Republican president, Judge Caris was a staunch Democrat, serving many years as Portage County Democratic chairman and twice as a delegate to his party's national convention. He was a devoted admirer of both Lincoln and George Washington and was called upon many times to deliver sparkling speeches about both presidents.

Judge Caris held three different public offices. At only 22, he was elected clerk of courts in 1912, and he won reelection. Although not yet an attorney (at that time it wasn't required), he was appointed probate judge in 1917 and then elected in 1919.

He passed the bar in 1922, left the probate bench the next year, and then joined H. R. Loomis in the practice of law, a relationship which would span 28 years. He left the firm in 1950 at age 60 to campaign for common pleas judge, an office he won handily. He held the judgeship for 24 years, until he was forced by a new state law to retire. As sharp as ever in retirement, he was kept busy as a judge by assignment.

Judge Caris died in 1978 at age 88, ending an outstanding, respected career . . . a career achieved without a college degree except for an honorary doctor of laws conferred by Kent State University to a self-taught man who learned Greek and could read the Bible in that language.

It is prescribed in courts of law that attorneys and witnesses address the judge as "Your Honor." The appellation is automatic and routine. Not so in the court of Judge Caris. "Your Honor" had a true meaning!

———

## WHAT'S IN A NAME? HISTORY, SERVICE, HONOR

*July 24, 1988*

"Seabury" isn't exactly a household variety among given names. And coupled with the surname of Ford, it seems quite unlikely that two Seabury Fords, both lawyers and both involved in public service, would exist in the same geographic area.

One of these Seabury Fords is 85-year-old Seabury H. Ford of Aurora, dean among Portage County's practicing attorneys. The other was Seabury Ford (no initial) of Burton, in neighboring Geauga County, who served many years in Ohio's House of Representatives and Senate and in 1849–50 as the 20th governor of Ohio, the last Whig to hold that office. The first Seabury Ford was the great-grandfather of the present-day, well-known lawyer and former public official.

The roots of both Seabury Fords are equally deep in the Western Reserve. The eldest Seabury was born in 1801 in New Haven County, Connecticut, and migrated to Burton with his family when he was only six years of age. Following his local schooling, he returned to New Haven to enter Yale and upon graduation came back to Ohio to study law in the office of his uncle. He practiced law in Burton, became a major general in the state militia, and joined the Whig party when it was organized in 1834. That was his introduction to politics, which would consume most of his later years.

The elder Seabury served in the Ohio General Assembly either as representative or senator from the 34th through the 46th sessions with the exception of one. He served as speaker of each of the Assembly's houses.

At 37 he lost the Whig nomination for Congress, but his defeat did not diminish his political ambition. Ten years later, he was the Whig nominee for Ohio governor.

As most Whigs, Ford was a devout opponent of slavery, and when he ran for governor he was firm in his conviction that slavery should be excluded in any territory acquired as a result of the Mexican War. He was sadly embarrassed when the Whigs nominated Zachary Taylor, a southern slave owner, for president. For that reason, he ignored Taylor's candidacy, which exposed him to taunts from the Democrats.

Ford's election to the governorship was the closest in Ohio history. He won by 311 votes in an election during which nearly 300,000 votes were cast. His inauguration was delayed six weeks while the General Assembly examined the voting returns.

His administration was not without its problems, among them a controversy over the repeal of laws that discriminated against blacks, a constitutional convention election that succeeded, and a cholera outbreak in Columbus which created chaos when it spread to the Ohio penitentiary. He solved that problem by granting pardons to deserving prisoners and promising additional pardons to those who helped keep order and nurse the sick.

Ford's term as governor ended in December of 1850. On the first Sunday following his return to his home in Burton, he suffered a paralytic stroke from which he made only a partial recovery. He died in May of 1855, six months short of his 54th birthday.

Attorney Seabury Ford, onetime prosecuting attorney and former Portage County Republican chairman, has emulated his great-grandfather in more ways than just his given name. He was born in his great-grandfather's hometown, Burton, in 1902. His family moved to Aurora when he was a child. His roots in Aurora date back to 1815, when his maternal great-grandfather, Hopson Hurd, arrived from Connecticut. He ran a general store in Aurora at the corner of Garfield and Chillicothe Roads. His home was in the old Singletary tavern and stagecoach stop, a house built in 1805, and now still in the family as Seabury Ford's residence. The house is located at 12 West Garfield Road.

Seabury's grandfather, Frank Hurd, was known as the "Cheese King of the Western Reserve" during the days when Aurora was the cheese capital. At one time, Frank Hurd operated 25 cheese factories throughout the Reserve.

The present Seabury also emulated his great-grandfather on the political scene. An ardent Republican, he has been described by some as the "last surviving Whig." Besides the county chairmanship, he has served as a precinct committeeman and was a onetime state central committeeman.

Seabury received two law degrees from Western Reserve University in 1925 and he has been a practicing lawyer ever since—63 years—briefly in Cleveland and since 1934 in Ravenna. At nearly 86, he still goes to his office daily.

As with his great-grandfather, public office also has been an attraction to him. He has been an Aurora justice of the peace, councilman, and law director, and he served two terms as Portage County prosecutor until 1953. During the state grand jury investigation of the shootings at Kent State University, he was one of the special prosecutors.

Both the Portage and Ohio Bar Associations have honored him for his many years in the practice of law. He differs in at least two respects from his great-grandfather. He has never run for state office. And he has outlived his distinguished ancestor by more than 30 years.

## MEMORY OF WALLS'S EDUCATION EFFORT
## REMAINS STRONG

*January 12, 1985*

Fifty years ago this month, one of the Portage area's most beloved educators began a new career as Ohio relief director under the governor's administration of fellow Kentite Martin L. Davey. Although William A. Walls, Kent superintendent of schools, has been a state and national leader in the crippled children's movement and has been active in welfare organizations, his new role in state government was an abrupt departure from his career in education.

Today, hundreds of youngsters who attend Walls Elementary School in Kent don't know why their school was so named. The same probably can be said for some of their teachers. Their acquaintanceship with Mr.

Walls is gained through his photograph and a handsome plaque that grace the school's main hallway.

For others, particularly older residents who were students during Walls's tenure as superintendent of schools, memories of him as a revered educator and as an active Kent citizen are among their most cherished. They recall him as a bright, warm person who always placed the interest of his charges at the uppermost level.

Bill Walls was one of Kent's most respected citizens. He was a leader not only in the schools, but also in his Rotary Club, in the Methodist Church, and in scores of organizations to which he loaned his talents.

He was a large man whose stature most times bordered on obesity, a condition which probably could be attributed to his voracious appetite. His closest friends referred to him by the nickname "Tubby," with no intention to voice disrespect. His persistent good nature and hale-fellow-well-met personality stood out among his many charming attributes. He was a bachelor, a marital status that busied would-be Kent matchmakers.

A native of Muskingum County, Bill Walls came to Kent in 1907, the same year he received his bachelor's degree from Mount Union College. His first Kent assignment was principal of Kent High School, then located in the old Union or Central School building. After three years in that position he was named superintendent in 1910.

Following the 1915 school year, he left Kent to become superintendent at Martins Ferry. He did an educational stint in France during World War I, held several more positions elsewhere, and then returned to head the Kent schools in 1920. During his Kent years, he also taught during summer sessions at Kent State. He continued as Kent superintendent until 1937, serving a total of 24 years, including 21 as superintendent. His tenure as Ohio relief director was a brief one; he returned to the superintendency shortly before his death in 1937.

Kent was plunged into deep gloom on August 14 of that year when word was received that Mr. Walls's car had struck a truck on S.R. 40 between Springfield and Columbus. He was in that area on business for the Kent Board of Education. His broken body was taken to White Cross Hospital in Columbus where he underwent surgery and where he died on August 22. His funeral services at the Kent Methodist Church attracted educators, politicians and close friends from across the state. John Spangler, then principal of Theodore Roosevelt High School, succeeded him as superintendent.

Twenty-eight years later, a new elementary school was erected in the northeast section of the city. The Kent Board of Education honored Mr. Walls by placing his name on the building, a move which achieved instant public acclaim. Walls is the only school in Kent to bear the name of a former superintendent.

———

## CLOSING OF KLINE'S MARKET ENDS AN ERA IN KENT
### November 12, 1989

Once there were three independent grocery stores in a two-block span along Kent's Water Street—Kline's and the Longcoy store on South Water and Kneifel grocery on North Water. A horse-drawn hack each day made the rounds of all three stores and picked up crates of groceries for delivery to waiting householders. The crates were collapsible so that they might be stacked in neat piles after they were emptied. Later, the horse and wagon gave way to a motorized delivery service. Kneifel's and Longcoy's disappeared from the mercantile scene many years ago, and now with the closing of Kline's following 79 years of operation, the death knell of independent markets has been sounded.

My longtime friend, Emmet J. Kline, founder of the market in 1910, never feared competition from supermarkets. He was known to say many times, "Competition? There has always been competition. It's good. That's what keeps you on your toes." That was his response when A&P built a store practically across the street from his market.

During its lengthy existence in the business world, Kline's offered many special touches. Who can forget the smell of the store's freshly roasted peanuts? A pedestrian on Water Street was treated to that special aroma. Or the store as a mecca for historical materials, an expression of Emmet's (and his sons') love of local history and appreciation for heritage? To the very end, Kline's sold copies of *Portage Heritage* (a history of Portage County that Emmet helped to publish), Christian

Cackler's *Recollections of an Old Settler,* and other memorabilia. And Emmet's tulip bulbs! Each year he ordered tulip bulbs from Holland and potted them at the proper time so as to have them blooming and available for customers at Eastertime. Any gardener or florist knows such a schedule takes know-how and proper timing. In the fall, choice tulip bulbs always were available at Kline's.

Prior to opening his store at the South Water Street location in the same year Kent State University was established, Emmet operated a milk route in Kent, ladling dippers of milk to housewives from containers hauled on a horse-drawn wagon.

Kent was a town of only 4,400 when Kline's opened for business. It was a railroad town with the car shops, yards, and a busy depot, all now only memories of another era. Cars were few. (Emmet had one of the first ones in town.) Streetcars carried passengers on regular schedules from Akron through Kent and on to Ravenna.

That was the Kent scene when Emmet opened his store, which would endure for eight decades and into four generations of customers and three generations of Klines.

Although he worked from dawn to dusk, Emmet didn't confine his activity to his business. He was active in his community—St. Patrick's Church, city affairs, and historical matters. He served three terms on city council and ran unsuccessfully for state representative, mayor of Kent, and city treasurer. He was one of the founders of the Portage County Historical Society and a charter trustee. An achievement of which he was most proud was his association with the publication of *Portage Heritage* in 1957, the first county history in nearly 80 years. He teamed with his good friend J. B. Holm, the volume's editor, serving as biography manager for the book.

Following his retirement, Emmet turned over the business to his sons, Francis, Maurice, and Ralph. Francis has been the main man on the scene these past years, with Maurice, Portage County treasurer, spending many of his spare hours in the store. Ralph is deceased. After he retired, Emmet turned to travel, visiting 20 European and African countries with his longtime friend, Dr. Joseph Renouf, a Kent dentist. He also visited Ireland (the ancestral home of his wife, Julia McMahon),

Australia, New Zealand, and the Arctic Circle. For a onetime farmboy, Emmet Kline really got around the world.

But his real world was centered around his hometown and 156 South Water Street in Kent, where, he, his sons, and grandchildren served with genuine interest, honesty, and innovative spirit the needs and wants of an admiring and appreciative public. And so, now another passes!

---

## FRED BECHTLE'S STORE WAS A GEM IN A BYGONE ERA

*October 20, 1991*

A cigar store Indian which he wheeled daily to a place of honor on the sidewalk was a trademark of Fred Bechtle's store at 113 South Water Street in Kent.

There were other trademarks of this unique business. One was the strange combination of Bechtle's mercantile offerings. Besides operating a newspaper distribution agency, he also, as the main staples of his store, sold all types of men's furnishings and a variety of tobacco products. And in the late years, Hickman's jewelry business shared the north side of the storeroom.

For many businessmen in Kent's downtown area, Fred Bechtle's store was a daily gathering place. Many went there each morning ostensibly to buy their cigars and their newspapers, but people who knew Fred Bechtle would surmise that of more importance was an opportunity to chat with the "sage of South Water Street." After all, he was more than a storekeeper. During his career he held village, township, and county offices and, even in his advanced years, kept a close ear and eye on the public domain. He knew what was going on about town, and he liberally shared what he knew with his customers.

Fred Bechtle was born on South Water Street in 1872, the son of a baker and confectionery store owner whose business also was on South Water Street. Following his attendance at Kent schools, Fred Bechtle went to work for Frederick Merrill, who operated a clothing store in Kent. Later, he became a news dealer, handling out-of-town newspapers and hiring his own newsboys to hawk them. He sold the news dealer business in 1928 and then devoted all of his energy and enthusiasm to the men's furnishings and tobacco business.

It wasn't all work and no play for Bechtle. He was a baseball player on some of Kent's better teams. It was said that he had the ability to play any position. At one time he managed one of the town teams. He also was a boxing fan. On many an occasion while they were waiting for newspapers to arrive, he put on the gloves and boxed with newsboys who worked for him.

Interspersed with his business career, Fred Bechtle had a career in public service that spanned more than a half-century. He served as village and township clerk beginning in 1898. He served until 1906 and then again for another five years starting in 1912. He was a member of the Kent Board of Education for four years and then from 1917 to 1919 was Portage County auditor. He returned as Franklin Township clerk in 1928, serving 23 years, until 1951. I have fond memories of Fred Bechtle. A slight, thin man, he was quiet of demeanor, with a soft voice. He smoked cigars. He always wore high, stiff collars. When corduroy trousers became popular in the early 1930s, I bought a pair at the Bechtle store. As I remember, they cost $2. They were rust colored. I had seen many country stores in which disorder was not considered an evil, but I had never seen a store quite like Bechtle's. It wasn't exactly disorderly, but his arrangement of goods for sale was a bit baffling. But he always knew where everything was and could find the needed item in a jiffy.

Fred Bechtle cared about his native town, its culture and its heritage. I vividly recall a day in the spring of 1950 when a demolition crew arrived to tear down the old wooden *Courier* building at 138 East Main Street to make way for a more modern brick structure. Fred made a special trip to the site to witness the building's demise. The old building had housed many generations of publishing a weekly, semi-weekly, and, finally, a daily newspaper. "This is a sad day," he told me. "I so well remember Will Kent when he owned the paper and Johnny Paxton when he was the editor. I hate to see old buildings torn down." The beloved building went down amidst the rubble wrought by the wrecker's expertise.

Despite the many changes that have come about in all of our towns, the Bechtle name lives. Take a look at the top of a block at the southwest corner of the first alley south of Main Street on the west side of South Water. There you will read, "Bechtle, October 1912."

---

## CRANE

### His Troubles Overshadowed His Poetic Genius

*November 15, 1987*

Hart Crane was a major American poet whose works today are studied in high schools and colleges for their technical perfection and experimental daring. He was a troubled man whose poetry expressed an optimism in America, yet he deemed his own life a failure, and at the young age of only 32 he chose the path of personal annihilation.

Hart Crane was a native Portage Countian. He was born in Garrettsville on July 21, 1899, the son of Clarence Arthur Crane and Grace Hart Crane. Although christened Harold Hart Crane, he chose Hart as his given name in deference to his maternal grandparents.

His father was a wealthy and energetic businessman who operated a Cleveland candy manufacturing company and numerous confectionery stores including one in Akron. He is credited with the invention of Life Savers candy. Despite attempts to involve his son in his business, Clarence Crane never succeeded. Neither did he succeed in his expressed mission to "knock that poetic nonsense" out of his son.

The Crane family first moved to Dayton and then to Cleveland. Crane biographers say the poet as a youngster attended public schools in Cleveland and Warren. His writing of poetry began at the age of 13, but he found little encouragement except from a few small magazines which were his main publishing outlet. Incompatibility of his mother and father led to their divorce in 1916, a family situation to which Crane attributed his personal unhappiness. He described it as "the curse of sundered parentage."

When he was 17, he spent a year with his mother on her father's plantation in the Isle of Pines, Cuba, an experience that undoubtedly gave him an appreciation of the sea which was reflected with bombastic emphasis in some of his later poetry. The other theme which dominates his poetry was the big city, which he experienced the following year in New York and Paris.

When the United States entered World War I, Crane abandoned thoughts of college and returned from New York to Cleveland where he worked as a laborer in shipyards and munitions plants. Still intent on shaking his son's poetic dream, Crane's father enticed him into his business, but young Hart would have none of that for any considerable period. He broke away several times and went to New York, where he wrote advertising copy and turned out poetry for several avant-garde periodicals. From 1916 to 1925 he divided his time between Greenwich Village and Ohio, working as a salesman, warehouse helper, and reporter.

One of his biographers in *American Authors*, edited by Kunitz, writes that the only congenial companionship he found in Ohio was at Herbert Fletcher's bookstore, which was next-door to one of his father's candy shops in Akron. The final break with his father came in 1920 after a bitter quarrel, and young Hart again turned to New York, where, according to his biographers, he drifted into habits that led to alcoholism and homosexuality.

In the early 1920s he produced his first major poems, "For the Marriage of Faustus and Helen" and "At Melville's Tomb." *White Buildings*, Crane's first of two books of poems, was published in 1926. Its publication led to two grants from banker philanthropist Otto Kahn, a recognized patron of the arts in that day. Inspired by acceptance and by those grants, Crane was enabled to work on an ambitious, long poem, *The Bridge*, his best-known effort, published in 1930.

*The Bridge* attempts to express the myth of America, its vitality, and its strength. The Brooklyn Bridge is the central symbol as Crane offers a mystical interpretation of the past, present, and future of America. One of his biographers describes *The Bridge* as the most important volume of American poetry since Whitman's *Leaves of Grass*. Kunitz's *American Authors* says of *The Bridge*: "A subjective mysticism renders the poem highly obscure and robs it of organic unity, but it is filled with vivid images." At any rate, critical success of *The Bridge* earned Crane a Guggenheim Fellowship, which enabled him to go to Mexico to research and to write an epic poem on Cortes and Montezuma. He had hoped to do for Latin America what *The Bridge* had done for America.

But this was not to be. Crane's personal habits were ruinous. His alcoholism became more intense, so much so that his quarrelsome nature and lack of discipline caused even his close friends to give up on him. He was headed for personal destruction. The Mexico trip turned out a colossal failure. Crane felt that he had squandered his fellowship time in Mexico, and he never started the poem which the fellowship was designed to support.

In despair, Crane sailed from Mexico to New York. Shortly before noon on April 27, 1932, he went to the deck of a steamer, the *Orizata*, took off his coat, and leaped into the Atlantic. His death came just three months short of his 33rd birthday. The following day, the death of the young poet rated only a five-paragraph story on page 1 of the *Record-Courier*, his home county newspaper. The story described his passing by drowning with no mention of suicide.

Crane's own words provide his eulogy:

> Sleep, death, desire,
> Close[d] round one instant in a floating flower.

---

## DOOLITTLE'S DEATH RECALLS OUR OWN BILL BOWER

*October 3, 1993*

There was plenty of excitement in Portage County in the spring of 1942. World War II was on in all of its fury. Only a few months before, the Japanese had staged their sneak attack upon Pearl Harbor. Like all Americans, Portage Countians were incensed and humiliated that the United States should be so violated. The war against Japan and Nazi Germany was not going well. Desperately, the United States needed a single victory to buoy spirits. Enter, Col. Jimmy Doolittle. News in the *Record-Courier* on April 19, 1942, provided the tool to lift the American spirit. He and his band of intrepid flyers had bombed Tokyo,

Yokohama, Kobe, and Nagoya the day before. That took place only 132 days after Pearl Harbor.

It is now more than 51 years later. I reflected upon those days this week with the death of Gen. Jimmy Doolittle in California at age 96. His passing at such an advanced age provides the capstone to an era which will long be remembered by Americans. And especially by Portage Countians. After all, we here in Portage County, and particularly Ravenna, had an endearing connection with the famous general.

Although the raid in "30 seconds over Tokyo" had taken place a month before, it would not be until May 20 that the *Record-Courier*, with an eight-column headline, would bring the news to local folks that 1st Lt. Bill Bower of Ravenna was one of the pilots of the B-25 Mitchell bombers that surprised the Japanese with a bombing raid against their principal cities.

In a letter that May, Doolittle informed Bill Bower's mother, Kathryn, that her son was happy and well. That set into motion a local excitement seldom experienced in Portage County. To say that local people were exceedingly proud and pleased that Bill Bower was a hero and that he had been spared would be an understatement. Here was a 1934 graduate of Ravenna High School who would be forever a World War II hero.

Colonel Doolittle went to the White House in May of 1942, and President Franklin D. Roosevelt conferred the Congressional Medal of Honor upon him, and the 79 other participants in the Tokyo raid the Distinguished Flying Cross.

Bill Bower, born in Ravenna in 1917, had briefly attended Hiram College and then Kent State University before enlisting in the Army Air Corps in 1939. He had been a member of the onetime National Guard troop in Ravenna when it still was a "horse" troop. He was well known in his hometown.

No wonder people, so accustomed to bad news from the war fronts, were so excited. When it was learned that Bower had been a pilot on the bombing raid, the Ravenna Junior Chamber of Commerce (now the Jaycees), immediately swung into action. I was a member of the Ravenna Jaycees at that time. We immediately voted Lieutenant Bower an honorary life membership in the organization. (I wonder if any present-day Jaycees would be aware of that.) And we made plans. Big plans. The Jaycees named Dick Webb general chairman of the "Welcome Home Bill Bower Day." Dick Webb later would enlist in the Air Force and, as a pilot, would participate in some fierce engagements in the Philippines.

In June of 1942 Bill Bower made it to the nation's capital where he and 22 others were decorated with the Distinguished Flying Cross. On June 28 he took a train from Washington and returned home. The next evening, a Sunday, editor Angelo Sicuro and I went to Edinburg, where we met Bill at the Wishing Well, a fine country dining place operated by Mr. and Mrs. Andy Austin. We went there because that was where Bill's mother worked.

I thought at the time that, for a hero, I never had met a more modest man. During the course of the interview, Bill said, "We went there, dropped our bombs. And that was about it." He did say that he saw bombs hit a ship at Yokohama. And that he never had flown so low without landing. (Planes flew above their targets only 15 or 20 feet.)

I wrote an interview story which was printed the next day in the *Record-Courier*, accompanied by a photo taken at the Wishing Well. The circumstances for the interview were not ideal. "Uncle" Andy Austin had died that day. Bill had seen him only briefly before taking off for Cleveland for a picnic with relatives, including his grandmother.

Plans for the Bill Bower Day in Ravenna went forward. The Ravenna Arsenal was booming at that time, and Maj. Marvin Kafer, commander of the depot side, was exceedingly cooperative. He turned loose his carpenter and painting crews to build floats for the parade, as well as for the making of posters and signs to decorate the town.

On July 3, 1942, Ravennans witnessed the biggest parade they had seen before and probably since. There were floats, marching units, and bands which stretched for blocks and blocks. Airplanes flew over the parade in tribute to the local hero. Earlier that day there was a luncheon at the Ravenna Arsenal and tours of the ammunition plant.

That evening a dinner was held at the Vale Edge at which Judge Walter Wanamaker of Akron, a World War I flier, was the speaker. Gordon Kelso, Jaycee president, was the emcee. He presented Bill a plaque denoting his life Jaycee membership. City and county dignitaries made appropriate remarks. Also appearing on the program was Paul

Derthick of Ravenna, father of a son killed at Pearl Harbor, Portage County's first World War II victim. Bill Bower Day concluded with a dance at the USO Center. (Before that time and again today, it's the Ravenna Armory on North Freedom Street.)

Bill Bower remained in the Air Force after World War II, eventually was promoted to the rank of a colonel, and now lives in retirement in Colorado Springs, Colorado. I had not seen Bill Bower for several years when about a year ago I chanced to meet him at the East Park Restaurant in Ravenna. He was affable and congenial as ever. The biggest difference I noted was his considerable loss of hair.

I shall always remember what Bill, really a modest person, said to me that evening 51 years ago at the Wishing Well at the conclusion of our interview. Noting that Andy Austin had died that day, he said, "If any of this gets in the paper, make certain it doesn't detract from Uncle Andy." The story of his heroic exploits for his country did not do so; it appeared on page 1, alongside an obituary and a photo of Uncle Andy.

When Gen. Jimmy Doolittle is buried at Arlington National Cemetery, you may be certain that many of his surviving airmen, including Bill Bower, will be there.

———

## GABLE, "SLOB FROM OHIO," IS REMEMBERED AT 95

*February 11, 1996*

Clark Gable, 95 years old. That is difficult to imagine. We are more inclined to think of him as the handsome, debonair "King of Hollywood," an actor who charmed the ladies and will be forever remembered as Rhett Butler in *Gone with the Wind.*

A week ago a television documentary traced the life and times of Clark Gable. But it made no mention of his onetime residency in Portage County prior to his days of stardom. Clark Gable at the height of his acting career described himself as "just a slob from Ohio." What a slob! A slob, born in Cadiz, who reached the very pinnacle of Hollywood stardom in the 1930s.

February 1 was Clark Gable's birthday. He died in 1960 at only 59 years of age. The people in Cadiz always celebrate Clark Gable's birthday with all sorts of remembrances. Here in Portage County, where he once resided, his birthday causes not even the slightest of mentions. He once lived with his father, William Henry Gable, and his stepmother at Yale. Probably some people in Portage County haven't the faintest notion the location of Yale, once a prosperous center at the confluence of Edinburg, Palmyra, Deerfield, and Atwater townships.

Upon the death of his mother when he was only seven months old, Clark went to live with his grandparents. Then, his father, an oil contractor, remarried. Exactly when Clark Gable and his father moved to Yale is not certain, but it is known that he attended Edinburg schools in 1915, when he was 14 years of age. In school he had a girlfriend named Treela. It is said that that schoolchild romance ended when the Gable family moved to Palmyra. Considering that Yale is near Palmyra, that wasn't a distant move. In Portage County, Gable went by the name of Willie; his correct name was William Clark Gable.

The late Mary Ensinger of Edinburg recalled that her family sold their farm on Alliance Road to Gable's father and that her family stayed on to keep house for the elder Gable and his son Clark until the stepmother arrived, after which the Ensingers departed. That was in 1917. That was the same year that Clark convinced his father and stepmother that he should "strike out on his own." That he did. He went to Akron and got a job at the Miller Rubber Company, and he also attended night classes. His love affair with acting began when he wandered into the Akron Music Hall, where *The Bird of Paradise* was playing. He took an unpaid job as a callboy with the Lilly stock company, and he was given a walk-on part in which he uttered only three words. In that brief moment his acting career was launched.

Then he received word that his stepmother was gravely ill. He returned to Portage County and remained at her bedside until she died. That was in 1920, and it is said that the snow was so deep at the time that her body was placed on a bobsled for removal to Edinburg Cemetery for the burial.

Gable and his father then went to the Oklahoma and Texas oil fields, but Clark was disenchanted with such work. His father never agreed that an acting career was fitting for him. Despite his father's objections, Clark went to Kansas City, where he joined a touring company that ultimately went broke. Then he hopped a freight and went to Oregon, where he worked briefly as a lumberjack. There he met Josephine Dillon, director of a theater group, who later became his first wife. Gable appeared on Broadway in 1924 in *What Price Glory* and then he went to Hollywood, where he failed several screen tests. Finally, he won several bit parts.

His first major picture was *The Painted Desert* in 1930. He then signed on with MGM, a move which assured his success. He became the nation's movie sex symbol. Gable reached the pinnacle of movie fame for his role in *It Happened One Night* with Claudette Colbert, for which he won an Oscar for best actor in 1934. Then came *Gone with the Wind* and his role as Rhett Butler opposite Vivien Leigh. The movie won an Academy Award in 1939 and continues its popularity even today.

Gable's most distressing time came in 1942 when his current wife and deepest love, Carole Lombard, was killed in an air crash. In his despondency he joined the Army Air Corps in World War II, serving on bombing missions over Europe for which he was awarded the Air Medal. He returned from World War II with the rank of major.

In 1954, he ended his long relationship with MGM, after appearing in 67 films. In 1960, he appeared with Marilyn Monroe in *The Misfits*. Shortly after finishing the film he suffered a heart attack, and 10 days later he was dead at 59. He left his fifth wife, the former Kay Williams Spreckles, and an unborn child. That child today is John Clark Gable.

The self-described "slob from Ohio" had an illustrious acting career. And Portage County and the little settlement of Yale can claim at least part of him.

―――――

## TITANIC'S ALVIN A BRAINCHILD OF
## GARRETTSVILLE'S ALLYN VINE
### *August 9, 1986*

Dr. Allyn Collins Vine was born in Garrettsville on June 1, 1914, two years after the "unsinkable" *Titanic* sank in the Atlantic on its maiden

voyage, killing 1,513 of the 2,224 people aboard. Yet his inventive genius played a key role in the explorations last month—74 years later—
which led to the location of the *Titanic* on the ocean floor.

Allyn was the inventor, in 1964, of the two-man, 22-foot oceanographic sub *Alvin*, a name contracted from the inventor's first and last
names. Under sponsorship of the Woods Hole Oceanographic Institute, the mini-sub last month made 11 dives two and a half miles to the
ocean floor to locate and photograph wreckage of the ill-fated ship.

Findings of the exploration team headed by Robert Ballard, ocean-
ographer and marine geologist at Woods Hole, have been much in the
news these past three weeks. Among other findings, the explorations
revealed that the Titanic did not sustain a huge gash in her hull when
she struck an iceberg, as had been theorized. Rather, the explorations
confirmed that steel plates separated, letting in the sea and sending the
882-foot ship to the bottom on April 15, 1912. Thousands of photographs were taken by robot cameras to confirm the team's findings.

Dr. Vine, senior scientist at the Woods Hole Oceanographic Institute, retired two years ago, capping a 44-year career as an oceanogra-
pher at the Massachusetts institute. He and his wife, Adelaide, reside at
Woods Hole in a home they developed from a former carriage house
once owned by the well-known Crane plumbing family. He maintains
an office at the institute and serves as a consultant. They have two sons,
Norman and David, and a daughter, Vivian.

Dr. Vine comes from Garrettsville's prominent and talented Vine family. His father, Elmer (Mike) Vine, operated a Garrettsville butcher shop
for many years. His mother was the former Lulu Collins, a Wayland
native. It was in her honor that the sub *Alvin's* mother ship, the *Lulu*,
was named.

Allyn is the second of four Vine sons. He graduated in 1936 from
Hiram College, which honored him in 1967 as outstanding alumnus.
He received a Master of Science degree from Lehigh University in 1940
and joined the Woods Hole Institute that same year. In 1973 Lehigh
conferred upon him an honorary doctor's degree. His wife also is a Hiram
graduate.

His elder brother, Everett, a Hiram College graduate, is a retired
Garrettsville postmaster. He resides on a 175-acre farm on S.R. 303.

Another brother, Victor, a graduate of the U.S. Naval Academy, where he starred in football three years, retired in 1976 as a navy commander. He was the navy backfield coach when Joe Bellino and Roger Staubach, both Heisman Trophy winners, were members of the navy team. He resides in Horseshoe Bay, Texas. Victor's twin, Vernon, an artist, died at 27.

Allyn Vine's proud parents were on hand on June 5, 1964, when the *Alvin* was dedicated at Woods Hole. His wife christened the sub. Allyn was absent, and for a valid reason. He was exploring the depths of the Puerto Rican Trench in the bathyscaphe *Archimedes*. The next year, the *Alvin* was used to locate a lost H-bomb off the coast of Spain.

When the *Alvin* was dedicated, it was hailed as the first U.S.-built submersible with appreciable depth capability with a 30-mile range. Its motors are battery-powered, driving three propellers. Four portholes permit viewing ahead and beneath the vessel by the pilot and the observer. Special escape devices are provided. When it was dedicated, the sub was described by an assistant U.S. Navy secretary as a tool of ocean research that ultimately would lead to exploitation of the "oceans' abundant living and mineral resources."

In 1980, the *Alvin* sub was used in a dive to the Pacific Ocean off the shore of Ecuador. That was the exploration when the Woods Hole team found giant worms never before known to man.

Now, the mini-sub has become part of exploration history by enabling the revelation of secrets of the *Titanic*'s sinking. And a Garrettsville native's ingenuity and talent have made a major contribution to man's knowledge of a historic sea disaster.

————

## WOMEN IN HISTORY
### They've Come a Long Way
*March 10, 1991*

"You've come a long way, baby" has become almost a standard exclamation of women's progress. This comes about as a result of the graphic Virginia Slims cigarette ads which appear each month in slick magazines. The ads feature inset photos of women in the dark ages pulling a plow or performing some other mundane task with a gloating husband standing by in disapproval or approval, as the case may be. Then, in contrast, there's always a beautiful, svelte model, an obvious representation of today's liberated woman. Not that it's exactly prim and proper to see the liberated woman glorified in an ad for tobacco products, but at least it makes a valid point and a sound case for the progress the female gender has made in recent decades.

In the 1990s, when women deservedly want to be given equal esteem, compensation, and opportunity as their male counterparts, it is interesting and significant to note that right here in the Portage area, the difficulty for women to make their voices heard above the crowd is well established in the annals of local history. In a review of printed volumes on Portage County history, you will find scant few biographies of women. From the time of our earliest settlements until the mid-twentieth century, it was pretty much a man's world.

Even so, there were some refreshing exceptions. There exist some historic examples of strong women in this area who rose to prominence, self-respect, and expression of their talents despite the common notion that women were to keep the home fires and care for the children while their spouses brought in the wherewithal to support the family. There are examples, too, of women coming to the forefront on issues they considered important to the well-being of their communities.

Like in 1908, when Portage County women became concerned with the abuse of alcohol and led a bitter campaign to get all of Portage County voted dry. They succeeded; every saloon in the county was forced to close, not to reopen until 1933 when the Eighteenth Amendment was repealed. They did this despite the fact women were not permitted the right to vote until 12 years later. Which brings up another point. Eastern states considered themselves more sophisticated than western areas, yet it was Wyoming territory that granted the vote to women in 1869, a half-century before Ohio did so.

During our earliest days, some women distinguished themselves as being strong willed despite the fact they did not enjoy the same privileges as male early settlers. Eleanor Garrett was one of them. She and her husband, John, settled Garrettsville in 1804. After establishing the

settlement and a mill (which still stands), John Garrett died at only 46.
Eleanor was not deterred. She furthered the development of the infant
settlement and with the help of her sons built the community. She was
the community's first postmistress and the "mother confessor" to people
of the town. Several times she made the trip on horseback to her native
Delaware with only a small son to keep her company. She died at 96.

Rebecca Woodard was another. She and her husband, Joshua, came
to Ravenna in 1810. Imagine the perils in the unbroken wilderness when
Rebecca, with baby Sally in her arms, rode horseback from Ravenna to
Geneva, New York, and back again in 1816.

Sally Haymaker was another. With her husband and three small children, she came to what is now Kent in 1805, and they stayed throughout that first winter in a tiny hut which had been used by Western Reserve surveyors several years before. Amenities were scant in those days;
the women "made do" to keep their families together and to help their
menfolk build a new community.

During the passing years, some fairly prominent women emerged.
Portage has produced only one first lady of the land, Lucretia Rudolph,
daughter of a Hiram farm couple who had the good fortune of marrying
James A. Garfield, our 20th president. And another Hiram woman, Jessie
Brown Pounds, the wife of a Disciple minister, wrote the words to that
grand old hymn "Beautiful Isle of Somewhere," which older residents
will recall.

During olden days, women who stepped away from housekeeping
chores usually became schoolteachers. One of the best-known among
them was Alameda Booth, a Nelson native, who taught in area schools
and ended her career on the faculty at Hiram College. True or not, she
was known as the "smartest woman in Portage County."

The more daring entered upon other pursuits—Etta Reed Payton
and Emma Vaders, for example. Those Ravenna ladies became stars
on the Broadway stage in New York City. And then there was Mary
Brayton Woodbridge, the daughter of a onetime sea captain whose
house still stands on South Chestnut Street in Ravenna. Mary
Woodbridge became nationally known as a leader in the temperance
movement, one of the most volatile issues of her day. She became a
national officer and leader of an unsuccessful campaign to pass an

amendment to ban alcoholic beverages. She was a devout woman and a most eloquent speaker.

In more recent years, women have won public acceptance after paying their dues for many long years. There was a time when few women aspired to public office and high positions in business. Not so today. In local politics, the late Gertrude Cunningham became the first woman mayor of Ravenna. Edith Olson broke the male barrier when she was elected to Kent City Council in 1923. Ethel Sivon did likewise on the Ravenna City Council.

Today, female public servants are numerous. Helen Frederick is county recorder; Janet Esposito, a county commissioner; Glenda Enders and Gerry Lewis, the generalissmos of the county board of elections; Barbara Watson is a judge; and Nancy Hansford, former Kent mayor, just completed a term as commissioner.

And as a capstone to this discourse, consider this: The four most important public positions in the city of Kent all are at present under the stewardship of women. Kathleen Chandler is mayor. Priscilla Blanchard is city manager. Donna Lightel is superintendent of schools. And to complete the quartet, on March 16, Carol Cartwright will become president of Kent State University.

As the ad says, "You've come a long way . . ."

---

## "AUNT LAURA" LOVED AURORA, DESPITE HARDSHIPS

### May 13, 1990

In contrast to today's standard—speedy transportation, numerous household conveniences, and the comforts of home—it is difficult to comprehend the exhausting, and sometimes dangerous, trials of our early pioneer women. Women's rights were unknown. Only the menfolk could vote, and women were pretty much relegated to lives of drudgery—helping to clear the land, keeping house with only the most meager staples and crudest of utensils, and raising children.

Such was the life of "Aunt Laura" Cannon, except that her hardships actually began at the tender age of 13 and seemed to follow her throughout much of her lifetime. Obviously she was a strong woman who appeared undaunted by pioneer hardships, a woman whose reputation for helping others became legendary in the Aurora community. Aunt Laura's story is chronicled beautifully by William J. Dawson, who compiled a history of Aurora for the community's sesquicentennial in 1949.

Laura Cochran Cannon was born in 1792 in Blandford, Massachusetts. It was in 1805 that she and her parents, Mr. and Mrs. John Cochran Sr., and Laura's sister, Rhoda, 20, who was crippled, set out in a wagon train for the Ohio frontier. A son, John Jr., had arrived in Aurora in 1804. When the party reached Buffalo, New York, the father fell ill. The mother, hoping for a quick recovery for her husband, remained with him and the two daughters were told to continue with the wagon train. Rhoda, unable to walk, was carried in one of the wagons.

The parents had engaged one of the men in the pioneer party to look after their daughters. What happened during the remainder of the journey through the wilderness is almost too repulsive to imagine. The man and his wife and the two Cochran girls, apparently by the couple's design, gained considerable distance ahead of the other wagons in the train. Laura was forced from her wagon and was made to walk alongside the wagon in which her disabled sister was riding—to walk not for a little distance, but all the way from Buffalo to Burton in Geauga County. Laura in later years told how blistered her feet became and how tired she became walking along the lonesome road.

The hard-hearted couple abandoned the penniless and friendless girls in Burton. There Laura, with a crippled sister to look after, found employment with a pioneer Burton family. When she had earned enough to pay the "fare," she and her sister rode on a log wagon to Mantua. There they received the sad news that their father had died in Buffalo.

Finally, the daughters and their mother were reunited in Aurora, where the handicapped sister died shortly thereafter. Her funeral was said to be the first in the Aurora settlement. Obviously the father's death caused a crisis in the Cochran family. Laura went to work for 16 shillings per week to help sustain the family.

Laura became the belle of Aurora. She was pretty, with a good sense of humor (she needed it). Also, she had a good singing voice. At only

18, she married Stephen Cannon in 1810. He was fairly well-to-do and was a handsome young man.

Laura Cochran Cannon made quite name for herself in Aurora. She was everybody's friend. Many communities had and still do have ladies who are "aunts" to everyone, a title usually bestowed upon those who are thoughtful, kind, and caring . . . those who forget their own troubles to lend a hand to others.

And lending a hand was part of Aunt Laura's very being. In the early days when physicians were not too learned and also were scarce, she took upon herself the task of nursing the sick. Doctoring with herbs and roots, she acquired quite a reputation for her medical skills. "Call Aunt Laura" apparently was a routine message in Aurora. Besides ministering to the ill, she "officiated" at more than 500 births during her lifetime.

She also possessed great skill at the loom. In seven months she wove 600 yards of woolen cloth, five blankets, nearly 100 yards of carpet, five plaid shawls, plus many other articles. She did all her own warping, spooling, and coloring. All of this she accomplished in addition to her housework and her calls upon the sick.

When fortunes dimmed for her and her husband after 44 years of marriage, they decided to pioneer in Iowa. She helped to build a second log home there, and shortly thereafter her husband died. Aunt Laura followed a daughter and her husband into Wisconsin. She made the 300-mile trip in a wagon drawn by four yoke of oxen. There she helped to build a third log home in the wilderness. After three years in Wisconsin, she yearned for more familiar surroundings and longtime friends. She returned to Aurora. Aunt Laura was happy again. In Aurora she was welcome in every home, and she attended all parties and public events.

Aunt Laura died at 88. To say that she had experienced a full life would be a gross understatement.

———

## RAVENNA GAVE SUSAN B. ANTHONY "BAD PRESS"

### November 18, 1990

"She seems inclined to force from the selfishness of man what she seems hopeless of accomplishing by an appeal to his sense of justice or of right." Sound familiar? The quotation could have been attributed to Betty Friedan of the National Organization for Women or other prominent leaders in the modern women's rights movement. But guess again.

The words were in a published report of a lecture delivered by Susan B. Anthony, a great woman's suffragist, at the Congregational Church in Ravenna on April 28, 1870. That's 120 years ago, but the words insofar as equal rights for women are concerned strike a familiar chord. They could have been spoken yesterday.

A present-day reader of the 1870 *Portage County Democrat*, a Ravenna weekly newspaper, can assume that the paper's editor and publisher, Lyman W. Hall, was a top-drawer chauvinist. In the first instance, the four-paragraph report of Miss Anthony's talk was buried on page 3, below the fold. That, in itself, was not too unusual, inasmuch as papers of that era customarily filled their front pages with poetry, stale national news, and advertisements. Local news (what there was of it) was sprinkled on pages 2 and 3.

It was the report's tone that would have infuriated today's women. "There was a fair audience," the paper said. "The house was far from filled," as much as to say, "Why would anyone want to go hear Susan Anthony, who's trying to upset the way of running things?"

Miss Anthony's talk, sponsored by the Ravenna Lecture Association, was entitled, "Work, Wages and the Ballot," the three ingredients of the suffrage movement which she and others launched in the mid-1800s. She and her followers set their sights on the same goals as the more current women's movements—equal opportunities for women in all matters.

Here is another quotation from the *Democrat*'s report (extremely editorial in nature) of Miss Anthony's speech: "She seems to regard the ballot as the panacea for all ills that womankind is heir to. In regard to the importance, necessity and justice of widening the field of women's activity, in opening avenues to a greater range of employments, trades and occupations, her views must meet the ready assent of all candid, thoughtful persons."

The paper observed that Miss Anthony called on women to act vigorously in the upcoming two years and they might win the right to vote in the 1872 presidential election. She *did* vote in 1872 in Rochester, New York, and was promptly arrested for doing so. She was summarily hauled into court and fined $100, a fine which the male-dominated justice system never bothered to collect.

A smidgen of sarcasm is noted in the final sentence of the *Democrat's* report on Miss Anthony when it noted that "she advised the women to take her paper, *The Revolution,* read it and pay for it, price $3 a year."

All of this talk concerning women's right to vote seems rather strange in today's scheme of things, in view of the recent election of three women governors, a number of women jurists, and other public officials. It is obvious that women have early leaders such as Susan B. Anthony, Carrie Chapman Catt, and Elizabeth Cady Stanton to thank for their pioneering and highly unpopular leadership in the woman's suffrage movement.

But, Susan B. Anthony did not live to enjoy the thrill of women winning voting rights. She died in 1906 at age 86; the Nineteenth Amendment to the U.S. Constitution became effective in 1920. But she did witness several states grant women voting rights long before that year. Wyoming Territory did so in 1869, and thus when Wyoming became a state in 1890, it automatically held the distinction of being the first state with voting rights for women. There lies a strange twist in the course of American history, considering that new western territories—supposedly far less developed and sophisticated than the aged eastern states—granted women voting rights before their eastern counterparts. Ohio, for example, didn't come aboard until 1919, although it won statehood in 1803.

In more recent times, we have witnessed another proposed amendment, one that would grant women equal rights under the law. In more specific language, the amendment read: "Equality of rights under the law shall not be denied or abridged by the United States or any state on account of sex." In 1979, the Equal Rights Amendment failed to achieve approval by three-fourths of the states. Following an extension, only 35 of the necessary 38 states ratified the amendment in 1982. Susan B. Anthony's battle still goes on!

————

## FAMOUS PORTAGE WRITER BURIED IN MAPLE GROVE

*October 9, 1988*

Fannie B. Ward was ahead of her time. She challenged a man's world a century ago when such actions were not popular and a woman's world was her home. She placed herself many times in the face of danger. She achieved success in a field once closed to females.

Fannie Ward was a journalist; more specifically, a pioneering travel writer. Travel writers were not common in her day and women travel writers were virtually unknown. Her insatiable appetite for travel took her into southwestern United States, Mexico, Cuba, and Central and South America. Her syndicated dispatches were published during the 1880s and 1890s in more than 40 newspapers in the largest of American cities. In at least one instance she was on the scene while a memorable event in history was being forged.

Fannie Ward died 75 years ago this month, and her obituary and photograph were prominently displayed on page 1 of the old *Kent Courier*. And for a valid reason—Fannie Ward was a onetime resident of both Kent and Ravenna. Maple Grove Cemetery in Ravenna was her final resting place, her repose from delirious days in Washington, D.C., and countless trips to faraway scenes.

Fannie was born in 1843 in Monroe, Michigan. Little is known of her earliest days. Biographies fail to list her maiden name. It is known that in 1873 she went to Washington to accept a temporary appointment in the U.S. Treasury Department, and next we learn that she was sending dispatches from D.C. to the *Cleveland Leader*, predecessor to today's *Plain Dealer*. She spent considerable time in the editorial departments of several eastern newspapers. By 1882 she was sending her dispatches from the southwestern United States during a Senate committee investigation of Indian agencies.

In 1884 she took up travel writing in earnest. Her travel letters appeared in Sunday newspapers from Mexico and throughout Central America. Her two-and-one-half-year stay in Central America almost did her in; she contracted yellow fever and mountain fever, forcing her return to a more placid life in the nation's capital.

Following her recuperation, Fannie was on the road again, that time with her daughter into the wild countrysides of South America, where she became the first woman to write travel news from that continent. During her 19 months there, she and her daughter were subjected to danger many times, mainly from uncivilized Indian tribes and the demands of primitive travel. They crossed the Andes on the backs of mules.

Fannie then returned to a comfortable life in her spacious home on Massachusetts Avenue in Washington, which was filled with pottery, baskets, and other artifacts representing several civilizations, which she had gleaned from her extensive travels.

By 1898 she again was bitten by wanderlust. At 55 years of age she joined her friend, Clara Barton, on a trip to Cuba, then a hotbed of military and political intrigue. Clara Barton, a nurse and humanitarian, was the founder of the American Red Cross in 1881. Fannie always seemed to be blessed with being at the right place at the right time, a real plus for a newsperson. She was in Cuba on February 15, 1898, when the U.S. battleship *Maine* blew up, an event blamed by Americans on the Spanish. "Remember the *Maine*" fired Americans to enter the Spanish-American War.

Fannie probably would have traveled still more except that declining health intervened. In 1905 she suffered a cerebral hemorrhage, which cost her most of her eyesight. She gave up her large home in Washington and went to Berwyn, Maryland, to live for a brief period with her son. Then she returned to D.C. to make her home with her daughter, Nelly. Her daughter was married to Walter Jex, a onetime Kent doctor.

The end to Fannie's interesting life spiced with extensive travels came on October 10, 1913, at her daughter's home. Services were held in Washington, and she was returned to Ravenna for burial beside her youngest daughter in the family's plot at Maple Grove. Fannie was home at last!

## PORTAGE WOMAN A TOP "GENERAL"
## IN TEMPERANCE BATTLE

*March 23, 1985*

Two unusual historical trends helped to shape the career of one of Portage County's most renowned and revered women. The first of these was the migration in the decade between 1840 and 1850 of 16 sea captains from Nantucket to Portage County towns, primarily Ravenna and Rootstown. The second was the anti-alcohol movement that gained strength throughout the country in the 1870s and 1880s.

Among the migrating sea captains was Isaac Brayton, who began following the sea as a boy and is said to have commanded a ship that carried the first missionaries to the Sandwich Islands. A religious man, Captain Brayton united with a church during one of his voyages to Honolulu and he is said to have established a family Altar and Bible Society aboard ship. He abandoned the sea in 1833 and came to Ravenna in 1839. The attraction of Portage County, an area far removed from the eastern shore, to former sea captains never has been explained.

Captain Brayton made his influence felt in Ravenna. He was a leading force in the establishment of Ravenna's first high school, and he served as an associate county judge. The Brayton family later moved to Cleveland, where he was elected to the Ohio General Assembly, and he served with the Sanitary Commission during the Civil War. He served as superintendent of the National Soldiers' Home when it was located in Columbus.

Captain Brayton returned to Ravenna in 1873 to spend the remainder of his life with the family of his daughter and son-in-law, Mary and Frederick Woodbridge. Frederick, as a young man, clerked in Zenas Kent's Ravenna store and later was the secretary-treasurer of Crown Flint Glass Company, one of Ravenna's several glass factories of that era.

Frances E. Willard, noted educator and reformer, wrote a touching biography of Mary Brayton Woodbridge in the 1885 *History of Portage County*, in which she referred to the Ravenna woman as "a most gifted child." She describes little Mary as a prodigy. Educator Horace Mann, witnessing Mary's accomplishments at only age six, remarked, "Persevere, my child, you will make a notable woman."

Mann's words were prophetic. Mary Woodbridge became a nationally recognized leader in efforts to drive the evils of strong drink from the face of her country. From earliest days (even in dealings with the Indians), alcohol had been a Portage County problem. Mary Woodbridge became immersed in the anti-alcohol movement. Frances Willard writes that "God put his own message on her lips" and that when she spoke the strong were "melted to tears."

The history of Mary Woodbridge became part and parcel of the Woman's Christian Temperance Union. She first served as president of the local WCTU unit in Ravenna, then for many years headed the Ohio WCTU. In 1878 she was chosen recording secretary of the national organization (when it was only four years old) and in 1884 became national superintendent of the department of legislation, an office that took her across the country to address large gatherings in leading centers of influence.

Her crowning achievement came when she was selected to conduct the constitutional amendment campaign. Political leaders in Ohio, when assessing Mrs. Woodbridge's efforts, said they simply were "outworked, outwitted, and out generaled." Hardly could "wet" advocates compete with groups of women kneeling in the dusty streets and praying in front of saloons, asking God's help to rid the country of the evils of liquor. On occasion, the campaign took on serious implications. For example, in 1881 in Garrettsville an old church building was blown up by an explosion of gunpowder. The act was attributed to "whiskey apologists" in retaliation against temperance organizations.

Success did not come easily to Mary Woodbridge and other temperance advocates. Yet, their persistence caused the closing of thousands of saloons across the country even before the ratification of the Eighteenth Amendment in 1919. Here in Portage County, the "dries" prevailed in a countywide vote in 1908, and saloons were closed from that year until 1933, when the Eighteenth Amendment was repealed.

Despite its legality, liquor causes immense problems today. Mary Woodbridge, the strong Ravenna lady who led the fight a century ago, would be appalled by the present "evils of strong drink."

## FAME WAS FLEETING FOR HIRAM
## LYRICIST JESSIE POUNDS

*August 4, 1984*

Fame has an unflattering inclination to diminish with passing years.

Certainly Jessie Brown Pounds of Hiram achieved a full measure of fame in the late 1800s and early 1900s as a prolific author of words for church hymns. Her best-known hymn was "Beautiful Isle of Somewhere," which she wrote in 1896 and which older Portage County area church-goers may recall singing as youngsters.

Jessie is said to have written about 600 hymns in addition to short stories, poems, plays, and cantatas. Yet you would be hard pressed to find any of them in modern church hymnals. Revised hymnals seem to have a way of deleting many of the old hymns in favor of lesser-known numbers, many of them more difficult to sing.

Jessie Brown Pounds was born in 1861, two doors west of Hiram Christian Church, where her husband, Rev. John Pounds, later served as minister. Except for a few years, she spent her entire life on that street and died there at age 60 in 1921.

Portage County history volumes make only passing reference to Jessie Brown Pounds. Portage County has had many women of achievement, and she certainly deserves a place among them. The bulletin of the First Christian Church in Ravenna recently did pay tribute to Jessie, who is described by those who knew her as a "great little lady; a charming woman; always cheerful."

As a child, Jessie was of frail health, a condition which caused her to miss a considerable amount of formal education. She made up for that with persistent reading and instruction under the tutelage of her mother. She became well versed in the classics, Shakespeare, the Bible, and the writings of New England poets. Early in her life she began writing verse, and by 12 she had seen some of her writings in print. By the time she was 20, many of her stories and poems had been published in religious journals.

How sad it is that today one must conduct an extensive search for her hymns. With the help of two church secretaries and the library, I searched several hymnals and other religious publications and could find only one of her hymns, "The Way of the Cross Leads Home." "Beautiful Isle" could not be found. Finally, Helen Chadwick Hoskin, office secretary at the First Christian Church in Kent, located the famous hymn in her home library.

Tennessee Ernie Ford included "Beautiful Isle" in his book of favorite hymns. He referred to it as a special hymn that is sung many times in gospel services. He described it as particularly adaptable for solo rendition. "Beautiful Isle" achieved national fame when it was sung at the funeral of assassinated President William McKinley in 1901.

Jessie related to her nephew, Rev. Kenneth Close, now a retired minister, how she came to write the words of the hymn. On a cold Sunday during the winter of 1896, she was persuaded to remain home from church services "much against my will." She was inspired by the thought that although the weather on earth might be miserable, somewhere (in heaven) the sun would be shining. She wrote the words in about an hour, and to this day not a single word has been changed. And beautiful words they are:

> Somewhere the sun is shining,
> Somewhere the songbirds dwell.
> Rush, then, thy sad repining,
> God lives and all is well.
> Somewhere, somewhere,
> Beautiful isle of somewhere,
> Land of the true where we live anew,
> Beautiful isle of somewhere.

It is said that Jessie received $5 dollars for writing the words for hymns. In her day, that was worth more than today, but even then it was not considerable money for work that would live far beyond her life span.

The Hiram Christian Church where Jessie attended and her husband served as minister also was the church of fellow townsman James A. Garfield. He attended Hiram College shortly after the institution was founded by the Disciples of Christ in 1850 as Western Reserve Eclectic Institute. Garfield later was a teacher, principal, and trustee of the college.

Garfield, who in 1881 became our second martyred president, was a scholarly man who also was widely known as a preacher. Many times he filled the pulpits of Portage County churches on a guest basis. His wife, Lucretia Rudolph Garfield, was a native Hiram girl. To his dying day, Garfield considered Hiram his home.

When you attend church services tomorrow, leaf through your hymnal. If you're lucky, you might find "Beautiful Isle" or others of Jessie Brown Pounds's hymns, including "The Touch of His Hand" or "The Way of the Cross." But probably you won't find them. Fame is fleeting.

## METEORIC CAREER ON STAGE TOOK
## ETTA REED TO THE TOP

*August 31, 1985*

There was a time when heads turned as Etta Reed Payton walked into a room. Fawning women were quick to note her latest apparel, and in a few days her latest fashions were mimicked among the elite.

At the turn of the century, Etta Reed Payton, an accomplished actress who was toasted throughout the theatrical world, was considered a trend setter. Following stage appearances in Brooklyn and other centers around the country, she invited fans to join her on stage for tea—and a look at her latest fashion fads. She was considered the best dressed actress of her day, and none of the admiring housewives of that time would order a hat with ostrich plumes or a new bustle until they had seen them on Etta. Her husband, noted actor Corse Payton, who owned several theaters in Brooklyn and a number of traveling road companies, deemed it good business to dress his beautiful actress wife in the latest fashions.

Etta Reed Payton was born in Ravenna in 1868, the daughter of Gustavus and Carrie Reed who resided at 213 West Riddle Avenue. Her father, a Rootstown native, served as a member of the 104th Ohio Volunteer Infantry during the Civil War, seeing service, among other places, at Kennesaw Mountain, where he lost a leg. In 1871 he built a home at the West Riddle address. He served as Portage County treasurer and auditor and was a member of the Ravenna Board of Education. He was part-owner of Reed's Opera House in Ravenna, a fabled theatrical house, where his talented daughter in later years would appear frequently in dramas of that era.

At only 16, Etta Reed joined the Bennet and Moulton Opera Company as prima donna soubrette. Then she took up drama and headed her own company, with which she starred during tours of the West. Nowhere was the popular actress more wildly acclaimed than during appearances in her native Ravenna.

Following her western theatrical tours, Etta took off for New York's playhouse big time. There she appeared in Corse Payton's Lee Avenue theater and the Grand Opera House, as well as in Payton's various road companies, which operated primarily in the New York and New England areas.

Payton was one of the best-known actors of his day. So popular was he that he had a 10-cent cigar and a soda—the Corse Payton Special—named for him. In the early 1900s, he earned $100,000 a year, and he spent every cent of it on good times. Upon his death in 1934, his long-time press agent, Edwin Reilly, recalled that Payton didn't give a second thought to buying bottles of champagne "for the house" in high-class bars in the afterglow of a successful stage appearance. Reilly said he mislaid $5,000 cars and never seemed to miss them. Those were large sums during the early days of this century.

Apparently Etta Reed was completely captivated by her theatrical mentor, so much so that she married him. Payton treated Etta as queens should be treated. He dressed her in the most expensive latest fashions and paraded her eloquence before her fans. The tea sessions on stage following performances in Brooklyn and other cities were his idea. A promoter first, last, and always, Corse Payton deemed it a necessary business practice to esconce his leading lady in lavish fashions. After all, his Broadway successes and old-time favorites such as *East Lynne*, *St. Elmo*, and *Camille*, plus a smattering of Shakespeare, featuring Etta and himself, were hits; the money was flowing in, and adoring fans must be served.

As with most ventures in such halcyon days, the bubble burst. Corse Payton spent his money as fast as he made it and saved nothing for leaner days. Prior to his death in 1934, he was appealing to close friends for eating money—close friends because pride prevented him from seeking help elsewhere.

Etta Reed Payton died in the prime of life. At only 42, she was stricken by a paralytic stroke while riding in a car in New York City. She sustained serious injuries from which she only partially recovered. She attempted a return to the stage, but following several weeks on the road was forced into retirement. In May 1915, she joined her husband in an attempted comeback at the Court Square Theater in Springfield, Massachusetts. Longtime fans were shocked by the change in her appearance. Illness and injuries had taken their toll. The comeback was not to be.

She was taken to a Springfield sanitarium and then to a hospital in that city, where the end came in mid-October 1915. Her mother went to Springfield to be with her daughter when she died and returned with her body to Ravenna, where services were held at the home of Mr. and Mrs. A. C. Williams on North Chestnut Street. She was buried in Maple Grove Cemetery. One of Ravenna's favorite daughters—and one of the most famous and fashion-bedecked actresses of her day—was gone at only 47.

———

## STINAFF SOARED AS A PIONEERING WOMAN AVIATOR

*November 6, 1988*

Women pilots are not a rarity these days. But a half-century or so ago they were not common, and females who were attracted to the skies were considered by "ground" people as being daredevils.

It was in that era that Mildred Stinaff, a descendant of a pioneer Kent family lived . . . and died. A plucky young woman with a sunny smile and sparkling eyes, Mildred loved to fly. So much so that she took a job as a secretary and terminal hostess at Akron Municipal Airport to gain an opportunity to fly in her spare time in order to qualify for a Department of Transport pilot's license, a certificate few women held in those early days of aviation. She already held a limited commercial pilot license, for which she qualified at only 17.

She soloed in 1929, the same year she graduated from Akron's North High School, and the following year she achieved national recognition when she set a women's world record for executing 42 consecutive inside loops at the old Mid-City Airport, which now is the site of the Terex plant on S.R. 91 in Hudson. That record bettered one of 28 loops set in Houston, Texas. Mildred lost her record when a Kansas City aviatrix made 46 loops.

Mildred got her first plane ride as a result of her brother's generosity. Girdwood Lincoln Stinaff went to Cleveland to give a pint of blood to a desperately ill young man. For that he received $50. He gave his sister $15 of that sum for a 15-minute ride at the Stow Airport, now the Andrew Paton Airport owned by Kent State University. That brief plane ride hooked Mildred on flying and led to her brief aviation career.

On June 23, 1931, Mildred concluded her day's work for B. E. Shorty Fulton at Akron Municipal Airport and took off in her biplane to practice loop flying. Her parents, Charles and Lillian Stinaff, were at the terminal and saw her take off.

Her father was quoted in the *Kent Courier*'s June 30 edition as saying that his daughter was not stunting when her plane went into a spin and crashed near the airport. She had made a loop or two and was flying at about 1,000 feet when the plane went into a spin. She straightened out the aircraft at about 300 feet and had started to climb when the plane again went into a spin. The plane crashed about a quarter mile from the airport. Mildred's parents saw the plane go down, and they followed her to the hospital.

Aviatrix Mildred Stinaff was dead at only 19. Funeral services were held for the well-liked flier at the High Street Christian Church in Akron. The family decided to hold burial services at Standing Rock Cemetery in Kent because her pioneer ancestors were interred in Kent.

Two hundred cars, led by two motorcycle policemen, were in the motorcade from Akron to Kent. Five planes, flying in formation, swooped over the grave site and another plane, piloted by Forrest Miller of Kent, quietly dipped to a low altitude and dropped a wreath on Mildred's grave.

Although she was born in Akron in 1911, Mildred Stinaff had close ties to Portage County. Her great-great-grandfather, William Stinaff, came from Massachusetts to Ravenna in 1819, later moving to Kent. He was a carpenter, as was his son, Henry, Mildred's great-grandfather. He and William built the old Central School in Kent in 1867 and the Erie Railroad shops, south of West Summit Street, in 1865.

Stinaff Street in Kent, west off North Mantua Street, was named for the Stinaff family who resided in that area. Mildred's brother, Girdwood Lincoln Stinaff, now 80, still resides in Akron. Another brother, Charles, of Cuyahoga Falls, died seven years ago.

I was set onto the Mildred Stinaff story by onetime Kentite Jeane Wolcott of Columbus. Jeane, daughter of the late Kent postmaster Oliver Wolcott and his wife, Dorothy, feels a close kinship with Mildred, although it has been 57 years since her ill-fated crash.

Jeane also is a flier. And she was born in the Wolcott home on Stinaff Street in Kent during the month of September, also Mildred's natal month. Jeane holds membership in the 99s, an organization of women fliers which was established in 1929. Mildred was a charter member.

The marker on Mildred's grave at Standing Rock chronicles in brief her aviation history. Engraved on the stone are her pilot's wings, her pilot's license number (No. 10491-LC), and the 99s symbol which dominates the inscription.

"Jesus Saviour Pilot Me" is the final line.

Mildred Stinaff is remembered for her role in women's aviation history.

#### PART THREE

———

# COMMUNITIES, LANDMARKS, AND LANDMARK EVENTS

Kent Square (Main and Water Streets) in the late 1880s. The watering trough in the foreground was later moved to Standing Rock Cemetery and there served as a planter; unfortunately, it was stolen in 1995 and has not been recovered.

# IF ONLY THE FRANKLIN HOUSE
# REGISTER COULD TALK

*September 4, 1988*

Its pages speak of the life and times in an era now 130 years gone. And also leave much to the imagination for what is not recorded. A guest register of the old Franklin House, which opened in 1839 on the northwest corner of Main and Water Streets in Kent (then Franklin Mills), today is one of the most perused artifacts in the Rowe Museum, operated by the Kent Historical Society in the historic railroad depot.

The register, which spans a period from May 18, 1858, through August 29, 1863, includes the names of local people as well as travelers from across the country. Most of the names are written in fine Spencerian hand, some of them with artistic flourishes. One guest even wrote his name backwards. The writing on early pages would indicate that names were written by the desk proprietor, because the writing is identical.

There are many group registrants representing sleighing parties, circus troupes, and musical groups who were playing the town. For some strange reason there are dozens upon dozens of signatures of local folk, including members of the Kent family—Zenas, Marvin, Charles, Henry, and William S.—one wonders why they stayed in a downtown hotel. Why didn't they save their money and put up at home?

There are notables, too, including James A. Garfield on several occasions, and Horace Greeley, the noted journalist and politician, on March 10, 1861. What he was doing in Kent is anyone's guess. Greeley was a well-traveled man, as the advice he popularized, "Go west, young man, go west," would confirm. (Incidentally, that advice did not originate with Greeley. The phrase was coined in 1851 by an Indiana newspaperman by the name of John Soule. Apparently Greeley, who had traveled in the West, was taken by the words and popularized them through his *New Yorker* magazine and the *New York Tribune*, both of which he established.)

Greeley ran for president of the United States in 1872 under the banner of liberal Democrats and disgruntled Republicans but was overwhelmed by Ulysses S. Grant. It was probably just as well that he failed in his bid for the presidency; he died one month following the election.

In a big, bold hand Thomas Jefferson signed the guest register on
April 28, 1859. Either the name was written as a prank or by another
man with the same name, because President Jefferson died on the Fourth
of July in 1826.

It could be said with accuracy that the old Franklin House and the
1837 Town Hall on Gougler Avenue launched the political career of
James A. Garfield, then a resident of Hiram. He signed the register and
was a hotel guest on August 23, 1859. That day he was nominated in
the old Town Hall at a district Republican convention for his first political office, state senator. That office led to the U.S. House of Representatives, the Senate, and, in 1881, the White House.

Garfield was well known in Franklin Mills, having preached many
times in the Disciples churches, and as a youth he drove mules on the
Ohio Canal through the village and stayed many times with other canal crewmen at the old Cuyahoga House on North Mantua Street.

The historic register would indicate that the pre–Civil War years
were male oriented. Women's signatures are noticeably absent; and when
men and women registered as guests simultaneously, the register lists
merely the man's name and "his lady." No doubt, the lady referred to
was his wife, but skeptics might make a different deduction. After 130
years, who cares?

There are numerous signatures from nearby cities—Akron, Cleveland, Cuyahoga Falls, Canton, Columbus, Warren, and Ravenna among
them. It must be remembered that travel was slow and tedious in those
days, mainly by horse and buggy, and travelers, even from rather close
distances, couldn't get back home the same day.

Speaking of horse and buggy, travel, the hotel register included a
column headed "Horses." Guests filled in under the heading the number of horses in their party. The hotel probably arranged for the horses'
housing in a nearby livery stable. Another column was headed "Destination." Under that column, many of the guests merely wrote "Home."
Apparently, every age has its wiseacres; one guest wrote under the residence column "Earth" and under the destination column "Heaven."
An Alliance man wrote that he had stopped at the hotel merely to
"warm." Several Ravenna men didn't know how to spell the name of
their hometown. They spelled it "Revenna."

The hotel also catered to many traveling men—salesmen, musicians, speakers, entertainers, politicians. One wonders how they arrived in Franklin Mills. The village did not get its first railroad until March of 1863. Apparently they came by train to other centers and then took a hack to the hotel.

One guest, Gabriel Ravel, listed his residence as Paris, France. There were many from other large cities: New York, Philadelphia, Boston, Milwaukee. What brought them here would make many interesting stories.

One unusual registration was that of Daniel R. Tilddtifacts, belonging to William S. Kent following his death the previous January. The register was at that time on display in the lobby of the Kent National Bank, today's Huntington.

The last day's registration in the historic volume was August 29, 1863. But that was not the end of the Franklin House. Historical writings tell us that the Franklin House opened on April 1, 1839, in the giant business block built by Zenas Kent at the northwest corner of Main and Water in 1836–1837. The hotel and its successors, the Continental and Revere hotels, continued in business until 1899.

The big block, larger when it was built than any in Akron or Cleveland, was destroyed by fire on August 28, 1972. With that disaster went a huge chunk of downtown Kent's heart.

———

## EVER HEAR OF REEDSBURG? PEOPLE IN KENT DID

*March 3, 1991*

Many towns in Portage County underwent name changes during their early days. For example, Brimfield was originally known as Swamptown, an appellation attributed to the swampy character of its terrain. Then the settlement was called, at various times, Beartown, Briartown, Wylestown, and Thorndike before residents settled on the name of Brimfield for Brimfield, Massachusetts. There are many other examples of the name-changing trend in Portage County, but they will await another time for recitation.

Those acquainted with Kent history are aware that what is now Kent was known as Franklin Mills almost from the time of its settlement in 1805 until 1867 when residents renamed the village Kent as a tribute to the Kent family. The name change was executed in appreciation to the family, particularly Marvin S. Kent, for the community prosperity that resulted from his success in bringing the Atlantic and Great Western Railroad and its railroad shops into the town.

And for several years the upper village (that area north of Cuyahoga Street) was called Carthage. In 1825, that area was platted and it was officially entered in Portage County records as Carthage. The name had only a brief existence, residents apparently preferring the name Franklin Mills for the entire community. Even during the Carthage years, people in the lower village in the Stow Street area still clung to Franklin Mills name. But in one instance the name stuck; Carthage Avenue still exists.

But who ever heard of Reedsburg? Actually, for a brief span of time in the early years, Reedsburg was the designation for what now is Kent. To develop this strange sequence of pioneer events that inspired the Reedsburg name, we need to turn back to November of 1805, when John and Sally Haymaker and their three children arrived to settle land that had been acquired by John's father, Jacob. They spent the winter in a dirty hut located along the west shore of the Cuyahoga River on what today is North Mantua Street. The hut previously had been used by a surveying party.

The following spring, John's father and brother George arrived. They built a cabin west of the river in today's Stow Street area. Brother Frederick Haymaker arrived in the fall of 1806. His claim to fame, besides fathering 27 children with three wives, was his service as secretary to Aaron Burr during the latter's ill-fated expedition that led to his trial for treason. He was acquitted; but Burr, also remembered as the slayer of Alexander Hamilton in a duel, saw his political career diminished to zero.

The Haymaker family in 1807 built a crude mill on the shore of the river. Its grinding stones were hard heads. Crotched poles held a roof, and a piece of coarse cloth served as a bolting cloth. Primitive as the mill was, it could provide meal. And its presence gave rise to Franklin Mills as the name for the new settlement.

Then came Jacob Reed. He and his brothers, Charles and Abram, had settled in Rootstown in 1804. After operating the mill for only four years, the Haymakers sold it in 1811 to Reed. He made several improvements, installing a real roof and siding. Apparently residents were pleased with his improvements and the service Reed offered the community. As a result, the settlement came to be called Reedsburg, so says the 1885 history of Portage County.

Apparently Reed tired of the milling business; he sold the mill in 1816 to George B. DePeyster and William Price, whose enterprises in the Stow Street area comprise an interesting period in local history. DePeyster was the community's first postmaster in 1820. He kept the mail in a cigar box.

Following the Price and DePeyster acquisition of the mill, the Reedsburg name was dropped and the community returned to its original designation as Franklin Mills, a name that would remain for 50 more years. But for five years, Reedsburg was the name.

Jacob Reed was quite involved in public life during Portage County's pioneer days. He was a member of the grand jury at the first session of the Common Pleas Court in 1808. He served on another grand jury the following session with Owen Brown, father of the famed abolitionist John Brown. His name appears frequently on lists of other juries. In Rootstown, when the community was officially organized as a township in 1810, Reed served as one of the judges at the first election.

Last week's "Portage Pathways" sought information concerning the office and printing plant location of the *Ohio Star*, a weekly newspaper established in Ravenna in 1830. A response has come from Ravenna resident Harold Nading, who relies upon A. B. Griffin's history of Ravenna for the answer. Griffin said the *Star*'s headquarters were located on West Main Street, three doors west of Meridian Street.

Griffin's writings are well known. A native New Yorker and a master cabinetmaker, he came to Ravenna in 1838. Some of his elegant pieces were displayed at the Philadelphia Centennial Exposition in 1876. After he gave up his cabinet making business, Griffin owned and operated a Ravenna hub factory.

In 1856 he served as mayor, Ravenna's fourth following the community's incorporation as a village in 1853. Apparently at the outset of village government, mayors served one-year terms.

———

## ONCE-THRIVING EARLVILLE REMAINS
## IN HISTORIC OBLIVION
### January 18, 1986

Earlville, U.S.A.!

Thousands of motorists on S.R. 43 pass through Earlville each day, oblivious to its presence and to its once-robust history. To the unaccustomed and to those unacquainted with local history, Earlville is a spot along S.R. 43 north of Kent. Today, Earlville appears on maps only by accident. At one time, it was a thriving shipping point on the old Cleveland and Pittsburgh Railroad.

Local histories would indicate that Earlville, located north of Kent along S.R. 43 in the Rusty Nail area, pre-dates the arrival of the Cleveland and Pennsylvania on March 13, 1851. That's the date when daily railroad service was started over that railroad between Ravenna and Cleveland. On that inaugural trip, the train was pulled by a locomotive named *Ravenna,* and it carried members of the railroad's board of directors.

On March 18 of that same year, regular trains began connecting train passengers with a packet on the old Pennsylvania and Ohio Canal which ran to Beaver, Pennsylvania, where passengers took a steamer into Pittsburgh. The entire trip was made in 26 hours and the fare from Cleveland to Pittsburgh was $3.50. Unbelieveably, the fare included meals and a bed on the boat. In April of 1851 daily service began between Ravenna and Cleveland, affording traveling facilities that didn't arrive to other towns for some years hence.

No one seems to know how Earlville got its name. The 1885 Portage County history, which details the coming of the C. & P. Railroad (later the Pennsylvania), simply states that the new railroad passed through

Earlville, leaving the obvious impression that Earlville was known by that designation prior to the arrival of the C. & P.

Kent had a physician named Thomas Earl who was involved in railroading. In fact, he was one of the original incorporators of the Atlantic and Great Western Railroad (later the Erie) in 1851, which Marvin Kent as its president induced to run through Kent beginning in 1863. Kent was disgruntled when the C. & P. chose to operate over a right-of-way north of Kent at Earlville instead of tracing its route through Kent.

Many area residents can remember the old C. & P. station located in a gully between Diagonal Road and S.R. 43. Yet, a drawing in the 1874 atlas of Portage County shows a busy station which may have been located higher, on the level of the present S.R. 43 in the area of the Rusty Nail and Hill's Grocery. The same drawing hangs in the Rusty Nail Restaurant operated by Don Bentley. The Earlville station once was a busy place. Prior to the coming of railroad service to Kent, passengers went to Earlville to board the train for Cleveland, or, if they chose to go south, to Wellsville on the Ohio River.

Passengers traveled from Kent to Earlville by hack. In 1862, the hack business was taken over by Obed Chase, who became somewhat of a character around Kent. His hack, which resembled an old stagecoach, was painted bright yellow with dark trimmings. He ran the hack until 1875, when he sold the business to Luther and Levi Reed and then was employed as a deliveryman for the Wells-Fargo Express Company in Kent. Incidentally, Levi Reed was the father of W. W. Reed, Kent civic leader, postmaster, and founder of the W. W. Reed insurance firm.

In 1882, when the Forest City Ice Company of Cleveland leased East Twin Lake for the harvesting of ice, a railroad spur was laid from the C. & P.'s main line to the icehouse that was located on the south shore of the lake, approximately where Dr. and Mrs. Walter Lang's home is located today along Overlook Drive. That spur crossed what today is the No. 5 tee, fairway, and green of Twin Lakes Country Club.

Roy Pierce, Diagonal Road resident and a Streetsboro native, has vivid recollections of the old Earlville station located in the hollow between

Diagonal and S.R. 43. As a young man he worked for Otis Green, grandfather of David Green, who operated a farm along Diagonal Road near Dollar Lake. Roy hauled milk from the Green farm to the Earlville station, where it was put aboard a train for Cleveland for distribution by the old Telling Belle Vernon Milk Company. Pierce also recalls cutting swamp grass at the Green farm and hauling it to Cliff Callahan's sand quarry at Twin Lakes to use as packing material for sand that was shipped by rail from the Earlville station. That sand operation today is known as the Hugo Sand Company, operated by Mrs. Ralph Strohm. In more recent years, many Kent commuters boarded the Pennsylvania train at Earlville to travel to work in Cleveland.

At one time John Sprague, who also operated Sprague Coal, was the Earlville station agent. In those days, considerable coal was shipped into the area via the Earlville station. And prior to that time, particularly in the 1880s and 1890s, Earlville was a busy shipping point for area farm products, including cheese manufactured in Streetsboro, Franklin, and surrounding townships.

The old station, the last remaining remnant of Earlville's railroading days, was torn down in the 1950s with the decline in railroad business. Today, only a designation on historical maps and the memories of a few old-timers serve to recall Earlville's days of glory.

———

## LEGACY OF KENT'S FOUNDING FAMILY
## IS AN ENDURING ONE
### December 10, 1983

Historical speculation is a questionable practice. History speaks for itself, and facts are facts. Yet, it can be interesting to speculate upon the implications of the various "what ifs" that invariably are contemplated as one assesses the twists and turns which arise in any historical review—world or local. For example, in the grand scheme of worldwide significance, would World War II have come about had Adolf Hitler never been born or had he been throttled early in his career?

Or, indeed on a far less important turn of events, would the city of Kent still be known as Franklin Mills had Zenas Kent elected to continue his highly successful mercantile business in Ravenna instead of transferring his interests to the banks of the Cuyahoga River? Or, had he remained in Ravenna, would our county seat city have changed its name to Kent in grateful appreciation of the Kent family's community spirit and business contributions to the town? All such speculations are interesting to contemplate but constitute an exercise in historic futility.

What prompts such historical challenges is today's 75th anniversary of the death of Marvin S. Kent. At 92, Kent's benefactor, whose good works inspired the change in name from Franklin Mills to Kent in 1867, was Ohio's oldest bank president. He worked until his death on December 10, 1908, as head of the Kent National Bank, today's Huntington.

Certainly most communities can boast pioneering families whose unusual business acumen and public contributions served to build their towns and cause them to prosper. Yet, the Kent family was an unusually successful one in Portage County, one whose pioneering efforts live on today in many institutions and business establishments. Besides their keen business sense, the Kents were known for their fairness, rapport with others, and their ability to get things done.

Zenas Kent came from sturdy English stock whose ancestors came to the United States in the 1600s. Zenas was born in 1786 in Middleton, Massachusetts, the son of Zenas Sr., a Revolutionary War soldier. The elder Zenas migrated westward with his wife and nine children, settling in Mantua in 1812. Zenas Jr., then 26, left his bride of a year back in Massachusetts, returning a year later to bring her into the Western Reserve wilderness.

Zenas Sr. and Jr. both were carpenters and joiners, but for young Zenas it was the mercantile business in which he found his life success. His first such venture was in Hudson, then a township in Portage County, where he formed a friendship with Capt. Heman Oviatt. While there, he built a tannery for Owen Brown, father of the famous abolitionist, and he taught school during the winter months.

In 1815, Zenas Kent transferred his interests to Ravenna, with Captain Oviatt furnishing the capital for a store. Kent erected a combination business building and residence at the corner of Main and Chestnut Streets on a site which for many years was the location of the former Second National Bank building and now is the headquarters of the Kane, Bangas, and Sicuro law offices. The store later was moved to the south side of Main Street. The Oviatt and Kent partnership terminated a few years later, and Mr. Kent became the sole proprietor.

Mr. Kent permitted few diversions from his mercantile career. One of those was his contracting to build a new Portage County courthouse in 1826. Completed in 1832, it was described as an architectural wonder despite its meager $7,000 cost. That courthouse replaced an old frame building, erected in 1809, and served until a new courthouse was erected in 1881. The latter center of county business was razed and replaced by our present courthouse in 1960.

That same year (1832) Zenas Kent was attracted by prospects of water power along the Cuyahoga. He and David Ladd purchased vast holdings along the river, erected a flouring mill on the original Haymaker mill site, and in 1835, with John Brown, built a tannery on Stow Street. He sold the land for the planned silk business, which turned out to be a disaster; built in 1837 the large block at Main and Water (now the site of the gazebo); and erected the Town Hall on Gougler Avenue that same year.

Meanwhile, son Marvin S. had entered business with his father in Ravenna, and in 1845 he and brother Charles, later mayor of Kent, bought out the business. Zenas Kent continued to reside in Ravenna until 1851 when he built a home on South River Street (later the American Legion home). In 1849, Zenas founded the Franklin Bank of Portage County, which later became the Kent National, and still later, the Huntington. Three generations of Kents—Zenas, Marvin and his son, William S.—served the bank as president.

Marvin's greatest achievement was bringing the Atlantic and Great Western Railroad into Kent in 1863. He served as its first president and later established the railroad shops. In 1881–1883 Marvin built the mansion we know today as the Kent Masonic Temple. It was the era of prosperity which followed the coming of the railroad that prompted the name change from Franklin Mills to Kent.

The good works of the Kent family are legion. Besides business developments, they provided sites for several churches in Kent and for the Kent Free Library. And in 1910, it was William S. Kent's gift of 52 acres on Kent's east section that won the location of Kent Normal School for Kent.

Historians make the claim that history is held in the hands of people. They cause the events that alter the course of history. So it was with the Kent family on the local scene.

---

## KENT IS REAPING BENEFITS OF KENT FAMILY GIFTS

### October 1, 1995

Some time ago someone asked me an interesting question. The Kent family was wealthy. Why, then, when the last of the Kents died, did heirs not donate their landmarks? Instead, they sold the Marvin Kent home on West Main Street to the Masonic Lodge and the old Zenas Kent home on South River Street to the American Legion.

It's a good question, but there is an inference that the Kents were penny-pinchers and did nothing for the community of Kent. That is far from the truth. It has been said that heirs of the Kent family needed to sell all the family's holdings to settle an estate. Of course, the estate could have been settled if bequests had been made to organizations. When William S. Kent died in 1923 he left no heirs. Therefore, all of the family's holdings were sold by heirs of his father, Marvin S. Kent.

In their time, the Kents were wealthy. When Zenas Kent died in 1865 it is said that he left an estate exceeding $300,000. In 1865 that was a lot of money. The family owned all of the water rights along the Cuyahoga and lots of properties. They erected many buildings in Kent; they operated many businesses; they were entrepreneurs. It is not inaccurate to say that most everything they touched turned to money. In a business way, they were highly perceptive, and their judgment never appeared to go astray.

William S. Kent

But there was another side to the Kent family, whose members entered the Portage County scene at Mantua in 1812. That was when Zenas Kent Sr., his wife, and son, Zenas Kent Jr., then 26, came from the East. Their ancestors had come to the New World from Gloucester, England, in 1643.

Three generations of the Kent family built a vibrant economy in Kent, and there are at least a dozen instances when they shared their wealth

Residence of W. S. Kent, Kent, Ohio

The Marvin S. Kent home, on the corner of West Main and North Mantua Streets in Kent, was built beginning in 1881. The stately Victorian is now the Kent Masonic Temple. Marvin Kent bought the Atlantic and Great Western Railroad to town in 1863.

with the community. As one writer put it, "The Kents were generous to a fault." That they made generous donations is true. Take a look at some of them:

In 1854, the Kent family provided stone (valued at $100) for the erection of the Disciples Church at the corner of North River Street (now Gougler) and Park Avenue.

Marvin and his brother, Henry, gave land south of West Main Street, which was valued at $10,000, as a site for Kent's first railroad depot.

In 1864, the family gave the site on Portage Street for the first Catholic church in Kent. The Kents were not Catholics.

In 1867, they provided the site on North River Street for the Universalist Church.

In 1881, they provided land, estimated in value at $15,000, to induce the Pittsburgh, Youngstown, and Chicago Railroad to come through Kent. Later, that railroad became the Baltimore and Ohio, and now it is CSX.

In 1901, the family donated a site at the corner of West Main and

South River Streets for the Kent Free Library. That gift induced another from Andrew Carnegie to make possible the establishment of the library.

In the 1860s, after inducing the Atlantic and Great Western Railroad to come through Franklin Mills (now Kent), Marvin Kent provided a site along Mogadore Road for railroad shops, which for many years provided employment for hundreds of men. The site was valued at $15,000.

In 1879, Marvin Kent brought the Turner Manufacturing Company into Kent to occupy the long-vacant alpaca mill on the west side of the Cuyahoga River. The Turner plant provided employment for several years and eventually fathered the Cleveland Worsted Mills Company in Cleveland and Ravenna. The building they erected still stands and is occupied by the Portage Packaging Company.

Influence of Marvin Kent helped to bring the Connotton Railroad into Kent. Today, the railroad is the Wheeling and Lake Erie.

In 1830 Zenas Kent, then a Ravenna resident, built a new Portage County courthouse. It cost $7,000, and he said he lost money.

Historical writings tell us that the Kent family did not seek glory for its good works. For example, in 1864, when people in gratitude to Marvin Kent for bringing the railroad into the community and its attendant prosperity, wanted to change Franklin Mills's name to Kent, Marvin Kent objected. He wanted to call the town Rockton. People of the community went ahead with their plans, and Franklin Mills officially became Kent in 1867. Rockton became the name of the Masonic Lodge.

Undoubtedly, the Kent family's most prominent contribution to the community was a gift from William S. Kent, son of Marvin. When a Kent committee in 1910 was campaigning to make Kent the site of a new state normal school, William S. was a tireless worker on behalf of the effort. His gift of 52 acres (the old Kent farm) at the corner of East Main and South Lincoln streets was a generous move that turned the heads of the state selection committee. He could not have visualized that the infant normal school someday would become Kent State University.

The university is named for William S. Kent, as is Kent Hall on campus. It is the only public university in Ohio named for a person.

When William S. Kent died in 1923 he didn't forget two favorite organizations. He willed $5,000 each to the Red Cross to help feed the poor and to Christ Episcopal Church to help finance a remodeling project.

There is no doubt that the Kent family knew how to achieve wealth. But in so doing they provided many opportunities to enhance the community's economy. And, at the same time, they shared their means to gird the town's religious, educational, and cultural climate.

———

## LANDMARK DAM SHAPED THE GROWTH AND DESTINY OF KENT

*June 9, 1984*

The Kent Dam is in the news again as it has been many times during the 180-year history of the town! Ten days ago, Kent City Council's utilities committee scuttled a five-year plan to harness the energy of the Cuyahoga River to provide hydroelectric power for the city's sewage disposal plant. Economic infeasibility was offered as a reason for abandoning the hydroelectric plan.

Actually, the plan to harness the energy generated by the waters of the Cuyahoga River was not without some merit. But, like most things these days, ideas such as the hydroelectric plan cost a lot of money, and economic tradeoffs must be considered. Can sufficient money be saved to make the initial investment an economically sound one? Obviously, the council's utilities committee decided against the economic prudence of the idea.

The river and the dam comprise a large hunk of Kent history. After all, it was the Cuyahoga and its potential for water power which attracted our earliest settlers into this Western Reserve wilderness back in 1805, when members of the Haymaker family came from the East to settle this land. And, subsequently, the river and its source of power have played an important role in our economic well-being.

In the fall of 1806, the Haymakers built a crude dam about seven feet high across the river a little north of the present Main Street dam. It was built of earth, logs, and stones. The next spring, thaws came, and the waters rose and townspeople were concerned whether or not the dam would hold. It did, and the first step toward making a settlement in the wilderness had been achieved.

The dam and its promise for power spawned a grist mill, such a simple one that it could be said that it was a bare improvement over the earlier hominy blocks of the settlers. Later, came Kent's mill along South River Street near Stow Street, an enterprise that for many years utilized the power of the river.

Then, in 1836, came Kent's ill-fated silk business, an enterprise that was intended to inject a new dimension into local industrial progress. A group of investors from Cleveland, Boston, and Ravenna, feeling that Franklin Mills (now Kent) had the potential to become the largest industrial center of Ohio, formed the Franklin Land Company and purchased 150 acres and the water site from Zenas Kent for $75,000. Additional land in the "upper village" also was purchased for $40,000. The company rebuilt the old dam (which had washed away in the flood of 1832), started the present Portage Packaging Company building, erected the Town Hall as an office for the Franklin Land Company and the large building at Main and Water Streets that burned down in 1972.

The silk-venture bubble burst, but the town had a good dam, several new buildings, and a good Main Street bridge, which served until the present one was erected in 1876. No doubt, the coming of the canal (that materialized in 1840) had much to do with the get-rich scheme. All was not lost, and the town enjoyed a new prosperity. Later, a mill raceway started above the dam and went south to the present packaging company building to power the looms of the Turner mill, which opened in 1879.

The dam was not to see the last of its travail. During May 1904, a ravishing flood washed away the top of the dam and the impounded water rushed down the river to uproot trees and undermine the Baltimore and Ohio Railroad tracks. Then, during the big flood of March 1913 came more trouble. Traffic on both the Erie and B. & O. was held up. The reservoir at the Kent waterworks went out, and the B. & O. tracks were washed out in downtown Kent. Water rose to the floor of the Stow-Summit bridge. The old canal lock gave way as hundreds of townspeople watched. And the dam was damaged, all but washed away.

Although repeated efforts to repair the dam were made during the following decade, nothing tangible materialized until 1924. During that

Kent circa 1850s. The covered Main Street bridge was built in 1831.

year, a successful movement was launched to repair the dam under the administration of Mayor Roy H. Smith, father of Alexander Smith of Whittier Avenue. The Lamson and Sessions Company (with which the mayor was associated) purchased the dam along with other property from the Kent family estate. Mayor Smith said Lamson and Sessions would pay $500 of the dam repair cost despite the fact that the dam no longer had any commercial use, only aesthetic and civic importance. The people of Kent subscribed $5,855 toward the repair project, which was completed in November of 1925.

That's the dam we have today, a dam which is a focus of Franklin Mills Riveredge Park and a central point of Kent's historic industrial district, which enjoys an honored designation in the National Register of Historic Places. That district includes the dam and the Main Street

Downtown Kent scene.

Erie Railroad Station, Kent. Today this building serves as the home of the Kent Historical Society as well as one of Kent's best-known restaurants, the Pufferbelly.

bridge, the old alpaca mill building, the 1875 railroad station, the P. & O. Canal lock site, and the old livery stable building that has been restored to house the Williams, Zumkehr, and Welser law firm. The dam continues to dominate the Kent historical scene!

---

## OLD KENT JAIL KEPT THE PEACE IN INFANT COMMUNITY

### March 29, 1986

The small town of Franklin Mills in the mid-1860s was basking in the glow of prosperity. Marvin Kent had induced the Atlantic and Great Western Railroad to run through the town, a move that increased the population, prompted the opening of new stores, and accounted for the construction of many new commercial and public buildings.

Franklin Mills residents were happy . . . so pleased and so indebted to Marvin Kent for the railroad and the car shops that they began a movement to honor him by changing the name of the community from Franklin Mills to Kent in his honor. Kent would have none of such tomfoolery. He proposed, instead, the name of Rockton, a suggestion that fell upon deaf ears. As early as 1864, the U.S. Post Office Department accepted the name of Kent for the community, but it wasn't until 1867 that the Ohio General Assembly made the name change official. The new village became Kent, and the name remains the same today, 119 years later.

The village of Kent was incorporated in 1867 when Kent had 2,300 residents. On July 30 of that year an election was held to select the first mayor, other officials, and members of council. Three candidates—John Thompson, Luther Parmelee, and Sylvester Huggins—contested for the mayor's office. Thompson won over Parmelee by 145 to 143 votes, with Huggins trailing at 116 votes. This was the same Sylvester Huggins, three years later again a mayoral candidate, who dropped dead in downtown Kent on election day.

The first piece of legislation approved by the infant village council ordered two kerosene lights erected in the covered bridge on Main Street, a move hailed in a Kent newspaper in glowing language: "These two beacon lights send forth their warning rays to guide the lonely footman through this heretofore obnoxious passage." Wow!

Despite the infusion of glory occasioned by the establishment of incorporation status and the community's new name, all apparently was not ideal in the new village. Most of the residents were hard-working, law-abiding people. However, there was a minority exception of wrong-doers, particularly hobos who rode the rails and stopped off in town to create trouble. What was the town to do with the nonconformists?

Mayor Thompson came up with an obvious solution. He would build a jail to house them until they could mend their ways. In 1869 he ordered the construction of a small, one-story, brick building at 124 West Day Street to serve as a town jail. It was complete with bars across all its windows. That jail building stands today, 117 years later, as a reminder of Kent's infant days of municipal government. The building, now a rental residence, is located just west of the AmeriTrust drive-in bank's exit.

Older Kent residents have recollections of the building serving as a jail until the 1930s, when the jail was moved to the basement of City Hall, located just across South Water Street at the intersection of East Day Street. During the late 1930s, the old jail building served as headquarters for the city service director and the city engineer. Then, vacant for several years, the property was purchased in 1950 by the late Tony Ferry, and in 1970 it was sold to its present owners, David Green and Gordon Seaholts.

It may come as a surprise to many residents who drive along West Day Street that the old jail building eight years ago was included as a historic site in the National Register of Historic Places by the U.S. Department of Interior. This is one of more than 30 places in Portage County which are included in the National Register. (This number is rather misleading, inasmuch as some of these designations are districts that include multiple historic sites.) Not many old Ohio jails have been designated as historic sites. That makes Kent's old jail distinctive and unique.

———

## KENT'S TOWN HALL A CENTER OF
## COMMUNITY HISTORY

*July 13, 1985*

Many communities have ancient public buildings which throughout the passing years have been woven into the very fiber of community life. Regretfully, in far too many instances, some of these public buildings have fallen victim to the wrecker's ball.

Not so with Kent's 148-year-old Town Hall, located at 218 Gougler Avenue. Owned by the Franklin Township trustees, the venerable hall, a striking example of New England architecture, lives on to serve its public purpose and to recall for community residents its dominant role in forging significant events of history.

Most communities in Portage County have township halls that to this day continue to play a leading role in public life. Important as they have been in helping to mold the course of community life, few of them can match the Kent Town Hall's stature, which extends even to major national events.

The Town Hall was not intended for public use. In 1836, when the fledgling Franklin Silk Company spawned visions of sudden wealth, the hall was planned as a headquarters for the Franklin Land Company, the real estate arm of the silk manufacturing venture. Construction on the hall started in 1837. Bricks for the building were made at a plant located near the present intersection of South Water and Summit Streets, and native timber was sawed by the old Caris mill located near the present Stow Street bridge.

Then the silk-business bubble burst, and construction on the hall was halted. Through the leadership of Zenas Kent and other influential citizens, plus the Franklin Township trustees, funds were raised to complete the hall in 1839 for use as a center of local government and as a community center.

Zenas Kent, who then resided in Ravenna, and Frederick Wadsworth of Edinburg, were the architects and contractors. The hall's classic design is a likeness of a public building that once stood in Hartford, Connecticut. The building's walls are 20 inches thick. Originally, the hall was heated by four fireplaces, which in later years were removed. The four chimneys remain to add beauty to the hall's lines. The hall's most attractive interior feature is a circular stairway located to the left of the main entrance. The stairway was suggested during the building project by Nathan Button, one of the Franklin men who aided financially in the completion of the project.

Several years ago the late Dudley Weaver, eminent Portage County historian, compiled a history of the Town Hall. Dudley's interest was learned at the knee of his grandmother, Charlotte Weaver, and he learned his lessons well. Ponder these significant involvements of the Town Hall as recorded by Dudley.

From 1840 until 1867, the hall was the seat of our local government. Even today the hall is the center of township government and the site of meetings of township trustees Chuck Young, Glenn Frank, Bob Garrison, and clerk Ken Hankins.

The bell in the hall's steeple was shipped in by canal in 1841 and was installed the following spring. The first school of higher learning in Franklin, a select school, was taught there by a Mr. Bates in 1842. He later served as pastor of the First Congregational Church. In 1851, prior to the erection of a church building, the hall was the meeting place for people of the Catholic faith, and in 1855 the second bell was installed in the steeple. (Who knows what happened to the first?)

A most significant event, one with national implications, occurred in the hall on August 23, 1859. James A. Garfield of Hiram was nominated in a Republican convention for the first public office he ever held, that of state senator representing Portage and Summit counties. Garfield, martyred in 1881, became the 20th American president.

On December 2, 1859, from 1 to 2 P.M., the hall's bell tolled the news that fellow townsman, abolitionist John Brown, had been executed for his treasonous raid on Harpers Ferry. Brown had lived in Kent from 1835 to 1840. Two years later, the same bell called townspeople together to announce that the nation had gone to war against the South.

In the hall was formed the Franklin Mills Rifle Company, the first in Portage County to enter service under the Union banner. In the war years that followed, women of Franklin gathered in the Town Hall to make bandages and to assemble blankets and other military items for the men in service.

One of the biggest moments came on April 10, 1865, when a meeting in the hall celebrated the surrender of Confederate forces at Appomattox Court House. The saddest day in the history of the Town Hall was April 15, 1865, when the bell tolled in sorrow at the passing of President Abraham Lincoln, our first assassinated chief executive.

In 1867, J. F. Lukins, head of the Union School system, taught his charges in the hall, and the following year, because the new Union (or Central) School had not yet been completed, the hall became the site of Kent's first high school.

On September 19, 1881, the hall's bell sorrowfully tolled in memory of a second slain president, James A. Garfield. The front of the hall was draped in black, and a meeting of townspeople was held there that evening.

Hardly had the first summer school been held in the hall that a meeting was held in 1898 to discuss the entry of the United States in the Spanish-American War. The assassination of another president, William McKinley, drew area residents into the hall in 1901 to make plans for attendance at his funeral in Canton.

Following the turn of the century, the Town Hall served as a summer school for the public school system. The Davey Institute of Tree Surgery trained its young recruits there, and the hall became a public school (called Riverside) during the extensive remodeling of the DePeyster and Central buildings. Depression years found the hall used for WPA projects and for the city recreation department. The Town Hall Players, a drama group, rehearsed and produced plays there.

During World War II years the C. L. Gougler Machine Company took over the hall, as it did most other buildings on North River Street. At that time, the name of the street was changed by the Kent City Council to Gougler Avenue. Ted Rowe's Hamilton Kent Manufacturing Company succeeded Gougler in the building, and then in 1954 the first and second floors became the headquarters for the Kent Board of Education and the school administrative offices. That arrangement ceased in January 1978 when the board office and school system headquarters were moved to the DePeyster building. The school system's use of the building appeared a proper one inasmuch as the hall several times had served to educate young people. Today, the bell of old Central School (opened in 1869) reposes on the front lawn of the Town Hall.

For 148 years the Town Hall, now in the National Register of Historic Places, has figured prominently in community life. Let's make certain it continues to do so.

---

## LOCATION OF NEW KENT POST OFFICE
## REPEATS HISTORY

*August 3, 1985*

When the U.S. Postal Service begins construction on a new Kent Post Office building on the former Parsons Lumber Company site on Franklin Avenue, it won't be the first time the post office has been located on that street.

Except for three previous brief periods, the post office in Kent always has been located near the intersection of Main and Water Streets. The first post office—way back in 1820—was in the home of George B. DePeyster in the "lower village" in the Stow Street area. DePeyster handled all of the mail for Franklin Mills (the former name for Kent) in a cigar box. He charged 25 cents to deliver a letter, a price that caused mail to repose for days in his cigar box until householders could raise the delivery price.

At another time, Postmaster Benjamin Anderson's arbitrary action in 1856 of transferring the post office to the "upper village" in the Crain Avenue–North Mantua Street area irritated residents who were forced to walk all that distance to claim their mail. Such problems tend to pass, and in later years the post office never strayed far from Main and Water Streets.

The *Kent Courier* in a page-1 story on July 8, 1910, related in glowing terms a prospective move of the Kent Post Office to a new two-story block on Franklin Avenue, only a stone's throw from West Main Street. Elmer E. France, a former postmaster and at that time the agent for the Franklin Avenue property, announced that he would build a modern brick building adjoining the alley next to the Thompson block just to the south. That post office site today is occupied by Ray's Place.

William Wilson Reed, postmaster at that time and later head of the insurance firm which exists today, had campaigned for a new post office beginning with his term as postal head in 1905, and the France announcement came as the culmination of that effort. The Franklin Avenue site at that time was known as the France-Rockwell property. France said the 30-by-60-foot first floor of the new building would be the post office's center of operations, with the basement floor serving as a carrier room.

A ten-year lease was to be arranged, a move that apparently did not materialize because the post office in 1912, only two years later, was moved to the east side of South Water Street, where it remained until the present post office building (the first to be built by the federal government) was dedicated in 1936. The South Water Street location was next to the alley in what today is the AmeriTrust building.

Picture, if you will, the community of Kent in 1910. Only a few streets had been paved. South Water was paved in 1904 from Erie Street, and West Main was improved from Main Street to the Erie Railroad tracks the following year. It was not until 1914 that East Main Street was paved, despite the fact that paving of that thoroughfare was a stipulation by the state when the new Kent Normal School was awarded to the city in 1910. Franklin was paved from West Main to Summit in 1907, a move that no doubt was deemed an advantage for the new post office.

When the Franklin Avenue post office was opened in late 1910 or early 1911, all of the fixtures, including boxes and desks, were provided by the building owner. The government apparently didn't buy things of that nature in those days. Parking, a big consideration in the present post office relocation, was not an issue in 1910. There were few cars, and almost everyone walked to the post office anyway. Free mail delivery to homes and business places was an infant then; it did not begin until 1908.

W. W. Reed held the postmastership longer than any other person. He was postmaster twice—from 1905 until 1913 and again from 1922 until 1935, for a total of 21 years. Leo Bietz, postmaster for from 1935 until 1955, was second in tenure, and France was postmaster for 13 years. The latter held the distinction of serving as postmaster when the post office was advanced from third to second and, finally, to first class.

The community of Kent is about to begin a new era in postal history. The planned $1.7 million facility on the old Parsons property will have 10,000 more square feet than the present facility on South Water Street, the latest in postal equipment, facilities for large trucks, and 45 public parking places. When the new facility is opened next year, postal service in Kent will have progressed from George DePeyster and his lowly cigar box. Meanwhile, 165 years have elapsed.

———

## PARSONS MEMORIES STIRRED BY
## KENT POST OFFICE SITE

*August 11, 1984*

The site of one of Kent's oldest business firms is about to undergo a historic transformation. Back in 1866, Timothy G. Parsons and his brother, Edward, founded the T. G. Parsons Lumber Company. When the business ceased operations in 1974, the firm was the oldest business in Kent under continuous ownership and management by members of the founding family. Now the site of the former T. G. Parsons Lumber Company, at 624 Franklin Avenue, has been selected by the United States Postal Service as the location of a new Kent Post Office. Construction of the facility is expected to begin by the spring of 1985, and the building may be ready for occupancy by 1986.

Selection of the site culminates a lengthy civic discussion. Originally, the Postal Service favored a site at the intersection of South Water Street and S.R. 261, a move which generated sharp disagreement from the Kent Downtown Development Corporation and the Kent Area Chamber of Commerce, both of which objected to moving the post office from a downtown location to a site so distant from the downtown business area. For more than a century, the post office has been located at various sites in the downtown area and since 1936 has been housed in a government-owned building on the southwest corner of South Water and West Erie Streets.

Unable to achieve their goal of retaining the post office on a downtown site, both civic groups acquiesced and expressed favor for the Parsons site over the location near the Gold Circle store. The city of Kent now has accepted an offer of the Nypano Company for a gift of land to make possible the extension of Williams Street west of Franklin Avenue (a requirement of the Postal Service). It appears certain that the new post office will be erected on the Parsons Lumber site.

All of these intricate negotiations serve to put into historical perspective a family and a business that had broad civic involvement during a span of more than a century. An older Edward Parsons was the founder of the Parsons family in Ohio. A native of Northampton, Massachusetts, he bought a tract of timber and settled in Brimfield in 1831. He was the second postmaster of Brimfield, a fact in history that may make it seem logical that the location of a business which his sons spawned should become the site of a new Kent post office. Timothy G., Edward's second son, was born in Brimfield. During his early years, he answered a strong call to the young and robust California where he engaged in mining.

He returned to Ohio and became a farmer, but the Civil War beckoned and he volunteered. He moved to Kent in 1866, and he and his brother, Edward A., started the lumber business. T. G. was an active civic leader, serving on city council and the school board. Brother Edward A. was a Portage County commissioner in 1874–1875. Timothy died in 1923 at 91.

He had three sons, Edward S., John T., and Dwight L. Edward and Dwight operated the business for many years and were closely identified with Kent civic and business interests. Edward Parsons served as mayor of Kent in 1903–1904. He was the father of Dorothy Parsons, a Theodore Roosevelt High School teacher for more than 40 years who died in 1980. John resided in Pittsburgh and also held an office in the lumber company. He was the father of John Jr., whose wife, Eloise, is the daughter of Hale B. Thompson, druggist and banker. Dwight, an astute businessman, spent his entire working life with the lumber company. He had two sons: Dwight, a prominent attorney in Akron, and Charles, now a resident of St. Petersburg, Florida. When advancing years forced the elder Dwight Parsons to abandon constant direction of the business, son Charles returned to Kent from California to assume company leadership. Dwight Parsons died in 1959.

By that time, the new trend of chain and discount lumber operations offered keen competition to privately held lumber firms. Finally, in 1974 the T. G. Parsons Lumber Company ceased operations after 108 years as a solid business firm and corporate citizen. Soon the old complex of lumber offices and sheds, now owned by Leonard Tompkins, will be razed to make way for the new post office edifice.

---

## RICH IN HISTORY, KENT FREE LIBRARY IS "ON THE GROW"

*December 17, 1983*

Noteworthy institutions spring from humble beginnings. So it has been with the Kent Free Library. Back on September 29, 1875, employees of the Atlantic and Great Western Railroad met on the second floor of the Kent railroad station to organize the Atlantic and Great Western Railway Reading Association. The station, one that today is the headquarters of the Pufferbelly Restaurant, the Kent Area Chamber of Commerce, and the Kent Historical Society, then was only a few months old. George E. Hinds, the stationmaster and inspirational leader of that group, was elected secretary-treasurer. Annual dues were one dollar, and a member was allowed to draw one book at a time, to be kept no longer than three weeks.

The first library in Kent was the A. & G. reading room located on the second floor of the station. It is almost amazing to ponder that railroaders deemed literary improvement so important that they would be concerned with reading during their train changes. But, that was the case. The reading room association flourished for several years, and then interest waned. From 1884 until 1892 the collection of books was locked up in a room at the station.

At that time, there was no Ohio law to enable a town of fewer than 5,000 inhabitants to tax itself for library purposes. That situation changed through the efforts of Hinds and Scott Williams, who encouraged the passage of an enabling law by the Ohio General Assembly. The village council passed an ordinance to establish a public library to be known as the Kent Free Library. Voters subsequently approved a 1-mill tax levy to maintain the library. Kent was the first town in Ohio to avail itself of the new law's provisions.

The library was located in a downtown block, and Mrs. J. M. Woodard was hired as librarian at the magnanimous salary of $12.50 per month. Kent residents deemed it important to have a library building. How to achieve that goal was the tougher question. Then in 1901, through the efforts of Hinds and other members of the library board, Andrew Carnegie, the steel baron, became interested in the Kent venture. His $10,000 gift and a later one for $1,500 assured the library if the town could provide a site and $1,000 annually for maintenance. Both conditions were met without a problem. Marvin S. Kent donated the site at the corner of West Main and South River Streets, and the Barnett sisters donated the $1,000.

The building was completed in the spring of 1903. Nellie Dingley was the first librarian. Its opening precipitated an outpouring of public acclaim and these words from John G. Paxton, editor of the *Kent Courier:* "There may be more elaborate and more expensive library buildings than the one in Kent, but there isn't a more handsome library to be found anywhere. Kent people can be deservedly proud of the fact that they took advantage of Mr. Carnegie's offer and are now numbered among scores of cities which can boast of free libraries."

Amazingly, the library building in its original state served the community for 58 years, until 1961 when an addition containing 3,400 feet doubled its space. Then, in 1977 a two-story addition was erected, providing 4,800 square feet.

Obviously, even those additions have failed to accommodate the library's clientele. During busy times, there now is no room for patrons to sit, stack room is in short supply, and there is a need for increased facilities. As a result of these cramped conditions, 108 years after the Atlantic and Great Western Railway Reading Association first met, the Kent Free Library is embarking upon its most ambitious expansion project, its third, which will add 6,000 square feet of space to its West Main Street facilities.

Unlike most public institutions, the Kent Free Library has provided an excellent service to the people without requests for operating levies or bond issues. The two previous additions were financed without the need for such requests, and the cost of the current $447,103 addition is being met through a $300,000 bequest from the estate of Florence Turner, for 21 years a library board of trustees member, and a grant from the Emergency Jobs Bill. Operating costs for libraries have been met for many years through intangible taxes on stocks and bonds. The library board is asking community contributions to raise $40,000 for equipment and furnishings. Considering the above financial bonanza, that's quite a bargain for the community.

Andrew Carnegie, George Hinds, and Marvin Kent would be pleased to know that their efforts many years ago have been fulfilled in scope far beyond what they envisioned.

## STOW STREET LANDMARK HAS
## SEEN A LOT OF HISTORY

*July 12, 1986*

A stately house on Stow Street in Kent has figured prominently in the developing history of the community for at least 152 years. The home, owned for the past 35 years by L. A. Bachman, is one of the few surviving landmarks of what once was known as Kent's "lower village." Each day thousands of motorists on Haymaker Parkway, plus many more on Stow Street, pass this old homestead. Probably most of them are unmindful of the prominent role this house has played in Kent's history.

The exact year in which this house was erected with bricks made, no doubt, at the site, is hazy. The late Dudley Weaver, one of Portage County's most knowledgeable historians, placed its construction year in 1834 in writings some years ago. He said the house was built in that year by Chauncey Beach, chief miller for the Kent flouring mill that was built by Zenas Kent in the 1830s along the Cuyahoga River just north of the River-Stow Street intersection. However, Bachman says he was told many years ago that his house probably was built about 1825.

The house is only a stone's throw from the site of the town's first grist mill, a crude affair built by the founding Haymaker family in 1806. That mill, plus other buildings which followed—John Brown's tannery built in 1835 for Zenas Kent just west of the Stow Street bridge and many other historic businesses and homes—was the central concern in the lower village's early beginnings.

As with other historic Portage County sites, deeds to the property date back to the Connecticut Land Company. It is known that in 1817 George B. DePeyster and William H. Price purchased 500 acres in that area, including the Bachman house site, from Jacob Reed. At that time, the two entrepreneurs improved the old Haymaker mill and built a saw-mill and forge where they made scythes, pitchforks, and axes. Then in 1832, Zenas Kent and David Ladd bought all of the Price and DePeyster holdings along the river for $6,300, realizing a tidy profit when they sold the land to the Franklin Land Company for $65,000. That was in anticipation of Franklin Mills's ill-fated silk business and the coming in 1840 of the Pennsylvania and Ohio Canal.

Probably Price's untimely death influenced the sale of the land to Kent and Ladd. In 1831 Price went to New Lisbon, Ohio, to return a huge millstone by horse and wagon. On the way back, the millstone shifted and fell on him. He died of his injuries.

DePeyster was Kent's first postmaster, receiving the appointment from President James Monroe in 1820. He operated the post office in his Stow Street home, keeping the mail in a cigar box. He also operated a store in the basement of his home, and he built the Lincoln Tavern, a stagecoach hostlery which stood on the northwest corner of Stow and South Mantua Streets.

Apparently, Joseph and Elizabeth Dyson were the next owners of the old Stow Street property. Deeds in Bachman's possession indicate that they sold to John H. and Henry A. Davis of Palmyra in 1903. Frank H. Johnson, who sold to Robert and Hannah Dyson, also was an early owner, as were J. H. and Rose Evans. Deeds indicate that the property's title passed to Harry A. Davis and then to his sister, Cora Bascom, in 1834, and eventually to Philip and Reynolds Bascom. For more than 30 years, the Davis brothers, who were Palmyra sawmill operators, maintained an antique business in the old Stow Street house.

Bachman's association with the house goes back to 1933. He lived there, helping to care for Mrs. Bascom in her declining years, and in 1951 he and his wife, Irene, bought the property from the Davis brothers.

Originally an Akron resident, Bachman worked for General Tire, Davey Tree, arborist Sam Parmenter, the Twin Coach Company, and Fageol Products, before retiring from Kent State University.

Bachman's wife died in 1968. Today he occupies an apartment on the west side of the house and his daughter, Margaret Humbert, and her three children reside in the east side. All together, the house has ten rooms. For Bachman, the house is a treasure trove of memories. His affection for the house and its one-acre, well-wooded lot runs deep. And for Kent, the property stands as a stately reminder of its early days.

----

## CREATION OF LAKE ROCKWELL PROMPTED
## SPIRITED BATTLE
### December 15, 1984

Nearly 75 years ago, plans of the city of Akron to impound waters of the Cuyahoga River in Portage County to create a new city water supply sparked a bitter controversy extending over a three-year period that ultimately was settled in the Ohio Supreme Court. The current plan of the city to sponsor a massive project to upgrade the city's aging water system, particularly at Lake Rockwell, recalls that "turbulent" period.

It was in 1911 that the city of Akron announced plans to dam the "waters of the Cuyahoga River north of Kent." That announcement aroused the ire of William S. Kent, banker, merchant, publisher, and philanthropist, who represented the third generation of the Kent family to control the water power of the Cuyahoga. His grandfather, Zenas, in 1830 had purchased holdings along the Cuyahoga in what then was Franklin Mills and in the area north of the village. Each generation of Kents had zealously guarded these water rights for more than 80 years.

William S. Kent had a powerful weapon in his battle to preserve his interests in the Cuyahoga River's water power. He owned the *Kent Courier*, a weekly newspaper that was one of the ancestors of today's *Record-*

*Courier.* Kent people watched with intense interest William S. Kent's battle against the municipal giant. Kent claimed the dam and reservoir would destroy his water power. Naturally, the *Kent Courier* took up the fight for its owner.

Karl Grismer's *History of Kent*, published in 1932, recalled Kent's contention that the reservoir would constitute a constant menace to the town and "might someday cause a disaster greater than the Johnstown flood." The paper went on to say, "The people of Akron are going to wake up some day and realize that they have been made partners to one of the worst injustices ever perpetrated upon a neighboring community."

Kent sought an injunction to prevent the city of Akron from damming the river and impounding water. After losing in the local courts, he carried his case to the Ohio Supreme Court, which ruled on July 14, 1914, that the city of Akron had a right to divert the water. Kent finally settled his claim with the city of Akron for $75,000 in payment for his water rights. He also received $25,000 for land at Pippin Lake that was needed for the reservoir.

Its case won, the city of Akron lost no time in creating its new water system. A dam 280 feet long was constructed in the river east of Twin Lakes to impound water in an area that eventually was to cover 769 acres. The body of water was named Lake Rockwell after a family which had been prominent in Franklin Township and Kent for several generations. The city of Akron acquired a total of 2,174 acres at a cost of $319,000, approximately $150 per acre. A water treatment plant and pumping station were erected along Ravenna Road, a line was laid through Franklin Township and the cities of Kent and Tallmadge, and in 1915 water was turned into the Akron mains. To protect its reservoir area, the city planted trees that still today guard its banks.

The Akron water development in Portage County was only one of several that were to follow. Portage has Lake Milton at its eastern border, the mammoth Berlin and West Branch reservoir projects, as well as the city of Akron's Mogadore reservoir in Brimfield and Suffield townships. Later, LaDue and East Branch reservoirs in Geauga County were developed by the city of Akron to augment its Lake Rockwell water supply. East Branch contains 420 acres and LaDue 1,500 acres.

Now, the Akron water system is in trouble, particularly at Lake Rockwell, where heavy vegetation buildup has caused an algae that gives the water a bad taste. Akron Mayor Tom Sawyer has called for a 20 percent water rate increase to help finance a $57.5 million water improvement program over the next six years. Besides lake improvements at Rockwell and the city's two backup reservoirs in Geauga County, the program calls for upgrading in the Chapel Hill, Firestone Park, and Kenmore areas.

But what of William S. Kent's warning of impending doom for Kent nearly 75 years ago? There have been no floods of Johnstown intensity. On occasion during hot, summer months the Cuyahoga River in downtown Kent has been reduced to a trickle when more water was impounded at Lake Rockwell to satisfy the needs of the City of Akron and its customers in surrounding communities.

Akron's water passes through Kent on its way to Akron, but, fortunately, Kent residents need not drink it. Kent gets its water from wells, and it's far superior!

———

## MANY KENT VENTURES ROSE UP FROM
## SENECA CHAIN FIRE

*December 8, 1984*

Fires are killers. They destroy property and sometimes account for the loss of jobs. Yet, on occasion they are blessings in disguise. Such was the case 75 years ago—on December 10, 1909—when a fire destroyed the Seneca Chain Company plant in Kent.

The blaze caused an estimated damage of $50,000 and resulted in 400 men losing their jobs. Seneca Chain was located on West Main Street in a building which today is the site of the Forest City Materials Company, a manufacturing building which previously housed headquarters of the Twin Coach Company. Next to the Erie Railroad and its car shops, Seneca Chain at that time was the community's second largest employer.

Kent then was a village of 4,500. Coming as it did only two weeks before Christmas, the fire and a loss of jobs nearing 10 percent of the population plunged the community into a period of deep gloom and dimmed its Christmas spirit. How to recover 400 jobs was a real concern for a community of that size. Yet the fire took on a far different aspect. The blaze spawned the organization of the Kent Board of Trade (today's Kent Area Chamber of Commerce) and ultimately inspired the location of Kent State Normal School (today's Kent State University) in Kent. For a community tragedy to eventually result in happenings of such a major thrust must be considered of historical significance.

Like a phoenix, the sunbird of Greek mythology that rose from the ashes of its ancestor to begin a new life cycle, the community of Kent responded in similar fashion to the wrenching disaster. Immediately, public-spirited people responded in an effort to rebuild the plant. Company officials said the plant would be rebuilt only if the people of Kent raised $100,000 to finance the issuance of preferred stock. That was a tall order for a community in which money was not in plentiful supply. Alert to the need for organizational support for such a venture, a group of businessmen met in the council chambers on January 14, 1910, to discuss ways and means of achieving the goal.

Martin L. Davey, 25-year-old general manager of the infant Davey Tree Expert Company, presided over the meeting. Among those in attendance were David Ladd Rockwell, vice president of the Seneca Chain Company, former mayor, and ex-probate judge; Postmaster W. W. Reed; Mayor N. J. A. Minnich; John Wells, superintendent of the Williams Brothers Mill; and William S. Kent, president of the Kent National Bank.

The meeting resulted in the organization of the Kent Board of Trade on February 15, 1910. John Wells was its first president. Shortly thereafter, Ralph Heighton won the board's slogan contest and received a $5 prize for his entry, "Kent—Home of Hump and Hustle." Elmer France headed the fund drive to put Seneca Chain back in business, and the $100,000 fund was subscribed by Kent people by May 13.

About that time, John Paxton, editor of William S. Kent's *Kent Courier*, noted that the Ohio General Assembly had approved the Lowry Bill to create two normal schools in northern Ohio to train teachers, who at that time were in short supply. He challenged the village of Kent to file an application. The Kent Board of Trade took up the challenge and appointed Rockwell, France, and Duncan B. Wolcott, a lawyer then serving as Portage County prosecutor, to a committee to investigate possibilities.

Wolcott was the prime mover of the Kent effort. He prepared Kent's application for the school, which was submitted in Columbus the following September. An important part of the application was William S. Kent's willingness to contribute the 52-acre Kent farm in the eastern section of the village as a site for the institution.

More than 40 cities and villages contested for the location of the two schools that today are Kent State and Bowling Green Universities. They included Ravenna, Warren, Hudson, Chagrin Falls, and Wadsworth. Members of the General Assembly's site selection commission made the first of two visits to Kent on September 27, 1910. A dense fog shrouded the Kent site that day, and it was necessary to provide boots for commission members who trekked the Kent farm site. That's the day when members of the commission were treated to a bluegill and hard cider lunch at the Frank Merrill home at Twin Lakes, delaying their departure for Ravenna where they were to inspect the old Beebe property as a possible site.

The commission made a return visit to Kent on December 1 and soon afterward said Kent would need to raise $13,200 to buy property adjacent to the Kent farm and to pave East Main Street. The money was raised in a few days and then Gov. Judson Harmon announced that Kent would get the normal school. Kent Courier headlines referred to the announcement as an early Christmas present.

And all of this organizational planning and rapid turn of events began with a costly industrial fire almost exactly a year previous. As for the Seneca Chain Company, the community's confidence as expressed by their purchase of stock apparently was misplaced. The company reopened, flourished briefly, and then passed out of existence.

————

## SEVENTY-FIVE YEARS AGO TODAY OHIO WAS HIT BY MONSTER FLOODS

*March 27, 1988*

Seventy-five years ago today, Portage County, as well as other areas throughout Ohio, was in the grip of probably the most disastrous and widespread flood in the history of the state. Following week-long torrential rains, practically all Ohio rivers and streams overflowed their banks. Dams broke; bridges by the hundreds were washed out; reservoirs burst; railroad beds were washed away; gas and electric services were cut off; industrial plants were crippled; thousands of houses were flooded, and many were destroyed; the loss of life reached into the hundreds and the monetary damage into the millions.

Here in Portage County, 70 bridges were washed out. Areas along the Cuyahoga River were hard hit, with Kent bearing the brunt of this natural disaster. The flood's fury was concentrated from March 24 to 27, but it would be weeks and, in some instances, years before damage would be repaired.

In an almost miraculous stroke of good fortune, there was no loss of human life in Portage County. However, many chickens and livestock died. Several other Ohio areas were not so lucky; in Dayton, news reports at the time estimated that 650 were drowned and more than 22,000 were homeless.

An "extra" edition of the *Kent Courier* on March 28, 1913, told a graphic story of the flood, including photos taken by Arthur J. Trory, which now may be viewed in the Kent State University archives. Kent residents watched anxiously as the Cuyahoga River rose.

Their worst fears came to pass: the B. & O. Railroad's tracks in downtown Kent were washed out; Erie trains were delayed, and 116 passengers from one train spent 50 hours in Kent before they could proceed. The Plum Creek bridge washed away, as did the village waterworks reservoir. Some Kent residents in low-lying areas were taken out second-story windows and rescued by boat. In Munroe Falls, the paper mill was flooded out. In Aurora, the Erie bridge was washed away, and with it went a cheesehouse. Streetcar tracks were under three feet of water at Silver Lake. Akron had 500 homeless families.

Kent during the 1913 flood.

To get an idea of the water's depth, consider the fact that water was two feet over the top of huge Standing Rock in north Kent. In Mantua, retired banker Earl Mizer, then 15, recalls that the flood was concentrated around the lumber company, whose lumber piles washed away. In Ravenna, streets in the north section of the town were under water.

The old canal lock at the river's edge in downtown Kent was destroyed, leaving the remnant still in place today. The Main Street dam, built in 1836 by Zenas Kent, was badly damaged. By 1913 the dam served no commercial purpose, but Kent residents viewed so strongly its aesthetic appeal that they raised more than $5,000 to finance its rebuilding in 1925. That's the same dam which today is listed in the National Register of Historic Places.

The flood provided plenty of fuel for Kent residents' protest of the planned construction of a dam and reservoir north of Kent by the city of Akron. A flood relief benefit at the Kent Opera House after the waters abated turned into a full-scale protest session against Akron's plans, residents claiming that had such a dam broke when the flood hit, Kent would have been wiped out. Their protests were to no avail. The project went forward following several lawsuits, and today we know the Akron reservoir as Lake Rockwell.

Probably some of Portage County's older residents (they were mere children then) can recall the disastrous 1913 flood. They can attest to nature's fury and the havoc it created.

---

## AMERICAN LEGION BAND SOUNDED A FINE NOTE FOR KENT

*October 8, 1983*

The glory years of one of this area's most famous musical organizations came into sudden focus when Martin L. "Brub" Davey, former president and chairman of the Davey Tree Expert Company, handed me a voluminous scrapbook. The book, filled with newspaper clippings, programs, and other memorabilia, comprised the complete history of the Kent American Legion Band, sponsored by Portage Post 496.

Throughout the years of the band's existence, from 1946 through early 1953, George Gallaway, trombone player and arranger for the band, meticulously kept the scrapbook to provide for future years a firsthand, backward look into the seven-year history of one of this area's finest and most famous musical organizations. The scrapbook will find a permanent home in the museum of the Kent Historical Society now being completed on the second floor of Kent's 108-year-old railroad depot, where the band's fame may be shared by future generations.

The book and the recapitulation of the band's success has a strong personal association. John Farinacci, the band's founder, director, and commander throughout its existence, is a longtime friend, Kent State University classmate, fraternity brother, and one of the finest musicians I've ever been privileged to know. World War II had ended only a year before when Farinacci, then supervisor of instrumental music at Kent

State University School and a former U.S. Army major, organized the American Legion band in 1946, with Wilford Cook as manager and Merle Andregg as vice commander.

The time was ripe. The old Twin Coach band, which was prominent in the community for 15 years, had disbanded. So, too, had the American Legion drum and bugle corps, organized by World War I veterans in 1929. The corps had won a state Legion championship and had appeared in the early 1930s in competitions in Boston and Detroit. Kent always had been a band town, having been the home of the Post's Mason and Erie bands.

The infant band made its first public appearance in Kent's 1946 Memorial Day parade. And only 35 strong, the band went to the state Legion convention in Cleveland and walked away with the Class B championship. Then in 1947, resplendent in new uniforms, the band, now 50 members, captured first place in Class A at the Cincinnati Legion convention, the first of six Ohio Class A championships. To the national Legion convention in New York City they went, taking fourth place in competition with Joliet, Illinois, a turn of events which launched five more years of the "Joliet jinx." The Kent band marched along New York's Fifth Avenue in a gigantic American Legion parade.

In 1948, the band again won the state title and went to Miami, where it took third place, again with Joliet as the top winner. The story was the same in 1949 in Philadelphia, except that the Kent aggregation climbed to second place behind Joliet, topping bands from Nashville and Dallas.

That year, Farinacci departed from Kent State University School to become supervisor of instrumental music in the Cleveland Heights schools, but he commuted to his duties as director of the Kent band. The Kent musicians played for the dedication of the new High Level Bridge between Akron and Cuyahoga Falls and at a Browns game in Cleveland and was feted at a community appreciation dinner.

The following year, after winning the state championship, the band was destined for the national convention in Los Angeles. Transporting a band that distance for so long a time takes money, so a community campaign was launched to raise $5,000. When the drive fell short of its goal, band members agreed to pay their own meals to ensure the trip.

Again, the band was second to Joliet. That same year, the Kent musicians won first place honors at the Ohio State Fair.

The next year—1951—is one I shall not forget. The state titlist band was due to compete in Miami but money was in short supply. A benefit Guy Lombardo concert in the then new KSU gym, which was to raise funds, was a failure. Hardly had Lombardo started to play when a storm doused electrical power which was not restored until 10 P.M. Electric firm owner Dick Keller, who was band president and had arranged the concert, was dismayed. The ill-fated power outage definitely had discouraged a larger crowd.

Enter the Davey Tree Expert Company, specifically Brub Davey. He viewed the band as a "traveling Chamber of Commerce," so much fame had it brought for Kent. The company supplied $5,000 toward the trip, a 1,510 mile journey on two chartered Greyhound buses, in exchange for playing six concerts en route to and during return from Miami in cities where Davey Tree did prominent business. My wife and I went on the bus trip to chronicle daily experiences for the *Record-Courier*. It was a memorable trip, one which impressed upon me the fine musicianship of the band members, most of them World War II veterans, and the intense finesse of their directors.

Concerts were played en route in Louisville, Atlanta, and Orlando. The third concert, held in a park, was "old home week" for former Portage Countians residing in that area. By the scores, they hailed the band and exchanged news of home.

At Valdosta, Georgia, near the Florida line, one of the buses broke down earlier that day. Intent upon not idling away time, Farinacci marched the band in a cotton field on a scorching day. The cotton had been harvested and only sharp stubble remained, not exactly an ideal site for marching.

Joliet again took first place in Miami. Kent was second and Milwaukee third. The Joliet band was made up of musicians who had been championship players throughout their high school years, and the Milwaukee band members were on the payroll of the Blatz beer people. That was stern competition and tells plenty about the excellent musicianship of the Kent band, whose members, for the most part, were not professional musicians. En route home, the band played concerts in

Jacksonville and Charlotte and appeared during the Richmond-Davidson football game in Richmond. The band returned to "the wars" in 1952, again winning the state title and losing to Joliet in New York City.

Certainly the crowning event came in 1953, when the American Legion band represented Ohio in Washington during President Eisenhower's inauguration. Local residents and former residents around the country hardly left their television sets as they sought to get a glimpse of the hometown band in the "big parade." Our own John Fowler, then on our staff and now in the public relations department of the Firestone Tire and Rubber Company, went to Washington to cover for the hometown paper.

An announcement on April 20, 1953, sent shock waves throughout the community. The band voted to disband. Cited as reasons were lack of community acceptance and support and increasing competition tension on the state level. Despite its long history of state championships, the band had a perpetual fight on its hands as delegates attempted to alter the contest rules. As for the first reason, it was recalled that annual community appreciation concerts had attracted only a handful of people and that supporting funds were difficult to come by.

When the band disbanded, 13 original members remained: Farinacci, Gallaway, Keller, Joe Escott, Harold Bechtle, Fran Amodio, Sam Apicello, Bill Savory, Harold "Casey" Jones, Don Hursell, Dave Echleberry, Merle Andregg, and Wilford Cook. Three—Escott, Jones, and Cook, World War I veterans—had been members of the old drum and bugle corps.

Thus ended a glorious period in Portage County band history—six state championships in Class A and another in Class B; one fourth, one third, and four seconds in national competition. And, paraphrasing an ancient quotation, the fame of people and institutions all too often is more appreciated elsewhere than in their hometown.

———

## IKE'S INAUGURATION BIG MOMENT
## FOR KENT BAND

*January 22, 1989*

The inauguration of George Bush as the 41st president of the United States recalls one of this area's greatest moments in the national limelight. Kent's famed American Legion Band, sponsored by Portage Post 496 and representing the state of Ohio, marched in the inaugural parade when Dwight D. Eisenhower became the 34th president.

For the Kent band it was the culmination of a seven-year drive toward a national Legion championship, a goal which barely eluded this outstanding musical organization. During its existence, the band won seven state championships and four seconds, one third, and one fourth in national competition.

The thrill of passing the presidential reviewing stand and receiving the new president's crisp salute eclipsed all of the band's brilliant successes and disappointments on the national scene. As for the home folk on January 20, 1953, they shirked their work to get a glimpse of the Kent marchers on national television. They were not disappointed; the cameras homed in on the band as it made a parade turn.

The good news that the Legion band would be the only Ohio band in the parade came from Ray Bliss, then Ohio Republican party chairman. Preparations began quickly as plans needed to be made to move a 65-piece band to Washington for the march down Pennsylvania Avenue. Bandsmen left Kent at 10 P.M. Monday from the B. & O. station, rode all night, and arrived in the capital at 7:30 A.M. on Tuesday's inauguration day. It wasn't all pleasure; sleep was difficult to come by. Following their appearance, band members entrained at 9:30 P.M. and returned to Kent the next morning at 6:40. Despite the grueling trip, it was a grand, once-in-a-lifetime experience.

Harold Bechtle, probably the oldest surviving member of the band, recalls the long hours of rehearsing for the Washington appearance. "It was quite an experience," says Bechtle, a World War II Navy Seabee veteran who will be 88 on February 3. "The weather was good. Besides marching, we had some free time to see some of the other units in the parade."

The band was led by drillmaster Scotty White, majorette Ruth Bowen, and a color guard. Band director John Farinacci marched alongside. As the band approached the presidential reviewing stand, Farinacci flashed a snappy salute to the new president. Eisenhower returned the salute.

The band struck up "Across the Field," the Ohio State University fight song, and bandsmen shouted "K-E-N-T," allowing four beats between each letter. There was little doubt of the band's hometown. Ohio governor Frank Lausche, riding in a car directly ahead of the band, turned and applauded when the band played the OSU song.

There was a contingent of Kent people who witnessed the parade firsthand. Mr. and Mrs. Martin L. Davey Jr. made the train trip with the band. John Fowler, *Record-Courier* newsman, also accompanied the band to provide news reports and photo coverage. Others from Kent in the capital for the inauguration included Mayor Bob Garrett, Mr. and Mrs. Hugh Brown, Redmond Greer (later a Kent mayor), and Lu and Maxine Lyman. Lyman then was Portage County GOP executive chairman. It was a great day for Republicans. They had waited a long time for such a day; Eisenhower was the first Republican president in 20 years.

Farinacci organized the band in 1946 while he was serving as director of instrumental music at Kent State University High School. A World War II veteran, Farinacci, who now resides in Florida, is a KSU graduate. He later joined the Cleveland Heights school system and commuted to Kent as he continued as band director.

The blush of the band's inauguration appearance hardly had faded when in April 1953 an announcement that the band would disband sent shock waves throughout the community. Lack of community support and continuous attempts to change the Legion's band competition rules were offered as prime reasons for the band's demise.

For seven years, the Kent American Legion Band had achieved glory on the state and national scenes. And the invitation to march in the inaugural parade certainly was its crowning moment.

———

## CLOSED KENT EATERY LEAVES WEALTH
## OF MEMORIES BEHIND

*August 10, 1985*

This week's announcement that the Captain Brady Restaurant in Kent had closed its doors pricked my nostalgic conscience. For nearly 60 years, the restaurant named for the legendary Indian scout who leaped the Cuyahoga River to evade his Indian pursuers has been a fixture on the KSU campus and city scene. Now this once-bustling spot has been stilled. And, like the thousands of other Kent State University students who passed through its portals, I experienced a twinge of regret as memories of another day are unleashed as nostalgic food.

In my younger days, "Brady sitting" was the "in" thing. The Brady was a meeting place . . . the scene of untold numbers of planning sessions for campus events, a study spot in lieu of a trip to the university library, the scene of social gatherings for the exchange of the latest campus and town gossip, a mecca for northern Ohio diners who were attracted there to partake of late lunches and dinners.

To me, the Brady was more than any of those. The restaurant was my employer, as it was for so many students who needed a financial lift to meet college expenses. In the 1930s, when the Captain Brady was operated by the Misses Mary and Pearl Cook, I hired on as an evening dishwasher, a job which required me to dispatch the dirty dishes and silver through a contraption so strange-appearing that it could have been put together by Rube Goldberg. For three hours each evening, it seemed to me that the stream of soiled dishes would never come to a merciful end. Part-time Brady help was paid 35 cents per hour, and we worked three hours for three meals. The meals were 35 cents, thus our day's food intake totaled $1.05.

I finally graduated from that menial chore to one of late-evening cook, a designation which was not nearly as important as the title. When the cooks, Ada Barnard among them, left after the dinner-hour rush, it was my assignment to fry hamburgers and to concoct other culinary delights for the late evening crowd. This assignment did not require any particular mastery of the culinary arts, a condition probably resulting from the inexpensive nature of the product as well as from customers less discerning than those we have today.

There was one source of irritation to that job. In the late evening after I cleaned up the kitchen, several hamburger customers would arrive just before closing time to order a snack . . . and dirty up my clean kitchen. I distinctly recall one group of "regulars" which included men who later became friends—Cy Porthouse, Rod and Ike McSherry, Bud Grubb, and Bob Green. They never knew of my irritation . . . it was all part of the job.

There was a special bonus to my Brady association on Saturday nights (or early Sunday morning), Otis Graber and I moved all of the chairs and tables and scrubbed and waxed the floors. (For the most part, these are the same chairs and tables which will be offered at auction on August 15.) As part of that assignment, the Cook sisters permitted me and Otis to cook up a real meal for ourselves—steaks and the works, including the elite of sundaes—which we consumed at about 4 A.M. We looked forward to this best meal of the week.

The list of coworkers at the Brady was almost endless. Some of them come to mind. For example, there was Bill Langell, retired circulation director of the *Record-Courier*. Admonished several times concerning his too-frequent breaking of glasses, he finally was told by the Misses Mary and Pearl, "Bill, you're just too expensive for us." That took care of his employment. There was Ernie Williams, now a retired vice president of the First National Bank in Alliance; Carl Hageman of Tallmadge, who became an air controller in Miami and is now retired in Pigeon Forge, Tennessee; Dean Kisseberth, onetime school principal at Mantua Center; Ken Jacobson, later an Erie railroad detective, who now is deceased; Ruth Jones of Palmyra, now a retired school principal in Canton; Ora Crum, a waitress who married Garner Spencer, who was co-proprietor of the Cardinal Restaurant in downtown Kent.

The Captain Brady building was built in the late 1920s by the Donaghy family, which still owns it. Following the tenure of the Misses Pearl and Mary, the family operated the restaurant with Oka Stonestreet as its manager. Strange as it may seem, the Captain Brady once was the Robin Hood. Doug Miller was its operator, and then in the early 1930s he built the new Robin Hood diagonally across the street. That building today houses a bar.

The Captain Brady was the site of some pretty heady developments. For example, early in 1935 Kent State was conducting a search for a new football coach. Everyone surmised that after many disappointing athletic years, the university would hire a name coach. Among the applicants were Alonzo Stag Jr., Jimmy Aiken of Canton McKinley, Ray Watts of Baldwin Wallace, Sid Gillman of Ohio State, and Stu Holcomb of Findlay College. President Engleman surprised everyone by announcing the selection of George (Rosy) Starn as the new coach and athletic director.

There was a veritable floodgate of opposition which culminated in a mass protest meeting of 400 students, alumni, and townspeople at the Captain Brady. The appointment prevailed, and Starn proceeded to achieve a good record as a coach. I attended that mass meeting, and I still remember Kerm Taylor, former KSU star, pleading with the crowd to "give the new coach a chance." Among Starn's stars were Ravenna's Ernie Sullivan in basketball and football; Harry Lohr, former Central School principal, in basketball; and Marvin Garner, a baseball pitcher who later became a dentist in Canton. The latter married Gene Gettrust of Kent.

Despite its closing by the Hahn-Burgess family, the Brady's life as a restaurant is not at an end. Later this summer or early fall, Plaza Sweets of Akron will open a combination deli, bakery, and ice cream parlor in the building. The new business has quite a heritage to live up to. We hope it succeeds.

———

## OLD BRAYTON HOUSE POSES
## HISTORICAL DILEMMA
### Landmark Ravenna Residence Rich in History
*November 12, 1995*

Many people in Portage County know the old house. It is located on South Chestnut Street in Ravenna just north of the Portage County Administration Building.

This old house has been much in the news of late, the result of a fire last April 23 which severely damaged a portion of the structure. Here's the dilemma: Either the house must be renovated and placed in livable shape, or city of Ravenna officials will have no choice except to seek a court order to have it razed.

For one of Portage County's most memorable homes, that is a difficult choice. Officials of Portage County have hinted a mild interest in purchasing the house inasmuch as it adjoins property already owned by the county. But certainly that interest is not written in stone, and if it were the county's property, it probably would be razed rather than restored for occupancy.

So what is so special about the old house on South Chestnut Street? Only that this was the home of Capt. Isaac Brayton, one of the many sea captains from Nantucket, Massachusetts, who came to Portage County back in the late 1830s, 1840s, and 1850s. Why did they come so far inland after long years at sea? That's a valid question for which there is no ready answer. Suffice it to say that these seafaring people and their long-suffering families added much to the culture of Ravenna and Rootstown where they settled.

Isaac Brayton came to Ravenna in 1839. He had followed the sea from the time he was a mere boy. He was born in Nantucket in 1801 and is said to have commanded a ship that carried the first missionaries to the Sandwich Islands. Today we know those islands as the Hawaiian Islands. A religious man, Isaac Brayton during one of his voyages united with a church in Honolulu, and historical writings tell us that he established a family Altar and Bible Society aboard ship.

He abandoned the sea in 1833 and six years later came to Ravenna. In the county seat town he made his influence felt. He is credited with being a leading force in the establishment of the first high school in Ravenna. Also, he served as an associate judge in Portage County in the early 1850s when judges were appointed by the Ohio General Assembly rather than being elected.

He had served in the legislature of Massachusetts before moving to Ravenna when Horace Mann was superintendent of that state's public schools. In 1853 he moved from Ravenna to Newburg (now part of Cleveland) and then was elected to Ohio's General Assembly. He served on the Sanitary Commission during the Civil War and afterward was superintendent of the National Soldiers Home in Columbus. He returned to Ravenna in 1873 and spent the remainder of his life with his daughter, Mary, and her husband, Frederick Woodbridge. The latter became secretary-treasurer of the Crown Flint Glass Company in Ravenna, one of the community's leading industries.

There have been claims that Abraham Lincoln may have visited the storied Brayton home on South Chestnut Street. There may be some doubt in that claim; the only written record of a Lincoln visit to Ravenna was in February 1861 when he was on his way to his inauguration. His train stopped for a few minutes at the old C. & P. station on West Main Street, and he gave brief remarks. Following his assassination, the train bearing his body passed through the county on its way to Springfield, Illinois, for his burial.

As for poet Edgar Allen Poe having visited in the Brayton home, there appears more logic. Edgar Allen was a cousin of Adam Poe, who ran a hotel in Ravenna, and it is quite believable that he may have visited here.

Isaac and Love Mitchell Brayton's daughter, Mary, eclipsed both of them in national prominence. Married at a young age, Mary nevertheless pursued her studies and her eloquent speaking abilities, which led her to the peak of her chosen mission—ridding the country of Demon Alcohol.

She became immersed in the anti-alcohol movement through the Woman's Christian Temperance Union. Frances Willard wrote of her: "God put his message on her lips and when she spoke the strong were melted to tears." The history of Mary Brayton Woodbridge became part and parcel of the WCTU. In that mission she began at the grassroots. She served as president of her local WCTU unit and then for many years was president of the Ohio organization. In 1878 she was named national recording secretary and in 1884 became superintendent of the Department of Legislation, an appointment which took her across the country to address large gatherings. Her crowning achievement came when she was selected to conduct the constitutional amendment campaign against alcohol. One political leader in Ohio, speaking after one of her campaigns, said they were simply "outworked, outwitted and out generaled." Hardly could "wet" advocates compete with groups of women kneeling in dusty streets and praying in front of saloons. Even before the ratification of the Eighteenth Amendment, which prohibited the sale of liquor, work of Mary Brayton Woodbridge and her cohorts resulted in the closing of thousands of saloons across the country.

The old house on South Chestnut Street is said to have been a stop on the underground railroad for helping slaves from the South seek freedom in the North. Knowing the historical, caring background of the Brayton family, that's a fair conclusion. At any rate, the old house is steeped in history. Hopefully, it can be spared.

———

## RAVENNA CHAMBER'S ROOTS SEEN IN EARLY 1900s

*April 2, 1989*

The year was 1914. Harper Brothers, the Ravenna men's clothing store, was advertising Kuppenheimer suits for Easter at $15 to $25. You could buy a Buick runabout roadster for $950. Sirloin steak was going for 18 cents per pound and choice ham for 17 cents. Men's Walkover shoes could be had for $3.50 to $6, depending upon the style.

In that economic climate, 135 Ravenna businessmen convened in the Elks clubrooms to organize for the promotion of Ravenna's betterment. The date was April 1, 1914—75 years ago—and the result of the meeting was the organization of the Ravenna Chamber of Commerce.

A month before, Ravenna businessmen had pledged $3,600 to help bring an industrial concern into the county seat. H. Warner Riddle had offered a four-acre site for the potential firm. The outcome of that effort, the name of the firm, and the location of the site were not mentioned in the *Ravenna Republican*'s article. At any rate, that effort probably was responsible for the meeting a month later that saw formal organizational plans for the Ravenna chamber.

The *Republican* in its April 2 weekly edition reported the chamber's organization in colorful language. The 135 businessmen "united for the larger development of the city with common pride and common interest and of a quiet, firm purpose to mould the affairs into a better and

Looking east on Main Street in Ravenna.

Riddle Block No. 1, Main and Chestnut Streets in Ravenna. At the turn of the century, H. W. Riddle built 12 downtown blocks, most of which remain in use today.

The Portage County Courthouse, and combination jail and sheriff's residence, in 1881. The present courthouse was built in 1960.

larger municipal destiny," the article reads. Inasmuch as A. D. Robinson, editor and manager of the *Republican*, was chairman of the new chamber's executive committee, it is suspected that the article was done by his hand. The story went on to say that "the meeting indexed a fine popular sentiment most gratifying to all who believe in the future of Ravenna." The constitution and bylaws unanimously adopted at that first meeting upon recommendation of Robinson's executive committee stated a direct and simple purpose—"to promote the social, commercial and industrial welfare of Ravenna."

The first corps of officers reads like a Ravenna "Who's Who" of that day. W. H. Marsh was the first president. Albert L. Caris, later a renowned common pleas court judge, was vice president, and William J. Dodge treasurer. The executive committee was charged with selecting a secretary at a later date. Members of the executive committee, in addition to chairman Robinson and the officers, included Albert Dietrich, J. A. Bennett, Walter A. Lyon (a onetime Ravenna mayor), H. Warner Riddle (also a former mayor), and F. D. Pitkin.

During the proceedings at the first meeting, members prescribed four regular meetings per year—in January, April, July, and October—plus an annual meeting. And in its final action at the initial meeting, the organizers selected as the new chamber's slogan "Ravenna—10,000 in 1920," an apparent reference to city population.

While researching old newspaper files, one finds the advertisements as interesting and revealing as the news columns. Sometimes we may think towns change little during the passing of years. The changes among advertisers reveal otherwise. In the same edition as the Ravenna chamber article, it is quite obvious that few of the business places remain today. Even most of the banks operate under different names today.

The April 2, 1914, *Republican* presented a large ad sponsored by the Ford Seed Company at 742 North Chestnut St., a firm founded in 1880 and discontinued only several years ago. Austin's grocery, where cheese was selling for five cents per pound, is gone. So, too, is Chapman and Green, the predecessor of Kertscher's store, now also out of business.

Even two Akron department stores, the M. O'Neil Company and C. H. Yeager Company, both of whom were advertising in the *Republican*, have ceased business. The former is now the May Company, and Yeager's many years ago left the business scene. O'Neil's advertised tots' dresses for 39 cents and Yeager's a 9-by-12-foot rug for $11.95. In that same paper, an Atwater farm of 85 acres was advertised for sale at $4,000, including all of the farm's buildings; and a photo of a young Burritt Allen advertised his auctioneering business. All of which tells us that the business scene has changed. New stores, new products, new technology, new people.

But the Ravenna chamber, now at a healthy 75 years, goes on. It continues to fulfill its original goal of promoting the social, commercial, and industrial welfare of the community, under the leadership of David Frank as president and Ruth Shields, veteran secretary.

## LIBERTY BELL MADE 1915 STOP IN RAVENNA

*October 15, 1989*

The Liberty Bell, along with the Statue of Liberty as the most cherished symbols of American freedom, has not always quietly reposed at Independence Hall in Philadelphia. Actually, the 237-year-old bell is much-traveled. And during its travels it made two stops in Ravenna.

The last of those stops was on November 23, 1915, when the special railroad car carrying the bell back home from the Panama-Pacific Exposition in San Francisco was displayed at Ravenna's Pennsylvania Railroad station for all to see.

Thousands of Portage Countians went to the station to see the bell during a 10-minute stop. Among them were 2,000 county schoolchildren who marched two abreast to get a good look at the bell that they had learned from their history studies was tolled when our nation declared its freedom from Great Britain. No doubt among those children are many present residents who will recall that crisp November day when a light sprinkling of snow covered the ground. From such events are spawned indelible memories.

Local residents knew ahead of time that the bell would pass through Ravenna en route from Cleveland to Pittsburgh. Mayor Walter A. Lyon appointed a special committee to make arrangements for an organized ceremony on the appointed day. Above all else, painstaking plans were made to make the event available to schoolchildren. The *Ravenna Republican*, then a weekly newspaper, described the ceremony as a "demonstration as enthusiastic as it was appropriate." The *Republican* continued: "It is safe to say that the sentiment of love inculcated in the schoolroom for the herald of '76 was enlarged by the sight of the bell itself, and that every child or youth thus favored will cherish the memory of the day as one of the golden possessions of life."

So near could people approach the bell that they could read its inscription: "Proclaim liberty throughout all the land unto all the inhabitants thereof," a biblical quotation from Leviticus. As children filed past the bell, each was handed a photo of the bell. Spectators arrived at the station on foot or by automobile or horse-drawn carriage.

This was not the first appearance of the Liberty Bell in Ravenna. It passed through the city in 1893 en route to the World's Columbian

Exposition in Chicago.

Truly, the Liberty Bell has a glorious history and is one of our most precious symbols of American independence. But, also, the bell has had its troubles. Originally cast in London, the 2,080-pound bell arrived in August 1752 in Philadelphia to hang in the State House to commemorate the 50th anniversary of the Pennsylvania Commonwealth. It cracked a month later while being tested in the State House yard.

A Philadelphia firm recast the bell, adding copper to make it stronger. The copper ruined its tone, and it was again recast.

In 1753, the bell was hung in the steeple of the State House, which became the meeting place for the Continental Congress. The bell rang out in defiance of British tax and trade restrictions, proclaimed the Boston Tea Party and the first reading of the Declaration of Independence. In 1771, when the British were about to occupy the city, the bell was moved to Allentown, Pennsylvania, where it was secreted.

In 1781, the bell was lowered into the brick section of the tower. There it was hanging when it cracked again when tolled for the funeral of Chief Justice John Marshall in 1835. It has not been recast and still bears its crack.

As far as can be learned, the Liberty Bell has not traveled out of Philadelphia since its 1915 trip across the country. For many years, the bell was displayed in a glass case in the hallway of Independence Hall, the former State House. Then, in the 1976 Bicentennial year, it was moved to a new glass and steel pavilion behind Independence Hall for easier viewing by the American people.

———

## GLASSBLOWERS' TRAIN WRECK
## PROMPTS FAMOUS QUOTE

*April 26, 1986*

"I said to myself, that's a hell of a way to run a railroad."

That statement made by Barney Dyer, a Ravenna crossing watchman, became a classic remark among railroaders throughout the country. He gave that response during a coroner's inquest following the worst railroad wreck in Portage County history, when asked to describe his reaction as he saw a fast freight bearing down upon a passenger train standing at the Ravenna Erie Railroad station.

The date was July 3, 1891. Train No. 8, running 45 minutes late, left Kent at 2:11 A.M., bound for Ravenna and on to the East. John Pendergast, the passenger train engineer, decided to stop in Ravenna to repair the locomotive's whistle after it failed to function as the train approached the Cleveland and Pittsburgh Railroad crossing west of Ravenna. He was atop the locomotive making the whistle repair. Two warning lanterns were on the rear of the train.

Running in the same direction behind the passenger train was train No. 82, a freight heavily loaded with meat and fruit. A flagman was sent back to warn the approaching freight of the halted passenger train at the Ravenna station. It was too late. The freight engineer saw the danger and shut off the steam, but was unable to stop his train in time. Both he and the fireman leaped from their cab. The freight crashed into the rear of the passenger train.

The result was a railroad disaster the magnitude of which to this day is the worst in Portage County railroading history. Nineteen passengers, most of them glassblowers from Corning, New York, en route back home from a vacation-closed factory in Findlay, Ohio, lost their lives. Twenty-one passengers were injured. During the 95 years since that fateful day, the accident has been known as the "glassblowers' wreck."

A July 10, 1891, edition of the Kent Courier related the horrible story of the disaster. The glassblowers, 47 in all, were riding in the last coach. Naturally, it bore the brunt of the crash. Both that car and the sleeper directly ahead were demolished in the crash and the fire that followed. The scenes, said the news report, were heart rending. Many were killed instantly. Others were pinned by the car's timbers and were held prisoner as they burned to death.

The story told by a young lad following the crash was particularly touching. James Clark was riding with Willie Kane, 16, who was elated that he soon would rejoin his parents in Corning. He had not seen them for a year. He was proud that he had saved a considerable sum of money, and he intended to give his mother a happy surprise. The Clark boy was thrown through a window and went back to look for his young friend. He found him dead, pinned among the timbers.

The bodies (the story referred to them as corpses) were taken to the Etna House in downtown Ravenna, the same Etna House we know today, except at that time it was the town's main hotel. There they were placed into sacks. Doctors were summoned from throughout Portage County. The Ravenna fire company, plus scores of citizens, were called out to halt the blaze, but nothing could be done until the first coach was destroyed and the second severely burned.

The inquest, which took place within days of the fatal crash, was conducted by Dr. A. M. Sherman of Kent, then the coroner of Portage County. He called into questioning all of the crew members on both trains as well as the now-famous Barney Dyer.

Of course, the engineer of the halted passenger train testified that it was incumbent upon the engineer of the freight train to pay heed to the warning signals and to the lights on the rear of his train. That didn't help much, because 19 people had died horrible deaths.

Even members of the news media got into the act. An item in the July 10, 1891, paper took issue with a "dude reporter" from the *Cleveland Plain Dealer* who described those who came from Kent to help clear the wreck as "a lot of dirty and greasy workmen." "Wonder what he expected," said the *Courier*. "Would he had the men hasten out of bed at three o'clock in the morning, don satin clothes, white shirts, standing collars, and plug hats to go out and clear up the wreck? The *Plain Dealer* dude is too fresh." Me thinks the local media objected to out-of-town reporters entering upon their turf.

But certainly one of the chief witnesses at the inquest was Barney Dyer, who was employed by the Erie and the C. & P. Railroads as a watchman at an interlocking switch west of Ravenna. "I saw 82 coming fast and jumped and gave the signals," Barney testified. "It couldn't have been more than two or three minutes between trains. I had no difficulty seeing the taillights of No. 8 a mile away." That's when he made his famous statement, "That's a hell of a way to run a railroad." Who can dispute Barney? He was right!

———

## 1923 SCHOOL BUS HOLOCAUST SENT
## EDITORS SCURRYING

*July 28, 1984*

A week ago, the *Record-Courier* published an interesting "Back Then" photograph. Taken in Hiram, the photo showed a lineup of horse-drawn school buses. For older residents, this photo brought back happy memories of those more spartan times when all of Portage County's country school districts operated a "fleet" of these buses. They were most often referred to as "kid hacks."

Not all of the memories inspired by the recent photo publication are happy ones. Indeed, for some Portage Countians, the photo probably revived memories of one of the darkest days in Portage County history, nearly 61 years ago. The date was October 11, 1923. At 7:55 A.M. two horses pulled a Rootstown school bus onto a railroad crossing on New Milford Road, three miles south of Ravenna and a half mile north of New Milford. There it was struck by a Pennsylvania Railroad train known as the *Clevelander*. Local residents and railroaders called it "the flyer."

The fragile school bus was dashed to bits by the train, said to be traveling 50 mph. Eight children, ranging in age from three to 15, were killed almost instantly. Three children and the driver were injured. Six children leaped from the bus and were spared. The accident holds the dubious record as the worst school bus disaster in county history.

The next day, a Friday, was a publication day for the thrice-weekly *Ravenna Republican*, predecessor of today's *Record Courier*. One can imagine the scramble of the *Republican's* publisher and editor so near their deadline to chronicle the disaster in words and photos in a time when newspapers did not have the benefit of a large, well-trained staff and speedy technical facilities. But the *Republican* in its day-after edition offered complete coverage, devoting its entire page one (except ads) and most of page three to detailed stories and six photos.

The list of dead and injured told the story of the gruesome accident. The Grover Shaw family lost three children: Mildred, 11; Harold, 9; and Verna, 3. The youngest child was sitting on her sister's lap when the train struck the bus. Apparently, although she was too young to be attending school, Verna was going to school with her sister that day, a prevalent custom of the time. Others killed were Julia Wancik, 13; Ella Stianche, 14; Thelma Benshoff, 9; Richard Silvasi, 8; and Margaret Kunst, 12. Injured were Lawrence Shaw, 8; Steven Wancik, 11; Stanley Benshoff, 6; and the driver, Louis Cline, 42. Six children leaped to safety: Andrew Kazimer, 14, the boy who saw the train and warned his classmates; Valeria Silvasi, 14; Frank Kunst, 15; Glenn Benshoff, 6; Edward Sorenson, 14; and Roy Benshoff, 13.

As soon as the train could be stopped, trainmen, passengers, and farmers in that area began the gruesome task of picking up the mangled remains of the dead and administering to the injured. Photos in the *Republican* showed only fragments of the ill-fated school bus. Schoolbooks, dismembered limbs, and lunch boxes were strewn along the tracks.

As with all such disasters, a probe of the dreadful accident began immediately. Dr. R. D. Worden of Ravenna was the coroner at that time. He questioned the bus driver, witnesses, and survivors.

The six uninjured children said that the train usually had passed the crossing before the arrival of their bus. But that morning, the train was about 15 minutes late. Whether or not the engineer had sounded the train's whistle also was a matter for investigation. Witnesses said the engineer, F. L. McCaslin, sounded a long whistle before the train approached the crossing and several shorter blasts just before the train struck the wagon. Whether or not the driver saw the approaching train or stopped his horses before driving onto the tracks were matters of uncertainty.

The Public Utilities Commission of Ohio investigated the wreck and some days later issued its report. The commission placed blame for the tragic accident with the Rootstown Board of Education for not properly instructing its drivers in safety regulations, the Portage County commissioners for failing to keep shrubs and trees at the crossing site trimmed to provide a clear view, and the railroad with failing to observe simple precautions. And the driver was given part of the blame for failing to bring the vehicle to a full stop before starting to pass over the crossing. The latter point was a matter of dispute. No criminal charges were brought either by Coroner Worden or by Abner Heisler, then prosecutor of Portage County.

Investigations most always follow tragic accidents. They cannot restore lives but may prevent a repetition of such tragedies. In the case of the Rootstown disaster, the investigation could not erase the scars of the worst school bus accident in history. For the families involved and for the entire community, the scars remain 60 years later.

————

## PALMYRA HOTEL STANDS AS REMINDER
## OF FRONTIER DAYS
*April 12, 1986*

One hundred and fifty years ago, the coachman's horn alerted residents to the daily coming of the stagecoach. They flocked to the old hotel to get the latest news from the outside world, to claim their mail, and to exchange conversation with travelers. Historical writings record that scene at the old Palmyra Hotel for modern-day Portage Countians.

Palmyra was an important junction for the stagecoaches, then the principal means of travel prior to the coming of the Pennsylvania and Ohio Canal and, later, the railroads. The old hotel, located on the northwest corner of the town square, was more than a stagecoach stop. It was an important stage station for both freight and passengers and for the change of horses. Palmyra was served by two stage routes, one from Cleveland to Pittsburgh and another from Cleveland to Wellsville.

The imposing three-story brick building still stands, a silent reminder of those glory days in Portage County's early history. The building, entered in the National Register of Historic Places in 1976, is owned by Nicholas Stone, an antique dealer, escape artist, and magician who for many years traveled across the country to display his magical talents and prowess in escaping from his bonds while submerged beneath the waters of lakes and ponds. That's another story, one that bears more definitive repetition at another time. For now, the old hotel grasps our attention.

Historical writings differ on the age of the hotel. Local writings place its beginnings at 1832, when Francis Lewis built the structure from bricks that were fired in crude kilns across the road. The clay was hauled to the site with teams of oxen. Mr. Stone is convinced that the first excavations took place as early as 1808 and that work was suspended during the War of 1812, then resumed shortly after the war in time for opening in 1818 for stagecoach business. Research of the Ohio Historical Society bears out his version.

In any event, the hotel has had various owners and has been home to a variety of businesses—an inn, a saloon, a blacksmith shop, several stores, a physician's office, a harness shop, a post office. Originally, the building had only two stories, the third being added in 1888 after it was acquired by the Knights of Pythias lodge, which used the third floor as its meeting room.

Francis Lewis, a prominent Palmyra businessman and farmer, operated the hotel for many years. It is said that at one time he owned farms in each direction from Palmyra Center. He bought and dressed hogs, curing and storing the meat in the hotel's basement. He shipped meat by way of the Ohio River and the Canal. Lewis died while on a business trip to Cincinnati.

Other owners or operators included John Lewis, D. E. Wilson, one-time Portage County sheriff James Jones, John Breeze, Tib Jones, Wade Wilson, Gerald Williams, and Harry Six, among others. The K. of P. lodge owned the building until it was purchased in 1974 by Mr. Stone.

When the Stones—Nick and Betty—bought the building, they planned a renovation project and the establishment of an antique business. They came from Akron, where at one time they operated six antique shops.

The building was much in need of repair. The Stones drilled a well, put in a septic tank, and did other renovation work. Then, in 1984, Mrs. Stone died. Only recently, Mr. Stone sold the collection of antiques to a Youngstown man, reserving for himself his vast collection of locks and keys, some of which he has on display in the building. He says his lock and key collection totals several tons.

Now, he's preparing to place the old building at 9401 Tallmadge Road on the market for either sale or lease. What will be the old hotel's future? As we ponder that question, we see in the mind's eye happier days when stage passengers who had been jostled about on muddy roads finally arrived in Palmyra, there to seek the comforts of the hotel, a meal of home-grown food, libations of corn whiskey or brandy, and the warmth of the hotel's six fireplaces.

One need only look to the easternmost of the three sandstone door-steps for evidence of which of the hotel's facilities was the most popular. The step to that entrance, which led to the office and bar, has been worn down six inches from its original level.

---

## RUM, MONEY TALKED AND GAVE HIRAM A NAME

*July 21, 1991*

Names of places—towns, townships, and cities—evolved from various sources. Some were named for people. Others received their identification from the original New England areas where their settlers once lived. For example, Brimfield takes its name from Brimfield, Massachusetts, the onetime home of the Portage County township's settlers. Suffield is another; it gets its name from Suffield, Massachusetts.

For other areas in Portage County, name sources are more obscure. The name of Hiram is one of the more interesting sagas in Portage County history. It is the only area in Portage County named for a figure associated with the Masonic Order.

Nine men were the original landowners of Hiram Township, an area that once embraced the present areas of Mantua, Shalersville, Freedom, Windham, and Nelson. Their total payment to the Connecticut Land Company for ground was $12,903, not a bad price for such prime land in the Western Reserve. Among them was Col. Daniel Tilden, a Revolutionary War veteran, whose $3,600 was the largest contribution among the landowners. All of the original landowners were residents of Lebanon, Connecticut, none of them had seen the land they had purchased, and all were Free and Accepted Masons.

As in these modern times, money talked. The good colonel, as a result of his major contribution toward the purchase of what today is Hiram, won the right to name the township. Plus, he had to supply alcoholic beverages for a social gathering, which added a measure to his privilege.

At the time (late 1790s), Daniel Tilden, prominent in the affairs of Masonry, was high priest of his chapter. It is said that in those days it was customary to hold a social hour after the affairs of the lodge had been conducted. On many occasions, it still is. At one such gathering, the subject of the group's possessions in the West was a matter of discussion. One of the number proposed that the brother who supplied the punch might name the township. As the principal landowner, Tilden was accorded that privilege. The punch, incidentally, had as its principal ingredient Jamaica rum, to which sugar and milk were added.

At the appointed moment, the colonel arose and offered a toast, saying, "Brethren, let us drink to the widow's son. May peace, prosperity and brotherly love prevail for all time throughout our possessions for such an extent as to add luster to our patron saint, Hiram, whose name we now give." Hiram, the name became, as a result of an alcoholic toast. And Hiram it is today, not only the name of the township and the village but also the name of the revered Hiram College. The Hiram patron saint to whom Tilden referred was Hiram Abift, an accomplished artificer in brass and a mason who is said to have been a worker on Solomon's temple.

Daniel Tilden is believed to have been the only one of the original purchasers to come into the Western Reserve to live on his holdings. Most of those who bought Western Reserve lands here did so with the expectation of making a tidy profit and not with an intention of relocating here.

In addition to being the only Portage area named for a lodge's patron saint, Hiram has another distinction. With an elevation of 1,300 feet above sea level, it is the highest spot not only in the county but in the vast Western Reserve.

Colonel Tilden was the grandfather of Edwin B. Babcock of Shalersville, a prominent farmer who once owned 500 acres in that township as well as another 500 acres in Michigan. He served Portage County as coroner, trustee, and infirmary director and was a director of the old First Savings Bank. Colonel Tilden was also an uncle of Samuel J. Tilden of New York, a Democrat who lost the presidency in 1876 to Ohioan Rutherford B. Hayes in perhaps the most controversial election in the nation's history. Although Tilden polled over two million more votes than Republican Hayes, he failed to win the presidency by one electoral vote, and that decision followed a long and bitter controversy. Tilden received 184 electoral votes to Hayes's 165, one short of a majority. Confronted with that impasse, Congress created a special electoral commission to determine the winner. Lucky for Hayes, the commission had a Republican tilt. Only 56 hours prior to inauguration day in March of 1877, the commission named Hayes the winner.

Neither Tilden nor his descendants ever forgot. Forever, they claimed their famous namesake had been gypped out of the presidency. From 1937 to 1944, Ted Tilden of Hiram served as Portage County prosecuting attorney. Despite the passing of many years since Samuel Tilden had missed by a hair eternal fame as a U.S. president, Ted continued to berate Congress for its action, which seated Hayes. He could not make the claim that one of his ancestors served the nation as president. So go the ways of politics!

———

## STORY OF BRADY'S PAST PUTS PRESENT
## INTO PERSPECTIVE
*February 26, 1983*

Brady Lake always has been in the news! Ever since Indian fighter Capt. Samuel Brady in 1780 leaped the 21-foot chasm of the Cuyahoga River in today's Kent, fled with Indians in pursuit to that beautiful body of water in eastern Franklin Township, and saved his life by hiding beneath a submerged tree, Brady Lake has been prominent in the affairs of Portage County. The ensuing 200 years have not dimmed—but have enhanced—the stature and prominence of this small village as a generator of news.

Consider, for a moment, events of this past week that serve to fill current news columns. Mayor Claude Brown is hauling fresh water from a public well a mile and a half from his home. His own well fails to provide sufficient water for family needs, a circumstance repeated many times over in the Brady Lake community. Brady Lake has a water plant, built by the county with federal funds, that hasn't pumped a drop of water because there are no distribution lines and, so far, no money to build them. Meanwhile, six residents of the community, angered over the deficient water supplies, filed suit against the City of Kent, charging that the city's Breakneck Creek well field has lowered the level of the lake and the water table, thus causing their water problems.

While all the foregoing was transpiring, the Kent Board of Education was wrestling with the problem of disposing of land bequeathed to the schools and the Brady Lake United Methodist Church by the Emma Williard estate. The board, by law, cannot sell the land without a public auction, which obviously causes concern among residents who maintain houses on land they do not own. Complicating the problem is the fact that the board and church own the land jointly. Then, add to current developments, the Brady Lake Village Council's negotiations for an $18,000 bank loan to buy the lake itself, now owned by the Portage County commissioners. The commissioners bought the lake from Kent State University, which was given the lake and parcels of land by the late H. R. Loomis, prominent Ravenna attorney.

Brady Lake has a glorious—and sometimes inglorious—past. And the fine people who reside there hardly need these kinds of problems. A look into the dim pages of the past serves to put the current issues into perspective.

Brady Lake came into its heyday in 1890 when A. G. Kent of Geauga Lake purchased lakefront property, spent considerable money, and opened an amusement park. He built a dance pavilion, summer theater, bath house, miniature railroad, and a toboggan slide. Among the attractions were a 75-passenger steamer and 40 rowboats. Chester Bishop, the heartthrob of that day, made regular theater appearances. The amusement park opened in June 11, 1891, an event which was widely heralded. Several thousand turned out despite unfavorable weather. Many people reached the park by excursion trains run by the Nypano and P. & W. Railroads. At the end of the season, the park was purchased by an organization of Spiritualists who ran it for several years. They failed and sold out. They later purchased property north of the resort, which has remained as a headquarters.

Meanwhile, in 1902, W. H. Donaghy, C. M. Davis, Milton Kneifel, and Warren Lane purchased the park and reopened it as an amusement resort called Brady Lake Electric Park. They were aided by the coming of the interurban line from Akron through Kent to Ravenna. The streetcar line had come to Kent in 1895 and was extended to Ravenna in 1901.

The Brady Lake Amusement Park opened in about 1898 and remained in operation up until the late 1940s, when it deteriorated into a gambling and nightclub resort.

Karl Grismer's *History of Kent* chronicles an event that took place on July 4, 1902, at the park. A crowd of 6,000 fought madly to get on the few interurban cars which the Northern Ohio Traction Company provided. A riot ensued, one man sustained a broken leg, and some of the amusement seekers didn't reach home until almost morning.

Naturally, the amusement park sparked the development of the Brady Lake area as a vacationland. Summer cottages blossomed along the shores of the lake as people sought the pleasures of the amusement park for warm weather living. Many of those cottages today are year-round residences.

Brady Lake gained prominence for quite an unrelated reason in that period. It was the home of a large ice center. Henry Spelman and his son, Burt, ran the operation, cutting ice and storing it in a large building at the north end of the lake. Historic files today contain photographs of a fire on June 6, 1924, which destroyed the ice house as well as 19 cottages.

Brady Lake Village, encompassing areas on the south and east, was incorporated in 1927.

In the 1930s, the park was operated by the Wilson family of Ravenna. By this time, it had been upgraded with the addition of a rollercoaster and other amusement facilities. I can recall radio advertisements billing the park as "Ohio's Most Perfect Playground." Big bands and some of the most prominent entertainers of the day appeared at Brady Lake. It was there that I got my first glimpse of Rudy Vallee and the famed Cab Calloway.

In the 1940s, World War II years, a Cleveland combine reopened the amusement park, including a night club, bingo games, and an ample supply of slot machines.

The late Mayor Joe Cox, who headed the village for 20 years, ran headlong into the antigambling designs of then Gov. Frank J. Lausche. The governor removed Cox from office in the late 1940s for failure to halt the gambling, but the mayor was reelected the following election. Meanwhile, a Lausche-sponsored bill passed by the Ohio General Assembly doomed slot machines when their possession was made a felony. Mayor Cox in the early 1950s was defeated by one vote by the late Richard Lewis.

Today, the rollercoaster and the large park buildings are gone. The park area is a trailer campground operated by the Pertick family. The amusement park area stands a silent reminder of more halcyon days. But, Brady Lake's troubles, albeit a different kind, persist.

––––––

## BRADY LAKE PARK WAS OPENED A CENTURY AGO

*July 28, 1991*

A century ago this summer, Brady Lake Amusement Park was brand spanking new, and it was drawing immense crowds from throughout northeastern Ohio. Only the previous February, A. G. Kent, who previously had been the proprietor of Geauga Lake Park, had announced that he would develop a resort alongside beautiful Brady Lake. Unlike some whose plans go awry, Kent kept his promise.

Swarms of workers arrived on the 150 acres that Kent purchased or leased. They built a pavilion. Kent contracted for a switchback railroad attraction; the Donaghy brothers of Kent erected a bath house; a steamer to accommodate 75 passengers was ordered; picnic areas were developed, as was a pony track; and 40 new rowboats were placed into lake service.

On May 22, Kent announced through a *Kent Courier* article that the park would be officially opened on June 11. The tight schedule was met, to the delight of thousands who arrived by trains operated by the Nypano, C. & P., and P. & W. Railroads.

Said the *Courier* in reporting on opening day activities in its June 12, 1891, edition: "Manager A. G. Kent was a happy man yesterday. The opening was a grand success. Nearly 2,000 people were on the grounds when a heavy rain came up in the afternoon, which doubtless kept many people away who intended to go later. All the attractions, including the switchback railway, steamer, rowboats and dance hall were crowded all day." An Akron band gave a concert, and a well-known Cleveland orchestra played for dancing.

Popularity of the new park grew as word of its presence circulated throughout Ohio and western Pennsylvania. Only three weeks following the opening, a picnic arranged under the auspices of Ravenna merchants attracted 10,000 people. Proprietor Kent directed his recreational appeal to Sunday school and church groups, lodges, business people, literary clubs, and the like. He sold no alcoholic beverages and allowed none on the grounds.

Kent remained as the park's operator only that opening season. He sold out to the Spiritualist organization, which ran the park several years before running into financial troubles. The Spiritualists later bought property north of the resort where they located their national headquarters. This is the property currently in the news as a result of plans for the Crescent Woods development.

The park then was purchased by a combine which included W. H. Donaghy, C. M. Davis, Milton Kneifel, and Warren Lane, a group said to have been backed financially by the N.O.T. interurban line.

The park received its greatest impetus when the streetcar line was extended in 1901 from Kent to Ravenna via Brady Lake. The line had started service to Kent in 1895. Thousands rode the interurban from Akron and other Summit County areas directly to the park.

The huge crowds of recreation seekers were enthusiastic. Sometimes too much so. An example of their overenthusiasm occurred on July 4, 1902, when 6,000 people fought madly to board the too-few cars which the N.O.T. provided. Several fights ensued, and one man sustained a leg fracture. Some of the picnickers didn't arrive home until the wee hours of the morning.

I can recall hearing, as a youngster, radio advertising which billed the park as "Ohio's most perfect playground." At one time, many of the country's most famous bands were booked for the pleasure of dancers. Rudy Vallee, whose megaphone was his trademark as he sang his theme, "My Time Is Your Time," appeared there, as did Cab Calloway and his New York–based orchestra. No doubt many older Portage County residents can recall dancing to the music.

Under various ownerships, the park operated nearly 60 years. During the late 1940s, it became a gambling and nightclub resort, a move which proved its undoing. The park drew sharp attention from Ohio's anti-gambling governor Frank Lausche, who shut the gambling operation down. Today, the park area is a silent reminder of its glory years . . . and in another generation it likely will be of interest only to historians.

And what happened to A. G. Kent, whose vision started it all? In apparent robust health, he dropped dead on February 2, 1900, at the Masonic Hall in Kent amidst a throng of dancers.

#### PART FOUR

---

# GROUPS AND INSTITUTIONS

# ACADEMIES ONCE MET COUNTY EDUCATION NEEDS

*February 12, 1995*

Today when we think of academies, we turn to such famous names as the U.S. Military Academy at West Point, New York; the U.S. Naval Academy at Annapolis, Maryland; the U.S. Air Force Academy at Colorado Springs, Colorado; or, closer to home, the Western Reserve Academy in Hudson.

What is difficult to comprehend is that Portage County was sprinkled with academies for young students in the mid–nineteenth century. They were considered to be far superior to earlier schools, where classes were first taught in homes or in cabins with oiled-paper windows. Reading, writing, and arithmetic were the sole subjects, and at one time only the Holy Bible was available as a textbook in schools.

And qualifications for those early teachers left much to be desired. For example, back in 1836 a young man from Randolph presented himself to the Atwater teacher examining board which consisted of a minister and two unlettered farmers. He was asked three questions: "Can you repeat the Ten Commandments?" "What do you think of the temperance question?" and "What do you think of profane swearing?" Apparently the young man satisfactorily answered the trio of questions. He was issued a certificate and was hired.

Portage County's schools date back to 1803, shortly before Ohio was admitted to the union that same year. All were pretty much select schools with a group of parents teaming up to pay the meager salaries of teachers. Teacher salaries many times were in the form of farm produce or whiskey. Classes were held only during the winter months; kids were needed for work on the farm during milder months.

The Connecticut Land Company was supposed to back arrangements for education in the Western Reserve, as was the Northwest Ordinance at even an earlier time. It was not until 1825 that an Ohio law authorized local school districts and set up boards to examine qualifications of teachers and not until 1853 that Ohio passed laws to set up the framework for modern schools. Local boards were authorized to establish districts, attendance became compulsory, and superintendents were hired.

In earlier days women were not permitted as teachers (until new laws were passed), and at one time Ohio actually had laws calling for the establishment of separate schools for black children.

Local school systems progressed to the days of one-room district buildings, meager high schools that did not come along until the 1850s; then to centralization with higher-grade high schools in each community; and, still later, further centralization into the systems we now have in Portage County.

But back to the academies, or institutes as they many times were called. Because there were no public schools for the higher grades, academies met the need for education beyond the common grades.

Many Portage communities had academies—Ravenna, Kent, Windham, Nelson, Palmyra, Aurora, Randolph and Brimfield among them. Perhaps there were others. In November 1854, the Brimfield Institute announced that a new term would begin on December 4 with A. F. Butts as a principal and J. Blake as superintendent of the geography department. For the term of 11 weeks three subjects would be taught— English branches, mathematics, and foreign languages. Cost to parents, depending upon the course of study, ranged from $3 to $4.50. The committee which made the announcement consisted of William Kelso, Edward Parsons, Henry Sawyer, and Hiram Ewell, who said, "We believe the course of instruction to be sufficient, thorough, and progressive." Obviously, the later development of better public schools rendered these "pay for study" academies obsolete.

The first owner and builder of the Beebe house (the Tappan Female Institute) in Ravenna was John Hood, a man of means who eventually failed in business. The house passed to a man named Curtiss in 1840, and upon his death title of the land reverted to the Tappan family, which still held a financial interest. The institute apparently lasted only three years, after which A. M. Pease became the property owner. He was a cheese dealer who used the house both as a residence and his business. The next owner, A. M. Hazen, added the cupola, and in 1869, D. C. Coolman bought the house, made some changes, and gave it a new name, "Clinton Terrace." The next owner was William Beebe, cashier of the Second National Bank. He was the son of Horace Y. Beebe, also of Ravenna, who induced the Ohio delegation to use its vote to break a stalemate and give Abraham Lincoln the Republican nomination in the 1860 Chicago convention.

The old house also was featured on another page of history. In 1910, when Ravenna made a bid for the northeastern Ohio normal school, the Beebe property was the local committee's selected site. Today that normal school is Kent State University.

————

## HARKEN BACK TO DAYS OF ONE-ROOM SCHOOLHOUSE
### October 8, 1989

If you're old enough, you probably will remember your days in a one-room school where the teacher fired the heating stove, did the cleaning, and in time wedged between those chores imparted basic learning to all eight grades. Portage County's landscape once was dotted with such small country school buildings. Kids walked to school or later rode in horse-drawn "kid hacks." Four-year high schools were the exception rather than the rule.

Teachers called their young charges by grades to benches at the front of the room to recite their lessons as they kept a wary eye upon the conduct of the other pupils assembled in the room. Such was the educational program in Portage County even into the 1910s and early 1920s, until all one-room schools were centralized into a single building at the center of the community. Even then, in some areas students did not have the advantage of four-year high schools, and they were forced to take their final year of schooling in either Ravenna or Kent.

Seventy-five years ago, H. B. Turner, county superintendent of schools, announced the completion of a canvass of all schools in the county system. In his report, announced in the September 24, 1914, *Ravenna Republican*, he enumerated 80 school buildings in the system but said little about the academic programs that took place in them. He was either impressed or dismayed by the physical condition of the buildings, but only in rare instances did he mention that the course of study had been enhanced by the inclusion of manual training, domestic science, games, and recreation. There was no mention of the more solid subjects—English, mathematics, languages, or history.

His stated objective of the survey was high-sounding, but his conclusions offered little substance. He said the canvass provided "a working basis for better buildings and better teaching and commanded the county to assess needs and to realize the power of the educational unit." He did, however, encourage continuing centralization of schools.

Turner did have some nice things to say about certain of the 21 school districts he surveyed. For example, he noted a new trend in the schools of the Charlestown district, the innovation that children were being furnished with individual drinking cups and towels. No more water pails, dippers, or collapsible drinking cups which many pupils carried! And no community towels. He also noted that the Charlestown district was providing free textbooks to the pupils. All students today, by law, are furnished with free textbooks. This was not true at one time. In my youth, parents were provided a list of necessary textbooks and they had to buy them, usually at a general store that had been designated as an outlet.

In the Turner report, Aurora schools received a special mention for their progressive spirit and for their then recent completion of a new brick and stone building. Incidentally, Aurora schools, centralized in 1897, were the first of the Portage County schools to do so. Brimfield High School was lauded in the Turner report as the only school in the county to display photographs of graduating classes on the wall. And in the Rootstown system, which then included a two-room building at New Milford, it was noted that the schools had designated plots to test chemical treatment of farmland and to test experimental wheat crops.

Seventy-five years ago, approximately 3,200 children were attending schools in the county system, which did not include Kent and Ravenna schools. There were 18 high schools in the 21 districts, and several districts, including Paris, were praised for raising their high schools from third to second class. Ravenna Township in 1914 boasted the highest school enrollment, 243 pupils in 10 buildings. The report urged centralization, a move that began the following year. Franklin at that time had five one-room schools. Brady Lake School was termed a "model school," a designation resulting from its affiliation with the Kent Normal School, today's KSU. Centralization of Franklin's schools was not completed until 1920, when the present Franklin building was erected. The report enumerated the school population, district by district. Almost unbelievably, Hiram Township had a school at Hiram Rapids with only 12 pupils.

The 20 high schools of 1914, which included Kent and Ravenna, have been reduced to 11 present high schools as a result of consolidations in the 1950s and 1960s, when the Field, Garfield, Crestwood, Southeast, and Waterloo districts were organized. Rootstown remains a separate district, and Windham is an exempted village district. Kent, Ravenna, Aurora, and Streetsboro are city districts. All of these districts, plus the Maplewood Joint Vocational School District, comprise Portage County's elementary and secondary system.

During the county's pioneer days, teachers boarded around at patrons' homes, and many times their meager stipend was paid in whiskey or farm produce. Those teachers could not have envisioned the present extensive school curriculum and our modern school facilities. Nor teachers' salaries!

———

## EDUCATION HAS HAD TOP PRIORITY
## IN PORTAGE COUNTY
*November 19, 1983*

Education, from the earliest beginnings of Portage County, always has had a high priority. Aurora and Ravenna had schools (located in log houses) in 1803, the same year the state of Ohio was admitted to the union. Ravenna's first school began in a log house at what is now Ryedale, the Riddle family complex east of the city. Nelson opened its first school in 1804, also in a log cabin, and Mantua's schools date back to 1806. The bell with which Nelson's first teacher, Hannah Baldwin, summoned her children to classes remains with us today—in the trophy case at James A. Garfield High School in Garrettsville.

Granted, the first of Portage County's schools would be considered crude by today's standards. The first buildings had oil-paper windows and open fireplaces to provide heat. The early settlers, who had come from Connecticut and Massachusetts to find a new life in the Western Reserve wilderness, were concerned mainly with providing a working knowledge of reading, writing, and arithmetic for their children. The Bible was the chief textbook.

When the state of Connecticut sold its Western Reserve holdings to the Connecticut Land Company, a move that heralded the settlement of the area we now call home, education was among the considerations. Some of the land was reserved as "school lands," which later were sold to raise funds for school support. The state of Ohio in 1825 passed legislation to provide for school districts, and then in 1853 laws set up local boards of education and superintendent positions.

Many areas of the county established academies. One of the earliest was in Nelson Township in 1833. It was a private institution, supported by popular subscriptions. The academy apparently went out of business in 1876, inasmuch as its last minutes are dated in that year. The building later became the home of Nelson's first high school.

Educationally, Portage County has come a long way since those early schools. Today, we have consolidated and city districts, plus Maplewood Vocational School, offering a wide variety of subject matter. Modern school buses have replaced the horse-drawn "kid hacks" of the early 1900s.

Portage County is educationally unique. The county is one of the few among Ohio's 88 counties that can boast three higher education institutions of national stature. Hiram College, founded in 1850 as Western Reserve Eclectic Institute, holds a distinguished position among the nation's arts and sciences colleges. James A. Garfield, who as a boy worked on the P. & O. Canal, which traversed through Portage County, was one of its earliest students.

He showed such scholastic promise that he was made an assistant teacher at Hiram in those early days. He entered Williams College in Massachusetts in his junior year, graduated in 1856, and returned to Hiram as a teacher. He was 28-year-old principal of Hiram when he was nominated in 1859 in the Town Hall in Kent (then Franklin Mills) for his first political office—state senator. The Civil War cut short his senatorial service and he served with distinction, rising to the rank of major general.

He became a U.S. senator and then went to the 1880 Republican convention in Chicago as campaign manager for another candidate. As a result of a deadlock, the convention turned to him as the GOP candidate. He was elected president in 1880, was shot by an assassin in July of 1881, and died in September. He was serving as a Hiram trustee at the time of his death.

James A. Garfield, although born in Orange in Cuyahoga County, truly was the "president from Portage." He spent most of his years in Hiram, married Lucretia Rudolph, a Hiram girl, and raised his family there. He is said to have been our country's most scholarly president.

What is now Kent State University came much later—in 1910, when the Ohio General Assembly approved a bill creating normal schools for northeast and northwest Ohio. Kent was selected as the site for the northeast school, which today is a major university with nearly 20,000 students. Also, there is the Northeastern Ohio Universities College of Medicine, in Rootstown.

Not even the sketchiest history of education in Portage County could pass mention of Orville Nelson Hartshorn. Hartshorn was born on August 20, 1823, on a farm located on Prentiss Road in Nelson Township, the eldest son among five children of Norris and Asenath Hartshorn who had come from Connecticut to seek a better life in the untamed Portage wilderness. Hartshorn, at only 23, became the founder and first president of Mount Union College in Alliance in 1846. Mount Union long has held a place of high regard among Ohio's private colleges.

In 1923, the 100th anniversary of Hartshorn's birth, Mount Union erected a monument in his honor on the old Hartshorn farm in Nelson. It was created from boulders collected around the farm and bore two bronze plaques, one depicting the seal of Mount Union and the other displaying his motto, "Take a square view, trust God, then act, leaving to Him the consequences." Like too many edifices in today's world, the monument to this visionary and dedicated educator has been vandalized in recent years.

Alliance, a community particularly familiar to residents of southern Portage County, is known as the "Carnation City." How the city achieved that name is an interesting story. Back in 1876, Dr. Levi L. Lamham was the Democratic candidate for Congress. William McKinley of Canton was his opponent. During the hotly contested campaign, Lamham gave McKinley a red carnation for his lapel. McKinley won the election and ever thereafter he wore a red carnation as a symbol of good luck. Apparently, it worked, guiding his political fortunes to the White House. In 1904, following President McKinley's assassination, the Ohio General Assembly passed legislation to make the red carnation Ohio's state flower in memory of the martyred president. The course of history sometimes takes strange and interesting turns!

------

## OBJECTIONS DOOMED ATWATER
## AS COLLEGE TOWN

*October 6, 1991*

During the course of Portage County history, several abortive attempts have been made to establish institutions of higher learning. Despite those attempts, Portage today has the distinction of having three such institutions, two public, one private.

One of the most notable of those abortive attempts occurred in Atwater Township shortly prior to the mid-1850s. Atwater at that time was the home of Linnian Academy, which was located on the village green, a wide piece of public land laid out by Capt. Caleb Atwater at what we today refer to as Atwater Center. This space of land was 65 feet wide and extended from the Center south to the cemetery. This land belongs to the township, and all private properties are located back of this line, affording a fine piece of public greenery.

Orville Nelson Hartshorn was a student at the Linnian Academy, which prompted him in later years to view Atwater as a fine community in which to establish a college. Apparently a group of women in the Atwater community objected to his proposal, and his vision to found a college there never materialized. Hartshorn, born in a home on Prentiss Road in Nelson Township in northeastern Portage County, moved his proposal a few miles south into the Alliance area. He chose that section of the Alliance community known as Mount Union for his college, and that's how Mount Union College, one of Ohio's most distinctive private colleges, came into being in 1846 with Hartshorn as its first president.

In 1923, on the 100th anniversary of his birth, Mount Union College dedicated a memorial to Hartshorn in Nelson Township. Then President W. H. McMaster presided at the dedication ceremony. The monument was constructed of boulders picked up on the Hartshorn farm. One of the monument's two bronze plaques was inscribed with Hartshorn's favorite motto, "Take a square view, trust God, then act, leaving to Him the consequences."

One never knows at the time what effect opinion will have in future years. Had there not been objections, Atwater today probably would have been the location of a major private college.

Another abortive college attempt took place in Kent in 1869–1870. At that time, the Universalists of Ohio were considering northeastern Ohio locations for a college to represent their denomination. One of the prime movers was John R. Buchtel, well known in Kent because he attended the Kent Universalist Church. At that time, there was no Universalist Church in Akron, where he resided.

Marvin Kent was the chief negotiator for the Kent forces. He and Buchtel signed an agreement under which Kent would be the new college's location. Such was not to be. A few days later, Kent announced that the deal was off; Buchtel had offered $100,000 if the college were located in Akron. It was. That was the beginning of Buchtel College, today's University of Akron, now a state institution of higher learning.

In later years, Raymond Manchester, onetime Kent State University dean of men and math professor, had another version for Buchtel's change of heart on the new college's location. Manchester was one to smell a promotion a mile away. He latched on to the fable that Buchtel had become so incensed when his buggy became stuck in the mud in Kent that he changed the location of his proposed college. Hence, the Buchtel buggy-wheel trophy would go to the winner of the KSU–Akron University football game, a gimmick Manchester, onetime Kent mayor and state representative, promoted to the hilt, always with an all-knowing smile.

And then there was another abortive college location scramble. Ravenna in 1910 was in the intense scramble among northeastern Ohio locations for the proposed normal school. The old Beebe homestead at the corner of Clinton and Lafayette was the Ravenna site. Supposedly, the Ravenna committee was left waiting for hours for the state selection committee. Members of the committee were detained by Kent backers at the famous bluegill and cider lunch at Twin Lakes, and due to the lateness of the hour, they gave only cursory inspection to the Ravenna site. A few days later, word came from Columbus that Kent had been selected as the site for the new normal school, today's Kent State University.

Portage, by no stretch of the imagination a metropolitan county, rightfully can boast that it is the home of three higher education institutions. Kent State; Hiram College, founded as Western Reserve Eclectic Institute in 1850; and the Northeastern Ohio Universities College of Medicine in Rootstown comprise this educational trinity.

---

## RED CARPET WELCOME (AND BLUEGILLS)
## PAID OFF FOR KENT

*September 21, 1985*

September 27, 1910, was an important day in Kent history. The town had been spruced up as never before. Weeds had been cut. Streets had been scrubbed. Rubbish piles had been hauled away. All of these preparations had taken place to welcome into the village the five members of the Ohio site selection commission charged with the responsibility of recommending a location for a new state normal school.

During sunny hours the town would have glistened. On Tuesday morning, September 27, the reverse was true. On that day the village was blanketed in fog, and a steady drizzle hardly made the town an attractive one. The spirit of the people, buoyed by the impending visit of commission members, sagged with the inclement weather.

Members of the Kent Board of Trade, intent upon granting a fine welcome to the visitors, took up their posts on roads leading from Wadsworth, where commission members had visited the day before. Confident that the visitors would arrive by automobile, Kent officials waited to escort them. At 11 o'clock that morning, Postmaster W. W. Reed, secretary of the Board of Trade, spotted five strangers standing near the Erie Depot. A quick inquiry revealed them to be the commission visitors. They had left their cars in Wadsworth and had come to Kent by train.

Quickly, cars were rounded up. Boots were acquired at Coe Livingston's store, and the commission members and Board of Trade guides set out to trek two potential sites—the Engelhart farm in southwest Kent and the William S. Kent farm, south of East Main Street and east of Lincoln Street. The Kent farm of 52.89 acres which had been offered as a site for the new normal school was overgrown with briars. On a clear day the state visitors would have had a magnificent view of the town from the hilltop of the Kent farm. The impenetrable fog on that day ruled otherwise.

The disconsolate Board of Trade members thought all was lost. The commission members were due in Ravenna at noon to inspect the Beebe site, which had been proposed by the county seat committee. Damp, chilled, and hungry, the commissioners were set to leave when it was proposed by the Kent committee that they have lunch "on the way." They agreed. "On the road to Ravenna" turned out to be the Frank Merrill home at Twin Lakes where a sumptuous lunch awaited. The commission members gorged themselves on freshly caught bluegills from East Twin Lake and fried chicken, all washed down by generous servings of hard cider. Thoughts of time evaporated during the lunch, and it was after 3:30 P.M. when they finally left for Ravenna, where they had been anticipated by noontime.

Perhaps the Kent Board of Trade had scored a coup. Who can determine, after 75 years, the state of mind of the five commission members? Yet, there were those during the passing years who firmly believed that the bluegill dinner evoked more than passing appreciation from commission members and exerted a powerful influence upon the selection process. The fact that David Ladd Rockwell, one of the influential members of the Kent committee, had been a lieutenant governor candidate on the same ticket with Gov. Judson Harmon probably did not detract from Kent's chances for the new school.

The commission returned to Kent—unannounced—on November 11 and 12, and on November 25 unofficial dispatches from Columbus reported the good news that Kent had, indeed, won the location of the new northeastern Ohio normal school, a report that was confirmed on December 1 when Governor Harmon made the official announcement.

The announcement culminated a long and arduous campaign on the part of the Kent Board of Trade (today's Kent Area Chamber of Commerce) and others in the community. Only the preceding February, the Board of Trade had been organized to rally the community in a campaign to rebuild the Seneca Chain Company, then located at the present site of the Forest City enterprise, following a disastrous fire the preceding December. Kent townspeople oversubscribed a stock offering, and Seneca Chain eventually was rebuilt.

Martin L. Davey, then only 25, had presided at the organization sessions of the Kent board. John Wells of the Williams Brothers Mill was elected president; W. W. Reed, secretary; and George W. Hinds, treasurer. The board officially adopted the slogan "Kent, Home of Hump and Hustle," following a contest won by Ralph Heighton.

It was John Paxton, *Kent Courier* editor, noting the passage of the Lowry Bill by the Ohio General Assembly, who challenged the Board of Trade to campaign for the normal school. Kent's application, prepared by then County Prosecutor Duncan Wolcott, was submitted in July 1910, and on September 8, a delegation including Wolcott, Rockwell, William S. Kent, Davey, and school superintendent William A. Walls presented Kent's advantages during a hearing in Columbus.

Seventeen communities vied for the normal school site. Today, four of them—Canton, East Liverpool, Warren, and Ashtabula—are locations of Kent State University regional campuses.

There were several stipulations required of the Kent community to ensure the coming of the normal school: Funds must be publicly subscribed to finance the purchase of the Sawyer and Meyer properties on East Summit Street to add to Kent's donation of 52.89 acres. The community must guarantee 250 students for a training school. East Main Street must be paved. The community quickly raised $13,200 for the land purchases, and the other conditions were met with ease.

Editor Paxton, pleased that his challenge had met with success, had a field day with *Kent Courier* announcement stories. In a late November edition, he wrote: "Santa came early for Kent; that Normal just fits our sock." Seventy-five years later, it still fits, except that the "normal" has developed far beyond the dreams of that small band of community leaders who campaigned to achieve it. That normal school is today's Kent State University, one of the nation's leading higher education institutions, with 20,000 students, a faculty of 800, a campus with 1,200 acres and 100 buildings, and extensive curriculum offerings. And now, with the opening this coming week of the School of Fashion Design and Merchandising and the Kent State University Museum, another dimension is being added to the dream which began so many years ago.

## MERRILL HALL WAS THE FIRST
## BUILDING ON CAMPUS

*May 9, 1987*

President William Howard Taft and former President Theodore Roosevelt had visited Kent in a heated campaign for delegates in the Ohio Republican primary election. Even such important events in June 1912 did not dissuade the attention of area residents from "Normal Hill," the site of the new normal school that the town of Kent had won in a bitter contest two years previously.

On June 18, 1912, Kent had gone "all out" to make historic note of its elation that the normal school would, at long last, become a reality. Every store in the community closed at 10 A.M. The streets were draped in colorful bunting, Phillip R. Shriver wrote in *Years of Youth*, published in 1960 in observance of Kent State's semicentennial.

Post's band led a procession of automobiles, bicycles, and marchers on East Main Street to the Kent farm, a 52.89-acre tract whose contribution by William S. Kent had clinched state officials' decision to locate the new northeastern Ohio normal school in Kent. The parade ended atop the Kent farm hill, where awaited a group of dignitaries on a specially erected platform.

That day so long ago marked the laying of the cornerstone for Merrill Hall, first building on the infant campus that today is the massive, multifaceted Kent State University, one of the Midwest's largest and most comprehensive institutions of higher learning.

Only in recent days, the first board of trustees had taken official action to name the new institution Kent Normal School in honor of William S. Kent, whose contribution of the campus site won for him a "solid
silver" loving cup, a gift authorized by the trustees.

Merrill Hall has served the university as an administration building,
first library, training school, and classroom building. The hall, with its
tall pillars, dominates the original circle of buildings on the beautiful
front campus.

Edwin F. Moulton, representing that first board of trustees and for
whom Moulton Hall is named, stepped forward to introduce President
John E. McGilvrey as "the man who has the ability to make this school
the finest in the world." McGilvrey delivered the principal address, out-
lining his educational philosophy and declaring that "This normal school
should send into the schools each year an average of 200 teachers." As
he concluded, a light rain began to fall . . . a rain described by President
McGilvrey as a baptism of the infant school.

Frank Merrill, superintendent of schools in Ravenna and a descendant of the Haymaker family, Kent's founders, stepped forward to lay
the cornerstone. Before he drove the stone into place, Merrill inserted a
copper box containing photographs of the trustees, the commission on
normal school sites, Marvin S. Kent, William S. Kent, President
McGilvrey, and 50 views of Kent village and its surrounding area. Also
among the cornerstone items were a brief filed by the Kent Board of
Trade, the prime mover of the campaign to obtain the school for Kent;
a report of the commission to the governor; a list of subscribers to the
normal school fund; a copy of the enabling Lowry Bill; and minutes
from that first board of trustees' meetings. With a final blow of the mal-
let, Merrill sent the cornerstone into its final resting place, where it
reposes to this day.

Next month, we will celebrate the 75th anniversary of that cornerstone laying, an event which heralded what Kent State University has
become in its relatively brief history. Phil Shriver wrote 27 years ago:
"The rains of a thousand storms have pounded against this foundation
stone, which supports to this day the massive westernmost pillar of Merrill
Hall. Twined about it is the ivy planted by McGilvrey while its contents
remain safely shielded within."

# NORMAL SCHOOL OPENING IS
# KENT'S TURNING POINT

*May 15, 1988*

Mid-May of 1913! Conditions were ideal for the robust business climate. The very first classes began at the new Kent Normal School on May 19. The promise of a regeneration of the economic spirit in Kent inspired a boom in the sale of building lots, construction of homes, and lusty business at the community's retail stores and manufacturing or service firms. What would it have been like living here 75 years ago? The mid-May files of the old *Kent Courier* and the *Ravenna Republican* offer a fairly complete slice of the business and social scene of that day.

Spurred by the opening of the normal school, building lots in Pleasant View Allotment in Kent (that's the Crain-Willow-Columbus and Highland area) were selling from $125 to $350, payable on a plan of $5 to $10 down with monthly payments of $2 to $7. The plan called for no interest, and payments were forgiven during periods of illness.

The City Garage in Ravenna was offering a brand new Studebaker for $1,050, and Harper Brothers' store was selling men's suits from $7.25 to $17.50. Heriff's store in Kent was suggesting Bavarian china as an ideal gift for graduates, and another Kent store, Straight and Company, advertised wallpaper at 25 cents for a double roll and rugs from 25 cents to $20.

Ohio governor James Cox addressed the Kent Board of Trade at its third banquet, the first such affair held at the Normal's Lowry Hall. Brady Lake Park planned its Memorial Day opening with band concerts, two performances of *The Girl from Out Yonder* each day in its theater, and a high-wire act featuring a "human" elephant. Silver Lake Park did likewise, offering "aeroplane" and hydroplane rides and its new lake steamer, the *Chautauqua*. An Indian and vaudeville show was staged at the corner of West Main and River Streets in Kent. Reflecting the dominance of the railroad business, the *Courier* traced the comings and goings along Kent's three railroads in a weekly column headed "Track and Train."

It was commencement time at area high schools and at the White Hospital School of Nursing in Ravenna, where seven young women received their caps.

Forty-seven students arrived for that first summer session at the Normal School in 1913. Going to college in those days was a good financial deal—tuition was free, rooms in Lowry Hall went for $1.25 per week, and dorm residents received a weekly meal ticket (good for 21 meals) for $3. After high promotion on the part of President John E. McGilvrey, 290 students arrived for the second summer session.

The new Normal School was properly launched and everyone was enthused with its pronounced economic effect, so much so that John R. Burns, a realtor of that period, took it upon himself to conduct a survey of Kent business and service firms. His glowing report in the *Courier* would score with any chamber of commerce. Almost without exception, Burns, whom I remember as a jaunty Irishman with a quick wit and an opinion on almost all matters, learned from his survey that companies and smaller businesses were lavish in their praise of the economic climate. For example, plumber J. A. Harris, who employed five men, said he was "too busy to eat." Homebuilders Ed Lutz, F. A. Coffeen, M. M. Corl, and Fred Green were in a real frenzy as they sought to complete new houses. Naturally, lumber firms Beal and Parsons were enjoying lush business as they supplied materials for new homes.

The Erie yards and roundhouse employed 100 men and still needed more, while the Erie shops (builder and repairer of railroad cars) had a crew of 450 and needed 100 more. A similar story was reported by the infant Davey Tree Expert Company, which employed 150 and planned to increase its staff to 200 to meet work demands. The Falls Rivet and Machine Company, predecessor of the Lamson and Sessions Company, today's R.B.&W., voiced bright prospects for business and reported employment of 125. The Kent Telephone Company had a staff of 14 women and four men, and the Kent Water and Light Company reported employment of 18. Another utility, the East Ohio Gas Company, reported a crew of three and a need for four more.

House painters were among the busiest in town as new homes went up. F. Jacobs and Company was wondering how it was going to complete 40 promised jobs with its crew of seven, which needed to be expanded by at least five. The Miller Keyless Lock Company, maker of combination door locks, many of which still grace older area homes, with its crew of six, had difficulty keeping up with orders. Even a Dr. Raub was feeling the effects of the developing economy. He planned to expand his fence post business. And so, on and on went the Burns survey and its cheering responses. Only the Williams Brothers Mill, then with an employment of 25, reported a dull time. This was natural—May is not the wheat season.

Some of the surveyed businesses many years ago passed out of existence. The Erie yards, shop, and roundhouse are gone, as is much of the railroad business. Others are familiar and still in business, some of them on a much-expanded scale. Seventy-five years have wrought many changes. One thing appears certain—75 years hence will bring many more. And people probably will be talking about the "good old days" of 1988.

------

## OVERLOOKED LANDMARK TRIBUTE
## TO EARLY KSU EDUCATOR

*July 20, 1985*

For many people in whose names public landmarks and memorials are dedicated, fame is a fleeting thing. A case in point: Each day thousands of motorists pass in front of the May H. Prentice Memorial Gateway at the intersection of East Main and South Lincoln Streets in Kent. Few of them know or would even care who May Prentice was or why she should have a gateway named in her honor. That thought was inspired by the current maintenance work on the gateway being performed by Kent State University masons.

May H. Prentice really was a remarkable woman. She was the first female faculty member at Kent State, arriving in 1912 at the behest of the university's first president, John E. McGilvrey. Actually she was the second faculty member to arrive at the new normal school, coming only a short while following George E. Marker, who later terminated his KSU association to found the Commercial Press, a printing firm, in Kent.

Miss Prentice first taught extension courses, and later she became director of teacher training and also elementary training. Thousands of students came to know her and to love her for her patient guidance, understanding, and democratic spirit. She came from Macomb, Illinois, where she had received her educational training at Macomb Illinois State Normal School. When she arrived in Kent in the fall of 1912, there were only four houses on East Main Street east of Lincoln Street—three on the north side and a small cottage on the south side. Houses at that time were renting in Kent for $12 to $15 per month. Miss Prentice retired in 1930 after continuous service on the faculty from 1912 and in teaching since 1873. Beginning in 1928 and extending through 1934, graduating classes contributed funds to finance the memorial gateway.

On March 12, 1934, the university's board of trustees voted to change the name of the William A. Cluff Training School to the John E. McGilvrey Training School in honor of the first president and to name the memorial gateway marking the entrance to the college campus (already built), the May H. Prentice Memorial Gateway, subject to the consent of both educators. McGilvrey deferred on the basis that he deemed it inappropriate, inasmuch as Cluff had been one of the trustees who caused his dismissal and such action probably would bring unfavorable publicity to the campus. He was to wait until 1938 to have a building named for him, when the new science structure (now undergoing renovation) became McGilvrey Hall. In typically modest fashion, Miss Prentice accepted the honor, at the same time expressing the opinion that it was difficult to justify her name on the archway. Donors of funds to build the gateway, who remembered Miss Prentice with affection, were thrilled by the designation. (She was to be honored again in 1959 when Prentice Hall, a residence hall, was named for her.)

On January 15, 1935, the May H. Prentice Memorial Gateway was dedicated. Thousands of words were spoken that day as a compliment to Miss Prentice and her affection for the infant university. I well recall the day; as a member of the men's glee club, the dedication ceremonies constituted a command performance. Miss Prentice, who had written the song "Climbing the Hill to Kent," which we sang that day, was not in attendance at the ceremonies. In frail health, she remained at home and her words of appreciation were read: "I like to think of the thousands of homecomers, new students, visitors and friends who will pass through it." She described the gateway as a "fitting symbol of this college as an entrance into the larger life." How prophetic were her words! Three weeks later she passed away, entering a larger life at 79.

--------

## IT'S BEEN FIFTY YEARS SINCE KSU
## PICKED BOWMAN

*January 30, 1994*

At 18 years of age, with only a high school diploma and armed with a teacher's certificate after passing an examination, George Arvene Bowman arrived at a rural school in Morrow County to begin his career in education. He had been working at a general store while unsuccessfully seeking a teacher's position. Finally, he received a call inviting him to teach at the rural school "because we can't find anyone else." That was the last time George Bowman ever sought a job; from that year on people always sought him out.

A lesser man might have despaired when he saw the condition of that first country school building. But young George Bowman grabbed a broom and cleaned up the schoolroom, which bore the obvious signs of having had chickens as its chief tenants during the previous summer months. In that sparse building he greeted 23 students extending from the first through eighth grades. That was the humble beginning of George Bowman, which carried him to other teaching assignments, principal ships, and four superintendencies prior to a 19-year, illustrious span as president of Kent State University, the longest tenure of any KSU president. Despite his ultimate successes, George Bowman always said the greatest compliment anyone could receive would be to be considered a great teacher, a lofty status he denied.

George Bowman died in 1976 after 13 years of retirement. But his love for Kent State University and his years of achievement as its head have become legendary. That's why so long following his tenure we remember him on the 50th anniversary of his acceptance of the KSU presidency.

It was in August 1943 that KSU trustees Bob Dix and Joseph B. Hanan went to Youngstown, where Bowman was superintendent of schools, to approach him about the KSU presidency, then vacant following the resignation of Karl Leebrick to enter military service. Bowman expressed little interest and said he had many programs in Youngstown he needed to see to completion and that he could not come for six months "if I come at all." Apparently Dix and Hanan took that for a "yes," and on January 24, 1944, Bowman was announced as the fifth KSU president. He arrived on the job the following July 1. From that date on George Bowman and his wife, Edith, also a teacher, whom he married in Zanesville in 1923, began a love affair with Kent State University that spanned his presidency and many years thereafter. He literally lived at KSU 24 hours a day, with true support and like feelings from his helpmate.

George Bowman came at a good time. As Dr. Phillip Shriver, former KSU dean, president of Miami University, and Bowman biographer, wrote: "Under his leadership a new era of progress would emerge. He 'lived' the university 24 hours a day so that stability and stature might come to an institution whose youth had been beset with so many un-happy episodes." In his inaugural address, Dr. Bowman observed, "We have not come to take anybody's place. We have come to make a place for ourselves." He made KSU a good place.

When he came to the university, he found 14 buildings, some of them in disrepair. When he retired in 1963, there were 41 on a campus which had expanded from 105 acres to 556. In 1944, there were 114 teachers, of whom 26 were still in the military in World War II. When he left there were 628, all but 48 of whom had been hired during his tenure. Wracked by an absence of young men, who were in the service, campus enrollment was 891 in 1944. When he retired, enrollment neared 15,000. Dr. Bowman was a man dedicated to the development of human re-sources. Indeed, during the university's semicentennial in 1960 that was the celebration's slogan.

But George Bowman's success as KSU president should not be mea-sured only in bricks and mortar. He developed many academic programs to meet the demands of the hordes of students which followed the end of World War II. His additions to the areas of curriculum and services were many and meaningful. New doctoral programs were added in many disciplines; the College of Fine and Professional Arts came into being, as did the Honors College and a 10-unit regional campus system; the library was expanded; the athletic program was upgraded.

A tall, stately person, Dr. Bowman might have been considered austere at first meeting. He was not; he had a keen sense of humor and a contagious attraction to others.

Following his retirement, the Bowmans moved from the East Main Street president's home to one the couple built on Overlook Drive across the street. They considered the location a real plus; they could still be closely associated with the campus they loved and for which they worked so tirelessly for so many years. A man with almost an uncanny memory, President Bowman could greet many students and alumni by name. He cherished and remembered them. And now, so many years later, those who were privileged to know him remember and cherish his memory.

---

## "AKRENT U" PROPOSAL NOT FIRST
## THREAT TO KENT

*November 27, 1982*

The bombshell proposal of Gov. James A. Rhodes to merge Kent State University and the University of Akron is reminiscent of another battle on the Ohio higher education scene nearly a half-century ago during which Kent State figured prominently.

That tempest was spawned by a proposal advanced by the welfare section of the Ohio House of Representatives finance committee calling for conversion of one of Ohio's teacher training institutions (Kent State University, Ohio University, Bowling Green State University, or Miami University) into a state hospital for the mentally ill. The year was 1933, and the date was April 28. I was a Kent State freshman, and the nation was in the depths of the Depression. The student registration fee of $20 per quarter was symbolic of the difficult economic times.

I have vivid recollections of the frenzy precipitated by the legislative proposal. It was reasoned that Ohio's public schools were saturated with 4,000 unemployed teachers and that the state's mental institutions were in a deplorable state. The legislative committee viewed conversion of one of the state teacher training colleges as the easiest way to solve the dilemma. After all, the colleges had buildings to house patients and ideal facilities.

State representative William R. Foss, chairman of the welfare section, told the *Evening Record* and *Daily Courier-Tribune* (the *Record-Courier*'s predecessor) that "We're not bluffing. Our plan, we believe, is feasible. We intend to investigate this proposition fully and to determine which college can most readily be converted."

With that, Foss set up an inspection tour by his committee of the four schools. Kent State's visit was designated for May 4 (a date that was destined to become historically significant for Kent State 37 years later). Phillip R. Shriver's book, *Years of Youth*, written to commemorate Kent State's semicentennial in 1960, said "the news struck Kent like a bombshell." Indeed, it did.

The Kiwanis Club mobilized community organizations in northeast Ohio into a force to prevent the conversion of Kent State College into an insane asylum. Postmaster W. W. Reed, president of the Kent Chamber of Commerce, assumed the committee chairmanship. (Mr. Reed 23 years earlier was chairman of the community committee to bring Kent State to Kent.) He appointed Martin L. Davey, Attorney Blake C. Cook (father of Judge Robert Cook), and H. G. Taylor, treasurer of the Twin Coach Company, to meet with students, faculty, and administration to map strategy to oppose the asylum move.

Their efforts culminated in a college assembly on May 1 of that year. I remember the assembly as a heated affair with more than 1,200 students and faculty crowded into the university auditorium. Mr. Davey, one of the speakers, exclaimed, "I might be tempted to run for governor again to kill the damn thing." (He did run in 1934 and was elected.) Names and addresses of legislators and then governor George White were furnished to the crowd. Protesting letters by the thousands found their way to Columbus. Area newspapers and community organizations voiced their opposition. Our own newspaper suggested that "Nutwood, Ohio would be a more ideal place," and the *Akron Times-Press* appropriately labeled the idea as "imbecilic."

Students, despite concern for the future of their school, had a field day with tongue-in-cheek references to Kent State as "Nut U.," "Looney

Bin College," and other uncomplimentary designations. President James O. Engleman was not taken with such humor. He viewed Ohio University and Miami as safe because of their ages and thus thought the axe would fall on Kent or Bowling Green.

The Kent committee's fortunes took a turn for the worse when the Foss committee, after its May 4 visit, reported to the legislature that Kent State was "so adapted to welfare needs that it would be difficult to distinguish it from those built for that specific purpose." For Kent State supporters, that statement spelled real danger for the future of their beloved college. Chairman Reed called for a statewide protest, which elicited a thunderous response from northeastern Ohio organizations.

Then, the Kent State Board of Trustees approved a resolution which expressed the opinion that "neither the Ohio General Assembly or Governor White will take steps which would abolish or seriously impair this institution." With that, the trustees asked that no further protest be voiced. The resolution, plus word from Columbus that Bowling Green most likely would be the college sacrificed, brought an end to the Kent campaign. Chairman Reed asked that support be thrown to the "Save Bowling Green" forces. Then opposition to the sacrifice of any college solidified in the legislature, and the entire proposal was scrapped.

Kent State was spared to live another day . . . to become a university in 1935 and to grow into one of Ohio's major institutions of higher education. And to become, once again, the target of a shift in fortunes through Governor Rhodes's merger proposal.

———

## STATE CHAMPION KENT SQUAD WAS THE TOAST OF THE TOWN

### Kent State High Basketball Team

### Netted State Crown 67 Years Ago

*March 20, 1994*

"March Madness" has begun. That's a term usually applied to the NCAA college basketball tournaments which kicked off this week. But "March

Madness" also appropriately can describe the current round of high school basketball tournaments which will culminate beginning March 24 with the state championship tournament in Columbus.

I seldom write about sports in this historical column, leaving such pleasures to more skilled writers in the sports department. But I am a basketball fan and have attended the state tournament for at least 35 years. To my mind, the state tournament is one of the most exciting capstones in the prep athletic arena.

My interest in the state tournament was sparked in 1954, when Theodore Roosevelt's Rough Riders lost their first game to a Columbus team when the tourney was played in Cleveland. The Riders made out better in 1957, when Charlie Boykin and company won their first game and then took on the famed Jerry Lucas and his Middletown teammates. After a hard fight, the Riders lost the championship game to the perennial state champs.

This column, however, concerns the only Portage County team ever to take a state championship in basketball. It happened 67 years ago this month, when Kent State High School won the Class B title by defeating Oberlin by the low score of 20–16 after taking its semifinal game against Hillsboro Marshall 20–18.

There were reasons for the low basketball scores during those years. After each basket the ball was returned to the court's center ring for a jump. And guards didn't shoot as much, concentrating on blocking shots of opposing players. In addition, jump shots and one-handed shots were taboo. Players shot with both hands on the ball positioned at knee or waist height. Run-and-gun basketball was unknown in those days.

Many younger residents may not be aware that Kent State University for many years included a training school attended by students from kindergarten through the twelfth grade. Besides a regular staff of supervising teachers, the University School provided training for student teachers. The high school was the first to close, with the elementary school following soon thereafter.

But back to Kent State High School's place in the basketball sun. The Blue Devils, as State High teams were known, defeated East Liverpool 25–19 and Bedford 38–20 in the regional tournament held at Goodyear gym in Akron to win a trip to Columbus. Probably few fans held out hope for a state championship, because Oberlin had won the Class B title the previous year and its team was heavy with returning players.

Members of the State High 1927 team were Clay Johnson, right forward; Lowell Van Deusen, left forward; Wilbert Manes, center; Dick Mercer, right guard; and Dan VeNard, left guard. In the championship game Johnson and Mercer each scored eight points with Van Deusen adding four. Manes and VeNard went scoreless. Glenn Francis was the Kent State High coach, with Frank Harsh as faculty manager and Louis Warner as manager. Francis, who became a well-known coach, was a student teacher that year, and Harsh, who later became principal, had served as coach. Substitute players were Lowell Kilbourne, Vernon McHenry, and Alex Ludick.

For a firsthand report on the excitement surrounding State High's success so many years ago, I talked several days ago with a longtime friend, Lowell Van Deusen, a member of that famous team. Eighty-four and retired, he formerly served as an assistant principal of a junior high school in Shaker Heights. His wife, the former Alice Sturgill of Kent, retired as a Shaker Heights junior high principal. Both are KSU graduates. Van Deusen is the son of Clinton S. Van Deusen, onetime head of industrial arts at KSU for whom Van Deusen Hall is named.

"It was really something," said Van Deusen, whose sharp recollections add interesting sidelights to that athletic achievement so many years ago. The tournament was played at the Columbus fairgrounds, there being no good basketball courts such as the present St. John Arena on the OSU campus. Van Deusen said the facility was quite spartan; four corner furnaces provided heat in the gym.

Two team members, cousins VeNard and Mercer, were not Kent natives. Their aunt, a teacher here, wanted them to have a good education, so she brought them here from their native Illinois. Mercer went on to Lombard College, and VeNard became a professor at Knox College in Illinois. Johnson played his college ball at Notre Dame and became a well-known New York City attorney; Manes and Van Deusen both graduated from KSU and both became teachers. Van Deusen has lost touch with most of his onetime teammates. He knows that Ludick is deceased but has no recent word of VeNard, Manes, Kilbourne, and McHenry. He believes Johnson resides in Westchester County, New York.

In those days Kent State, Roosevelt, and Ravenna were members of the Trolley League, so named for the interurban line which traversed from Akron through Cuyahoga Falls, Silver Lake, Stow, and on into Kent and Ravenna. It was a good league which was succeeded by the Western Reserve and today's Metro League.

Teams in those dim days did not enjoy all the amenities that school athletic programs possess today. For example, when the Kent State team went to Columbus it remained for townspeople to arrange for transportation. Van Deusen recalls that Fred Gressard Sr. arranged for townspeople to provide cars for the team's transportation to Columbus. And Dr. Nick Ulrich and Dr. Gerald Stevenson also were the team's benefactors. They provided osteopathic treatments for Kent State team members during the busy and strenuous tournament season.

When Kent State won the state championship, the story of the team's success was published on page 1 of the *Kent Courier*. The games were covered and the stories written by Oliver Wolcott, longtime *Record-Courier* sports writer who later became Kent postmaster. Naturally, the home folks were proud of the Kent State team's pinnacle atop the state's basketball elite. When they returned home, team members were kept busy on the hometown banquet circuit. And why not? They were the toast of the town.

## PORTAGE SPELMAN FAMILY DATES BACK TO 1810

*June 3, 1990*

Last month when Dr. Johnnetta Cole was the commencement speaker at the College of Wooster, she challenged graduates to make a difference toward ending bigotry in America. "Racism," she said, "is not a private possession of the South; it is learned, it ain't genetic."

You may ask, who is Johnnetta Cole? A truly gifted scholar and a respected anthropologist, Johnnetta Cole is the first female black president of Spelman College in Atlanta, Georgia.

Also, you may wonder, what kind of institution of higher learning is Spelman College? Spelman College is a 109-year-old institution, a highly prestigious liberal arts college that attracts and graduates the nation's best and brightest young African-American women. In fact, last year, Spelman for the second consecutive year made the *U.S. News and World Report's* list of America's best liberal arts colleges. In addition, Spelman took the number-two spot in a listing of the southern region's top liberal arts colleges.

Dr. Cole, who became president in 1987 after distinguished service at Hunter College, has even higher hopes for Spelman. She sees Spelman as an eventual renowned center for scholarship by and about black women and as a premiere institution for educating black women leaders from around the world.

And, a third question, of what interest is Spelman College to readers of "Portage Pathways"? For that answer we dig deep into the history of one of Portage County's most prominent families. The Spelman family, long prominent in business, cultural, and religious activities, dates back to 1810 in Portage County.

In the same breath of historical recollection, we turn to another family—the Rockefellers—whose industry, wealth, and good works are legendary and whose prominence extended to an international reputation. For the Spelman-Rockefeller connection and Portage County's connection with Spelman College, we need to turn back the pages of history 180 years. That was the year when Samuel B. Spelman left his home in Massachusetts to settle in the eastern section of Rootstown Township.

Samuel and his wife had a son, Harvey B., whose wife was Lucy Henry Spelman. The Harvey Spelmans moved from Rootstown and resided in Kent for a time before he became a prosperous Akron merchant. Eventually they moved to Wadsworth, where Laura Celestia Spelman was born in 1839.

Laura became the bride of John D. Rockefeller Sr., who later became an oil tycoon, in 1864 in Cleveland. That union spawned a long association of the Rockefeller family with the small Atlanta college.

In 1882, just a year after the Atlanta Baptist Female Seminary was founded in the basement of an Atlanta church, John D. and Cettie (that's what he called his wife), went to hear the seminary founders, Sophia Packard and Harriet Giles, in Cleveland when they made an appeal for funds to construct the school's first building. John D. donated a $100 on the spot and promised more if the women demonstrated their intention to stick to their mission.

More Rockefeller gifts . . . many more . . . would follow. Indeed, for many years the Rockefeller family and its various benevolent units, including the Laura Spelman Rockefeller Foundation, were the major supporters of the school. So grateful were the infant school's administrators to the family that the institution was renamed for John D.'s mother-in-law, Lucy Henry Spelman. John D. rejected an overture that the school be named for the Rockefellers. However, many other Spelman campus landmarks bear that name. There are a John D. Rockefeller Hall, a Laura Spelman Rockefeller Memorial Building, and a John D. Rockefeller Jr. fine arts building.

This college, with an enrollment of more than 1,700 female black students, now is getting national recognition. Not only for the scholastic achievements of its students and the success of its graduates, but recognition in the form of endowments. Two years ago when Johnnetta Cole was inaugurated as "sister president," comedian-educator Bill Cosby and his wife, Camille, donated $20 million to Spelman for an academic center, now in the planning stages.

And Spelman College is so-named because a descendant of a Portage County pioneer family met and married a future oil baron.

---

## REVEREND BADGER'S FRUSTRATIONS LED TO FULL CONGREGATIONS

*April 6, 1985*

This Easter Sunday many area worshipers will attend services in pretentious edifices—large church complexes with well-appointed sanctuaries, educational wings, chapels, and administrative offices. Contrast these religious trappings with the primitive churches attended by early settlers of the Connecticut Western Reserve. People went to church on foot or on horseback. For the most part, their ministers were circuit riders who experienced many hardships to bring the word of God into the wilderness. Prior to erecting crude church buildings, pioneers worshipped in spartan school buildings or in homes. There were no fire-places in our early churches; the first fires were built in holes dug into the earthen floor with smoke emitting through holes in the roof. Seats were planks laid on blocks.

Contrary to what we may be inclined to believe, many of our first Portage area settlers were not consumed by the need for religious teach-ing. They were busy carving a new existence from the deep Western Reserve wilderness. Writings of Rev. Joseph Badger, who was sent into the Western Reserve frontier by the Connecticut Missionary Society in 1801, offer testimony to his heroic efforts and his difficult mission to introduce formal religion among the first settlers. It is said that he vis-ited every settlement in the Western Reserve. He traveled by horse-back, forded streams, fought off wild animals, and suffered deprivation and humiliation. He was not enamored of the wilderness and he was disappointed with his reception. After preaching in the infant Aurora settlement, Reverend Badger described the people in these words: "They are as stupid as the woods in which they live." In Ravenna, after preach-ing to 20 early families, he wrote, "I doubt that there is a praying family among them." Despite his travails and disappointments, Reverend Bad-ger was responsible more than any other man for laying the groundwork for the organization of our earliest Portage County churches.

For Portage County's first settlers, the establishment of churches did not appear to be of first priority. With the exception of Deerfield, most settlements waited 10 or more years to formalize religious organizations. Deerfield, founded in 1799, began holding Methodist classes in 1802, a move which led to the organization of a Methodist church the follow-ing year. Aurora's Congregational Church (now known as The Church in Aurora) was founded in 1809, a decade following the community's settlement. Ravenna's first church was the Congregational Church, or-ganized in 1822, a span of 23 years after Benjamin Tappan founded the settlement.

Other early Portage churches included a Methodist church in Mantua in 1807; Rootstown Congregational in 1810 and a Methodist church in 1815; Windham and Charlestown Congregational churches in 1811; Randolph Congregational and Methodist churches in 1812 and 1814, respectively; Kent Methodist in 1817 and Kent Congregational in 1819;

Atwater Congregational in 1818 and Methodist in 1821; and Nelson Congregational in 1813.

St. Joseph's Church in Randolph, which began in 1829 as a mission, is Portage County's oldest Catholic church. Kent's St. Patrick's and Ravenna's Immaculate Conception Catholic churches were established in 1863–1864, and St. Peter of the Fields came in 1869. Historical records indicate that Portage has had only two foreign language churches, a German Presbyterian and Lutheran Society in Atwater and the Welsh Baptist church in Palmyra. Both of these denominations conducted their services in their congregations' native tongues.

Although most of Portage County's first settlers were descendants of immigrants who fled England to achieve religious freedom, they many times displayed an intolerance for differing religious views. The most graphic example of this strange paradox was the tarring and feathering of Joseph Smith, founding prophet of the Mormons, and his colleague, Sidney Rigdon. They were removed from a home we know today as the Johnson House on Pioneer Trail in Hiram and "ridden out" on a rail. Symmonds Ryder of Hiram, a convert to the Mormon faith, was the leader of that raid after he broke faith with Smith because the latter misspelled his first name, a rather stern response to such a slight injustice. Ryder later became a Disciple minister. From Hiram, the Mormons set up a church in Kirtland, then Smith and his followers headed west. They were set upon by a mob in Illinois, and Smith was killed. Under the leadership of Brigham Young, the Church of the Latter-Day Saints (Mormons) eventually established headquarters in Salt Lake City.

Four early Portage County church buildings are classic examples of New England architecture—Atwater Congregational, erected in 1841; Freedom Congregational, started in 1843 and completed in 1845; The Church in Aurora, erected in 1872; and the old Streetsboro Baptist Church (later Methodist), built in 1851. The Streetsboro church was moved to Hale Farm and Village, where it is known as The Meetinghouse.

———

## SAINTLY VISITOR HAD LASTING EFFECT ON
## RANDOLPH CHURCH

*January 14, 1984*

One hundred forty-three years ago—in 1841—a 29-year-old priest was sent by his bishop into the sparse and heavily wooded Portage County to settle squabbling among German Catholics in the Randolph community. The mission assignment was a tall order for the young priest. The dissension among the St. Joseph's Church families had reached the point of grave concern, so severe that a frame church building, erected in 1838, had been burned during the period of difficulty.

That young priest was Father John Nepomucene Neumann, born in 1811 in Prachatitz, Bohemia, and then only recently ordained. Father Neumann apparently did his work well; he remained for only 10 days at the Randolph mission, preaching the gospel and baptizing two residents. And during the ensuing years, St. Joseph's parish, the first Catholic church in Portage County, has continued to prosper and today serves the religious needs of many families in southern Portage County.

The story of Father Neumann and his Portage County association is an interesting one. He graduated from the seminary in Prague, then came to the United States in 1836 at only 25. He was ordained in New York and did missionary work in New York state for four years. He joined the Redemptorist Order in 1840. Bishop Purcell of Cincinnati visited the strife-torn church in Randolph on November 12, 1841, with the intention of settling a quarrel among factions in the church, which was founded by immigrants from the German-speaking area of Alsace-Lorraine in France who had come to Randolph in 1826. Apparently he deemed it a more appropriate assignment for a young priest, so he dispatched Father Neumann.

A bit of St. Joseph's history: The first mass was held in the home of Anthony Miller by Father John Martin Henni, pastor of St. John's Church in Canton. Father Henni visited the mission in 1830 and in 1831 organized the settlers into a parish, said to be the sixth in the state of Ohio. Franz Adam Knapp contributed land from his farm in west Randolph for the first church and cemetery. The parish school, started in 1832, is believed to be the oldest English parochial school west of the Alleghenies.

In 1835, a log chapel was built, and then in 1838 a frame church building was erected on the hill at the rear of today's church edifice on Waterloo Road. In 1842 a larger building was erected to replace the burned church; a fourth went up in 1865; a frame school building in 1859; the priest's home or rectory in 1887. The fifth church—the present one—was built in 1904 to replace the burned-out fourth church building. The fourth, and present, brick school was erected in 1922, the convent in 1923, and a primary school building in 1961.

Another feature—the Our Lady of Lourdes Grotto—makes St. Joseph's a unique parish. The grotto was envisioned by Father Edward Spitzig when he assumed the pastorate in 1926. He considered the gravel hill at the rear of the rectory an ideal site for a grotto because the setting closely resembled that of the original shrine in Massabielle, France. Then Bishop Joseph Schrembs granted his approval for the project with a stipulation that the grotto must conform in every detail to the original in France. The Our Lady of Lourdes Grotto was dedicated on August 14, 1927.

The six German families who formed the nucleus of St. Joseph's parish in 1831 could not have envisioned the eventual scope of St. Joseph's. Today, 725 families are on the St. Joseph rolls. Two hundred forty-four children attend school at St. Joseph's in kindergarten through the eighth grade. There are a dozen teachers and a principal, including physical education, auxiliary, and music teachers. Some are lay teachers; others are sisters of the Order of Notre Dame. The Reverend John Ashton, who assumed his duties during the summer of 1982, is the present pastor of St. Joseph.

But what of Father Neumann? His unifying work at St. Joseph's won him widespread recognition. In 1852 he became bishop of Philadelphia, serving in that capacity until his death in 1860 at only 49. He was particularly interested in education. When he became bishop, there were two Catholic schools in Philadelphia. When he died there were nearly 100. He helped to bring several European sisterhoods to the United States to take charge of the schools. He founded a Philadelphia branch of the Sisters of St. Francis.

Father Neumann became a U.S. citizen in 1848. In 1963 he was be-atified, and in June 1977 he was canonized—the first male American citizen to become a saint.

---

## PASTORATE PUT RANDOLPH PREACHER
## IN RECORD BOOKS
*September 22, 1984*

There hardly is an area that cannot boast of many distinctions, records, and unusual happenings. Portage County is no exception. The outstanding career of a onetime Randolph minister gives Portage a claim to fame that few, if any, can match.

The Reverend Joseph Meriam, when he preached his final sermon in the Congregational Church of Randolph in 1888, set an American record—a pastorate of 64 years in the same church. While there is an outside chance that somewhere in the United States that record may have been surpassed during more recent years, it's a fairly safe bet that his record still stands.

Reverend Meriam, born in Grafton, Massachusetts, in 1797, was only 27 when he was installed as minister of the Randolph church. In 1888, at 91, he bade farewell to three generations of the Randolph faithful whom he had served through times of joy, celebration, distress, and sorrow.

He attended Harvard and graduated from Brown University and then from the Andover, Massachusetts, theological seminary. He went to Virginia in 1822 to do missionary work and then in 1823 came to Ohio, where he engaged in missionary endeavors throughout several infant counties. The Randolph Congregational Church, which had been founded in 1812, invited him in September 1823 to become its pastor. He preached his first sermon there during his installation service on January 7, 1824. When he assumed his pastorate, the Randolph church had 21 members. During 12 of his ministerial years, Reverand Meriam shared his time with the Rootstown Congregational Church.

In an article which appeared in the *Ravenna Republican* in the 1920s, writer E. Y. Lacey, himself a minister, wrote of Reverend Meriam: "He was a typical servant and savant of the faith whose mission of doing good suffered no lapse and whose voice was never lowered in preaching the Gospel of love and brotherhood and in directing the minds of his congregations to ethics and the teachings of the Holy Writ."

The influential Randolph minister allied himself with many moral movements of his day. He was an ardent antislavery supporter and a staunch backer of President Abraham Lincoln. He preached "liberty to the land and the inhabitants thereof." Gen. William Stedman, a fellow Portage Countian and onetime U.S. consul to Cuba, was one of his coworkers in the abolitionist movement. On one occasion, General Stedman, while visiting in Granville, Ohio, met two Negro fugitives, John and Harriet, who were fleeing to Canada. He brought them to Randolph where they were secreted in the attic of the old Mead and Brainerd mill. The slaves' owner tracked them to Randolph. As their master started to climb the stairs to their hiding place, the mill men and other Randolph citizens beat them away with axes. The plantation owner and his aides were sent on their way, and a week later Reverend Meriam officiated at the marriage of John and Harriet before a large assembly of Randolph residents. Reverend Meriam's first priority was ministering to the spiritual needs of his flock, but he found time for the educational and civic welfare of his community. He made himself one of his people.

The story of the courtship of his future wife is an interesting one. He heard of a young teacher in Madison, Ohio, who refused to equip herself with a prescribed number of birch rods to keep order in her school. "Tan 'em," her employers said. "Love them," was her response. "I'd like to meet that young woman," the young minister said, and soon thereafter he went to Madison where he wooed and won Emeline Bidwell. They were married for more than 50 years, and she shared his pastoral concerns for Randolph residents. She outlived him by four years.

Reverend Meriam was the grandfather of Oliver F. Meriam, prominent Randolph resident, farmer, and salesman who died in 1973.

The old Randolph Congregational Church building was erected in 1832 at the town center. No Congregational Church parish exists in Randolph today, and the old edifice many years ago was acquired by the township trustees. The building is now the community's Town Hall, serving as a government center as well as a meeting place for community groups.

The first year of Reverend Meriam's pastorate his annual salary was $200, all of it paid in produce. His record pastorate did not yield monetary riches. He found his treasure in the people he served.

———

## UNITED CHURCH OF CHRIST CELEBRATES
## MILESTONE IN KENT
### June 18, 1989

Today the United Church of Christ in Kent is celebrating a significant milestone—a birthday. One hundred seventy years ago—June 18, 1819—the church was established in Franklin Mills (Kent) with only eight members. That beginning of the first church in the settlement was only 14 years after John and Sally Haymaker and their three children arrived as the community's first residents.

In 1819 Franklin Mills was a tiny community along the banks of the Cuyahoga River, tenanted by fewer than 40 families and with only a grist mill and several other infant industries. Like others throughout the Connecticut Western Reserve, Franklin residents were busy establishing homes, planting their first crops, and taming the deep wilderness. It was into that wilderness that Rev. Joseph Badger, a graduate of Yale and a Revolutionary War veteran, was dispatched by the Connecticut Missionary Society in 1800. Traveling on horseback, Reverend Badger forded streams, slept in a tent, and lived off the bounty of the land as he visited every settlement in the Western Reserve to bring settlers the word of God. More than any of the early missionaries, he was responsible for pioneering work toward the organization of churches and schools throughout the area.

In November 1816, Reverend Badger preached a sermon at a service held in a small meetinghouse located in the triangle formed by Crain Avenue and Lake Street. That building, erected primarily through the effort of Deacon Samuel Andrews, served a combined use as a school and a church. Apparently Reverend Badger impressed the few settlers with his preaching, so much so that the following June 18 at a service in that same meetinghouse, Rev. Caleb Pitkin and Rev. Simeon Woodruff officiated for the signing of a Confession of Faith and Covenant. The church was organized under the auspices of the Connecticut Missionary Society and under the 1801 Plan of Union, which brought the Congregationalists and the Presbyterians together in taking organized religion into the Western Reserve.

The eight founders were Deacon Andrews and his wife, Triphena, from the Rootstown church; Samuel Andrews Jr. and Myra Jones from the church in Tallmadge; Roxana Newbury from Rootstown; Boadica Thayer from New York; Patty Loomis, also of Rootstown; and John Jones, listed as "from the world."

The church first was known as a Presbyterian Society, later became the First Congregational Church, and then in 1964 joined with the United Church of Christ following a merger of the Congregationalists and the Evangelical and Reformed Church.

As with most infant churches, the Kent organization was served by itinerant ministers during its first years. The Reverend George Sheldon, who had come to Aurora as a child with that community's founding family, became the first regular minister in 1825. It was he who occupied the church's first parish house, which still stands on the southwest corner of North Mantua Street and Earl Avenue.

Not counting the small community meetinghouse, the church has had three homes. In 1835 a new brick building, also located near the point of Crain and Lake, was dedicated. In 1858, the church moved to a new edifice at the corner of Park and Gougler Avenues, a building which was to serve 97 years until the present edifice was erected at the intersection of East Main Street and Horning Road in 1955.

Famed abolitionist John Brown was a member of the church during his brief residency in the village. He, his wife, and three sons joined the church in 1838 by letter from Hudson where Brown had come as a child with his family. Brown came to Kent in 1835 to build a tannery for Zenas Kent. Even then an outspoken critic of slavery, Brown was disciplined for taking Negroes to his pew. Formerly, they had been seated at the rear of the church. In 1859, when he was hanged following his raid on Harpers Ferry, the church's bell, as well as others in the community, was tolled in mourning.

The Reverend Edward Wilcox, minister from 1936 to 1951, holds the tenure record among ministers. The late Herbert Van Meter served 12 years from 1951 to 1963, and Rev. John Hull 11 years from 1914 to 1925. The Reverend C. Thomas Jackson has been senior minister of the church since 1985.

The United Church of Christ has one member more than 100 years old, Ida Fageol at 105. Another longtime member, Ora Taylor, who died last week, would have been 104 on Monday. Bernice Douglas, nearing 95, holds the record for continuous membership, with 82 years. Margaret Gressard, one of the church membership's several Haymaker family descendants, is 98, with 71 years of membership.

----

## MOGADORE PASTOR WAS NEWS FIFTY YEARS AGO

*July 23, 1989*

War clouds were gathering over Europe during the summer of 1939. Within a matter of weeks Adolf Hitler's legions would march into Poland. World War II would begin. Americans who two years later would be drawn into the war watched with more than passing interest the troubles abroad.

And in the village of Mogadore there also were tense moments, brought about by the kidnapping in the Holy Land of a young missionary, Rev. Gerould Goldner, pastor of the Mogadore Christian Church. Young Reverend Goldner and his father, the Reverend Dr. Jacob Goldner of Cleveland, were riding donkeys in the hills south of Jerusalem when they were accosted by a Bedouin tribesman. Almost instantly they were surrounded by 10 other desert bandits. The area where the kidnapping took place then was known as the "Valley of Fire," near the Dead Sea. The father-son ministers were taken by their captors to a cave where the father and his donkey boy then were released by the bandits. Gerould Goldner remained a captive.

The bandits demanded $5,000 in silver as a ransom for the release of the Mogadore minister. In today's world when captors are demanding millions for the release of hostages the $5,000 ransom figure appears paltry. But that was in 1939, and we had not yet become accustomed to present-day astronomical sums. The minister father returned to Bethlehem to raise the ransom money, a sum that the bandits subsequently reduced to $2,500.

The story of Reverend Goldner's kidnapping and progress of the negotiations for his release were top news throughout the world. Protestants, Catholics, Jews, even Moslems, prayed for the minister's safe release. And, especially, members of the Mogadore Christian Church prayed for the safety of their young pastor.

Negotiations were intricate and sensitive. The British were involved as were the U.S. consul general and Arab leaders in that area. One letter from the minister hostage was received by the father and authorities as negotiations progressed. Reverend Goldner said in the letter that he was being treated well and that he was being held in a dry well. He later said that his captors moved him nightly to prevent discovery as they awaited word from the negotiators.

The $2,500 ransom was raised without too much difficulty. Church members in Ohio contributed to the fund. An Arab emissary carried the $2,500 in silver (so that it couldn't be traced) to the Bedouin captors. The negotiators waited. Would the captors fulfill their part of the deal? Word finally came from the kidnappers to the same man from whom the two Reverends Goldner had rented their donkeys. News bulletins said Reverend Goldner had been turned over to monks at a Greek monastery. Later, he was sighted riding a donkey on the road between Bethlehem and Hebron. There he was greeted by the U.S. consul general who drove him to Bethlehem.

The senior Reverend Goldner, who had suffered a heart attack as a result of stress over the kidnapping, and his son were reunited at the Bethlehem YMCA in a tearful exchange of hugs. The overjoyed minister said, "Pops, I'm sure glad to see you." In subsequent interviews, the young minister said he never expected to see his father again when the elder Goldner was released and he remained a captive.

Reverend Goldner had been held for six days before his release came on July 24, 1939. He said he never knew his specific whereabouts during his period of captivity. He spent the time playing cards with his captors and trying to learn the Arabic language. Following his release, a physical examination revealed that he was exhausted but otherwise physically fit.

After his difficult experience, Reverend Goldner sailed home from Bremen, Germany. His 10-week leave in the Holy Land ended, and he returned to Mogadore and resumed his pastoral duties. In March 1940 he resigned to become pastor of the Christian Church in Warren and later served the Lakewood Christian Church. He now is deceased, and his widow resides in Westlake, Ohio.

But the onetime Mogadore minister who made international news so many years ago still has Portage County connections. The third generation of Goldner ministers, represented by his son, the Reverend Dr. Russell Goldner, last May became pastor of the First Christian Church in Ravenna, and his daughter-in-law, the Reverend Irene Goldner, serves the Ravenna church as minister of Christian education. The Goldner ministerial legacy lives on!

## PIONEER DOCTORS LED WAY TO GOOD
## HEALTH IN PORTAGE

*March 1, 1986*

The date was November 12, 1825. William McLaughlin was desperately ill, and there was little hope that he would survive. In those days of primitive medical procedures, surgical operations were almost unknown. Only the bravest of physicians, whose knowledge was scant at best, would even consider surgery.

Dr. Joseph DeWolf, who had arrived to practice medicine in Ravenna a few years after 1800, was one of those brave medical pioneers. William McLaughlin had a strangulated hernia, and it was deemed by Dr. DeWolf that his life could be saved only through surgery. Dr. DeWolf opened his abdomen, found a portion of his intestines gangrenous, cut off eight or nine inches of same, stitched together the several parts, and sewed up the abdomen. McLaughlin survived and lived many years thereafter. That was the first operation performed in Portage County, and it must be remembered that in those days anesthesia was unknown on the Portage County frontier.

Dr. DeWolf, the first physician on the Ravenna scene, was involved in another surgical procedure that same year. James Haymaker of Franklin Township was taken ill with a swelling in his neck and was virtually given up for lost. At that time, a Dr. Stocking, a noted surgeon from the East, was visiting in Brimfield. He was called in and observed that only an operation would spare Haymaker. Dr. DeWolf and others held down the patient while Dr. Stocking pierced the swelling in Haymaker's neck. From the incision spurted blood, pus, and a feather, the culprit that had become lodged in the throat and was the cause of the swelling.

Haymaker lived for many years. He was the son of Frederick Haymaker, member of Franklin Township's founding family and secretary to Vice President Aaron Burr, who was tried for treason in 1807. It is said that Frederick Haymaker had in his possession documents involving Burr's infamous trip into Louisiana Purchase territory, but he kept silent concerning events during those years.

These two operations in the earliest days of Portage County heralded medical progress and laid firm foundations for the outstanding medical community Portage Countians enjoy today . . . more than 100 physicians with medical specialties covering more than 40 fields and our Robinson Memorial Hospital, located on an extensive campus north of Ravenna with 325 beds, plus trauma, emergency, intensive care, and special care units as well as laboratories and many other medical facilities to serve the growing area population.

During the early days of the Western Reserve, personal health depended largely upon home cures, many of them learned from the Indians. Roots and herbs were considered adequate remedies. Whiskey was deemed a cure-all. Home remedies were concocted from birch and balsam, saltpeter, and sassafras bark. Even during my lifetime, I can recall my embarrassment when I was forced to wear an asafetida bag around my neck to ward off symptoms of the flu or colds. Obviously, mortality was high, especially among the young. Reading gravestones in our cemeteries will attest to that.

Our earliest physicians in Portage County carried all their medical equipment, including their own homemade drugs, in their saddlebags. Their instruments included tooth forceps because they also served as dentists when the need arose.

Our earliest doctors were revered men. In addition to Dr. DeWolf, there were Dr. Rufus Belding, who came to Randolph in 1807; Drs. Ezra Chaffee and Ezekial Squires, who started their practices in Palmyra and Aurora in 1810; Dr. Gilbert, a Palmyra physician as early as 1806; and Dr. Murray, in Deerfield in 1805. Dr. Joseph Price was a tailor in Randolph before he "read" medicine and started a Franklin Township practice.

This year marks a significant milestone in Portage County medical history. It will be 120 years this coming June that 16 physicians organized the Portage County Medical Society. It was Dr. Joseph Waggoner who called doctors to a meeting in Ravenna to effect the organization of the society. It is interesting to note that two physicians, Dr. DeWolf and Dr. Isaac Swift, who came to Ravenna in 1815, were granted honorary membership when the society was organized. Today the society includes more than 100 medical personnel, with Dr. Alan Yoho, a urologist, as its president.

A man who is unforgettable in Portage County medical history is Dr. W. W. White. He organized a private hospital in Ravenna before 1900. Located in a frame building on East Main Street where the Wright Store is now located, the hospital was intended primarily for emergency cases. Then, in 1903 the White Hospital was moved into a new building at the corner of North Chestnut and Cedar Streets, where the Ravenna Post Office now stands. That hospital had beds for 25 patients. Surgical work there was done by the famed Dr. George W. Crile. Dr. Bernard Nichols served that hospital, as well as the Cleveland Clinic, as roentgenologist. He retired from Robinson Memorial Hospital in 1952.

In 1917, Portage County purchased the old White Hospital from Dr. White, and then in 1932 Robinson Memorial Hospital was built on South Chestnut Street as a memorial to George and Mary Robinson. With the need for expanded medical facilities quite evident, our present hospital was built on North Chestnut Street and was dedicated in 1977. That complex underwent an expansion program in 1984.

Portage County's medical community has come a long way since that day 161 years ago when pioneer physician Dr. Joseph DeWolf performed that first surgical operation.

---

## SICK HORSE PICKED ONE RAVENNA
## DOCTOR'S LOCATION

*September 23, 1990*

Most of our earliest settlers located in this area by design. For others, it was almost a matter of chance or the result of a strange series of happenings. On most occasions, it was a sparkling stream, a lush forest from which to gain timber for a log cabin, or a particularly fertile parcel of land that beckoned them to select a certain site for a future home. None of the above was the reason one of our pioneer physicians picked Ravenna for the practice of medicine. For him, it was an ailing horse.

Dr. Isaac Swift came by his medical career naturally; his father, also Isaac, enlisted when the war opened at Lexington and was a surgeon in the Revolutionary War army. Young Isaac, born in Cornwall, Connecticut, in 1790, took medical classes in New York City and became licensed to practice in New Jersey. But, like many young men of his era, Isaac had the wanderlust. With all of his worldly possessions in saddlebags, he left New England to select a more desirable location to begin his practice of medicine.

His trip was far from uneventful. After rough riding through dense forests, he finally reached Cleveland City, as the infant city on Lake Erie was called at that time. Among other tribulations, he and his horse had been forced to swim the Grand River at Painesville. Isaac remained several days in Cleveland, which he apparently found uninviting for a young doctor to open his practice. So he and his struggling horse set out in a southeasterly direction from Cleveland. As he traveled, his horse, which had taken cold in the Grand River incident, became sicker and sicker. Finally, Isaac's steed could travel no farther.

Isaac looked around and liked what he saw. He was in Ravenna, the county seat of Portage. The year was 1815, and for 60 years he would call Ravenna home—for his medical practice, business interests, public service, and community endeavors. Thus, a rather trifling happening, the illness of a horse, had dictated the physician's career. Dr. Swift's practice of medicine was a rather brief one—only 13 years. He had a variety of pursuits—a drug store, associate judgeship, county treasurership, among others. He became prominent in all of them.

Only a year after he arrived in Ravenna, Dr. Swift formed a partnership with Seth Day, and they bought out a store kept by a man named Hazlipp. They added a stock of medicines. Dr. Swift continued his practice, and Day operated the store. That was 1816, and the store, through several changes in ownership, eventually became the Lyon and Morgan drug store on East Main Street. When it ceased business some years ago, the business was the second oldest drug store in Ohio.

Swift and Day dissolved the partnership in 1820 after Day became county recorder and clerk of the court. Dr. Swift retained the stock of medicines and ultimately continued the business in the store of Cyrus Prentiss, and later he built a new drug store on Chestnut Street.

Incidentally, when the doctor and Eliza Thompson were married in 1818, they commenced housekeeping in a home which then stood where the Etna House now is located.

In 1831, the doctor was elected county treasurer, an office he held for eight years. Apparently he took a liking to public service, because in 1828 he retired from the practice of medicine. From that year, he devoted his time and talent to public office and his drug store. He disposed of the drug business to his son, Dr. Charles Swift, in 1859.

Although he no longer was associated in the practice of medicine, he was included among charter members when the Portage County Medical Society was organized in 1866.

In 1846 Dr. Swift was appointed associate judge of the common pleas court by the Ohio General Assembly. He is said to have served admirably in that position for five years. By that time, Ohio had adopted a new constitution and associate judgeships were abolished.

The doctor-businessman-public servant, unlike his wife and most other residents, paid little attention to religious matters during his early married life. Finally, after hearing pioneer preacher Rev. Charles B. Storrs, he joined a church (most likely the Congregational), in which he served as church treasurer 40 years and assumed other responsibilities in the church organization.

Dr. Swift died in 1874 at 84. His years in Ravenna had been fruitful ones in a variety of endeavors. Historical writings tell us that he was much revered by his medical associates as well as by other fellow townspeople. And all that came about because his horse took sick and he was forced to halt his journey in Ravenna.

———

## RAVENNA WATER CURE WAS A SIGN OF
## THE MEDICAL TIMES

*December 2, 1990*

During the past two and a half weeks, I have sat several times each day, almost transfixed, amidst a sea of medical mechanisms, sentries of various life-supporting systems . . . silent guardsmen and reporters of the many bodily functions.

Arrayed within a forest of plastic tubing, these medical marvels—with their beeps, red lights, and occasional disruptive procedures—nourish the body, transmit drugs, measure blood pressures and heartbeats, and monitor many other matters unknown to us laymen. In the quiet of an intensive care room, there is time a plenty to contemplate, to recall, to wonder. They prompt a wonder concerning how our medical giants practiced medicine prior to the arrival of all this digitized paraphernalia. We're told they learned much of a patient's condition by feel, by sight, and even sometimes by smell. Despite their almost uncanny senses, their diagnostic procedures must have been inadequate, at best. But in the era in which you live, you do the best you can with what you have.

All these sophisticated techniques set me to thinking about the early Portage County settlers who treated their illnesses with a variety of nostrums, many of them learned from the Indians . . . herbal teas, barks, berries, salves made from the various animals, etc. And a bit later came the patent medicines. The following is an example.

The February 26, 1835, edition of the *Western Courier* (that was a Ravenna weekly paper) advertised a nostrum which claimed success in treating "hydrophobia, snake bites, cancers, scrofulous humors, piles, King's Evil, inflamed breast, and fleur albus," whatever that may be. Incidentally there was a testimonial in the ad from a man who said the medicine had healed his injured "ancle." He knew where his ankle was but he couldn't spell the word.

People in those days appeared to be prime suckers for medical con men. Our earlier history recordings tell us that they fell in great numbers to the persuasions of medical hucksters in their eager bent to try each new quick cure. Mineral springs seemed to crop up throughout our area, and their sponsors immediately became medical mercenaries. Among such findings were mineral springs from a onetime mining operation in Deerfield in the early 1900s.

So enamored with the healthful properties of these newfound waters were its sponsors that they recommended them for medicinal purposes. Among the sponsors was a Deerfield physician. The water was piped and bottled for market. Besides the medical market, the company used the water for soft drink purposes. By 1914, their annual sales totaled $100,000. The sponsors envisioned an operation rivaling White Sulphur Springs, West Virginia. They even planned a sanitarium, but a fire in 1920 dashed their dream. The plant never was rebuilt.

And then there was the Ravenna Water Cure! With a flourish, the Ravenna Water Cure opened in April 1870 in a mansion at the corner of North Chestnut Street and Cedar Avenue. The site these days is occupied by Society Bank. The *Ravenna Democrat*, a weekly of that day, was lavish in its announcement of the new medical operation. Dr. G. W. Strong of Cleveland bought the mansion from Andrew Poe, one of the various Ravenna cousins of the famed poet Edgar Allen Poe. Dr. Strong added to the home to accommodate a number of bathrooms for patients. Said the *Democrat*, "Dr. Strong is an intelligent, capable and experienced gentleman and, in all respects, well qualified to conduct successfully his important enterprise. He has the goodwill of the people of Ravenna."

The longevity of the Ravenna Water Cure isn't exactly determined, but we do know it prevailed at least five years, because its home is featured in the 1875 Portage County Atlas. The mansion later became the family home of A. C. Williams, who moved the company by that name to Ravenna from Chagrin Falls in 1893. And for many years in more recent times, the attractive home was occupied by the Ravenna Eagles.

Perhaps the water cure people were bona fide. After all, in Hot Springs, Arkansas, where hot mineral water emits from the mountainside at an average temperature of 143 degrees, five million people annually seek its relieving qualities for arthritis, neuritis, and rheumatism. And the operation enjoys national park status.

———

## FIRST STREETSBORO MEDICAL PRACTICE
## BEGAN IN 1839
*December 28, 1985*

An innocent statement sometimes pulls the rip cords of history. On December 16, a sidebar to a *Record-Courier* news article by Dr. Kenneth Rupp, Portage County health commissioner, which sought to end the confusion over AIDS, a disease which has aroused the conscience of most Americans, made the statement that Dr. Rupp became the first Streetsboro physician in 100 years when he decided to locate his practice there in 1958. While Streetsboro residents appreciate the caring services of Dr. Rupp, many of them take exception to the statement, not one of Dr. Rupp's authorship. Especially is this true of descendants of other practicing physicians in the community over the years. They point out that the statement simply is not true and offer evidence to the contrary.

All of which gives rise to an outpouring of historical material concerning at least six physicians who have practiced in Streetsboro, most of them more recently than the aforementioned 100-year time span. Such a spark prompts a bit of historical research into such matters as community medical resources.

As far as can be learned, Dr. Henry Lacy was the first Streetsboro physician. He arrived in 1839 and practiced there until his death in

1854. In 1839, Dr. Lacy built the historic Burroughs home on S.R. 303, currently owned and occupied by Royal and Jane Burroughs Reynolds.

In 1854, that home was deeded to Simon Burroughs, great-grandfather of Jane Reynolds, who purchased the property to settle the Lacy estate. Four years later, ownership passed into the hands of Howard Burroughs; in 1910 it moved to Fred Burroughs, then to Willis Keller Burroughs in 1970, and thence to Royal and Jane Reynolds.

Portage County's history of 1876 mentions a Dr. Charles A. May, then a practicing Streetsboro physician who was a member of the Portage County Medical Association, which was organized in 1866 in Ravenna. Incidentally, the medical association in that year included 22 members.

Historical records are clouded for the years immediately prior to the turn of the century. But, it is well established that Dr. Bayard T. Keller arrived in Streetsboro to practice medicine in 1902. Dr. Keller graduated from Johns Hopkins University Medical School at 21 and then went to Washington Courthouse, Ohio, and to Chattanooga, Tennessee, prior to coming to Streetsboro.

Departing Streetsboro in 1909, Dr. Keller then practiced in Stow, Hudson, and Cuyahoga Falls. He was the first of three generations of physicians. His son, Dr. Dan Keller, practiced in Cuyahoga Falls and his grandson, Bayard M. Keller, in Cuyahoga Falls and then Chardon. The elder Dr. Keller was the father of his namesake, Bayard T. Keller, founder of the Keller Electric Company, and Nelle Keller Straight, wife of Carl Straight.

Dr. Keller operated his practice from an office located at the present site of the Trans-Ohio Savings. Two other doctors followed in the same location. Dr. W. L. DeVaul, also mentioned in the annals of the Portage County Medical Association, was located there, as was Dr. F. A. Russell. Dr. DeVaul is said to have arrived in Streetsboro about 1911 and Dr. Russell, who later practiced in Kent from offices located in his home at the corner of North Mantua Street and Fairchild Avenue, followed him.

Roy Pierce of Diagonal Road has vivid memories of Dr. Russell. Roy, a third grader at the time, broke his nose in a tussle with a friend. There being no proper facilities in Streetsboro to attend to Roy's fractured nose, he and Dr. Russell boarded an Erie train in Kent bound for Cleveland to get medical attention. Without benefit of an anaesthetic, the doctor in Cleveland used a pair of pliers to line up Roy's fractured nose.

It was not until Roy was about 40 that his nose was properly repaired by corrective surgery.

Following Dr. Russell into a Streetsboro medical practice was a Dr. Allgood. He practiced in the Singletary house, located on the north-west corner of the Streetsboro square. And thereby hangs another sig-nificant segment of Streetsboro history. Col. John C. Singletary of Au-rora arrived in Streetsboro in 1825 when he built a log house at that site. Then, in 1828, he started to build the famed frame house which he completed and occupied in 1829. Singletary was the community's first postmaster. The house, known for its distinctive sunburst doorway, was purchased and moved by the late Henry Defer in recent years to a site off S.R. 14 near the Ohio Turnpike entrance. The doorway was used as a model for Streetsboro's World War II honor roll, which at one time stood on the southwest community green.

A considerable slice of medical history has transpired since those early days. Today, the community is served by three physicians: Dr. Rupp, who combines his practice with the demanding county health depart-ment commissionship; Dr. R. J. Custodio; and Dr. Philip Kennedy.

The bustling 1985 community, now one of Portage County's four cit-ies, got its start in 1822 when Stephen Myers became the first settler on lands owned by the original proprietor, Titus Street, of Connecticut.

––––––

## DOCTOR TRAVELED PATH TO
## INTERNATIONAL FAME

*January 21, 1990*

It's a long road from Atwater in southern Portage County to interna-tional fame. Dr. Bernard H. Nichols traveled that path. In the field of medicine he won worldwide prominence as an X-ray pioneer and spe-cialist. Yet he remained a humble, warm-hearted, kind man who made numerous contributions through community service and projects to help the less fortunate. His death 25 years ago, on December 18, 1964, on his 88th birthday, ended a life devoted to mankind.

Today, many in Portage County may not have heard of Dr. Nichols. But others, particularly older practitioners in the medical field and long-time friends, never will forget him. Likewise they will not soon forget his wife, Martha, an energetic, flamboyant woman who devoted most of her hours to collecting cast-off items, which she sold at rummage sales at her Ravenna home or from a Hartville auction booth to raise funds for charitable purposes. In the field of X-ray, Dr. Nichols's achievements have become legendary.

He was born in Atwater on December 18, 1876. He attended grammar school there, graduated from Edinburg High School, and then worked his way through Starling Medical School, now part of Ohio State University, receiving his medical degree in 1904.

Following a brief practice in Youngstown, he moved to Ravenna, where he established a medical practice which ultimately would earn him a place of eminence among the world's practitioners. He became associated with Dr. W. W. White, founder of the old White Hospital in Ravenna, predecessor to Robinson Memorial Hospital. On the White staff were Dr. George W. Crile, Dr. E. E. Bunts, and Dr. W. E. Lower. The three doctors later would establish the Crile Clinic in Cleveland, today's world-renowned Cleveland Clinic.

It was in 1906 that Dr. Nichols became a pioneer in the study of X-rays, or roentgenology. His first work in the field was done with a machine built in Ravenna in a factory located in the Sorenson Block on South Meridian Street. It was powered with a crank, a method which required considerable manual labor. The doctor's X-ray work in Ravenna was interrupted in 1917 when he was commissioned a first lieutenant in the World War I army. He served overseas as a roentgenologist at a base hospital in France. His work there won for him a distinguished service citation from General Pershing.

In 1921 he joined the Cleveland Clinic staff and became head roentgenologist, a position he held until he retired at 70 in 1946. Dr. Nichols throughout those years commuted daily by train from his Ravenna home to Cleveland. He was retired only a single day until he signed on as head of the X-ray department at Robinson Memorial, an institution that he had helped to establish and where he spent evenings and weekends analyzing X-rays. When he retired from Robinson in 1952, he left behind an X-ray therapy machine that cost him $7,000 and then was valued at $15,000.

His many publications, lectures, and designs of X-ray equipment made him internationally known. Probably his proudest moment was his meeting in 1911 in Paris with William Konrad Roentgen who, in 1896 in Wurzburg, Germany, announced the discovery of X-rays. Dr. Nichols did not confine his service to medicine. He served his community for 15 years as a member of the Ravenna Board of Education and two terms as a city councilman.

When he retired the second time, he vowed to spend leisure hours tending his beautiful and spacious garden at his home on Grant Street and to a longtime hobby of refinishing old furniture. And he joined his wife in staging rummage sales for charity. In 1952, the Ravenna Jaycees honored Dr. and Mrs. Nichols with their outstanding citizenship award. Upon his death, a *Record-Courier* editorial described Dr. Nichols as a warm-hearted, kind man who dedicated his life to serving mankind. "Portage Countians will long remember his contributions to the field of medicine and his distinguished service to his community," the editorial concluded. Indeed, they will!

―――――

## NO LONGER "POORHOUSE,"
## COUNTY HOME HAS COME OF AGE

*March 14, 1987*

There was a time when parents admonished the wastefulness of their children by exclaiming, "What are you trying to do—drive us right into the poorhouse?" Sometimes, that wasn't an idle threat. There were "poorhouses," and they were havens for people who had no means of self-support. Like other counties, Portage had a poorhouse and a "poor farm."

During the county's earliest days, care of the poor was the responsibility of each township. It was not an ideal system. Poor people were "farmed out" to those who would keep them in the absolute cheapest way, and most times the poor were victims of uncivil treatment.

As early as 1833, sentiment for a public poor farm began in earnest. Then, in 1839, the county commissioners purchased a 162-acre farm in the southwest corner of Shalersville Township from David McIntosh for use as a poor farm. Not only did the $5,000 purchase price include the acreage, but also all the existing farm buildings, farm implements, and livestock.

McIntosh, who would become an almost legendary citizen of Portage, had owned the farm since 1818, only 16 years after he had come from his native New Hampshire as a lad of eight. This is the same David McIntosh who rose to the rank of a major general in the Ohio militia and who was elected representative to the Ohio General Assembly in 1845. And the same patriotic David McIntosh who, upon his death in 1883, bequeathed $1,000 to Portage County to be used for the purchase of flags for townships, a fund that has been perpetuated to this day and is administered by County Auditor Vic Biasella.

Following the original purchase, the commissioners named a board of directors, which included McIntosh, Darius Lyman, and Frederick Williams. McIntosh was named the first director-manager of the "poorhouse and poor farm." The original farm buildings and home housed the county's indigent and served the farm operation.

Ten years after the original land purchase, the county acquired 129 additional acres adjoining the farm on the east side of what today is Infirmary Road. By 1885, the county owned more than 300 acres. In 1858, voters approved a $5,000 bond issue to build a brick structure, and in 1872 a wing was added and renovations were made, at a total cost of $15,000.

Entire families at one time were among inmates in the poorhouse. Besides quarters for poor people, the county home also had wards for insane inmates until 1903, when a new Ohio law was passed to prohibit housing the insane in county infirmaries. A home census report in 1867 lists 38 mentally ill and 70 paupers among the home's inmates. For many years, for want of other facilities, unwed mothers with no means went to the county home to deliver their babies. Homes then were sought for these children.

The poor worked for their keep, helping to operate the large farm which raised all types of crops, produce, hogs, cattle, and chickens. A cannery processed the vegetables and fruit for later use in the dining hall. Soap was made in a special house, and there was another house where ice, cut from the farm pond, was stored. Brick ovens turned out 100 loaves of bread in a single batch. Oxen and a stable of horses were housed in a carriage house. There was a laundry, ironing room, chapel, and a large sewing room, as well as a water plant and a "dead" house, an ever-present reminder that the Grim Reaper paid frequent visits. In the early days, paupers who died at the home were buried on the premises.

With the passing of the unflattering "poorhouse" designation, the home and farm became known as the Portage County Infirmary. That designation, too, passed when in 1952 voters approved a $450,000 bond issue to build a new facility on the same site which then became known as the Portage County Nursing Home, its present designation. In 1962, when Dick Thomas was administrator, the county discontinued the farm operation as a result of unprofitability. Eighty-four head of cattle, some of them prize Herefords, were sold at that time.

Meanwhile, the land of the old infirmary has been reduced. Some of the acreage went to the county airport, more to the juvenile center, some to the dog pound, and still more to the county sanitary engineer's department.

The Portage County Nursing Home today is a viable, county-owned, self-sustaining institution which serves as a haven for 99 men and women. Always there is a waiting list for admission. It's no longer a "poorhouse," although its point system for admitting patients is weighted heavily toward the indigent or welfare-type patient. County residents on Medicaid who have been living alone achieve the highest points on the admission chart.

With Jim Alexander, the administrator, as my guide, I toured the nursing home. It is a well-kept, well-programmed facility with a staff of 50. Alexander, who came from the Columbus area, has been the administrator for 10 years. One is impressed with the ease with which he relates to the patients. They exchange greetings with him on a first-name basis. Mary Lang is the oldest resident; she will be 104 next month.

The nursing home in this modern age is a far cry from 1839 when it began as a poorhouse or poor farm for the county's indigent and insane.

It has come of age. After all, the Portage County Nursing Home is 148 years old, and it has adapted to the changes wrought by time.

———

## TOM, DICK, HARRY GAVE PORTAGE
## HOSPITAL GIFT

*March 11, 1990*

In Ravenna, when they were youths, they were known as Tom, Dick, and Harry. Never mind that Harry's given name was Henry. He apparently bore the Harry tag to complete the legendary Tom, Dick, and Harry triumvirate.

More accurately they were Richard H. M. Robinson, Thomas L. Robinson, and Henry M. Robinson, whose own fame may have been lost in the luster of their prominent father and grandfather. And their accomplishments, some of which achieved national and international notice, did not take place in their native city of Ravenna.

Their father was George F. Robinson, noted judge who served on the Portage County Common Pleas bench longer than any of his predecessors or successors. Born in Ravenna in 1844, Judge Robinson first served as Portage County prosecutor and, from 1888 until his death in 1917, was common pleas judge.

As a memorial to their parents, George F. and Mary, the three sons in the early 1930s gave the Robinson family homestead on South Chestnut Street in Ravenna and $50,000 to the county for a new hospital. Opened in 1932, the hospital (although now at a different location), still bears the family name, Robinson Memorial. Tom, Dick, and Harry were proud of their Portage County heritage and held an obvious pride in their parents, hence their hospital gift as a memorial to them.

Their Portage County roots were deep. Their grandfather, George Robinson, born in 1801, was a civil engineer. He served as assistant engineer on the Ohio Canal beginning in 1830. When that thoroughfare was completed, he became chief engineer for the building of the Pennsylvania and Ohio Canal, which traversed east-to-west through Portage County.

After the canal's demise, he turned to railroading, serving as the first superintendent of the Cleveland and Pittsburgh Railroad, which came through Ravenna in 1851. He served in a like capacity with the Cleveland and Mahoning Valley Railroad.

The elder George was one of the partners who established the Diamond Glass Works in Ravenna in 1868, and in 1864 he became the first president of the Second National Bank, now Society Bank.

Among his seven children were three sons, all of whom served in the Civil War. George F., who would become the renowned judge, was a captain, as was another brother, A. K. The third, Henry, was the first Ravenna soldier to lose his life in the war.

Judge Robinson's sons won success in fields other than the law, although one son, Thomas, did practice law for a time. However, his reputation was achieved in the banking and government fields. He was president of banks in Youngstown and New York City, and he also headed a Youngstown rubber company. He gained an international reputation when he served with the Dawes Commission, which established a bank to replace Germany's Reichbank following the end of World War I, for which he was decorated by three governments. Under appointment by Gov. Alfred E. Smith, he headed a commission which raised $15 million for unemployment relief in the state of New York. Thomas ended his career with the National Recovery Administration. Illness forced his retirement in 1934, and he died in Zurich, Switzerland in 1940.

Brother Dick, a graduate of the U.S. Naval Academy; designed two battleships, the *Connecticut* and the *Pennsylvania*. The latter, launched in 1915, at that time was the largest American battleship, 600 feet long and with a beam of 98 feet.

He studied ship design at the University of Glasgow after achieving national honors in mathematics competitions. Following 22 years in the navy, Dick resigned to follow personal business pursuits.

Henry (Harry) spent most of his adult life in California, where he was prominent in the banking and philanthropic fields.

Like their father, a revered jurist, and their grandfather, a pioneer engineer, Tom, Dick, and Harry achieved outstanding success. And, through their generous hospital gift nearly 60 years ago, the Robinson family name lives on in respect and admiration in Portage County.

#### PART FIVE

# BUSINESS AND COMMERCE

The interior of Thompson's Drugstore in 1877.

# MAPLE SYRUP HARVESTING ALMOST
# AS OLD AS PORTAGE

*January 25, 1986*

If you have a sweet tooth, the upcoming maple syrup season should be tailor-made for you. There is nothing that quite equals in culinary delight a stack of hotcakes topped with a generous portion of Portage County's premium maple syrup.

The syrup season is fast approaching. The unseasonably warm weather of the past several days bodes an earlier than usual syrup season, while it would be a safe bet that we have plenty of cold weather ahead of us. Although we haven't heard of any sap being gathered at this early date, some harvesters have placed their sap buckets to be ready for the flow of sap from sugar maple trees. Ordinarily, February and March are maple syrup months.

Local harvesting of sap and evaporating it into maple syrup or maple sugar is almost as old as Portage County itself. It didn't take the hardy first settlers from New England long to transfer their knowledge of maple sugaring from their home states of Connecticut and Massachusetts to their new homes in the Ohio wilderness.

As early as 1849, the community of Garrettsville had become a major shipping point for maple products. A story from the *Mahoning Dispatch*, reprinted in the *Garrettsville Journal* in 1849, reported that as many as 50,000 to 75,000 gallons of syrup were shipped annually from that northern Portage County community. Likewise, Deerfield shipped large quantities of syrup from the old Day and Wilson stores in the late 1800s and early 1900s.

The 1885 *History of Portage County* tells the story of Portage County's once robust maple industry occasioned by the profusion of sugar maple trees throughout the county. The previous year (1884), 428,000 trees were tapped, rendering 104,600 pounds of maple sugar and 67,192 gallons of syrup. Windham Township was the leader in syrup production that year with the tapping of more than 36,000, trees which netted 9,438 gallons of syrup and 13,862 pounds of sugar. Nelson came in a close second with 34,400 trees tapped with a harvest of 32,200 pounds of sugar and 7,361 gallons of syrup.

All of Portage County's townships are listed as maple products producers for that year with the exception of Suffield. Other top syrup producers that year were Hiram with 6,190 gallons, Edinburg 6,174 gallons, Charlestown 5,231 gallons, Freedom 4,990, Randolph 4,500, and
Shalersville and Mantua with more than 3,300 gallons each. Brimfield
Township farmers tapped only 117 trees.

Apparently some earlier producers chose to produce more maple sugar
from sap rather than evaporate sap into syrup. Perhaps that can be accounted for by the relative inaccessibility of commercial sugar or other
market conditions of the period. The history lists production of sugar
and syrup separately.

Historians tell us that production of maple products dates back to
our North American Indians. History volumes print drawings of Indians tapping trees and gathering sap. It is said that the Indians considered the sap a good tonic, drinking it to condition their bodies in the
springtime. It is believed they learned of maple syrup quite by accident
when their fires reduced sap to syrup and they licked their fingers with
delight.

The Canadian province of Quebec is the largest producer of syrup.
According to reports of crop statistics that province produces more than
2.5 million gallons of syrup annually. In the United States, Vermont is
the leader with more than 300,000 gallons, and New York is in second
place with 275,000 gallons. The 1980 *Ohio Almanac* places our state in
third place, with $845,000 in farm income derived from maple syrup.

Here in Portage County, maple syrup production has dwindled in
recent years due to the declining number of sugar maple trees and the
high cost of production. The largest producers are Kres Monroe in Hiram
Township, the Gallaghers in Freedom, and Frank Goodell in Shalersville.
There are many others in the county with lesser commercial operations
and others who make syrup strictly for family consumption. At
Maplewood Joint Vocational School, the collection of sap and evaporating it into syrup is a learning experience. Total county production of
syrup is estimated at 5,000 gallons, a sharp drop from the historical figures listed above. Best indications are that syrup this coming season will
sell in the neighborhood of $22 per gallon.

Maple syrup buffs will be interested to know the dates of the Ohio Maple Festival at Chardon in Geauga County, Ohio's largest syrup producer. The big weekend is scheduled for April 4, 5, and 6.

———

## HEARTY BREAKFAST FAVORITE ENJOYED
## START IN RAVENNA

*November 12, 1983*

Massive stone walls, slots cut into tall silos that once held 1.5 million bushels of grain, and memorabilia of a glorious industrial period. All of these provide the grist of nostalgia. As I lunched in the Tavern in the Square in Akron's Quaker Square and Hilton complex, I reflected upon long-gone days and thrilled to the finesse of dreaming architects whose vision transformed the old Quaker Oats Company complex to once again play a vibrant mercantile and social role in a modern city. Remembering the days when the Quaker Oats Company milled rolled oats and packaged breakfast cereals in Akron to become known throughout the world, it almost seemed that someone had waved a magic wand to perform a modern miracle.

Then it struck me! The Quaker trademark that gains instant recognition for products sold on a worldwide basis did not originate in Akron but in Ravenna. And that's a story in itself—a tale embodying the industrious nature of Portage County businessmen who more than a hundred years ago gave to the world the visage of the calm, respected Quaker which portrays honesty, purity, and strength.

To provide the setting for that development, one must go even farther back—to the 1850s when Ferdinand Schumacher, a young German immigrant, came to Akron and started to grind oats into meal to be sold as a breakfast food. His industry paid off; he bought an old woolen factory along the canal in Akron to step up his production to 20 barrels a day. Schumacher's oatmeal was popularized during the Civil War period, when he sold the product to the Union army. As one always hopes, the business soon outgrew its quarters and Schumacher built a plant in 1863 along Mill Street.

In 1883 he erected what he called his Jumbo Mill, eight stories high. His operations covered the whole block from Mill Street along Broadway. A meticulous person, Schumacher acquired a quarry at Peninsula so that millstones could be produced exactly to his own specifications. Then disaster struck. His mills were destroyed by fire, leaving him with a solid reputation but no mill. The tragic fire resulted in a merger with the Akron Milling Company and the formation of the F. Schumacher Milling Company.

During Schumacher's days of success in Akron, things were happening in the cereal business in Ravenna. William Heston, who had learned the miller's trade under the tutelage of Schumacher in Akron, moved to Ravenna. Heston and four others organized the Quaker Mill Company in Ravenna. His partners were Henry D. Seymour, Francis B. King, John B. King, and Henry H. Stevens. The company came into being on May 3, 1877.

How did the oatmeal entrepreneurs settle upon the Quaker name? According to Harrison J. Thornton in his *History of the Quaker Oats Company*, there are two versions of the adoption of the Quaker name.

Thornton says, "Mr. Seymour had been searching the dictionary for a name to use in incorporating the new company, but finding nothing that especially appealed to him, he turned to the encyclopedia and became interested in reading an article on the Quakers. The purity of the lives of the people, their sterling honesty, their strength and their manliness impressed him. Soon the parallel between their characteristics and what was successful, caught his fancy and he reached the conclusion that Quaker was the name to use."

The other version: A contrary story is told by William Heston. Walking one day through the streets of Cincinnati, at the time when the new company was still unbaptized, he was, he said, suddenly confronted by a picture of William Penn, whose Quaker garb and character at once suggested an admirable name for the new creation.

Thornton continued, "There is no way of definitely determining, as between Heston and Seymour, to whom belongs credit for the notable appellation. The most that can be said here is that the balance of tradition and recollection inclines toward Seymour's account. Yet a telling point in Heston's favor is that he came of Quaker ancestry." Whatever, the trademark originated in Ravenna, and on September 4, 1877, it was officially recorded by the new company in the U.S. Patent Office.

The Quaker Mill Company was sold in 1881. The 1885 *History of Portage County* lists the officers as H. B. Crowell, president; J. H. Andrews, secretary; E. R. Crowell, treasurer; and R. L. Phelps, manager. The mill employed 40 men and produced 200 barrels of meal a day.

Despite its lofty name, the Ravenna operation was not a rousing success. Its chief asset was the Quaker name, a distinct advantage when, in 1891, the Quaker Mill Company was acquired by an amalgamation of oatmeal-producing firms in Akron known as the American Cereal Company, which included Schumacher's company. That firm in 1895 registered the Quaker trademark in its own name. The American Cereal Company, which started to package oatmeal rather than sell it by the barrel, was the nucleus of the Quaker Oats Company, which became incorporated in 1901.

So . . . when you take a Quaker product from your kitchen shelf and note the placid, sturdy countenance of the Quaker trademark, remember that it was born in Ravenna 106 years ago.

————

## "ICE AGE" ENTERPRISES HAD NO
## SHORTAGE OF CUSTOMERS

*March 3, 1984*

With the Portage area socked in by a vicious late-winter snowstorm, today's column topic—the onetime flourishing ice business—is ridiculously appropriate.

Young people who are accustomed to raiding the electric refrigerator for quenching drinks and tasty food may find it difficult to believe that householders and business establishment less than a century ago had to rely upon natural ice for cooling purposes. But such was the case, and, as a result, harvesting and delivering chunks of lake ice constituted a big business. Not until later years did the manufacture of artificial ice come about to meet food preservation needs.

Ice Harvest—1909
Lake Brady, Ohio

The 1909 Ice Harvest at Brady Lake.

Except for the farmers who cut ice from ponds, the local commercial ice business in Portage County had its beginning during the winter of 1882 when the Forest City Ice Company of Cleveland leased the ice rights of East Twin Lake, north of Kent.

This was a massive undertaking which flourished for many years. An icehouse with a storage capacity of 15,000 tons was erected along the south shore of the lake in the area where homes along Woodway Drive now are located. A railroad siding from the old Cleveland and Pittsburgh Railroad (later the Pennsylvania) was laid to provide transportation of the ice to Cleveland. That area then was known as Earlville Station.

At ice harvest time, as many as a hundred men were employed by Forest City to cut and store ice and to load railroad cars. Horse-drawn, ice-cutting machines replaced earlier hand sawing of the thick ice. In storage, ice was preserved in layers of sawdust.

Fickle weather and warm winters that failed to produce thick lake ice made the ice business a tenuous one. Winters with sub-zero temperatures, such as our weather earlier this winter season, were considered ideal for the ice entrepreneurs.

The Spelman family was best-known for prominence in the local natural ice business. Henry L. Spelman of Rootstown, son of early Randolph settlers, became interested in the ice business as early as 1889. He erected a huge icehouse at Congress Lake and then went into the ice and coal business in Canton.

His son, M. B. (Burt), who is remembered as a prominent Kent banker, real estate developer, and civic leader, went into business with his father. The family business then was expanded to include icehouses and harvesting facilities at Brady Lake, Silver Lake, and other locations. The company did a large wholesale volume throughout the area, including Akron. The Spelman family in 1903 moved from Rootstown to Kent where Henry and Burt added real estate development to their prominence in the ice and coal business.

The family ice business ended when a disastrous fire on June 6, 1924, destroyed the large icehouses on the northwest shore of Brady Lake. The late Art Trory, our area's best-known photographer of historic events, captured on film striking photos of the Spelman fire. The ice house was not rebuilt, probably because the advent of artificial ice-making already had made inroads into the natural ice business. Older residents no doubt will recall the local wags who spoofed the icehouse fire with remarks such as, "Ha, ha, who ever heard of an icehouse burning?" But it did.

Meanwhile, natural ice harvesting had been going for a number of years on Crystal Lake, south of Ravenna, by the Fitzgerald family; at Fritch's Lake in Suffield Township; and at Geauga Lake. Fritch's Lake we know today as Wingfoot Lake, so named after much of the area around the body of water was acquired by the Goodyear Tire and Rubber Company in 1914 and the subsequent building of the Wingfoot hangar for blimp construction in 1916.

In Ravenna, the Portage Ice and Coal Company was big in the natural ice business. It was operated by the Fitzgerald family. Tom Fitzgerald in the 1940s became mayor of Ravenna. His brother Bob was sheriff in the late 1930s and early 1940s, and brother Rohan was chief deputy sheriff.

We recall Bob Fitzgerald's accounts of delivering ice to home iceboxes and chests. Ice delivery men wore heavy, rubberized garments that covered their shoulders and they used tongs to carry the ice blocks as they hauled them into the homes and placed them into the wooden iceboxes. These iceboxes, now long gone, are today's collector's items. Ice picks, bearing company names, were common giveaway articles for customers.

The Kent Sanitary Ice Company, organized in 1915, was the first artificial ice plant in Portage County. The plant was located just around the corner from North Mantua Street, on West Grant Street. Donald and Charles Kelso of Kent and Charles Garrison of Ravenna were its original organizers. The plant at the outset had a capacity of seven tons of ice per day, later expanded to 50 tons per day. The company furnished ice to a wide area including Kent, Ravenna, Stow, Hudson, and Brady Lake. The ice company went out of business about 1950 and then became the headquarters of the Hamilton Kent Manufacturing Company, which now is located on Highway 59 between Kent and Ravenna.

For youngsters who followed the ice wagons—either horse drawn or motorized—to pick up ice chips on a sweltering summer day, the coming of electric refrigerators and the demise of ice chests signaled the end of an era . . . an era which was very much a part of Americana.

## PAST ALIVE AND WELL AT HOPKINS MILL IN GARRETTSVILLE

*July 26, 1986*

Portage County has several attractions that draw tourists by the thousands—Sea World, Geauga Lake Park, the Kent State University Museum, Carousel Dinner Theater. But perhaps the best-kept secret among tourist attractions is the Hopkins Old Water Mill at Garrettsville. Unquestionably, the 182-year-old mill qualifies as the oldest among these attractions.

Where else in Ohio can a tourist watch while a giant water wheel provides the power for ancient, 3,000-pound French milling stones to grind grain into flour and meal—and then buy the product?

It's billed as the world's largest operating water wheel. And well it may be, with a diameter of 19 feet, 3 inches and a width of 9 feet, 9 inches.

In the mill's lower floor, tourists are provided a good opportunity to watch the water wheel as they peer through a glass-enclosed aperture. A dam in Silver Creek, which flows through Garrettsville's downtown section, and a millrace provide the power for the village's oldest business. Actually, the mill is as old as Garrettsville itself. That's not precisely accurate. Garrettsville was founded in 1803 by Col. John Garrett, and his mill followed a year later. The old colonel, whose gravesite is marked by a millstone, would be pleased to know that a mill still is operating on the site he picked out a year after he arrived from Delaware.

For owner Mike Tushar, a native of Garrettsville, operating the old mill is a labor of love, albeit he needs to make a profit to sustain body and soul. He admits that he could use more tourist business, and he has listed his establishment with Ohio's tourism organizations to bring this about. He welcomes bus tours and is happy to provide guides for tourists to watch the giant wheel in operation. Right now, he has a problem. Six weeks ago, the shaft in the water wheel broke. As might be imagined, shafts for water wheels are not a stock item, so one had to be especially manufactured. He's waiting now for a bearing, and when that arrives he hopes to be in full operation again by August 1, the beginning date of the annual three-day Silver Crik Turkey Daze.

Hopkins Old Water Mill produces eight kinds of meal and flour—white and yellow cornmeal, buckwheat flour, whole wheat flour (both soft and hard), natural unbleached white flour, buckwheat pancake mix, and Hopkins pancake mix. No additives are used in this centuries-old process. All of these products are sold at retail and wholesale. Besides these products, the mill also sells Portage County maple syrup, nuts, candy, and garden supplies.

During its long existence, Hopkins Old Water Mill has had an interesting, and at times stormy, life. As in most other communities, a mill was the first industry in the Western Reserve community of Garrettsville. Farmers needed a place to have their grain ground and pioneer families had to eat.

It is said that Colonel Garrett died on the same day his mill opened. Mrs. Garrett and her sons took over, the mill continuing in that family until the 1880s, when John Varderslice and then his son-in-law assumed control. In about 1900, the old wooden dam in Silver Creek was replaced by a concrete dam.

Catastrophe struck in 1940 when an arsonist set the mill afire to get even with an area farmer for the farmer telling him he was not an appropriate suitor for his daughter. The farmer had grain stored at the mill. Bill Scott, son-in-law of Vanderslice, restored the burned-out mill, using lumber and sandstone blocks from the original mill. Scott later sold the mill to Bruce Ginther and he and his father-in-law, Robert Hopkins, completed the restoration. At that time, the name was changed to Hopkins Old Water Mill. When Ginther wanted to retire, he sold the mill in the early 1970s to Tushar, a young man not yet 30, who always wanted to be a miller.

The 41-bucket waterwheel was made in Damascus, Ohio, disassembled and moved to Garrettsville where it was reassembled. The dam was rebuilt, millstones were brought in, and the mill again was completely restored and placed into operation.

Today the mill is not only an important area business but also is a cherished historical landmark in Ohio.

————

## LANDMARK MILL HAS LENGTHY
## HISTORY IN KENT

*July 8, 1990*

For many years the lofty elevator tower of the Williams Brothers Mill has dominated the skyline of downtown Kent. More than 200 feet tall, the tower marks one of Kent's oldest business firms, one which today remains one of the few independent flour milling companies in the nation. Few residents of the area would be unacquainted with this landmark, but no doubt many of them would not have the faintest notion of what really goes on inside the giant structure or the magnitude of the business.

Nor would they realize that Williams Brothers produces approximately 100 million pounds of choice flour each year, plus 35 million pounds of wheat bran byproducts used in animal feeds. These products are milled from 2.5 million bushels of soft red winter wheat purchased annually from Ohio farmers. For many people, names of national products they buy may be more familiar to them than the flour from which they are made. For example, Archway Cookies and Pepperidge Farm baked goods and H. J. Heinz Company products are three of Williams Brothers' large commercial customers.

A week ago I toured the mill, as I had done several times over the years, and I was amazed at the new technologies employed in the milling process, technology that has enhanced Williams Brothers' historic reputation for excellence in the manufacture of choice flour. As I toured, I couldn't help but believe that the company's founders, Charles A. and Scott T. Williams, would be pleased to see their dream fulfilled and amazed with the modern methods of flour production. The brothers, grandsons of a pioneer family who came to Franklin Township from Massachusetts shortly after the War of 1812, established the company in 1879 under the name of Peerless Roller Mills. And the mill has been operating continuously for 111 years—right now 24 hours a day, six days per week.

Later, the name of the firm was changed to Williams Brothers, the brothers dissolved partnership, and the Williams Brothers Company was incorporated in 1900. Throughout the years, as the business continued to expand, numerous additions and improvements were made to increase grain storage capacity and to improve milling processes. The latest improvement project began in 1983 as a 10-year plan to renovate product storage, material handling, raw material preparation, and plant capacity. These improvements in milling technology were made in response to the many changes in the baking industry and to perpetuate the company's solid reputation throughout the northeastern United States and Puerto Rico.

Williams Brothers from the beginning has been a family company. Charles Williams's son, Dudley, who died in 1986, headed the company for many years. Today, Charles Williams II, a grandson, is the chairman and president, and Charles "Pete" Williams III, a great-grandson of the co-founder, is secretary-treasurer.

During its early years, the mill was powered by an engine with steam generated from water drawn from the Cuyahoga River. That system ended in 1947 when the steam-powered engine was replaced by a single motor. Also, during much of the mill's existence, finished flour was shipped from the mill by train. Today most of the flour is shipped in giant bullet-shaped bulk trailers or in hundred-pound bags. The company owns the trailers; the tractors that haul them, as well as the drivers, are leased.

During the early settlement days in Portage County, mills, crude as they must have been, were essential for the sustenance of pioneers. They had to eat. Corn and wheat were the first crops, and millstones ground the grain for bread making and other cooking needs.

Except for a few historic mills, millstones have passed into history. But milling is still around, albeit with a highly advanced technology. The Williams Brothers Company of Kent is part of that advanced flour-producing technology. Even more than that, Williams Brothers for more than a century has played an important role in the history of Portage County. And still is doing it!

———

## SILKWORM FIZZLE HAD LASTING
## IMPACT ON KENT GROWTH

*October 1, 1983*

It was boom-time in 1837 in Franklin Mills (now Kent). Savvy capitalists and residents eager to make an easy dollar or two were bitten by the "canal bug." Their hopes were not completely ill founded; for several years money was made at fantastic rates. But for some, there were eventual substantial losses.

That period 146 years ago constitutes one of the most interesting and dazzling eras in Portage County and, more specifically, Kent history. The stage was set in the early 1820s, when the state of Ohio authorized the building of canals. By 1825, the Ohio Canal was planned from Portsmouth to Cleveland, opening an all-water transportation system from Lake Erie to the Gulf of Mexico. That canal traversed through Akron. The empire-builders conceived another canal, this one from Beaver,

Pennsylvania, to Akron, passing through Portage County, including Ravenna and Franklin Mills. That was the project that fired the local business spirit.

Zenas Kent, prosperous Ravenna and Hudson merchant who made investments on the basis of inside knowledge, not hearsay, apparently knew the canal would pass through Franklin Mills.

About that time—1832—the village saw most of its fledgling industries washed down the Cuyahoga River in a disastrous flood. The time was ripe! Zenas Kent and David Ladd purchased 500 acres, including a valuable water power site, for $6,300. With later acquisitions, Kent became the biggest landowner in Franklin Township. Kent knew what he was about.

Enter the Franklin Land Company, an organization formed by Cleveland, Boston, Ravenna, and Hudson capitalists who believed Franklin Mills with its ideal water power capabilities could emerge as one of the country's foremost manufacturing centers. They pinned their hopes on the manufacture of silk, and except for a quirk of nature, they might well have seen their dream realized.

In anticipation of this venture, Franklin Mills experienced a real land boom. Zenas Kent sold his holdings, for which he had paid $6,300, for $75,000. The land firm bought "upper village" (the North Mantua–Crain area) land for $40,000. All of the Franklin Land Company holdings were then sold to the newly organized Franklin Silk Company for $372,000, a sum almost unheard of in those days. Ground was broken on the west shore of the Cuyahoga River for the silk mill and foundation stones were laid in 1837. That structure, Kent's oldest manufacturing building, remains today and is now owned by the BBH Company and occupied by the Portage Paper Box Company, manufacturer of paper boxes and cartons.

Coming of the canal was assured. People went "crazy" as they anticipated big prices for their land. James Woodard, onetime mayor and member of one of Kent's earliest families, wrote: "Lots in good condition sold for up to $300 a front foot. Farm land a mile from the village sold as high as $400 per acre. The lot in the fork of North Mantua and North River Streets [now Gougler Avenue] sold for $5,000. Three years before it would have brought $500."

Zenas Kent erected a tall block at the corner of Main and Water Streets—bigger at the time than any building in either Akron or Cleveland. (The building served Kent businesses until 1972, when it was destroyed by fire.) Pendleton and Beach built the block on the southwest corner (now owned by First Federal Saving and Loan Association). The present Town Hall on Gougler Avenue was built in 1837 as an office for the Franklin Land Company. Zenas Kent erected a flour mill along the river on South River Street. He and John Brown of Harpers Ferry fame built a tannery on Stow Street. A new dam in the river and a covered bridge were built at Main Street. Anticipating prosperity, professional and business people flocked into the village. Meanwhile, gangs of Irish workers—the canal diggers—arrived. Locks were built and the canal was completed through town on the east side of the Cuyahoga River (where the old B.&O. tracks are located).

Joy H. Pendleton, later an Akron banker, imported large shipments of young mulberry trees, started a nursery, and contracted with farmers to raise trees. Silkworms, which would feed on the mulberry trees, were shipped in by stagecoach. Barber Clark, a wealthy farmer, started building a large cocoonery. Then came the crash. The entire nation was then victimized by an economic panic. The Franklin Silk Company issued scrip to counteract the dearth of money. By 1840 it became obvious that the village's economic bubble had burst. The silkworms couldn't survive in this climate, a development which probably would have been anticipated by any knowledgeable entomologist of the time. Land values returned to their former status. Incidentally, all of the scrip was redeemed dollar for dollar as a result of Zenas Kent's foresight. Despite the fizzle of the silk venture, Franklin Mills had gained many improvements, including a real downtown business district, and it had a canal, which opened in 1840 to provide new markets for local products.

The exterior of the huge building on the west shore of the Cuyahoga was not completed until 1852 to accommodate a cotton mill which did not materialize. It stood empty for another 20 years. Then in 1878, it was leased by the Kent family to Turner Brothers who started an alpaca (woolen) mill. When an agreement could not be reached by the firm and Marvin Kent, son of Zenas, the mill moved in 1889 to Cleveland where it eventually became the Cleveland Worsted Mills. The latter firm for many years operated two large plants in Ravenna—a dyehouse and a finishing mill.

This classic building was for a brief time the home of the L. N. Gross Company, which later moved to North River Street; the first site of the Ferry Machine Company; the location for Loeblein, manufacturers of fine furniture, now located in Salisbury, North Carolina; the R. D. Fageol Company; and now, the Portage Paper Box Company. And this succession started in 1837 with the canal boom and an ill-fated silk venture!

## PORTAGE ENJOYED HEYDAY AS
## CHEESE CAPITAL OF OHIO

*November 30, 1985*

In these days of high technology and lessening concentration upon agricultural pursuits, it may be difficult to comprehend that Portage County at one time was known as the "cheese capital" of Ohio. During its glory years from 1860 to 1904, Portage made and distributed more cheese than any other county, and Aurora held the distinction of being the largest cheese producing center in the United States. At one time, Portage had 40 cheese factories, a real boon to the economic welfare of farmers from whom they bought milk. A Portage township without a cheese factory was rare in those days.

With improved railroad service and increasing demand for fluid milk from burgeoning large cities nearby, farmers were able to get a better return for their milk, and the cheese industry went the way of so many enterprises that once were the staples of the local economy. In the early days of the nineteenth century, cheese making was largely done on the farm, a rather laborious chore. The curd was stirred in a tub on the floor. Portage's prominence in the cheese business began as early as 1819 when cheese was purchased from farmers and taken into the southern markets where there was a high demand for cheese.

Perhaps it was by chance that Portage really got into the cheese business. As the story goes, two Aurora boys, Royal Taylor and Harvey Baldwin, helped themselves to some apples from the orchard of P. P. McIntosh in Mantua. They were charged in the theft. To avoid trial, they loaded a wagon with cheese and cranberries and set out for Wellsville on the Ohio River. There, they acquired a skiff, loaded their cargo, and headed down river, all the way to New Orleans. Along the way, they sold their cheese and cranberries, netting a tidy profit on adventure. Beginning with that experience, Harvey Baldwin was in the cheese business, achieving more than modest success. Aurora's fabled prominence in the cheese business is an interesting story.

According to Aurora's written history, published in 1949 in connection with the community's sesquicentennial celebration, a partnership of C. R. Howard and Harvey Eggleston erected a cheese factory in 1847 near the northwest corner of S.R. 82 and Eggleston Road. The Harmon family in 1852 built a huge cheese curing house, a building which later housed Calico Corners. Then in 1862, Elisha and Frank Hurd built a cheese factory along Silver Creek and a curing house on Chillicothe Road. Those operations continued for 50 years, and the factory is said to have reached a daily production of about 4,000 pounds of cheese.

So successful was Frank Hurd in the cheese business that he became known as the "Cheese King of the Western Reserve." At one time he had 25 cheese factories spread around the Aurora and neighboring areas. Aurora historical writings point out that for 40 years "Hurd's milk prices" were the accepted standard for being "fair and just."

W. J. Eldridge, a onetime partner of Frank Hurd, by 1905 had 16 cheese factories, one in Aurora and others in the surrounding area, particularly Geauga county. W. J. Eldridge was the father of John I. Eldridge, prominent Aurora resident and former mayor, who is now age 89. By 1904, W. J. Eldridge was said to have controlled the southern market for cheese in a year when more than four million pounds of cheese were shipped from Aurora. He sold his last factory in 1921, marking the end of a robust and memorable cheese era, not only in Aurora but also, on a lesser scale, throughout Portage County.

Frank Hurd was the son of Hopson Hurd, a pioneer Aurora storekeeper and great-grandfather of Seabury Ford, Portage County attorney and former prosecutor. Ford resides in the same house occupied by his great-grandfather, which was built by John Singletary in 1805. The house once was a stage coach stop between Painesville and Chillicothe.

## WINGFOOT COMES A LONG WAY
## FROM JOHN FRITCH'S DAY

*July 1, 1984*

John Fritch, a German from Pennsylvania, settled along a lake in Suffield Township in 1804. He and his family erected a house with handmade bricks. Fritch gave his name to the lake. For more than a century the pretty body of water and popular fishing spot was identified on old Portage County maps as Fritch's Lake. John Fritch could not have envisioned what would eventually take place at his old homesite. In 1914, the Goodyear Tire and Rubber Company purchased most of the land at Fritch's Lake, and with that transaction came a new name—Wingfoot Lake.

Goodyear's entry into Suffield Township marked the beginning of an unusual and interesting period in Portage County's history. Goodyear erected the huge hangar that still today commands the Wingfoot Lake skyline. During the early days of Goodyear's Wingfoot operations, ballooning was common; the company supplied more than a thousand balloons for use during World War I. Then came airships, more commonly known today as blimps. Goodyear built more than a hundred blimps at Wingfoot, and men were trained in lighter-than-air operations. During the World War II years and thereafter, building and training activity continued. The sight of blimps floating serenely over Portage and Summit Counties was a common occurrence.

Today, the sight of a blimp over the area landscape is a rare spectacle, so seldom do any of Goodyear's fleet of blimps return to Akron, home of the vast Goodyear operations. Younger area residents are acquainted with blimps only through the medium of television as they float over sports spectacles and other public events. Goodyear's blimp fleet now includes four ships: the *Columbia*, based in Los Angeles; the *America*, in Houston; the *Enterprise*, at Pompano Beach, Florida; and the *Europe*, with its home base in Italy. None of the blimps was built at Wingfoot. Actually, the *America* is a successor to another *America* which was built at Wingfoot and was retired in 1972.

Each year, Goodyear's blimps hover over about 75 nationally televised events, most of them sports spectaculars, including baseball, football, golf, and auto race events. According to Skip Shearer, Goodyear's blimp coordinator, blimps also appear in connection with about 50 community and public service events. In some of those, the blimps' night signs are used to promote and advertise. Only recently, Goodyear blimps appeared at the Rose Parade in Portland, Oregon, and also participated in a Salute to the Statue of Liberty to impress upon the American people the need to contribute to the statue's renovation fund. Two Goodyear blimps will hover over events during the Olympic Games in Los Angeles late this month.

Goodyear is planning a new blimp model for 1987, and there's a possibility it might be built at Wingfoot, Shearer says. If not, it will be produced in Houston, where members of the current fleet were built. Why is the blimp fleet not based in Akron, Goodyear's hometown? It's mainly a matter of weather. The winter months in this area are not ideal for blimp flights and, besides, many of the wintertime events where blimps appear are in southern and western cities. [Later, the *Spirit of Akron* was built and is based at Wingfoot.]

Today at Wingfoot, which is operated by the Goodyear Aerospace Corporation, classified work for the U.S. government employs fewer than a hundred. Besides the hangar operation, the Wingfoot area includes a picturesque, well-equipped park which provides recreational facilities for Goodyear employees.

---

## HISTORY LOCKED UP IN VERSATILE
## KENT PRODUCT

*February 5, 1983*

If you are among the hundreds of residents in the Portage area who have a combination lock on your front door, consider yourself among the historically elite. Depending upon the year of its purchase, yours is either a Miller or a Gougler door lock, and it could be 95 years old. At any rate, it's a museum piece and a product that figures prominently in an interesting Kent industrial story.

Revival of interest in a Kent product which has disappeared from the market came this past week when United Press International circulated a story about many area residents in this security-conscious world living behind doors protected by aging little dials . . . Gougler locks. The story is much bigger and historically significant than that.

Turn back the clock to 1888. That's the year James B. Miller of Kent incorporated the Miller Lock Company for the purpose of manufacturing a combination lock known as the "Douds Patent Permutation Lock," so named for its inventor, J. B. Douds.

Miller had been a railroader and, among other positions, had served as superintendent of the Atlantic and Great Western shops in Kent and Galion. He left railroading to establish the Railway Speed Recorder Company in Kent, which manufactured a device for recording the speed and stops of trains. The firm was located on North Water Street in a building which later was occupied by the Davey Compressor Company

The recorder business thrived for many years, but finally the product was made obsolete by introduction of the railway block system. That's when he turned to the production of this unique lock. He developed and refined Douds' lock invention, and for 57 years locks were produced under the Miller name in a plant on Lock Street, off Lake Street, in Kent.

The Miller lock, produced for doors as well as in padlock types, became nationally known. They were particularly popular in Kent, Meadville, Pennsylvania, and Marion, Ohio, because railroaders moving through Kent purchased them here and took them home to the two other cities, which were division points on the Erie Railroad.

Miller was one of Kent's most prominent entrepreneurs. He was a councilman and was among the first officers of the Kent Board of Trade, the forerunner of the Kent Area Chamber of Commerce. He was one of the first in Kent to own an automobile and was the city's first Ford dealer. Upon his death in 1927, the business passed to his two sons, Jamie and Ned, who ran the company and manufactured the lock under the name of Miller Keyless Locks until 1945. In that year, they sold out to the C. L. Gougler Industries, which produced the locks in its Lake Street plant.

Charles McGarry, who resides in Kent, was employed by the Miller firm and went with Gougler at the time of the sale. McGarry's wife, Juanita, and her brother, Paul, also of Kent, are children of Jamie Miller and are the only members of the Miller family (except for their children) still remaining in Kent.

The lock division of Gougler continued to manufacture the combination locks under its own name until the 1970s, when the division was sold to a family in Columbus. Coincidentally, that family also was named Miller. Robert Breckenridge, president of Gougler Industries, reports that the Columbus Miller family continued to make the locks for several years and then went bankrupt. Tragically, all of the lock tooling and parts were sold for scrap. Today, Miller or Gougler locks are unobtainable, as are new parts to repair them, much to the consternation of the many homeowners who swear by the locks and are reluctant to give them up after many years' service.

Bob Phillips, a 63-year-old retired rubber worker who does business in Rootstown as the Phillips Locksmith Shop, is a real believer in the old combination locks. He says they're safe, even by modern standards, inasmuch as they have a straight bar, rather than a tapered one, and they can't be opened by slipping in a credit card like some of the knob variety. "They're sort of a deadbolt," said Phillips, adding that the locks are handy if you have children, since you don't have to worry about lost keys.

Phillips, who has become a specialist in Miller or Gougler locks, gets many calls to repair the locks or change their combinations. Service calls for changes in the combination usually come from new tenants or widows, he says. Combination changes are not difficult to make.

Phillips scrounges parts wherever he can. He recently found a combination controlling insert in a hardware store, and he bought a complete lock from an area woman who took a dislike to the fussy old dial on her front door.

Passing of these locks is another example of the demise of long-revered products not available in today's technologically sophisticated world. The Miller lock certainly was such a product. I know; I've been using one for years.

———

## RAVENNA MAN DEVELOPED HISTORIC COKE BOTTLE

*July 17, 1994*

Under the category of "Did you know?" . . . Specifically, did you know that the classic Coca-Cola bottle which has become a collector's item was developed by a onetime Ravenna resident? The bottle had its roots in Ravenna, as well it should have had. After all, the man who developed the bottle appropriately was named Root. Actually, Chapman Root.

Chapman Root came to Ravenna many years ago. He married Nellie Russell, daughter of the town baker. When he was a young bridegroom he went to work as a clerk in a local drug store and then later took a job with one of Ravenna's numerous glass factories.

Historical writings do not list the name of the glass company. It could have been one of several, because Ravenna had many of them during the 1860s, 1870s, 1880s, and 1890s. First of these was the Diamond Window Glass Company, founded in 1867, followed by the Enterprise Glass Company in 1872, the Ravenna Flint Glass Company in 1882, the Crown Flint Glass Company in 1883, the Eagle Glass Company in 1880, the Ballinger Glass Company, and still another glass factory, which made only lamp chimneys.

Some of them made window glass while others produced artistic glass that, along with Mantua and Kent glass, has become a prized collector's item. Prized glass artifacts from the three communities can be found in the Portage County Historical Society Museum; in the Corning Museum in Corning, New York; and in family collections that have been handed down through several generations.

Chapman Root didn't develop the Coke bottle in Ravenna. When the glass factory in Ravenna for which he worked closed abruptly, Root was out of work. Although at the time such a stroke of misfortune was a personal tragedy, the plant's closing turned out to be a most blessed turn of events. He moved to Terre Haute, Indiana, where he developed a unique bottle, a move which eventually made him one of America's richest men. He sold the bottle to the Coca-Cola Company, and it became a fixture with the soft drink bottler. At one time, Root's wealth was estimated at $20 million, a tidy sum in those days when we weren't accustomed to estimating wealth on the basis of today's astronomical figures.

The Roots seldom returned to Ravenna after their move to Terre
Haute, but they did maintain some business, social, and church con-
tacts. At one time they owned two business buildings in the city on
Main Street, and they continued their contributions to Grace Episcopal Church. Mrs. Root purchased a window in the remodeled church in
memory of her family. The couple maintained a close friendship with
Mr. and Mrs. W. J. Beckley. Mr. Beckley was a prominent Ravenna attorney. The Beckleys resided in a hilltop home on Lakewood Road overlooking Lake Hodgson.

Manufacture of glass products once was one of Portage County's most
flourishing industries. Presence of the factories was due largely to the
abundance of silica sand in this area. The first of our glass factories was
established in Mantua in 1821 by David Ladd. Two years later he moved
the factory to Kent, where he went into partnership with Joshua
Woodard and Benjamin Hopkins. Their glassworks was on the west
side of the Cuyahoga River in what today is north Kent. Another early
factory was the Franklin Glass Works, which was established in 1824
on a part of Christian Cackler's farm in northwest Franklin Township.
In 1968, that old glassworks was located by Duncan Wolcott of Silver
Lake. The old ovens were unearthed in an archaeological dig sponsored by Case Western Reserve University and were moved to the Hale
Homestead in Summit County.

One of the more prominent glass factories in Kent was the Day and
Williams Company. Its factory, really started by the Kent family in 1850,
was located south of Kent's historic railroad station extending to West
Summit Street. Today, the area at one time occupied by the glassworks
is a parking lot. Day and Williams took over the business from the Kent
family in 1864. By 1877, when the company was employing as many as
200 men, the firm experienced serious labor trouble. To meet that problem, the company imported Belgian glassblowers willing to work for
lesser wages. The Belgians resided in small company homes on South
Water Street where the Kent City Hall now is located. For many years,
that area was known as "Belgian Hill." Day and Williams, which made
window glass and other products, finally ended its business in 1885.

Kent had another glass company known as the Dithridge and Smith
Company, which was located in a plant on Mogadore Road. The com-

pany started production in 1894 but survived only a short time.

It can be assumed from the speckled history of Portage County's glass business that not many people became excessively rich from their enterprises. That remained for Chapman Root. He had a better idea. He developed the Coke bottle.

---

## TWIN COACH DREAM BEGAN ON
## AN IOWA FARM

*October 30, 1984*

It all began on a farm near Des Moines, Iowa, when Frank R. and William B. Fageol experimented with automotive developments. It culminated with a vast complex on the west side of Kent, where the Twin Coach Company became the largest employer in the Tree City and where Twin Coach buses were turned out by the thousands for a transportation-hungry American public. Today, that large Kent complex is virtually silent, with only a small part of the building occupied. And the Twin Coach Company does not exist.

One of the Fageols' earliest automotive creations was a steam-powered vehicle that hauled passengers to the Iowa state fairgrounds. In 1902 the family moved to California and settled in the San Francisco–Oakland area. By 1920 their truck business developed rapidly. Products of the brothers' Fageol Motor Company were distributed throughout the Pacific Coast. The Fageol brothers were among the first to see the possibility of mass transportation. They designed and built Fageol Safety Coach in 1922, a development that heralded the passenger-carrying industry. Safety Coach sales spread rapidly.

After establishing a sales office in Cleveland, the Fageols searched for a body-building facility in the East. F. R. and W. B. found it in Kent, a plant on West Main Street that had been vacated by the Thomart Motor Company. From 1924, when the first coach was completed, to the middle of the next year, 30 to 40 vehicles were produced each month. Then the American Car and Foundry Company acquired control of Fageol Motors and the motor coach activities were transferred to Detroit. Frank Fageol

continued with the new company for a time, and then in 1927 the Twin
Coach Company was incorporated, with F. R. as president, W. B. as vice
president, and Paul Brehm as secretary-treasurer.

With that organizational structure, a new Twin Coach bus was born.
It featured twin power plants instead of one large one, an engineering
design that probably accounted for the coach's name. The first Twin
Coach rolled off the Kent assembly line on July 31, 1927. It was a revolutionary bus. Its front and rear lines were the same; one could not tell
(until the bus moved) which were the rear and the front ends. With the
introduction, 25 orders were received before production really began.

Many developments in the transportation field followed. There were
a combination rail and road coach; house-to-house dairy and bakery
delivery units; trolley buses which ran on tires rather than rails that
were referred to as trolley buses; highway post offices; Pony Express mail
delivery trucks; and diesel and propane-powered buses. In the 1950s,
Twin Coach received a single order for 500 propane-powered buses from
Chicago. During the World War II years, when Twin Coach employment was at an all-time high, the company built tail assemblies for war-
planes, control cabins for blimps, and tail sections for Corsair aircraft.

Following the war, Twin Coach also produced the Super Twin, a large
coach hinged in the middle, and its smaller delivery vans in Kent and
also operated an aircraft plant in Buffalo, New York. Eventually Twin
Coach turned over its bus production to the Flexible Company in
Loudonville.

------

## PORTAGE GUNPOWDER MILL WENT UP IN SMOKE

*November 29, 1987*

The Ravenna Arsenal during its World War II heyday was known worldwide as a shell loading plant. But it must take a back seat, timewise, by
nearly a century to another Portage County operation involved with
ammunition.

Today, motorists traveling on Highway 59 between Kent and Ravenna
buzz by the Powder Mill Road intersection at the Kent State University

golf course without giving a passing thought to that strange name for a thoroughfare. Likewise, probably, the same applies to people who have homes along the historic road. There's a valid reason for the Powder Mill Road designation. More than 140 years ago, the Gillette and Austin Powder Mill manufactured gunpowder in buildings located alongside Breakneck Creek.

Actually, the road more properly is known as Fox–Powder Mill Road, probably so named because a man named J. J. Fox at one time was the owner of a considerable tract of land along the road. In later years, the Fox name seems to have been dropped, even on county road markers. Perhaps the latter resulted from the rather unusual length of the name.

Portage County historical records indicate that a Mr. Gillette of Ravenna was the motivating force behind establishment of the powder mill in 1846. The land where the mill was located today is a biological area owned by Kent State University. Students at KSU working in that area, under the direction of Dr. Samuel J. Mazzer of the Department of Biological Sciences, have uncovered some interesting details of the powder mill operation. Their research reports that Gillette was involved at the outset with a Tilden in the plant's establishment. However, *Portage Heritage*, the Portage County Historical Society's 1957 history volume, designates the operation as the Gillette and Austin Powder Mill.

In any event, it is known that the original structures near Breakneck Creek consisted of six buildings, two fabricated with brick and four with wood. Water to power the mill's grinding operations was obtained from the nearby Pennsylvania and Ohio Canal for an annual payment of $175. The mill's lease with the canal people required that after the mill used the water, it had to be returned to Breakneck Creek, one of the canal's feeder sources. The mill's operators lost little time following construction of the six buildings to get powder operations under way. By the third week of June 1846, 40 kegs were filled and ready for use.

Obviously, the manufacture of gunpowder is a tricky operation. It is known that people of ancient China, India, and the Middle East used gunpowder. But its exact ingredients and methods of making it were not known in the western world until 1242 when Roger Bacon of Oxford University in England published a book in which he told how to make it. Modern gunpowder is a mixture of charcoal, sulfur, and saltpeter (potassium nitrate). One of gunpowder's early disadvantages was the cloud of smoke emitted when it exploded, a problem that was solved in 1884 with the introduction of smokeless powder.

The Powder Mill Road gunpowder operations were short lived. On July 10, 1846, about 4 A.M. more than 1,200 pounds of powder and 2,000 pounds of materials used in its manufacture went up in a big explosion. All of the company's buildings were leveled, and the explosion's boom was heard in Ravenna. In Franklin Mills (now Kent), the concussion shattered a large glass window in the Franklin Block in the village's downtown section. The explosion damaged the upper structure of a canal boat which happened to be passing by the site at the time. Two mules pulling the boat were killed.

Considering the speed with which the plant was rebuilt, gunpowder facilities must have been rather spartan. Buildings razed in the July explosion were rebuilt a month later. But the following January they, too, became victims of another accident. One of the proprietors, Festus W. Hill, was seriously injured and died a few days later.

Even this second explosion apparently did not daunt the owners of the powder plant whose buildings were rebuilt. The Gillette and Austin plant, also known in some historical records as the Oregon Powder Mills, is believed to have operated until the 1860s. Although it has not been historically confirmed, it is probable that when the plant ceased operations, some of its machinery may have been moved to the Austin Powder plant in Akron. That plant, which also involved the Austin family, was moved to the Cleveland area in 1867.

As far as is known, only one reminder of the powder plant exists. Karl Bruemmer of Dawley Road, Ravenna, a gun collector and gunpowder hobbyist, has in his possession a can that once held gunpowder produced by the Gillette and Austin plant. Its block print label shows two hunters shooting birds. The can was on display for several years in the Portage County Historical Society's museum in Ravenna.

———

# A REPORTER'S "DREAM SCOOP" BECAME THE RAVENNA ARSENAL

*August 23, 1986*

It was the first week of August 1940. That, if you've lost count, was 46 years ago. As a young reporter, it was my assignment to cover each day the doings around the Portage County Courthouse. To a newsman, a good news source is one who has integrity, doesn't mislead, and seeks no individual credit or notoriety. Bob Barrett was such a news source. Bob Barrett was the Portage County recorder. And even our current county recorder, Helen Frederick, would admit that the recorder's office, by its very nature, isn't one that makes big news. Not so on that particular day in 1940.

When I stopped in his office on that day, Bob Barrett had earth-shattering news. "There's something going on here that I think you should know about," he offered, as he presented a slew of options on land in eastern Portage County, mainly in Charlestown and Paris Townships. "Agents from the Bankers Guarantee and Trust Company in Akron are taking up options on large tracts of land in eastern Portage County," he said. Indeed, they were.

I called F. S. Carpenter, president of the Bankers Guarantee and Trust Company, to seek more information. Little was to be had. He said the customer for the options was a confidential one, but he confirmed that ten agents from his company were taking up options from farmers in that area, that his firm had obtained plat books from the recorder's office, and that the area involved could include as many as 15,000 acres. That was sufficient cause for a news story. I wrote an 11-paragraph story that included circulating rumors that the area was destined for an airfield. The story ran on page 1.

A week later, U.S. representative Dow Harter of Akron, who had been in touch with the War Department, confirmed that the area in question was to become an ammunition loading plant. What began as a simple inquiry in the usually news-barren recorder's office heralded perhaps the most interesting, revolutionary era in Portage County history. From a variety of standpoints—geographic, social, economic, military—the arsenal era had a powerful impact upon the lives of our people.

Now the Ravenna Arsenal, long in a state of near-dormancy, is in
the news again. First, Gov. Richard Celeste proposed that some of the
land be released for economic development. And the Olin Corporation
is competing against two other companies for a contract to produce
mortar shells at the arsenal.

These developments prick our nostalgic conscience and prompt recollections of the transformation of Portage County life as we once knew
it into a new realm of uncertainty, beset with all types of problems,
albeit with an economic surge never before experienced in Portage
County. The need for 223 farm families, many of them on the same
farms since their ancestors settled them in the early 1800s, to vacate
their properties within 30 days was traumatic. Some of them found other
farms; others never farmed again.

The beginnings of the Ravenna Arsenal comprised a fantastic story.
The area that was rumored as 15,000 acres edged over the 22,000-acre
mark within months of the first announcement. The cost increased from
a first reported figure of $11 million to $14 million, then to $46 million
and eventually to $83.5 million.

Who knows the actual cost? The arsenal was built on a cost-plus
contract, and speed was the primary concern, because in a few months
we would be involved in World War II. The first-estimated number of
employees at 10,000 was doubled when production first began but construction had not yet been completed. Likewise, the number of buildings first estimated at slightly more than 200 zoomed to nearly 1,000.
And what began as options in Charlestown and Paris townships expanded into slices of Freedom and Windham townships, plus 1,600 acres
in Trumbull County.

The Hunkin-Conkey Construction Company received the construction contract, and Wilbur Watson Associates was engaged as the engineering contractor. Both were Cleveland firms. Construction workers
at the arsenal will never forget Hunkin-Conkey's construction superintendent, Jim Bartholomew, whose barking orders, no doubt, had much
to do with getting the job done in record time. Certainly there was
waste—plenty of it. I saw enough wasted lumber in huge piles to build
several houses. Such was the price of speed.

In October 1940 I took a photo of the groundbreaking on the Pearl Thomas farm, located along S.R. 627 just north of Paris School. In mid-August 1941, I took another photo of 75 millimeter shells rolling off Loadline No. 1, the first of the loadlines to be completed. This was a fantastic performance—in 10 months barren farmland had been transformed into a shell loading plant.

During that construction period, I visited the area almost daily. Actually, a spot without a road on the particular day would have one the next. The same with railroads. Trailers were moved in to house workers. Each held four men, and each man paid $2.10 per week for housing. In droves, workers came from throughout Ohio and neighboring states.

I remember well going with Angelo Sicuro to the Ravenna Hotel, located in what is today the Etna House, to interview Capt. J. D. Hillyer, the first U.S. Army ordnance department officer on the scene. The *Record-Courier* committed its entire news staff for that purpose—Angelo and I were "it." And then came Col. R. S. Chavin as commanding officer. We liked him because he always was accessible. And then there was Col. Martin Kafer. He came as a warrant officer, and within a few months he was a colonel. He commanded the Portage Ordnance Depot, the west end of the aresenal used for igloo storage of ammunition. His headquarters was in the old Bolton barn north of Charlestown Center. He put all of his female staff in uniform, complete with overseas-style hats. When he retired he bought the Bar 10 in Ravenna, and he eventually became a candidate for mayor.

Ravenna took on all the aspects of a western town. Friday was pay day for arsenal construction workers, and all of their checks were drawn on the Second National Bank. For the first time in history, the bank stayed open on Friday evening. Workers lined up on Main Street to get their checks cashed. The bars also cashed checks. At the Buckeye Bar on West Main Street there was a cashier's booth. Above it, through a hole cut into the ceiling, a shotgun-toting man stood guard. John D'Amico's Royal Castle also had a check-cashing booth.

The shell and bomb loading plant was known as the Ravenna Ordnance Plant in those days. The storage area was the Portage Ordnance

Depot, pronounced with a short "e." Atlas Powder Company operated
the shell loading plant. Each had separate guard units. I saw Judge Blake
C. Cook, Judge Bob Cook's father, swear in 300 Atlas Powder guards as
sheriff's deputies in one swoop behind the old courthouse in what then
was a Ravenna city park.

Housing became a problem. That was partially solved by the construction of Maple Grove at Windham and dormitories for women workers at Cotton Corners in the "V" between old and new S.R. 5. Ravenna
had three USO clubs to help handle the social problems of arsenal workers. One was in the Ravenna Armory, another in the 600 block of West
Main Street, and a third at the Cotton Corners dormitories. The old
Bolton mansion north of Charlestown center became an officer's club.

The arsenal, despite the nature of its mission, had a good safety record.
I recall only one major accident. Eleven were killed when ammunition
being unloaded into an igloo blew up. The shock was felt as far away as
Youngstown, and pieces of the truck were found in Windham.

Those closely associated will not forget the arsenal in its booming
days. And, now, those days may return, albeit in a much, much smaller
dimension. [In 1998, the Ravenna Arsenal is a desolate area with no
production in progress.]

―――――

## HOTELS PLAYED VITAL ROLE IN THE
## AREA'S DEVELOPMENT

*April 17, 1988*

Rare was the Portage County town more than a century ago that could
not boast at least one hotel. And in some cases, even the smallest of
communities had two or three hostelries catering to stagecoach, canal,
or railroad travelers.

Some of these ancient hotel buildings still remain, although it has
been many years since they housed a guest or served a meal. The old
Palmyra Inn is a noteworthy reminder of the glory days of innkeeping.
Another, but with a far more resolute purpose, is Brimfield's old Kelso
House, which once stood on the southeast corner of Highway 43 and

Tallmadge Road to cater to weary travelers. Acquired by the Brimfield Memorial House Association after the site was purchased for a service station, the ancient inn was moved to its present site near Brimfield Elementary School. Today, the Kelso House is one of our area's most robust historical centers in its role as a meeting place and museum.

As early as the mid-1830s, Franklin Mills (now Kent) had five competing hotels or tavern-hotels. The earliest of these was the old Woodard Tavern, built in 1819 on the southwest corner of North Mantua Street and Fairchild Avenue. Not to be outdone, Price and DePeyster shortly thereafter erected the Lincoln Tavern on the northwest corner of Stow and South Mantua Streets. They competed for travelers who arrived by stagecoach from Ravenna. The stage's last stop before arriving in Franklin Mills was the Black Horse Tavern, west of Ravenna.

By the mid-1830s, three more hotels had opened for business in Franklin Mills, bringing the total to five. Future abolitionist John Brown, who in 1835 built a tannery on Stow Street for Zenas Kent, erected a hotel building on Summit Street; the Franklin House opened in the large block erected by Zenas Kent at the corner of Main and Water Streets in 1836, and the Cuyahoga House went up on the northwest corner of North Mantua and Cuyahoga Street.

All probably opened for business in anticipation of the canal boom. Canal diggers swarmed into town to build the Pennsylvania and Ohio Canal, which traversed the countryside from Beaver, Pennsylvania, to Akron, where it joined the Ohio Canal. Most of the canal crews stayed at the Cuyahoga House or Woodard's Tavern; the new downtown Franklin House was considered too high-toned for canal men. Others stayed at the Lincoln Tavern on Stow Street.

Beginning with the arrival of the first canal boat in April 1840, the sight of heavily loaded boats pulled by slow-moving mules became a common sight. Boats, some carrying freight and others passengers, arrived and departed daily. In those days, what was known as Carthage, or the Upper Village of Franklin Mills, was the most active area of the town. Food and drink were plentiful at the hostelries, and there no doubt was ample interesting conversation among travelers as well as the rough-and-ready canal crewmen. As a youth, James A. Garfield for a brief time drove boat-pulling mules and did other chores on a canal boat. Canal service of the future president terminated when he contracted ague, a disease characterized by chills and high fever.

Hotels continued to operate under various names in Zenas Kent's downtown block. However, John Brown forsook the hotel business for other interests, primarily the development of the Brown-Thompson addition in the south section of town, after which he left to work for Simon Perkins in Akron. The old Woodard Tavern later became a rooming house, which burned in 1881; the Lincoln Tavern went out of business.

The old Cuyahoga House, with its large ballroom and hiding places for slaves escaping to Canada via the Underground Railroad, prevailed for many more years. Finally, even this grand old house with its stately pillars succumbed to the ravages of time, a changing life-style and diminishing business. This outstanding landmark was condemned and torn down in 1907, after sightseers were allowed to go through the building for a final look. Only the beautiful pillars of the Cuyahoga House remain to this day. They adorn the front of a house in Ravenna, located on West Main Street across from West Main School.

---

## VANISHED HOTEL LEAVES LEGACY OF
## PLEASANT MEMORIES

*August 25, 1984*

Today's younger residents of the Lake Stafford (Sandy Lake) area probably don't realize that an elaborate hotel once dominated the north shore of the lake. The hotel, razed in the 1960s, was an influential landmark in Portage County's glorious past.

I knew the hotel as the Glencrest. Prior to that time it was the Aaltje. The structure was built in 1877 by a member of the Cady family, which figured prominently in Sandy Lake area history. For many years the hotel and its surroundings constituted a summertime vacation playground for guests who came from Pittsburgh, Cleveland, and other neighboring cities.

For this writer, the demise of the hotel, now surrounded by fine year-round as well as summertime homes, possessed more than historic interest. I was personally involved. During the summer of 1935, when jobs were scarce for college students, I worked in the hotel. My job was varied and menial. There were dishes to be washed, bluegills to be cleaned for hotel guests, floors to be scrubbed and waxed, rooms to be cleaned, weeds to be pulled. Guests were not plentiful in those waning days of the hotel's popularity, so the hotel operator was eager to offer a room, board, and eight dollars per week to someone who would perform the aforementioned jobs almost around the clock. Harry and Margaret Mullen Sheets then operated the hotel under their lease arrangement.

One of my coworkers, the late Jay Littlepage, onetime Kent State University football and wrestling star, was the lifeguard. In the evening, when chores were finished, he and I many times took to the lake to fish, mainly for bluegills.

At that time, the Portage County Fish and Game Association leased the lake and hotel. The association employed a gatekeeper, Jim Caris, who thrilled me with his stories of the hotel in its glory days. I recall Jim relating how the hotel in the old days kept a horse-drawn hack to transport guests from the old C. & P. Railroad (later the Pennsylvania) in Ravenna to the lake. At one time, the Cleveland Worsted Mills Company, which until it ceased operations in 1955 provided hundreds of jobs at its two plants in Ravenna, owned both Sandy and Muddy Lakes (Stafford and Hodgson) as a water supply source.

During the hotel's heyday, many prominent Americans were guests. Two presidents, a governor, a famous temperance lecturer, and many industrial tycoons visited the resort. President James A. Garfield was a guest in the hotel shortly before his assassination in 1881. President Grover Cleveland is said to have marveled at the elaborate construction and decor of the hotel.

Two construction projects expanded the hotel. One in 1902 added 10 rooms. Another in 1918 provided 25 more rooms. Lumber used in the original construction was obtained from a grove that surrounded the lake. The logs were taken to a Ravenna lumber mill for planing, curing, and finishing.

At least two tragedies occurred near the hotel. About 1902, Bill Davis, a carpenter working on a hotel addition, and a young woman who worked in the hotel drowned when their boat capsized enroute to Cady's Landing on the southeast shore of the lake. Two years later, George Douthitt, a prominent Ravenna attorney, and a companion, Perry Clark, burned to death in a fire at a nearby cottage.

At the peak of the hotel's popularity, Frank Stanford, a Randolph man, operated a 30-foot steamer on the lake. For ten cents, he transported guests across the lake from the hotel to Cady's Landing. In the 1940s, long after the hotel ceased to be a popular resort, it was a frequent site for Ravenna Elks stag parties, Jaycee picnics, Kent State parties, and the like. The KSU Rowboat Regatta, now a bygone event, once was held on the lake. Now, the once-prominent hotel constitutes a blip on the pages of Portage County history.

———

## PORTAGE AREA WAS ONCE INUNDATED
## WITH NEWSPAPERS

*July 23, 1983*

Imagine, if you can, a wife in 1855 saying to her hard-working husband, "I wonder what's wrong with the mail. Our *Hickory Flail and Fushion Thresher* hasn't been delivered yet." Or a Kent family only four years later perusing the *Omnium Gatherum*. Believe me, the *Hickory Flail and Fushion Thresher* and the *Omnium Gatherum* were names of two early Portage County newspapers. With names like those, it's small wonder that their publications were short lived. For the record, the *Hickory Flail and Fushion Thresher* died the same year it came on the Ravenna scene. Like many newspapers of that era, the *HF and FT* was a Democratic sheet put out to boost the fortunes of a certain candidate. When the candidate lost, the paper ceased to exist. *Omnium Gatherum* was Kent's first newspaper, started in 1859. When Dr. Alonzo Dewey, its publisher, fell upon hard times, he changed the name to the *Family Visitor* and then to the *Literary Casket*. Understandably, neither name brought success, and exit Dr. Dewey.

Portage County had a long list of papers in the old days. Most of them deserve only passing notice in county historical volumes. For example, there was the *Sharp Sickle* in Atwater (wonder what it printed); the *Western Pearl* in Garrettsville; the *Whig, Argus, Western Cabinet, Reformer, Canal Advocate, Watchman,* and *Western Courier* in Ravenna; the *Bugle Echo* in Hiram; *Wide Awake* in Palmyra; the *Register, Review,* and *Gazette* in Mantua. Early newspapers most times reflected political leanings. Ravenna at one time had the *Watchman,* the *Sentinel,* and even a *Plain Dealer,* all of them politically oriented. Most of these early papers enjoyed only a modicum of success, hence the frequent changes of name, which didn't seem to be the solution for success. The *Ohio Star* was an exception. It was started in Ravenna in 1830, and it still lives today in the pages of one of its great-great-grandchildren, the *Record-Courier.*

Actually, the *Ohio Star* was not Portage County's first newspaper. That honor goes to the *Western Courier and Western Public Advertiser,* a paper published by a Pittsburgh-trained printer named J. B. Butler. A hefty section of its first edition, in 1825, was taken up by the inaugural address of President John Quincy Adams, despite the fact that it was printed several weeks after Adams delivered his address.

By 1838, after eight different ownerships, the *Western Courier* ceased publication, leaving journalistic endeavors to the more successful *Ohio Star.* A man named Laurin Dewey took over the *Star* in 1833 and converted it into an organ of the Whig party, which then was emerging as an influential political arm. Lyman Hall, recognized as one of Portage County's most influential editors, changed the *Star*'s name to the *Portage County Democrat.* The *Star* eventually merged with Ravenna's *Portage County Whig* and was renamed the *Portage County Democrat,* despite its obvious Republican leanings.

And in that name hangs another tale in Portage County journalism. Hall developed a new heading, *Democrat and Republican,* as much as to say that he really couldn't make up his mind. He proceeded to make the "Republican" in the flag larger and larger and the "Democrat" smaller and smaller until he eventually eliminated "Democrat" altogether in what must have been considered sort of a political evolution to his readers. Meanwhile, another *Portage County Republican* was organized in 1878, and it was later merged with Hall's *Republican* and sold to a group of citizens. It is interesting to note that James A. Garfield of Hiram held ownership shares in the revitalized newspaper at the time of his assassination in 1881.

Another step in the evolution came about 1893 when the *Graphic* was founded in Ravenna, with C. W. S. Wilgus as publisher. He bought out the *Republican,* combined it with the *Graphic,* and continued as publisher until 1910 when his brother-in-law, A. D. Robinson, took over. The paper became a semiweekly and then a triweekly. In 1927 the company was purchased by Dix interests and converted to daily status. Thus, the old *Ohio Star,* founded 153 years ago and following numerous changes in ownership, still exists in today's *Record-Courier.*

While all of these journalistic maneuverings were going on in Ravenna, would-be publishers were trying their hands in Kent. Following the *Omnium Gatherum* and *Literary Casket* debacle, there were the *Saturday Review* and a *Commercial Bulletin,* neither of which met with outstanding success. Then Napoleon Jeremiah A. Minich arrived on the Kent scene from Pennsylvania in 1876. Renaming the *Commercial Bulletin* the *Saturday Bulletin* and then simply the *Kent Bulletin,* Minich did well.

An outstanding citizen, Minich served two terms as mayor of Kent beginning in 1909 following the sale of his paper in 1903. The beautiful home on Columbus Street, at the corner of Columbus and North DePeyester, now occupied by the John Hammelsmiths, was the Minich home.

Kent also had a paper called the *Kent News,* at one time edited by a lawyer, Scott Rockwell. Enter the Kent family who founded the *Courier* in 1886 with the express purpose of opposing a municipal water system, a move much favored by Minich's *Bulletin.* Journalism was a highly personal matter in those days. For example, a long-standing feud between editors Charles Scott of the *Courier* and Rockwell of the *News* in 1886 erupted into a nasty fistfight in Kent's downtown section.

John G. Paxton, famed *Kent Courier* editor for more than 40 years, started the *Kent Tribune* in 1915. That paper and the *Courier* were purchased by Martin L. Davey, Ohio governor, in 1929, and he sold to the Dixes in 1930. That transaction paved the way for a merger with the *Ravenna Evening Record,* resulting in today's *Record-Courier.*

Dix Newspapers were founded by Albert Dix, who once operated a general store in Atwater. He was Bob Dix's grandfather. Albert Dix left Atwater in 1880 when he acquired an interest in a Hamilton, Ohio, paper. He and his son, Emmett C. (Bob's father), born in Atwater in 1873, then turned their talents to Wooster and the *Wooster Daily Record*, which became the flagship newspaper of today's Dix Newspapers communications organization.

---

## A HUNDRED AND TEN YEARS AGO, PORTAGE GREETED THE TELEPHONE

*November 15, 1992*

"Mr. Watson, come here. I want you."

In that brief command the first words were spoken over a telephone. The year was 1876, and it was Alexander Graham Bell who uttered them to his assistant. Bell and Watson were in separate second-story rooms in a Boston boardinghouse, conducting experiments with a voice transmitter. The distinct transmission and Bell's demonstration of his telephone at the Centennial Exposition in Philadelphia in July of that year confirmed Bell's experiments, realized his dream, and heralded today's vast, worldwide telephone communication system.

Telephone service developed rapidly, particularly in the eastern half of the nation, and just six years later telephones came to Portage County. This fall we are celebrating the 110th local anniversary of what then was considered this "wonder of wonders." In its edition of May 10, 1882, the *Ravenna Republican-Democrat,* the county-seat newspaper of that era, observed that "If citizens of Ravenna move rapidly they can easily secure the benefit and advantage of the best telephone system now in use."

The Midland Telephone Company signed up subscribers, poles went up, and wires were strung. By October 25, a hundred-line switchboard had been installed in a room over the First National Bank. Meanwhile, a line was constructed over a distance of 35 miles from Cleveland to Akron and then on to Canton and Massillon. L. J. Towns, Midland manager, was pushing a connection with Kent, Akron, and Cleveland. Line construction was completed almost all the way from Ravenna to Kent before Ravenna telephone service actually began on November 1, 1882.

Miss Georgia Bassett was the first telephone operator in Ravenna. She answered "hello" to rings from the 55 original subscribers. E. F. Deming, a Ravenna grocer, on that day received the first message for goods, so said the *Republican-Democrat*. Miss Nellie Johnson was credited with speaking the first words into the new telephone system. A party in celebration of the telephone service's arrival was held in Ravenna. The newspaper said a large crowd "was quite agreeably entertained by vocal and instrumental music through the medium of the telephone from the residence of E. Q. Van Ness and G. P. Reed, nearly a mile away from the party site. The words and music were distinctly understood."

The list of first subscribers in Ravenna reads like a local "Who's Who"—John Byers, H. D. Seymour, Dr. Joseph Waggoner, D. C. Coolman, J. C. Beatty, besides many familiar business places, Merts and Riddle, Etna House, Atlantic Mill, G. E. Fairchild, among others.

The newspaper went on to say: "If anyone had suggested 20 years ago that in 1882 a person could hold a conversation with another person five miles away with as much ease as though he were present, the probabilities are they would have been pronounced a bevel-headed lunatic."

Kent service followed the Ravenna inauguration by two months. On December 8, 1882, the Kent exchange opened on the top floor of the Kimes building, corner of South Water and Erie Streets. Like Ravenna, the Kent exchange began with 55 subscribers. Fred Cone was the first manager and Emily France the first operator. Edward L. Day received the first call in Kent. In those early telephone days, young women from the exchanges in Kent and Ravenna went door-to-door to collect monthly service fees from inaugural subscribers.

A succession of companies operated local telephone service prior to the Ohio Bell Telephone Company's acquisition in 1921. During years that have followed, Ohio Bell has invested millions upon millions of dollars expanding the service, building new exchanges, installing lines, automatic switching equipment to take advantage of the latest scientific innovations in voice communications.

Those are the tangibles in the growth of the telephone system. There are many people who have added a personal contribution to that growth pattern. Who can forget people like the late Leon Hubbell, who grew up in the business under his father in Chagrin Falls and became the Portage County manager in 1919, serving until his retirement in 1942? Or the late Ray Cheetham, George Towner, Cal Hinds, or John Wunderle? As managers they guided Ohio Bell's operations in Kent, Ravenna, Mantua, and Rootstown and witnessed firsthand the development of new communication systems.

Those original 55 subscribers in both Kent and Ravenna have escalated into thousands upon thousands. Today it is a rare home that does not have at least one telephone. Many homes boast several telephones; some have portable instruments that can be used outside the home; and now cellular telephones have become commonplace. And there is great competition for long-distance service to enable subscribers to direct-dial to remote locations around the world. They have plenty of places to reach. The latest *World Book* tells us that 425 million telephones exist throughout the world.

---

## NO THEATER NOW, BUT RAVENNA
## PIONEERED IN THE FILM ERA

*June 1, 1984*

History sometimes takes strange twists!

Consider this paradox: The city of Ravenna, practically the mother of moving picture theaters, has had no movie theater for several years and now is engaged in a strenuous effort to attract one to the community. Yet Kent, only six miles away, boasts nine cinemas—seven screens in University Plaza and two more at Kent Cinemas on East Main Street. One can only hope that the Ravenna community's efforts will be successful. After all, it's not nice to treat history in such a cavalier manner. This situation causes us to reflect upon a time that was and on Ravenna's glory days as a leader in the motion picture industry.

It was in 1904—80 years ago—that a young man of 22, Van C. Lee, rented a vacant room on the first floor of the old Riddle Coach and Hearse factory building on East Main Street, just east of Prospect, borrowed several hundred chairs from a funeral parlor, and projected eye-straining images upon a white sheet. Some say this was the first motion picture theater in the nation. Motion picture historians dispute this, however, pointing out that the first theater for showing motion pictures was established in Los Angeles in 1902. Whether or not it was the first, Mr. Lee was honored by a movie industry publication as the first movie theater manager in the land.

In 1905, Laurence Bundy of Kent started another theater in Ravenna, selling out soon afterward to a group which included Mr. Lee's brother, Arthur. A year later, on November 5, 1906, the Liberty Moving Picture Company began showing movies at the Opera House at the corner of North Water and Columbus Streets in Kent. Reports in old newspapers describe that venture as having a "mighty array of pictures." Within a year, three more theaters opened in Kent—the Bijou, the Electric, and the Grand. Those theaters, except the one at the Opera House, are described by nonagenarian Karl Mosher as "nothing but storerooms with a white sheet for the picture." Karl recalls that he worked as a "sound man" at the Opera House. His assignment called for him to work behind the stage to rewind the film as the operator showed the picture slides. Typical of towns where entertainment-hungry patrons paid a nickel to see this new wonder, Kent had four nickelodeon theaters in those early days.

But, back to Van Lee. He truly was a local pioneer in the movie business. As a boy of 12, Lee talked Thomas A. Edison into joining him on a tour of the country to demonstrate Edison's invention of the first motion picture projector. Lee was inspired by what he witnessed. When he started his theater in what is known today as Riddle Block No. 6, where Drs. John and Frances Redmond, McGraw, and Eckler, and Bohecker's Business College are located, Lee had to meet the resistance of people who said the flickers were hard on their eyes and had to combat their opinion that motion pictures were simply a fad that, too, would pass.

But he persevered. By 1913, he owned more than a hundred store-room theaters throughout Ohio, controlling theaters in every major Ohio city. He was instrumental in starting both the Hippodrome and the Stillman theaters in Cleveland. In 1912, he and his brother, Arthur, took over a large wooden building on North Meridian Street, where the B. F. Goodrich store now is located. For many years, a movie house in that location later was operated as the Ohio Theater. It was in that theater that the Lee brothers presented the nation's first stage and screen show combination. Van Lee was visionary. He predicted that eventually a method would be perfected to synchronize voice and music to the screen action. And for many years, he and another brother, George T., a Ravenna optometrist, worked to perfect a system of three-dimensional pictures—pictures with depth and reality.

Over the years, Kent and Ravenna had several more small theaters (including the Princess) until the first modern theater was opened in Kent in 1927, in the same building where the Kent Cinemas are located today. A year or two later, a similar building was erected on South Chestnut Street in Ravenna by the same firm. These later were purchased by Schine's Theaters, which operated them, plus others at the Kent Opera House and the Ravenna Ohio Theater, for many years. Certainly any local movie history must include the late John Palfi, a "fixture" in the local movie business, who managed these operations.

Today, there are more than 15,000 theaters in the country, plus 3,800 drive-ins, including our own Midway. It's a vast industry, employing more than 175,000 with 44 million weekly patrons in this country and 130 million worldwide. Now, making movies for television adds a new dimension to the industry. We have come a long way from Van Lee's pioneering effort and the first full-length picture with a plot, *The Great American Train Robbery*, produced in New Jersey in 1903.

————

## CELEBRATING(?) FIFTY YEARS OF
## LIFE WITH TELEVISION

*April 30, 1989*

Today's youngsters may be surprised to learn that there was life before television . . . that the age of man did not begin with the introduction of the "boob tube." So much a part of our culture is the television set that it is difficult for the younger generation to comprehend an existence without TV. As Dennis the Menace has been known to tell his pal, Joey, "Dad says there was no 'telebishun' when he was a boy." Indeed there wasn't, and somehow we managed to exist.

Such reflections come about as we celebrate (or regret, as the case may be), the advent of television 50 years ago this month. It was on April 20, 1939, that the Radio Corporation of America made the first commercial television broadcast from the New York World's Fair, an exposition that commemorated the sesquicentennial anniversary of George Washington's inauguration as our first president. And ten days later, Franklin D. Roosevelt became the first president and the first politician to make use of the new medium.

Much has transpired since those days of infancy which opened an era in which television brings the entire world into our homes in sight and sound . . . as events are happening, even from outer space. We're told that the number of television sets in the U.S.—140 million of them—exceeds the number of flushing toilets. That should tell us something about TV's impact on society.

Although TV broadcasting had begun more than a decade before, the 1950s were the real pioneering days for television. It was in 1951 that Estes Kefauver's crime hearings in the U.S. Senate first brought the workings of government into our living rooms, albeit Harry Truman's inaugural ceremony in 1949 was the first to be telecast.

Television transmission in color began as early as 1951, but it really was during the 1960s that color telecasting came into its own. And no mention of color television would be complete without reference to a former Kent scientist who played a major role in its development. The late Dr. Harold B. Law, a 1930 graduate of Theodore Roosevelt High School, spent his career with RCA in New York and New Jersey, where he was honored several times for his major contributions to the development of color picture tubes. More specifically, he was instrumental in the fabrication techniques that made color television practical.

After stints as a high school teacher in Maple Heights and Toledo, he joined RCA in 1941 in New York to work on television camera tubes. He transferred to the RCA laboratories in New Jersey, and it was there that he won wide acclaim for his color television developments. He received numerous honors from RCA and the Institute of Electrical and Electronic Engineers, among them the Lamme Citation for his work in developing the color picture tube. He retired in 1977 as director of the RCA Electronic Components Materials and Display Device Laboratory at the David Sarnoff Research Center in Princeton, New Jersey.

Dr. Law received his bachelor's degree in 1934 from Kent State University, where he was among those honored as distinguished alumni during the university's semicentennial in 1960. He received his master's degree and doctorate from Ohio State University. He died unexpectedly in April 1984 at his home in Hopewell, New Jersey. Harold Law left an indelible imprint upon the progress of mankind.

Today's young people might wonder what people did in the pre-TV era for entertainment. We did lots of things. We walked in the woods and learned about plants, birds, and animals. We performed numerous household chores. We played card games and baseball, rolled hoops and did our homework. On occasion we saw movies. We learned the capitals of all the states and how to spell, and some youngsters even memorized the books of the Bible . . . in their proper order. And sometimes we even talked to each other!

## OHIO CANALMEN HAD A LANGUAGE
## ALL THEIR OWN
### April 9, 1995

Did you ever hear of "riprap" or a "gooseneck strap"? Probably not, because these were only two of many peculiar names associated with Ohio's long-past canal era. For the record, a gooseneck strap was a metal strap holding the heel post of a miter lock gate to the top of the lock. And riprap was loose stone laid in a pattern on an earthen embankment to provide some protection against water action.

These terms and a host of others are contained in an interesting book entitled *The Ohio & Erie Canal: A Glossary of Terms*, published recently by the Kent State University Press. Author of the small handbook is

Terry K. Woods, a senior mechanical engineer at the Goodyear Tire and Rubber Company in Akron. Obviously he is a canal buff; he has published articles on canal engineering, history, and lore in many publications, including those of the American Canal Society.

Although Woods's book centers upon the Ohio and Erie Canal which opened in 1825 on its route from Cleveland to Portsmouth, no doubt the glossary of strange terms would apply as well to the Pennsylvania and Ohio Canal. That canal, known as a feeder, ran from Beaver, Pennsylvania, to Akron, where it joined the Ohio and Erie. The P. & O. opened in 1840 on a route that took it through Portage County (from Newton Falls to Ravenna, on into downtown Kent, and then to Akron.)

From A to W, the unique canal terms are listed in the glossary. Room limitations do not permit listing all of them, but here are a few of some of the more unusual ones:

*Aqueduct:* Not an unusual word, but it is mentioned here because Kent has an aqueduct structure in the southwest end of town that carried the canal over Plum Creek. That's what aqueducts were for; they carried the canal channel and towpath across a stream or valley too wide or deep for a culvert.

*Canal grass:* An underwater growth of weeds that was a big maintenance headache for canal boats. State boats (they were operated by the state to provide canal maintenance) cut the weeds to provide unimpeded navigation for canal boats.

*Change bridge:* A bridge that carried the towpath from one side of the canal to another. Horses or mules walked on the towpath to pull the boats. Several types of boats were used on the canal. Some carried only freight. Other packets carried only passengers and some carried both freight and passengers.

*Deadeye:* A cast-iron bar or eyelet mounted at the edge of the top deck of a boat to which the towline was attached.

*Driver:* An obvious term. The driver was a young boy (and sometimes a girl) who drove the animals along the towpath. Our 20th president, James A. Garfield, as a youth was a driver on the P. & O. Canal as it traversed through Portage County.

*Feeder:* This term is repeated here because Portage County had a major feeder, the Feeder Dam at the Shalersville-Streesboro border. A feeder actually was a channel that directed water to a canal from a water source, in this instance, Feeder Dam on the Cuyahoga River.

*Medicine Spoon:* An open-ended bag or box filled with dried manure or sawdust. When passed along the bottom of a leaking boat the "medicine" would
be drawn into the leak by the water causing the material to swell and plug
the leak. Ingenious, those canal crews.

*Slackwater:* An area of water impounded behind a dam.

*Way station:* A facility along the canal that supplied spare teams of animals to
pull the boats. Some boats carried spare animals aboard.

Those are merely samples of a host of canal terms listed in Terry Woods's
book.

---

## GETTING PORTAGE "OUT OF THE MUD"
## WAS NO EASY TASK

In these modern times of good roads, turnpikes, and interstates, it is
difficult to comprehend that during the early 1900s, the rallying cry was
"Let's get Portage County out of the mud." From the earliest Portage
County days, crude roads were hardly more than clearings through the
dense brush, most often following the old Indian trails. Carts drawn by
oxen, and in later years horses, carried farmers' products to market.

The advent of the Pennsylvania and Ohio Canal in 1840 heralded a
new means of transportation for Portage County's agricultural products.
The canals declined with the coming of the railroads in the 1850s and
1860s, but Portage County residents were left wanting more local transportation of people and products.

The dawning of the new century in 1900 found county residents immersed in mud, particularly in the springtime, following the thaw of
winter's snow and ice. Travel was, at best, arduous and time consuming.
The need to improve roads, even prior to the coming of the automobile,
was evident. In 1904 a "good roads" convention held in Ravenna stirred
interest in better travel, not only in Portage County but also in the state
of Ohio. How to pay for new roads was the prime question during the
convention's deliberations.

The upshot of the convention was a decision to pave one and three-quarter miles of Infirmary Road in northwest Ravenna Township. Bids were taken in 1907 for the county's first strip of pavement. Naturally, the bids were too high and the job was rebid, with the new winning bid totaling $12,781. Today, that meager sum wouldn't accomplish the "shovel work." The original plan called for an eight-foot paved lane in the middle of the road. Property owners protested and petitioned for the paved lane to be located only along one side of the highway. That move set the pattern, not only in Portage County but for the entire state as well. Certainly, older residents can recall many oldtime highways where only one lane was paved, with highway users finding it necessary to get into the gravel lane for passing.

As early as 1892, during the Ohio administration of Gov. William McKinley, a commission determined that highways "could never" be more than a matter of local concern. This was not to be. Only 13 years later the state allocated money to counties for highway purposes. It was a meager amount; Portage County received $113 in 1905 for roads. That amount increased to $5,000 by 1911 . . . a mere drop in the bucket, even at prices in those days.

At the outset, it was visualized that improved roads would be of macadam surface. Then brick roads were built, with concrete material coming by the end of World War I. Blacktop, material in common use for streets and highways today, really did not arrive until the administration of Ohio Gov. Martin L. Davey of Kent in the 1930s. Garrettsville holds the distinction of having the first paved street in Portage County. The Main Street of the town was bricked in 1886, long before most Portage County folk dreamed of improved roads and before the county got its first automobile. Interestingly, merchants whose establishments abutted the newly paved street were required to keep the pavement swept and clean.

Ravenna got its first paved street—East and West Main—in 1898. Water Street from Erie to Lake was Kent's first paved street in 1903, with West Main following in 1905, Franklin Avenue in 1907, and South Water Street in 1909. About that time, Dan Hanna, owner of the beautiful Cottage Hill Farm east of Ravenna, became interested in improved roads. He and other influential Portage County citizens organized the Portage

County Improvement Association in 1912. Not only was the association interested in better roads for use by farmers, but also in improved strains of livestock, soil management, and better agricultural practices. Hanna was the association's first president, with H. Warner Riddle of Ravenna as first vice president, William H. Getz of Kent as second vice president, C. G. Bentley and Fred H. Carnahan, both of Ravenna, as treasurer and assistant treasurer, and Charles R. Sharp as secretary.

The improvement association sponsored the extension service, among other projects, and H. P. Miller was brought in as the first agricultural extension agent. At the same time, Frank M. Williams of New York, a recognized road engineer, was enticed into Portage County to plan an improved road system. The move evolved into a plan which eventually led to the passage of the Gren Law by the Ohio General Assembly, which provided for road construction on a state-sponsored basis. Yet, it was not until 1921 that a state highway department was organized to plan and build state routes and not until 1925 that the gasoline tax provided funds for state, as well as local, road construction.

Hanna in 1913 proposed to donate $50,000 for construction of good roads, provided that the county raise $30,000 a year for five years. Besides, Kent and Franklin Township were to raise $15,000 and Ravenna and the township $20,000. The plan was debated widely, but finally was not accepted despite the fact that the improvement association with its 1,300 members was considered quite influential.

Another function of the association was the sponsorship of cooperative sales, hence a cooperative store was established on South Sycamore Street in Ravenna, where Oak Rubber Company is located. The cooperative became inactive in 1920 and was succeeded, at least in the sponsorship of part of its program, by the Farm Bureau.

Although the improvement association was short-lived, it had a profound effect. It was said that as a result of the association's work, more miles of road were designated by the state as intercounty highways than in any other Ohio county. Through the efforts of the association, the Main Market Road No. 11 (today's S.R. 59 and S.R. 5) was laid through Franklin, Ravenna, Charlestown, and Paris Townships.

Several innovations came as a result of the better roads movement. In 1916, a state law required the erection of road signs at all centers; in

1922, the state inaugurated its highway numbering system, Portage get-ting its first numbered highway in 1923. The Cleveland Automobile Club started branch offices in Kent and Ravenna in 1924 to provide information and road service to travelers; in 1925 the present county highway department was organized under the county engineer, and pas-sage of a two-cent tax on gasoline financed its work. And who can for-get the white crosses erected at roadsides at the scene of fatal accidents, a move sponsored by Gov. Vic Donahey.

Today, Portage County is crisscrossed by many state and county routes which afford transportation into all of its areas. In addition, the Ohio Turnpike and I-76 traverse our county. We have come a long way from 1915 when a new road (today's S.R. 88) was built from Freedom to Ravenna at the unbelievably low cost of $47,436.

---

## TURNPIKE A WORTHY SUCCESSOR TO PIONEER ROADWAYS

*January 5, 1985*

The upcoming year, when we will celebrate the 30th anniversary of the opening of the Ohio Turnpike, seems an appropriate time to reflect upon the historic strides of transportation in Portage County.

In 1799, Benjamin Tappan Jr., the founder of Ravenna, cut a road through the wilderness from Boston in what is now Summit County to Ravenna. Coming from Connecticut, part of the way over land and the remainder of the distance by way of Lake Erie, Tappan landed at the mouth of the Cuyahoga at what is now Cleveland. He struck the great Indian trail a short distance east of Kent and followed it to his father's, Benjamin Tappan Sr.'s, lands in what today is Ravenna. This great trail extended from Sandusky to Beaver, Pennsylvania, and through Franklin, Ravenna, Edinburg, and Palmyra Townships.

Also about that time, a road was "underbrushed" from Atwater through Deerfield and on to Georgetown, Pennsylvania. That road now is the east-west road through southern Portage County. Ebenezer Sheldon cut a road northwesterly from Aurora to a bridle path into Cleveland, also in

1799. The present Mantua-Ravenna Road was laid out in 1802 but actually was not built for several more years. A road from Warren to Cleveland via Hiram and Mantua also was begun in 1802, and in 1804 a road was cut from the center of Rootstown east of Edinburg and then north.

In 1805, Amzi Atwater surveyed a road east from Mantua to Garrett's Mill, now Garrettsville, and the next year a road was cut west to Aurora. About that same time, a road later known as the state road was cut through Windham to Warren, and in 1800 Erastus Carter of Ravenna laid out the Ravenna, Rootstown, Randolph, Canton Road, which was not completed until 1812. David McIntosh in 1817 cut a road east from Shalersville to Freedom. That was a year before the latter township received its first settler.

It requires little imagination to recognize these old roads as today's state routes which crisscross Portage County to carry a heavy burden of traffic. These ancient roads, crude as they might have been, heralded our present transportation system, which evolved from the stage-coach era to the days of the Pennsylvania and Ohio Canal to the lusty railroad era and thence to the trolley lines and then modern paved highways, including the Ohio Turnpike and I-76. We have come a long way from blazed trails fashioned by Indian nations to speedy surface and air transportation.

The canal was another link in our early transportation in the Portage area. Agitation for construction of the canal began as early as 1825, and the following year a meeting was held in Ravenna to further the project. The canal became a reality on April 19, 1840, when a boat named the *Ohio City*, drawn by mules and loaded with merchandise, arrived in Ravenna from the east and went on to Kent and thence to Akron where the P. & O. canal connected with the Ohio Canal. In August of that year, a lusty celebration sponsored by an appreciative public was held along the canal route. The canal did a flourishing business for about 12 years, but it was abandoned several years after the Cleveland and Mahoning Valley Railroad bought a controlling interest in its stock. That sounded its death knell and signaled the beginning of another era of Portage County transportation.

The Cleveland and Pittsburgh Railroad opened in 1851 with the departure of the first passenger train from Ravenna to Cleveland on

March 10. The Cleveland and Mahoning Valley Railroad, later the Cleveland division of the Erie, opened in 1856. The Atlantic and Great Western, of which Marvin Kent was the guiding genius, was completed in 1863, running between Salamanca, New York, and Dayton. D. C. Coolman of Ravenna, who later became its chief engineer, was prominent in the A. & G. W.'s beginning years. This was the first railroad link between New York and St. Louis.

The Lake Erie, Alliance, and Wheeling road, which ran from Alliance through Deerfield and Palmyra, was completed in 1876, and the Wheeling and Lake Erie, originally known as the Connotton Valley, was completed in 1881 through Kent from Cleveland to Canton. A lot of grading was done in northern Portage County for another railroad, the Clinton Air line, between 1853 and 1856. The line never was built, although there were attempts to revive it as late as 1881. Only two townships in Portage County—Randolph and Shalersville—never had a railroad.

The first electric trolley line—the Walsh Rapid Transit—was extended from Cuyahoga Falls to Kent in 1895 and then to Ravenna via Brady Lake in 1901. The streetcar line discontinued service in 1932. A line also operated from Garrettsville to Chagrin Falls via Hiram and Troy. Another, the Cleveland, Alliance, and Mahoning Valley, operated through southern Portage County beginning in 1913, and the Warren division followed several years later.

Garrettsville was the first community to pave a road in Portage County. In 1885 a section of its business district was paved. The next was in Ravenna in 1898, when Main Street was paved from the old Pennsylvania railroad eastward for five blocks. Portage County, mainly through the efforts of Dan R. Hanna of Cottage Hill Farms, east of Ravenna, fathered the "Portage Plan" for road improvements, which was adopted by the state of Ohio. Hanna in 1912 organized the Portage County Improvement Association and is said to have expended more than $100,000 of his own funds for highway and agricultural improvements.

Hanna could not have envisioned the Ohio Turnpike. The opening of the Turnpike on October 1, 1955, put Streetsboro on the map. That community's No. 13 toll gate is the only one in Portage County. [Later another gate opened on S.R. 44 in Shalersville.]

We have come a long way since Benjamin Tappan cut our first road. It is said that the turnpike carries more traffic in a single day than did all Ohio roads combined 100 years ago.

———

## CONVERSION OF RAILWAY RIVALED
## MODERN-DAY MARVELS
*May 31, 1986*

In these days of high technology, we tend to disregard mechanical achievements of the past, believing, sometimes falsely, that what we perform today adds up to the ultimate in man's achievements. This is not necessarily so.

For a case in point we turn back to June 22, 1880. For some time, preparations had been made for the narrowing of the old broad gauge to standard gauge of the tracks of the old Atlantic and Great Western Railway. On the appointed day, 3,000 men reported for work at 4 A.M. The feat they performed on that day 106 years ago stands out as an amazing Herculean and cooperative effort. In order to narrow the gauge from broad to standard gauge, workmen had to stand alongside the tracks and with bars shove one track to the assigned narrow gauge. A crew which followed then had to spike the rail into place.

At 6:25 A.M., an engine was run from Kent to Akron on the narrow gauge, and by 8:25 an engine came into Kent from the old Cleveland and Pittsburgh railroad, later the Pennsylvania. At 11:10 A.M., Engine No. 134, with John Bull as engineer, came into Kent hauling a baggage car and coach. At 11:30 A.M., regular train No. 7 from the east arrived, only one hour late. In six hours, the entire line of the Atlantic and Great Western from Leavittsburg in Trumbull County to Dayton had been narrowed to the new gauge. The shortest time for the job was consumed between Urbana and Dayton, two hours and 55 seconds.

A week ago, I mentioned the narrowing of the track project to a friend, pointing out that the tracks for approximately 200 miles had been narrowed in six hours. "Impossible," he said. "You're blowing smoke." For authority, I refer to a June 26, 1880, article in the *Kent*

*Saturday Bulletin*, a weekly newspaper of that day, which provided the details described above. Somehow, we seem to believe in this day and age that only "moderns" are capable of such mechanical achievements.

Narrowing of the railroad's gauge came as another crowning achievement for Marvin S. Kent, the railroad entrepreneur whose lengthy struggle to induce the Atlantic and Great Western to run through Portage County is well documented. Disgruntled that the Cleveland and Pittsburgh Railroad elected to run through Ravenna and north of Franklin Mills (now Kent), Marvin was persistent in his efforts to gain a railroad for his hometown. In 1851, he received a railroad charter. But that was only the beginning of his railroad effort. In order to preserve the charter, a paid-up subscription of $20,000 was required. Mr. Kent risked the $20,000 from his own funds. In Franklin Mills, he lifted the first shovelful of earth to signal the building of his railroad. He was to wait 12 more years before he drove the last spike in the tracks in 1864 near Dayton, the fulfillment of a longtime dream.

Unquestionably, completion of the railroad was the culmination of lengthy public service for Marvin Kent. The A. & G. W. was particularly significant because it linked the Erie with the Ohio and Mississippi Railroad, thus forming a grand trunk line from New York to St. Louis.

Ten years elapsed between the railroad's groundbreaking and March 1863, when the first A. & G.W. train arrived in Portage County. Even then, to provide financial backing for the road, it was necessary to interest a couple of English investors who long had been convinced of railroading's future success to come forth with funds. Kent served as first president of the A. & G.W.

The blush of success resulting from the A. & G.W.'s coming was still fresh when Marvin Kent was heralded for another achievement—he established the railroad shops in Kent on land he contributed along Mogadore Road south of Summit Street. The shops, which made and repaired railroad cars provided employment for as many as 800 men before they finally moved to Susquehanna, Pennsylvania, in 1929.

So grateful were the people of Franklin Mills to Marvin S. Kent for their new prosperity that they changed the name of the village to Kent in 1867. But Marvin Kent was not yet done with public achievements.

He gave sites for churches and the Kent Free Library, and he served one term as a state senator, beginning in 1875. From 1881 to 1883, he erected a beautiful mansion on West Main Street, an edifice that today is owned by the Masonic Lodge.

He died in 1908 at 92, two years before his son, William S. Kent, offered 52.89 acres of the old Kent farm, a gesture which induced the state of Ohio to locate a normal school in Kent. That original tract is the nucleus of today's vast Kent State University campus.

---

## STREETCARS ENJOYED A SHORT-LIVED BUT BUSY PORTAGE ERA

*April 20, 1985*

The year was 1895. The date was November 21. That was the day regular streetcar or interurban service began between Akron and Kent.

Eras of history can be marked by successive transportation alternatives. The Indians and their canoes gave way to the oxcarts, the transportation mainstay of our early settlers. Canal transportation was succeeded by the railroads and interurbans. The automobile age doomed horses and buggies following the turn of the century. The airlines caused the demise of railroads, once a booming American industry.

Streetcar service into Portage County did not come without a legal struggle. Two companies vied for the business as early as 1894. The Akron and Cuyahoga Falls Transit Company, headed by Thomas Walsh, was in competition with the Akron, Bedford, and Cleveland Company, of which J. F. Seiberling was the president. Following several court maneuverings, Portage County judge George F. Robinson dissolved an injunction held by the Seiberling interests, and the Rapid Transit was on its way.

Tracks first were laid to the western corporation limits of Kent and then to west end of the Main Street bridge. When first service began in 1895, the fare from Kent to Cuyahoga Falls was 10 cents and to Akron 20 cents. The line was known as the Walsh Line, so named for its president.

From its inception it was the intention of the company to extend the line to Ravenna. That move was not to come without another legal battle, which at times involved physical participation.

The Rapid Transit was sold in 1900 to the Northern Ohio Traction Company. Laying of tracks on Kent's Main Street bridge was the next bone of contention. Eventually, the county commissioners granted that right, and the work went forward. During June 1901, workers swarmed into Kent to lay tracks on North Water Street to carry the streetcars over that street, onto Lake Street, through Brady Lake and ultimately into Ravenna. So incensed was Dr. J. A. Morris with the North Water Street work that he jumped into a hole dug for a pole in front of his home, refusing to get out until arrangements were made to relocate the pole. Late in the autumn of 1901 the line was completed to Ravenna, and the first car arrived in the county seat on November 15. In Ravenna, the streetcars turned south onto South Sycamore Street, then went east to Prospect, then turned east onto Main Street, and then back to Kent by way of Black Horse and Brady Lake. The amusement park at Brady Lake was of prime importance to the streetcar operators; thousands rode the cars to the park for weekend outings.

The Akron to Kent to Ravenna line was not the only interurban line in Portage County. The Cleveland, Alliance, and Mahoning Valley line, which operated between Alliance and Ravenna was opened in 1913 and the Warren division followed a few years later. A line also operated from Garrettsville to Chagrin Falls by way of Hiram and Troy but was abandoned following several years of unprofitable operation. Many other lines were proposed between Kent and Cleveland, but they never materialized.

The Akron-Kent-Ravenna streetcar line was a dominant form of transportation for 37 years. By January 1932, automobiles had diminished the number of streetcar passengers to the point that the Northern Ohio Interurban Company was losing money. The company petitioned the Ohio Public Utilities Commission to discontinue service. The last car ran over the line on March 31, 1932. John Paxton, legendary editor of the *Kent Courier,* was one of only a few people to ride on the first car into Ravenna in 1901 and the last car out of Ravenna in 1932. He wrote in glowing terms of both events.

A crowd of more than 500 gathered in front of the courthouse in 1901 to greet the dignitaries who rode the first car into Ravenna. Mayor Hanselman of Ravenna made a chiding remark to Mayor David Ladd Rockwell of Kent, labeling Kent as a suburb. An eloquent speaker, Mayor Rockwell was not to be outdone, reminding his host that Ravenna residents had yet to experience their horses becoming accustomed to the newfangled streetcars, an achievement for Kent residents six years prior to that time. "You'll become used to city ways," Mayor Rockwell chirped to his Ravenna friends.

In the wee hours on the morning of March 31, 1932, Editor Paxton rode on the last car from Ravenna to Kent. "At Ravenna, two candidates got on—Lincoln Garrett and 'Kentucky Colonel' Semler, one running for commissioner, the other for sheriff," Paxton wrote. "We made the trip back, and everybody said goodbye to the crew. The car sailed over the hill at 1:10 A.M. on its way to Akron. The next morning, there were buses, two of them." Another era had ended!

#### PART SIX

———

# POLITICS

# FIRST PORTAGE ELECTION, IN 1808,
# DREW EIGHTY-EIGHT VOTERS

*November 8, 1992*

Last Tuesday more than 61,000 Portage County voters cast ballots in the presidential election. Election officials and party leaders were jubilant with the voter response, approximately 74 percent of the 83,387 registered voters. Their elation was justified, considering that in recent years election observers were quite pleased with a turnout exceeding 50 percent.

Although the response was cheering, in view of past performances, the numbers tell us that 22,000 eligible voters did not bother to visit the polls. That's not exactly something to shout about, when in some European countries the percentage of eligible voters who actually go to the polls exceeds 90 percent. After many months of political hoopla, we can only conclude that many people were turned off and, therefore, ignored the polls. Too bad!

Contrast the more than 60,000 voters in the November 3 election with the first election in Portage County. The date was June 8, 1808. It was the first balloting after the Ohio General Assembly in 1807 approved legislation to set up Portage as a county. Eighty-eight pioneers trooped to a home one and one-half miles southeast of Ravenna, a temporary site for the transaction of county business. There was no Portage County Courthouse at that time. Only the county seat had been established in Ravenna, and a courthouse would not follow until two years later.

Historical records are a bit sketchy on the site of the first election. Some records tell us that it was the home of Benjamin Tappan Jr., the first settler of Ravenna, which was located along what today is S.R. 14. Other historical accounts indicate that the first election was held in the Robert Eaton home, also located southeast of Ravenna, which didn't even exist as a town in those dim times. What we do know is that the Eaton home was the site of the first session of the Common Pleas Court two months later.

In today's mechanized world it is difficult to imagine the extra effort residents had to put forth to get to the polling place. It must be

remembered that Portage County was considerably larger in those pioneer days. In 1840 two western tiers of townships were removed from
Portage County to join with others from Stark and Medina counties to
form the new county of Summit. Anyway, during the oxcart days of
1808 it must have been quite a trying effort to get to a polling place. But
our hardship-ridden pioneers were a sturdy lot (they had to be) so they
took in stride the need to walk or drive animal-drawn vehicles over
muddy roads simply to cast their ballots. Consider this today as political
parties and others offer free rides to the polling-places, and people still
many times disdain voting.

In Portage County's first election, the 88 voters came from Ravenna
Township, Mantua, Rootstown, Deerfield, Randolph, Suffield, Aurora,
Hiram, Nelson, Shalersville, and Atwater, plus Hudson, Stow, Tallmadge,
and Northampton, all then part of Portage but now part of Summit.
Some of the voters' names still are familiar in today's Portage County—
Campbell, Moore, Wetmore, Harmon, Eatinger, Boosinger, Baldwin,
Baker, Hudson, Robinson, Sabin, Day, among others.

The voters elected Abel Sabin, Joel Gaylord, and Alva Day as commissioners. Strangely, Alva Day also was elected sheriff and his brother,
Lewis, became coroner. Titus Wetmore was elected recorder; and the
commissioners appointed Elias Harmon of Mantua county treasurer and
Benjamin Wheedon clerk. Two people who were present on election
day did not vote. John Campbell of Charlestown was a candidate for
sheriff, and Abel Sabin of Randolph was seeking the commissioner's
post. Because they considered it unseemly to vote when they were candidates, they abstained. Not so with today's candidates.

The commissioners met that same day at the Eaton home to set the
new county's business into motion. Besides naming a commissioner's
clerk and making plans for a courthouse (which followed two years later),
the principal business was setting bounties for animals. For wolves and
panthers, the commissioners offered $2 per pelt. No doubt, $2 was a
considerable sum in 1808.

The absence of 10 Portage County communities from the first election list stands out. There was a valid reason. Franklin, for example, was
not organized as a township until 1815. Streetsboro was not settled until 1822 and was not governmentally organized until 1827. Paris, Palmyra,

Charlestown, Freedom, Garrettsville, among others, were parts of other townships and had not yet been organized as separate governmental units.

In 1808 the county's population was approximately 2,000. In the 1810 census (the county's first), our population was listed at 2,995. Considering the novelty of a first election and the difficult transportation from a widespread area, 88 voters perhaps was a pretty fair response. One thing appears certain. If we had to travel by oxcart, walk, or go on horseback, our voting record would be even more dismal. We drive when the polling place is located in the next block.

## PORTAGE POPULAR FOR TWELVE PRESIDENTIAL HOPEFULS

*October 14, 1990*

Ah, the joys of the political trail! From this day forward until November 6, we will be bombarded on all sides by the appeals of candidates and proponents or opponents of the various issues. Matters of the present tend to cause recollections of past campaigns and to place in historical perspective politicking in years now dimmed by time.

One of my most vivid and regrettable associations with the coverage of political campaigns dates back to 1940, when President Franklin Delano Roosevelt was running for his third term against Wendell Willkie. It was an exercise in futility. The date was October 11, not an especially significant one to most people, but an important one for me. That's my birthdate.

FDR, making a whistle-stop campaign across Ohio, was scheduled to halt at the Baltimore and Ohio station on South Chestnut Street in Ravenna. A tremendous throng had gathered, including three bands and two drum corps, schoolchildren, the usual array of politicos, and the curious who hoped to tell their grandchildren that they had seen an incumbent president.

Trusty Speed Graphic camera in hand, I sought out a crossing signal tower as a vantage point and waited and waited and waited. As I clung to my precarious perch, the Presidential Special finally rounded a bend to the east. It was plain to see, judging from the train's speed, that the train would not be stopping for FDR to greet the assembled throng. Indeed, it did not. As it sped through the crossing, we got a glimpse of the smiling president waving from the window of his special railroad car. My camera dutifully clicked and the train, already late for FDR's later campaign appearances, sped on. The photo my camera recorded was mostly a big blur, but it did show the smiling president. The photo was published on page 1 and its blur actually told a graphic story . . . the story that FDR's train sped on by, much to the disappointment of a heap of folks. Willkie didn't even do that well during a scheduled campaign appearance four days later in Kent. The onetime Akron resident remained asleep in his private railroad car under doctor's orders. They said he had a strained voice. Again, a large crowd was disappointed.

FDR was one of 12 presidents and at least seven unsuccessful candidates to visit Portage County, dating back to "Old Tippecanoe" William Henry Harrison during the presidential campaign against Martin Van Buren in 1840. Harrison, a Virginia native who moved to North Bend, Ohio, in 1814, had an image problem despite his military heroism during the War of 1812. So, he became the first candidate to take his campaign directly to the people. His Whig campaign slogan was "Tippecanoe and Tyler, Too," and Harrison was known as the "hard cider and log cabin" candidate. Hence, a log cabin was erected in Ravenna on West Main Street on the site of the present Immaculate Conception Church for the candidate's appearance. One might wonder what means of transportation Harrison used to reach Ravenna. There were no trains at that time. Perhaps he rode a stagecoach or was driven from place to place in a special horse-drawn hack. Harrison's opponents pointed to his advanced age (68) as a deterrent to his presidency. Perhaps they were right. Harrison, who defeated Van Buren, insisted upon taking his oath and delivering his long inaugural speech coatless and hatless. He caught a cold which turned into pneumonia, and 31 days later he was dead. John Tyler became president. Until Ronald Reagan, Harrison, one of eight Ohioans to become president, was our oldest chief executive.

Portage waited more than 20 years after Harrison's visit until Abraham Lincoln stopped and spoke from his train platform at the C. & P.'s West

Main Street station in Ravenna. That was in February 1861, when Lincoln was en route to his inauguration. A marker on the south side of the street today marks that historic spot. Lincoln's visit was not without humorous incident. Cannoneers were on hand to salute the incoming president; their volleys shattered windows on the train. And Lincoln's wide presidential car necessitated the removal of a corner of a station freight shed.

Of all visiting presidents, James A. Garfield was hailed as Portage's own. He was a student, professor, and president of Hiram College and he lived in Hiram for 25 years before moving to Mentor. He was a lay minister and had spoken many times in county churches. Indeed, Portage launched him on his political career, which ended in 1881 when he was shot only four months after he took office. Garfield was nominated in 1859 for the Ohio Senate at a Republican caucus at Kent's historic Town Hall.

Rutherford B. Hayes made a stop in Ravenna on his way back home to Fremont, Ohio, and Herbert Hoover, in his unsuccessful reelection campaign in 1932, stopped at Kent and Ravenna B.&O. stations. Hoover lost to FDR. The most recent visit of a sitting president to Portage was that of Richard Nixon, when in 1972 his motorcade went through Aurora, Mantua, Hiram, Garrettsville, and Windham. Teddy Roosevelt had completed his presidency when he campaigned here in his bid for reelection as Bull Moose candidate in 1912.

Four presidents in particular—Hayes, Benjamin Harrison, William McKinley, and Warren G. Harding—not only stopped in Portage County but also stayed here. All were entertained at the Kent family home (now the Masonic Temple) on West Main Street in Kent. A bedroom has been maintained to this day as the presidential room.

William Howard Taft, another of Ohio's presidential sons, campaigned here when he was opposed by William Jennings Bryan, the perennial candidate who came to Portage umpteen times during his three bids for the presidency in 1896, 1900, and 1908. Besides Willkie and Bryan, other presidential hopefuls who carried their campaigns into Portage include Horace Greeley, who opposed Ulysses S. Grant; James Cox of Dayton, Harding's opponent; Adlai Stevenson, the Democratic standard-bearer in 1952; Hubert Humphrey who addressed a crowd of 10,000 at

Kent State University in 1968; George McGovern in 1972; and Walter Mondale, who came here twice, 1974 and 1982, but not as a presidential candidate.

Greeley's visit here probably didn't make much of a dent in Grant's Portage popularity. Grant's grandfather settled in Deerfield, and his father was a Deerfield and Ravenna tanner before he moved to Point Pleasant, Ohio, where the future general and president was born.

The 12 presidents who have visited our county represent a hefty percentage, actually 30 percent of the 40 presidents who have served. George Bush is the 41st, but we've had only 40, because Grover Cleveland served split terms. That's the Portage presidential parade, which formed in 1840 and undoubtedly will be restaged many times in future decades.

———

## "KNOW-NOTHINGS" WERE POWERFUL
## POLITICOS IN EARLY OHIO
### May 2, 1987

It is most unbelievable that a political organization would label itself as the "Know-Nothing" party. After all, political parties profess to have the final answer to pressing issues, and they hope to gain wide public support of their views. Yet from 1852 to 1860, the Know-Nothings were a potent political force in national politics as well as in Ohio, including Portage County.

As next Tuesday's election looms, we dip into political history to recall one of the strangest developments in American politics. Political organizations today hope to achieve large outpourings of people at their campaign rallies and meetings. Not the Know-Nothings. They initiated their members in secret, and their meetings were not open to the public. When anyone who was not a party member asked a Know-Nothing a question regarding policies, the reply was "I don't know." Constant repetition of that phrase gave the party its popular name, although the proper name of this political organization was the American party.

Perhaps the party's tenets provide a reason for its clandestine nature. The Know-Nothings were against immigration and were strongly anti-

Catholic, protesting the election and appointment of Catholics and the foreign-born to public office. Despite such controversial positions, the Know-Nothings succeeded in electing some of their members and were a potent force in 1854 elections in eastern states. They also enjoyed a strong following in the South. Ultimately, it was a slavery issue that "did in" the party, following a wide split of its members on that national question in the 1856 elections.

Here in Portage County, the Know-Nothings became active following the demise of the Whigs as a partisan force. This was particularly so during the highly emotional period immediately preceding the Civil War, when there were intense feelings and many debates over the slavery issue. It was during that period of conflict that the Republican party emerged and sought to pin upon the Democrats the responsibility for keeping slavery alive. The *Portage County Democrat*, a newspaper published in Ravenna, in reporting election results in 1855 said: "Slave Democrats have carried Palmyra. In Brimfield, the Slave Democracy succeeded by a very light vote. The People's Ticket won in Franklin, Nelson, Edinburg, Freedom and Windham."

Actually, most Portage Countians at that time were strongly antislavery, including most Democrats. Anti-Know-Nothing rallies were common, a trend which decimated the ranks of the party, and by 1860 the Know-Nothings had disappeared from the American political scene.

In the county's political history, the Know-Nothings were not the only instance of questionable political persuasion. During the early 1840s, the anti-Masonic movement was a political force of considerable power. The *Ohio Star*, a newspaper founded in Ravenna in 1830 and the original ancestor of today's *Record-Courier*, took up the anti-Masonic and anti-Catholic causes. The paper's editor and publisher, Darius Lyman, ran for governor in 1832 as a Whig but with solid anti-Masonic backing. He came so close to winning that his political opponents held their breath. So widespread and intense was anti-Masonic sentiment that Unity Lodge in Ravenna, which had been established in 1810, was forced to go underground in 1832, not to emerge publicly until 20 years later.

Editors in every time period have an unusual opportunity to witness the passing political parade. As a result, they may upon occasion develop a measure of cynicism. A case in point: A woman who developed a sudden interest in government wrote her newspaper's editor, to ask, "I want to get into politics. Do the taxpayers have a party?" The editor wrote back: "Very seldom, lady, very seldom!"

---

## RAVENNAN'S VOTE HELPED PUT LINCOLN IN THE WHITE HOUSE

*February 11, 1984*

A Ravenna man's vote was one of destiny. It was his vote in the 1860 Republican convention in Chicago that swung the Ohio delegation to Abraham Lincoln and gave to the United States one of our most revered presidents. Tomorrow this nation will mark the 175th anniversary of Lincoln's birth on February 12, 1809, near Hodgenville, Kentucky.

When Horace Y. Beebe, influential Ravenna glass manufacturer and banker, went to the convention as an Ohio delegate, he was committed to Salmon P. Chase, former U.S. senator and then governor of Ohio, for the Republican nomination. Senator William H. Seward of New York held the strongest support for nomination. On the first ballot, Seward garnered 173 votes to Lincoln's 102, an insufficient majority for nomination. Lincoln came closer on the second ballot—181 to Seward's 184. As usually happens in national conventions, there were considerable political maneuverings. Beebe switched his vote from Chase to the Illinois "Rail-splitter" and induced the entire Ohio delegation to do likewise. Lincoln won the nomination over Seward with 233 votes. Chase, an also-ran, later was appointed secretary of the treasury and chief justice and Seward secretary of state by the 16th president. Lincoln did not forget his friends—he named Beebe assessor for the 19th congressional district.

And, thus, the course of American history was altered. Lincoln went on to lead the nation during the hour of its greatest travail, winning the Civil War against rebellious Confederates, setting in motion attempts to heal wounds between the North and South, and then becoming our first martyred president.

In February 1861, Ravenna had one of its greatest historical moments. Lincoln's train, carrying him from his hometown of Springfield, Illinois, to Washington, D.C., for the March 4 inauguration, stopped in the county seat. A crowd of more than a thousand (probably large for those days) was on hand to greet the incoming president. A military battery fired several rounds in greeting as the tall, raw-boned president-elect emerged from his railroad car onto the platform. Naturally, Mr. Beebe was conspicuously present.

Noting that he had little time to tarry, Lincoln quipped that he risked arriving in Washington after his inauguration was over. But he did make a few remarks. "There may be some of you here today who did not vote for me," he said, "but I believe now we all must make common cause for the Union." As he prepared to depart, the new president told Portage Countians, "I have little more time than to say, 'How do you do and good-bye.'" And he was off for Washington.

Portage County did its share to help President Lincoln win the Civil War, the nation's bloodiest. With a population of only 24,208 in 1860, the county sent 8 percent, or 2,007 men, to the battlefields. Of that number, 15 percent—312—did not return. Before the war ended with Lee's surrender to Grant at Appomattox Court House on April 9, 1865, more than 360,000 soldiers of a 2,200,000 total Union force had paid the supreme sacrifice. No one really knows the actual cost in lives to Confederate forces; however, it is estimated that more than 160,000 were killed or died of disease among a force said to have been between 600,000 and 1.5 million.

President Lincoln grieved over such heavy losses on both sides of the conflict. But he persevered. His Emancipation Proclamation freed the slaves in the southern states; he saw the bloody war through to ultimate victory. Through all of this he displayed an immense sense of integrity and forthrightness, all the while placing the future of the Union at the top of his priorities.

Following the fall of Fort Sumter on April 14, 1861, bells throughout Portage County had summoned citizens to meetings to rally behind the Union cause and to send its young men into arms. On April 4, 1865, with the fall of Richmond, Virginia, and on April 9, the day of the surrender which brought a welcome end to the war, bells were tolled again in victory. Portage County's biggest gathering was in front of the courthouse where the happy, large crowd listened to polished oratory. President Lincoln proclaimed April 14 as a day of thanksgiving for the end of the war and to mark the beginning of the healing years.

America's joy was short-lived. On that same day, April 14, President Lincoln went to Ford's Theatre in Washington to enjoy a play, *Our American Cousin*. John Wilkes Booth crept into the presidential box and fired a shot into the president's head. Removed to a neighboring home, the president died the next morning—our first, but not our last, martyred president.

Portage County bells tolled again . . . this time in response to the appalling sorrow that gripped the land. Ravenna, Franklin Mills, and other Portage County communities assembled their people in mourning. Local business places closed, public buildings were draped in black, and more subdued orators now offered their words in deep solemnity. President Lincoln, who perhaps more than any other had captured the American soul, had become a man for all ages.

## DAVEY VICTORY IN THE '34 RACE
## PUT PORTAGE ON THE MAP
### *November 3, 1984*

Tuesday, November 6, 1984! An election day when Americans will go to the polls to decide whether Ronald Reagan will have four more years in the White House or whether Walter Mondale will ascend to the presidency. November 6, 1934! An election day 50 years ago when Portage County voters and their fellow Ohioans elected Martin L. Davey Sr. of Kent as governor of Ohio. His election to his first of two terms is historically significant. "M.L." is still the only Portage Countian to hold the Ohio governorship in the 181-year history of the state.

The political arena was not new to Martin L. Davey by the time he was elected governor. In 1913, when he was only 29, he was elected mayor of Kent and was reelected in 1915 and 1917. He was elected to Congress in 1918, defeated for reelection in 1920, and then reelected to

Martin L. Davey served as Ohio's governor from 1935 to 1937.

three more terms in 1922, 1924, and 1926. His first bid for the gover-
norship took place in 1928, when he was defeated by Republican Myers
Y. Cooper. He sat out the 1930 election, instead coming out for fellow
Democrat George White. Likewise in 1932, when he served as an Ohio

delegate-at-large to the national Democratic convention when Franklin D. Roosevelt was nominated to the first of his four terms.

Martin L. Davey was born in Kent 100 years ago last July 25. His father, John Davey, left his native England in 1873 to seek opportunity in a new land. From a poor family and with no chance for an education, it was not until he was 21 that John Davey learned his ABCs. He had an unquenchable thirst for knowledge, and he eventually learned Latin, Greek, and astronomy. John Davey came to Kent in 1881 to become sexton at Standing Rock Cemetery. The family was poor. They raised vegetables and the four sons, Wellington, Martin, James, and Paul, sold them door-to-door to help sustain the family.

John was appalled by the ruthless destruction of trees in his adopted land. He wrote a book, *The Tree Doctor,* that described in detail his methods for treating trees. That book really was the inspiration for the Davey Tree Expert Company, which today is a far-flung firm that does business in 40 states and the Canadian province of Ontario, has 3,800 employees, and last year did a sales volume of $104 million.

M.L. as a young man sold typewriters in Cleveland to help meet his expenses at Oberlin, a college he left to help his father launch the infant tree care firm. He succeeded his father as Davey Tree president in 1923 and held that management position simultaneously with his political career until his death in 1946 when his son, Martin L. (Brub) Davey Jr., succeeded him.

Hundreds of homefolk went to Columbus by special train in January 1835 for M.L.'s inauguration as governor. His two terms (he was reelected in 1936) had a hometown flavor. Myrna Smith, his Davey Tree secretary, became the governor's secretary; Larry Wooddell was his director of conservation and wildlife; James Woodard was warden of the Ohio penitentiary; plus many others held lesser state appointments.

His two terms, in a period when money was scarce and relief costs were high, were marked by controversy. One of the high spots occurred in 1937 during the "Little Steel Strike," when M.L. proclaimed that workers not only had a right to strike but that they also had the right to work, a premise he backed up with the National Guard.

He took on Harry Hopkins, then federal relief administrator, charging that his administration was cruel, inhuman, and wasteful. To help the poor, he campaigned for and won a constitutional amendment which banned a sales tax on food. Kent State also achieved university status during his administration. A fellow Democrat, Frank Lausche, who later served five terms as governor, said at the time of M.L.'s death that he was mystified as to how M.L. could manage the state on the slim finances that existed at that time. Davey ran for governor two more times, losing the nomination to Charles Sawyer in 1938 and the election to John Bricker in 1940.

The Davey years are shared by many local folk who well remember them, and more intimately by his son, Brub, and daughter, Evangeline Davey Smith, both Kent residents.

---

## HISTORY PROVES ONE VOTE CAN MAKE QUITE A DIFFERENCE

*November 5, 1983*

Tuesday is election day. If you think your vote doesn't count, guess again. History proves otherwise. Take a quick glance back to November 7, 1961. Redmond Greer, a Republican, was running for his second term as mayor of Kent. His opponent was Bob Byrne, a Democrat, longtime council member, and president of the Kent City Council.

Early the next morning, after a tiring night of ballot counting, Greer was deemed the winner by 11 votes—2,221 to 2,210. Byrne sought a recount of votes by the Portage County Board of elections, which was set for November 17. The recount began in the early afternoon and was finished by about 8 P.M. Greer lost nine votes in the recount; Byrne picked up two, deadlocking the two candidates at 2,212. Ohio law provides only one solution to such an election dilemma—flip a coin. With Portage county election officials as overseers, the coin was flipped. Greer was the victor, and he served a second term through 1963.

Redmond Greer and Bob Byrne now are deceased. But both probably would agree that a simple coin toss, usually considered a mechanism to settle bets, is a poor way to determine the future of a city. In such a situation, either candidate can be bothered by campaign reflections: "If

I had made just one more house call, the result might have been different." But that's the law, and so be it.

The Greer-Byrne election was not without historical precedent. Back
in 1914 there was a similar situation on a county-wide level. Joseph
Jones and James Stevens were pitted in a close race for sheriff of Portage
County. When votes were counted, they were tied at 814. A coin toss
gave the office to Jones. However, Stevens's disappointment was short-
lived; four years later he was elected sheriff, minus the blemish of a coin
toss. Jones, who won the office again in 1922, was the father of LeRoy
Jones, who served as sheriff from 1931 through 1935.

So . . . your individual vote does count. No doubt you have seen
figures to prove that a one-vote variance in each of the nation's precincts would have caused a reverse result in a presidential race. On more
than one occasion we have seen the winner of the presidential race
decided in the House of Representatives.

For newsmen who follow campaigns and elections more closely than
the average citizen, elections provide a strange and exciting fascination. Portage County has not been without interesting political sidelights. During much of my news career, I spent most election nights in
the Portage County Board of Elections headquarters in the courthouse.
It was always an exciting time for me. The speeches and the campaign
promises were done with. Nothing more could be said or done. Now we
get down to what the process of democracy is all about—the will of the
electorate, free and unencumbered.

Usually the business of vote counting was painfully slow. Years ago,
election boards in the polling place opened up the booth in the dim
morning hours and stayed into the night before they finished counting
the ballots. The presiding judge had the responsibility of posting a tally
sheet on the door of the booth and taking the counted ballots and the
tally sheets to the election board in the courthouse. Some booth boards
were not as speedy as others, and time seemed to drag on and on in the
county board office.

I distinctly recall one election—I believe it was the 1940 presidential election which pitted Republican Wendell Wilkie against President Franklin Delano Roosevelt. All precincts had reported except one.
As I recall, the one holdout was Paris Township. Unable to wrap up the

deliberations and arrive at a final count until all precincts were in, the board called the presiding judge of the tardy precinct. By now, it was 6 A.M. the day following election day. The answer election board officials received from the presiding judge became a classic, told and retold every election night for many years. "I'll bring in the results just as soon as I finish milking my cows," responded the errant presiding judge. And he did . . . after he milked his cows. No way, obviously, in his mind, would the business of getting his cows milked take a back seat to the processes of a democratic society. Nature's demands must be served, first and foremost!

In our modern age, voting is done with punchcards and votes are counted by computer. The method of vote counting is a mechanism, a convenience of no particular interest to the average voter except that casting a ballot is simple, and he or she gets the results much quicker than in the hand-counting days. The outcome is the same. The mechanism doesn't change the fact that all votes count—yours and mine. And we need not wait until the cows are milked!

---

## IT ALL STARTED WITH SPORTING AND HUNTING ON A SUNDAY

*July 9, 1983*

It was in 1808 that William Simcock of Franklin Township got himself into trouble with the law and became the subject of the infant Portage County's first criminal case. During the ensuing 175 years, Portage County has had its share of crime. In accordance with modern views, Simcock's transgression would not cause the slightest ripple; law enforcement people are kept much too busy with more serious crimes—housebreakings, rapes, assaults, homicides.

Simcock's case is described in Docket No. 1, Page No. 1 in the county clerk's office. He was charged in these glowing words: "On or about June 15, last past, not having the fear of God before his eyes, and disregarding the good laws of this state, did, on or about said day which was the Sabbath, or Lord's Day, wickedly and maliciously, molest and disturb the religious society of said Franklin Township while in meeting assembled, and returning from divine worship, by sporting and hunting game with guns and hound."

In the first session of the common pleas court in August of 1808, Mr. Simcock was brought to justice. He pleaded guilty and was fined $1.50 and $5 court costs, a substantial sum in those pioneer days. Our first settlers didn't countenance breaking of the Sabbath, hence, Mr. Simcock's historic criminal case.

Only six more years elapsed before Portage County recorded its first criminal murder case. Henry Aunghst was charged with killing a peddler, Epaphras Matthews, on August 20, 1814, at what today is Cotton Corners east of Ravenna. He was convicted by a jury in June 1816 and sentenced to die. A scaffold was erected at the corner of South Sycamore and West Spruce Streets in Ravenna, and Aunghst was hanged on November 30, 1816, more than two years following the crime. Apparently the wheels of justice turned as slowly in those days as they do now.

A crowd of 1,800 witnessed the hanging. It is interesting to note that the county's population in 1810 (the first census year) was counted at 2,995. Our county was larger then; it included 10 townships that in 1840 became part of the new Summit County.

Sheriff Ross Jamerson and his corps of deputies would be envious of Sheriff Stephen Mason back in 1814. He had so little to do that he taught school and trained the militia on the side. His equipment included a horse, gun, and a pair of handcuffs. His jail was little more than a covered pen for hogs.

A hanging on South Prospect Street in Ravenna attracted an estimated 5,000 people on a bitter cold February day in 1838. So great was the crush of the crowd that the militia was on hand to keep order.

And there was "Blinky" Morgan, so named because he had a bad eye, who was involved in perhaps the most celebrated murder case in Portage County history. It took place in 1887–1888 and people still are talking about it as a result of details being handed down by their ancestors. There was a time when Ravennans with the surname of Morgan ran the risk of being nicknamed "Blinky." I knew at least one who bore that doubtful distinction.

Portage County actually had no direct interest in Blinky's original crime. A band of thieves staged a fur robbery at a Cleveland store in 1887. One member of the gang, a man named McMunn, was arrested in Pittsburgh and was being returned by Cleveland detectives on the C. & P. (later the Pennsylvania) Railroad. When the train stopped in Ravenna, three members of the gang, including Morgan, boarded and freed McMunn. Cleveland detective Hulligan was beaten to death with a coupling pin, and all of the gang except Morgan escaped. Three of the gang were apprehended in Alpena, Michigan, and returned to Ravenna for trial.

Naturally, the Cleveland Police Department threw all of its weight into the prosecution of Morgan during the trial in Portage County Common Pleas Court. A famous criminal lawyer represented Morgan. The Portage County jail was under heavy guard throughout the trial to prevent an attempt to free Blinky. He was convicted and was executed in Columbus in 1888. Two other members of the gang were convicted but won new trials. Another went free. McMunn never was caught.

Another murder that provided conversation for a generation took place in Edinburg in 1900 when Nathan Goss, a store owner, was shot by thieves who had entered his place of business during the night. The three thieves were apprehended a short time later by Sheriff John Goodenough. All were convicted and sentenced to the penitentiary for life. In five years, all had been paroled.

Portage County has recorded several unsolved slayings. On April 5, 1922, Arthur Carlile, former Kent marshall and ex-sheriff, was killed in his Kent home. His wife was indicted, but Judge A. S. Cole dismissed the indictment on grounds that the state had no evidence against her.

Kent merchant policeman Clayton Apple was killed on what is now Gougler Avenue in Kent on March 22, 1925. Two suspects were arrested. Basil Nicosia died of a gunshot wound the day following Apple's death, and the second suspect, Frank Mollica, was tried and acquitted. It was believed that Apple's slaying was associated with rum-running activities during the prohibition era. Ravenna's crime records are dotted with several unsolved gangland-style killings during the prohibition days.

Of more recent vintage, Harold DuBois, then owner of the DuBois
Bookstore in Kent, was shot and killed in his place of business in October 1957. His slaying has never been solved.

Over the years, the battle against Portage County crime has intensi-
fied as the population increased and as most types of criminal activity
expanded manyfold. And the legend of Blinky Morgan lives on!

---

## "WET VERSUS DRY" DILEMMA
## "AGED" MORE THAN 120 YEARS
### April 2, 1983

Two news happenings in recent days serve to bring into historical focus
the issue of consuming alcoholic beverages. The first of these developments is Ohio's tough new drunk-driving law. The second is the 50th
anniversary this week of Ohio's legalization of 3.2 beer sales after the
long prohibition era drought.

The liquor issue is of ancient local vintage. Drinking or moves toward abstinence have been steeped in violence and sometimes death,
distilled with political chicanery, and aged for more than 120 years.
History continues to repeat itself as communities exercise their local
option rights either to legalize or ban the sale of alcoholic beverages.

History tells us the issue has been belted around publicly since the
dim days of the Portage County area. Arguments of wet and dry forces
today are similar to those advanced more than a century ago: "Liquor
fees for public coffers. Saloons will move to fringe areas outside the
jurisdiction of communities. Liquor breaks up homes and causes public
lawlessness."

In the olden days, a horse usually knew the way home despite the
inebriated condition of its driver. The motor age added a whole new
dimension to drinking, a dimension that has involved thousands of highway deaths and has led to Ohio's new drunk driving law with new and
severe penalties for violators.

Actually, the prohibition movement had its beginnings in the 1860s,
when orators dwelt at length on the evils of demon rum and the iniquities

of those who manufacture and purvey alcoholic beverages. They hailed prohibition as a blessing that would empty jails, close poorhouses, and bring a sudden halt to divorce trends. As we know, the "grand experiment" of the 1920s and early 1930s disproved all of the above arguments.

As early as 1886, the "dries" in Kent, confident that they could force a public election, took their case to the council. They were rebuffed by a council controlled by "wets." Two years later, drinking won out in a public election by a scant 11 votes. The following year, prohibitionists leaped upon a drink-related slaying in their campaign for another election. They won, 347 to 326, but saloons did not close. Council, again controlled by wets, refused to pass the closing ordinance despite the public vote.

Two decades later, all of Portage County was immersed in a bitter battle over the liquor issue. The Anti-Saloon League, which had been organized in Ohio in 1893, and the Women's Christian Temperance Union, founded in 1874, led the prohibition campaign headed by Henry Spelman of Kent. Attorney Charles Newton, who later became a Portage County common pleas judge, chaired the antiprohibition forces. The prohibitionists won in the countywide vote—4,305 to 3,121—and all county saloons closed on December 9, 1908, not to reopen until repeal of the Eighteenth Amendment a quarter of a century later.

During the long dry spell in Portage County, residents provided considerable business to the trolley company, riding to Cuyahoga Falls to purchase their booze. On Saturday nights, Kent and Ravenna men took the last trolley home after an evening of imbibing, sometimes too freely. It is said that the trolley conductor armed himself with a good-sized club to keep order en route.

There were a couple of ballot-box flurries to reopen the saloons. In 1915, following an Ohio legal battle which obscured the right of an entire county to vote on a liquor issue, Ravenna and Kent both voted dry again. And in 1918, the entire county voted to retain its arid condition.

Dating back to the mid-1880s, prohibitionists were a force in American politics. As early as 1869, the Prohibition party advanced its own candidates for the presidency. The party joined forces with the Anti-Saloon League, which in 1913 took its case against liquor to Congress with a goal to offer a constitutional amendment that would ban the manufacture, sale, and transportation of alcoholic beverages. The House turned them down in 1914, but the prohibition forces prevailed five years later when the Eighteenth Amendment was ratified by a sufficient number of states.

The amendment became effective on January 29, 1920, accompanied by the Volstead Act, which defined alcoholic beverages and provided an enforcement arm. Thus were ushered in 13 years of alleged abstinence and the dizzy days of bathtub gin, gangsterism, and murder as rival mobs competed for the illegal liquor business. Ravenna witnessed a vivid sample of this during the bootlegging days. The wet and dry issue continued to be a force in politics. For example, it was said that his favor for repeal contributed to Alfred E. Smith's loss of the presidency in 1928. And in local elections, voters were swayed by the personal liquor persuasions of candidates for public office.

By 1933, the American people apparently had seen enough. The Twenty-First Amendment repealed the Eighteenth Amendment, preserving for states their right to retain or get rid of prohibition. By 1936, all but eight states had taken action to permit liquor, and by 1966 all states had so acted, albeit that many communities or specific sections thereof across the nation to this day have remained dry by public choice. Today, the public discussion over the liquor issue goes on. History continues to repeat itself!

―――

## PORTAGE WAS ONCE A MECCA OF
## ORGANIZED GAMBLING

*March 8, 1992*

There may be some readers who will not like this column. Usually, "Pathways" columns bring readers pleasant stories about people, places, and events that trace the history of Portage County since the first settler arrived in 1798. This column will not be filled with such niceties. Rather, it will deal with a seamier side of Portage activities in past years, particularly those associated with law enforcement. Or, more accurately, the lack thereof. It is concluded that some people might not like this recital of events during a period of long-ago because such reports revive unpleasant memories. Also, they might object to some of the graphic language. But, as they say on TV, some of the names will be omitted to "protect the innocent."

I was reminded of that period so long ago by the current tiff that raises a question about the eligibility of two candidates for sheriff, incumbent Ken Howe and former sheriff Jim Wilkens. Shucks. Had there been such an "experience law" on the books during earlier days, Portage County would not have elected many sheriffs. The first sheriff, Alva Day of Deerfield, who served from 1808 to 1810, was a Deerfield farmer—as were many sheriffs down through the years. James Woodard (1850) probably never had handled a gun except to shoot woodchucks on his Kent farm. But he rid the area of counterfeiters whose nefarious schemes had victimized this region for years. Untrained, sure, but he put them behind bars. Back in 1812, Sheriff Mason had so little to do that while in office he taught school and, as a major, had plenty of time to train militiamen. When sheriff duties called, he dismissed his classes.

The point is that sheriff candidates have been farmers, shopkeepers, basketmakers, tanners, et cetera. This by no means is intended to infer that professional experience and training in law enforcement or criminal justice are not important. I think they are of prime importance. But there is another prime qualification for law enforcement people—HON-ESTY! Most times, we have had that character trait among our public guardians of the law. Other times, we have not.

I think back to my days as a young reporter when I had daily contact for many years with lawmen, mayors, judges, and others charged with representing the public interest. I'm sorry to report that some of the things I witnessed then would curl the hair of today's honest public servants. And those they serve, as well. Portage County then was a mecca for organized gambling. Slot machines were in most corner gas stations, ice cream parlors, bars, and other public places. Punchboards also were on prominent display. School kids regularly squandered their lunch money in the one-armed bandits. Private clubs raised building or maintenance funds from the slots. Claims were made that one nickel slot machine would more than pay for an establishment's rent.

Casino gambling was running openly at Brady Lake. At one time, Portage County had two dog-racing tracks, one at Brimfield and another at Lake Milton, despite the illegality then and now of dog racing in Ohio. So open was gambling that I once saw a slot machine purveyor delivering his machines to public places exposed on the bed of a stake-body truck. Nothing could hardly be more open than that.

The problem with organized gambling is that it corrupts public servants. No major operations can run without at least tacit approval, and more often as a result of a solid arrangement between law enforcement heads and gambling moguls. Gambling, in those days, reached into the highest echelons of our local government. Whenever as a reporter I confronted a mayor or other law enforcement head with the question "Why don't you do something about this rampant gambling?" I received a standard reply, "If you see gambling, file a complaint and I'll serve it." Whoopee! Naive me always thought law-enforcement people were expected to enforce the law when they saw violations occur. And in those days, anyone would have had to be blind not to notice open gambling at every turn in Portage County.

Sometimes these law enforcement machinations took a hilarious turn. Like the time I was chatting in the sheriff's office with the top guy himself, several of his deputies, and a smattering of courthouse employees who had come in for their morning gabfest. Enter a lady (and I use the designation loosely). She reeked of cheap perfume and she bore the results of an overdose of cosmetics. She obviously was a "lady of the evening" and probably morning, noon, and afternoon, too.

Unabashed, and in a voice louder than necessary in the small office, she announced, "I came in to get a permit to open a whorehouse." Can you imagine the astounding blubbering and the blank, numbing stares of the sheriff and his deputies, most of them directed toward this reporter? Finally, when the sheriff recovered his composure, he answered, "We don't allow that kind of thing in this county." To which the woman responded, "Why not? This is where I was told to come." At that time, and even today, I didn't, and don't, think the woman was misdirected in her quest. Frankly, I don't know that she received a blessing for her mission. But I do know such recreational outlets were not exactly unknown in the county.

At one of the dog tracks, I witnessed a deputy sheriff many times go behind the ticket-selling windows. In a few moments he would emerge with a paper bag in his hand. He got into his cruiser and sped off to Ravenna. I doubt that he visited that park to play tiddleywinks, and doubt even more that the paper bag contained a ham sandwich.

And another time, a story bordering on hilarity. One public official, not wanting his wife to know he possessed that kind of money, hid a paper bag with $5,000 in the basement coal pile. Before he could get back to it, his unknowing wife went down to fire the furnace. She shoveled the bag and his valuable contents into the fire. Subsequently the couple divorced. Can you blame him? Five thousand dollars was a lot of money in those days.

And the scene and poor law enforcement didn't get any better for a while, at least. I once knew a police officer who each day walked into a drugstore, went behind the counter, and came away with a handful of cigars, a day's supply. The same officer each day halted a bread truck and received the family's day supply. All for free, of course. And he thought he was entitled.

Most thinking Portage Countians believed that organized gambling and other such goings-on could be halted by any law enforcement head if he simply said "There will be none." That was the trouble with open commercialized gambling—it tended to compromise the best intentions and integrity of public servants, especially if they were weak in the face of temptation.

Things changed several years later. A Good Government Group was formed under the leadership of lawyer George McClelland, a onetime probate and juvenile judge and one of the most honest public figures I've ever known. After one sheriff candidate went back on his written and circulated pledge cards to rid the county of gambling, Bob Stockdale was induced to run for sheriff on a similar pledge. The plan worked. Stockdale and Prosecutor Bob Cook brought organized gambling to an abrupt halt, aided by a strong governor, Frank Lausche.

In comparison with the era described above, Portage County is as clean as a hound's tooth today. Now our law enforcement people are confronted with a full schedule of other wrongdoings—drugs, rampant vandalism, assaults, robberies, shootings, thefts. You name it.

## PUBLIC HANGINGS
### They Were Family Affairs
*November 8, 1987*

Picture this scene in the mind's eye: Mounted members of the 1st Brigade, Ohio militia, resplendent in brilliant uniforms; a Garrettsville band playing marching music; a crowd estimated between 1,800 and 3,000, including many women and children; an air of sociability as Portage Countians greeted their friends; genuine warmth of friendliness despite the bitter chill on a winter's day.

Such an atmosphere might better describe one of our many community festivals or the social highlight of the season. But that was not the case. This is an apt and historically accurate description of the public hanging of murderer David McKisson from gallows especially erected along South Prospect Street in Ravenna on February 9, 1838.

Driven, perhaps, by morbid curiosity, Portage Countians always turned out by the thousands for such spectacles. Hangings were regarded as a necessity for achieving criminal justice, and execution in public was considered proper. No doubt parents, in their infinite wisdom, took their children along to learn an object lesson firsthand. Truly amazing it was that an 1838 hanging would attract such numbers when the county's population was only about 20,000. And even more amazing that an 1816 hanging attracted 1,800 from a county population of only 2,000.

Portage County historical records reveal that three murderers were executed by hanging in Ravenna, two of them in public and the last one in 1866 inside the old county jail. From that time forward, capital punishment for Portage felons was carried out in Columbus. The last Portage Countian hanged was Blinky Morgan in 1888 in the state capital. In more recent years, all Ohio executions have been carried out by means of the electric chair, albeit there hasn't been an execution in Ohio since 1963 and today 72 men, including Mark Wayne Wiles, sentenced for a Portage murder, and one woman await their fates while sitting on Death Row.

From Francis Strong of Hiram, one of the militiamen who saw duty at the McKisson hanging, we gained the historically graphic description of the hanging. A letter he wrote in 1883 captured the public sentiment of the day and offered a firsthand report on the doings.

> About nine in the morning, Gen. Lucius Bierce's aide rode through the town [Ravenna] with fife and drum, called the militia together and paraded them on vacant land where the Phoenix Block now stands. Soon the general appeared. He formed the militia into a hollow square and promptly at 1 P.M. all started to parade. Staff officers, mounted with drawn swords, placed two wagons within the hollow square, one for the sheriff and prisoner and one for the Garrettsville band. The sheriff [George Wallace] came out of the jail arm-in-arm with the prisoner and we marched to the gallows.

Condemned men always are asked if they have last words. McKisson had plenty of them. On that bitter cold day he rambled on for more than a half an hour as the militiamen and those in the crowd nearly froze. Strong added, "When he was through, the sheriff turned around and, taking his deputy by the arm, walked down the stairs. When they stepped on the last step the trap was sprung and the prisoner was hanging in the air." Appropriately, the band played "Bonaparte's March Over the Rhine."

On the previous day, Strong had asked an acquaintance, Smith Manley, if he would attend the hanging. "Yes," replied Smith, "Sabrina, my wife, never saw but three men hung, and we must see this man, sartin." Smith and Sabrina rode to Ravenna from Hiram in a lumber wagon. Such was the morbid attraction of executions in the early 1800s.

Portage County waited only nine years following the organization of its county government in 1807 for its first hanging. The murderer was Henry Aunghst, a German ne'er-do-well, who paid with his life for the 1814 killing of an itinerant peddler, Epaphras Mathews, in the Cotton Corners–Campbellsport area. Aunghst was trailed to Center County, Pennsylvania, where he was captured and returned to the county's log jail in Ravenna. Even in those days on the Ohio frontier the wheels of justice sometimes turned slowly. Aunghst's first indictment was deemed faulty; he was reindicted and finally tried and found guilty in September of 1816, more than two years following Mathews's death.

Aunghst was executed November 30, 1816, on gallows erected on South Sycamore Street near Spruce Avenue in Ravenna. His body was cut down and buried near the foot of the scaffold. The night following Aunghst's execution, his body was dug up, possibly for anatomical purposes, as was the custom in that day. The thieves were pursued, and they dropped the body at the corner of South Meridian Street and Riddle Avenue. Sheriff Asa Burroughs took possession of the body and guarded it that night in the courthouse. The next day, Aunghst's body again was taken but soon recovered. Intent upon preventing a third theft, the body was reinterred in its original grave. The coffin was filled with lime, and a huge log was placed atop the grave.

The last execution in Portage County was the 1866 hanging of Jack Cooper for the murder of John Rhodenbaugh, whose body was found near his home on Ravenna-Hudson Road north of Brady Lake. Historical notes reveal that Rhodenbaugh, an auctioneer, was fond "of company and the social glass" and when drinking was prone to boast of his financial means. The night of his death on October 24, 1865, he had been drinking in Kelso's saloon in Kent with Cooper and Joel Beery. Cooper was found guilty of murder in the first degree and hanged on April 27, 1866, in the jail. Apparently, Portage County's lust for public hangings had abated. Cooper had made three unsuccessful attempts to break out of jail and finally was chloroformed into submission and hanged inside the jail. Beery got life in prison.

# INDEX

Western Reserve Academy, 98
Western Reserve College, 87
Western Reserve Eclectic Institute, 8, 9,
　33, 216
Western Reserve Historical Society, 46
Western Reserve University, 103
West Virginia, 61, 62
*West Virginia History*, 61
Wetmore, Titus, 326
Wetmore, William, 38
Wheedon, Benjamin, 326
Wheeling and Lake Erie Railroad. *See*
　Connotton Valley Railroad
White, Scotty, 182
White, W. W., 251, 259
White Hospital, 251, 259; School of
　Nursing of, 225
Widener, W. H. and Mrs., 32
Wilbur Watson Associates, 294
Wilcox, Edward, 247
Wiles, Mark Wayne, 348
Wilgus, C. W. S., 302
Wilkens, Jim, 345
Willard, Frances E., 128, 129
Williams, A. C. and Mrs., 134, 255–56
Williams, Charles II, 277
Williams, Charles "Pete" III, 277
Williams, Charles A., 82, 277
Williams, Dudley, 277
Williams, Ernie, 184
Williams, Frederick, 261
Williams, Gerald, 199
Williams, Martin, 58
Williams, Scott T., 82, 166–67, 277
Williams, Zumkehr, and Wesler, 157
Williams Brothers Company, 277, 278
Williams Brothers Mill, 82, 227, 276–78;
　Kent Normal School and, 174, 222
Williard, Emma, 203
Willson, Andrew, 42
Wilson, D. E., 199

Wilson, Wade, 199
Wilson store (Deerfield), 267
Windham Township, 11, 12, 15, 200,
　267, 296
Wingfoot Lake, 273, 283
Wishing Well, 113
Wolcott, Dorothy, 136
Wolcott, Duncan B. (attorney), 174, 222
Wolcott, Duncan (Silver Lake), 288
Wolcott, Jeane, 136
Wolcott, Oliver, 136, 236
Woman's Christian Temperance Union,
　129, 187, 343. *See also* Temperance
　movement
Women's suffrage, 124–25
Woodard, James (early settler), 26, 27,
　30, 279, 345
Woodard, James (penitentiary warden),
　336
Woodard, Joshua, 23, 26–27, 30, 37, 47,
　68, 120, 288
Woodard, Mrs. J. M., 167
Woodard, Rebecca, 120
Woodard, Sally, 120
Woodard Tavern, 26, 30, 297, 298
Woodbridge, Frederick, 128, 187
Woodbridge, Mary Brayton, 120–21,
　128–29, 187–88
Wooddell, Larry, 336
Woods, Terry K., 309–11
Worden, R. D., 197
Works Progress Administration (WPA),
　161
Wright Store, 251
Wunderle, John, 305

Yale (Portage County), 115
*Years of Youth*, 223, 232
Yoho, Alan, 251
Young, Chuck, 160
Young, Oliver, 52